This book may be kept

FOURTEEN DAYS

A fine will be charged for each day the book is kept overtime.

JAN 2 3 1978 SEP 2 3 '97		
FEB 2 8 1978		
APR 1 2 1978		
AUG 7 1978		
NOV 2 7 1978		
AUG. 24 1981		
EC. 3 1 1981		
APR. 30 1982		
MAY 2 9 1982		
JUL. 23 1982		
OCT. 4 1982		
MAY 1 1984		
MAY 2 1 1984		
NOV 1 7 1987		
1-7-92		
AUG 1 3 1994		
JE 0 8 2		

The Saga of the Fist

JOHN V. GROMBACH

Member of the 1956, 1960, 1964, 1968
United States Olympic Games Committee

Member of the 1924 Olympic Boxing Team

Advisory Coach to the
U. S. Olympic Modern Pentathlon Team —
1924, 1966, 1968

International Amateur Fencer, Rifle and
Pistol Shot

Reserve Brigadier General

NEW YORK EVENING POST, THURSDAY, JULY 23, 1931

Familiar Faces—John Grombach By GUS UHLMAN

INTERCOLLEGIATE HEAVY-WEIGHT CHAMP!

GROMBACH NEVER LOST A SINGLE BOUT IN 3 YEARS!
1921-1922-1923
1924 OLYMPIC TEAM!

AT WEST POINT HE WAS ON SIX VARSITY SQUADS

NOW HE IS A PROGRAM DIRECTOR FOR A RADIO COMPANY, N.Y.C.

GROMBACH WAS RUNNER-UP IN THE NATIONAL FENCING CHAMPIONSHIPS

GUS UHLMAN

1. The Author (Frontispiece) (N.Y. Evening Post Inc., 1931)

The Saga of the Fist

The 9,000 Year Story of Boxing in Text and Pictures

by JOHN V. GROMBACH

South Brunswick and New York: A. S. Barnes and Company
London: Thomas Yoseloff Ltd

This is an updated and revised edition of *The Saga of Sock.*
© 1949 by A. S. Barnes and Co. © 1977 by John V. Grombach.
New material in this edition © 1977 by John V. Grombach.

A. S. Barnes and Company, Inc.
Cranbury, New Jersey 08512

Thomas Yoseloff Ltd
Magdalen House
136–148 Tooley Street
London SE1 2TT, England

Library of Congress Cataloging in Publication Data

Grombach, John V
    The saga of the fist.

    Previous ed. published in 1949 under title: The saga of sock.
    Includes index.
    1. Boxing—History. I. Title.
GV1121.G7 1976   796.8′3′09   75-20594
ISBN 0-498-01681-1

Printed in the United States of America

Contents

Preface

This book's purpose is to bring to all of its readers the dramatic kaleidoscope of boxing, its little-known, but romantic story, its historic association with democracy, culture, and command of the seas, its cavalcade of colorful personalities, and its unlimited future with the flight of sound and sight and a world reduced by television and satellite relay.

It is hoped that this book will entertain the followers of boxing, interest the uninitiated, and become a ready digest of the story of boxing up to the Atomic Age.

John V. Grombach

Acknowledgments

The author acknowledges with thanks the assistance of the following in the preparation of this book: Eddie Ahlquist, Miss Christine Alexander, Ray Arcel, Horace R. Bigelow, Colonel George Brett, Al Buck, Dave Burke, James Chapin, John Condon, Jack Dempsey, Eddie Eagan, Nat Fleischer, Erroll Flynn, Colonel Joseph I. Greene, Mrs. J. V. Grombach, Leo Houck, Gene Kearney, Jack Kirk, Fidel La Barba, Paul Magriel, Joseph Moncure March, Edward D. Moore, Bob Olin, Grantland Rice, Miss Gisela M. A. Richter, Major Monte Stone, J. Stacey Sullivan, Jr., Howard Trafton, Mrs. E. VanWagenen, Max Waxman, Maurie Waxman, Spike Webb, Al Weil, Mrs. John Hay Whitney, Joseph Woodman.

Amateur Athletic Union, Amateur Fencers League of America, Atkins Museum of Fine Arts, Kansas City, Missouri, Archives Photographiques des Beaux Arts, Paris, Bettman Archives, British Museum, London, Brown Brothers, California Aggies, Cleveland Museum of Art, Columbia Pictures, *Esquire*, Fédération de Boxe Française, Grombach Productions, Inc., *Infantry Journal*, Intercollegiate Boxing Association, Les Musées de France, Library of Congress, Macmillan Company, Madison Square Garden Corporation, Metropolitan Museum of Art, Miami and Miami Beach Public Libraries, National Boxing Association, National Collegiate Athletic Association, National Gallery of Art, Washington, D. C., Navy Athletic Association, W. R. Nelson Gallery of Art, New York Athletic Club, New York Athletic Camera Club, *New York Post*, New York Public Library, New York State Athletic Commission, *New York Times*, *New York Herald Tribune*, Pacific Coast Intercollegiate Boxing Association, Penn State College School of Physical Education and Athletics, Republic Pictures, Southern Intercollegiate Boxing Association, Stanford University, Twentieth Century Sporting Club, United Artists, Vassar College, Warner Brothers, Whitney Museum of American Art, Wide World Photos.

Commissioner Ed Dooley, Marvin Kohn, Mary Ann Marciano, Walt Disney Productions, Walter Wanger, Ring Magazine, Nat Loubet, The Smithsonian Institute, Twentieth Century Fox Film Corporation, Murray Goodman, and Michael Burke.

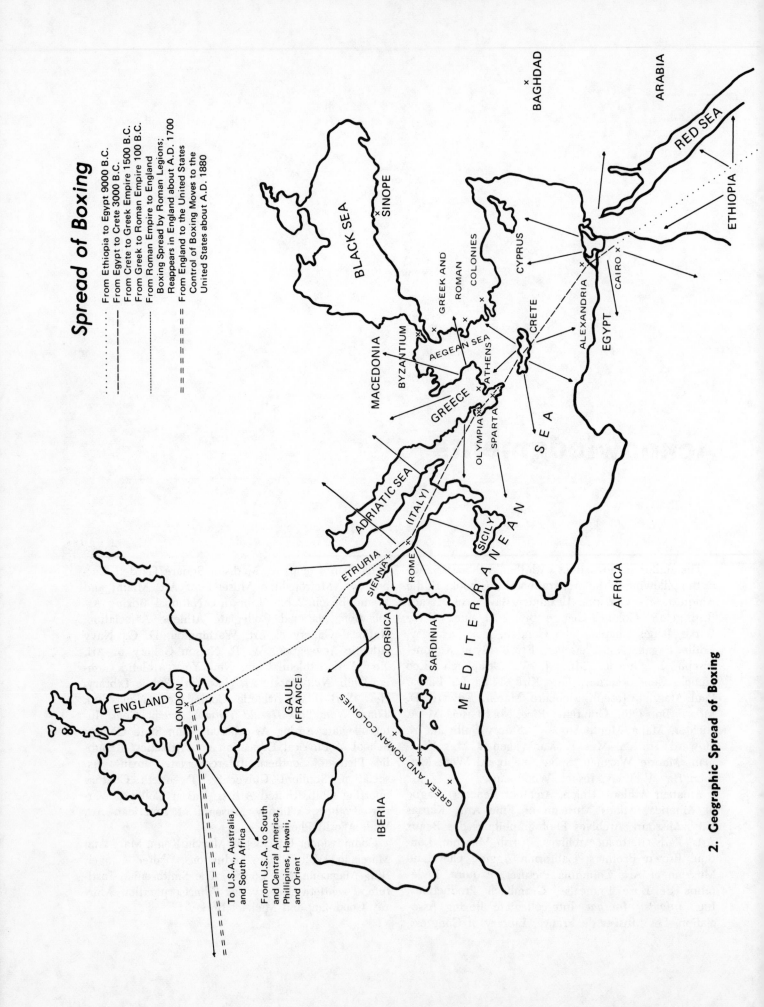

Spread of Boxing

⋯⋯⋯⋯ From Ethiopia to Egypt 9000 B.C.
━━━━━━━ From Egypt to Crete 3000 B.C.
━ ━ ━ ━ From Crete to Greek Empire 1500 B.C.
━━━━━━━ From Greek to Roman Empire 100 B.C.
From Roman Empire to England
  Boxing Spread by Roman Legions;
  Reappears in England about A.D. 1700
═══════ From England to the United States
  Control of Boxing Moves to the
  United States about A.D. 1880

To U.S.A., Australia,
and South Africa

From U.S.A. to South
and Central America,
Phillipines, Hawaii,
and Orient

2. Geographic Spread of Boxing

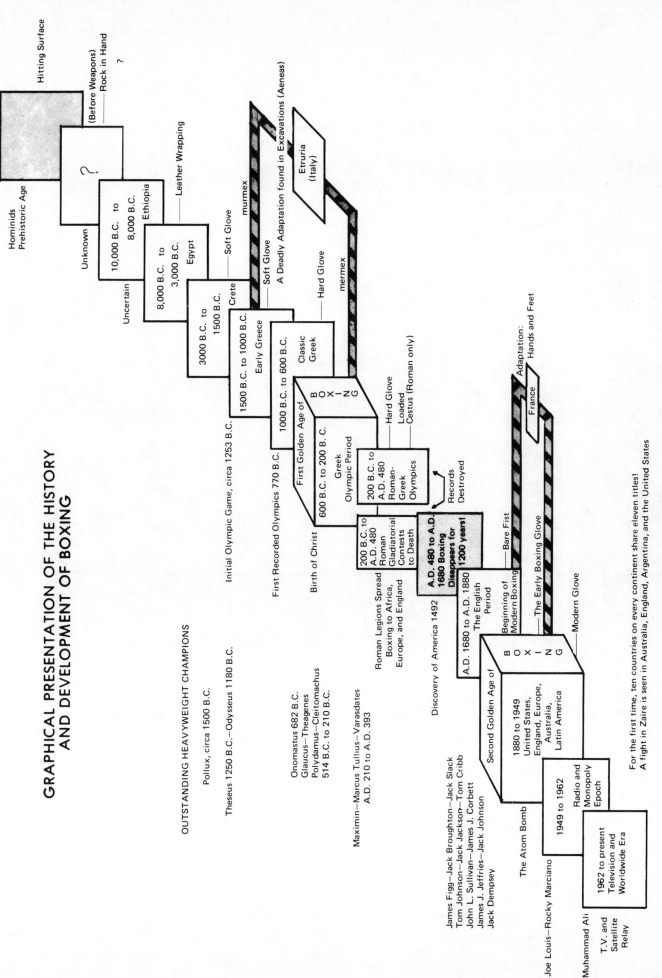

GRAPHICAL PRESENTATION OF THE HISTORY
AND DEVELOPMENT OF BOXING

Hitting Surface

Hominids
Prehistoric Age

(Before Weapons)
Rock in Hand
?

Unknown
10,000 B.C. to 8,000 B.C.
Ethiopia
Leather Wrapping

Uncertain
8,000 B.C. to 3,000 B.C.
Egypt
Soft Glove

3000 B.C. to 1500 B.C.
Crete
murmex

1500 B.C. to 1000 B.C.
Early Greece
Soft Glove
A Deadly Adaptation found in Excavations (Aeneas)

1000 B.C. to 600 B.C.
Classic Greek
Hard Glove

Etruria (Italy)
mermex

BOXING
600 B.C. to 200 B.C.
Greek Olympic Period

Hard Glove
Loaded Cestus (Roman only)

200 B.C. to A.D. 480
Roman-Greek Olympics

Records Destroyed

200 B.C. to A.D. 480
Roman Gladiatorial Contests to Death

A.D. 480 to A.D. 1680 Boxing Disappears for 1200 years!

A.D. 1680 to A.D. 1880
The English Period

Bare Fist

Beginning of Modern Boxing
The Early Boxing Glove

France
Adaptation:
Hands and Feet

Modern Glove

BOXING
Second Golden Age of
1880 to 1949
United States, England, Europe, Australia, Latin America

The Atom Bomb

1949 to 1962
Radio and Monopoly Epoch

1962 to present
Television and Worldwide Era

T.V. and Satellite Relay

OUTSTANDING HEAVYWEIGHT CHAMPIONS

Pollux, circa 1500 B.C.

Initial Olympic Game, circa 1253 B.C.

Theseus 1250 B.C.—Odysseus 1180 B.C.

First Recorded Olympics 770 B.C.

First Golden Age of

Onomastus 682 B.C.
Glaucus—Theagenes
Polydamus—Cleitomachus
514 B.C. to 210 B.C.

Birth of Christ

Maximin—Marcus Tullius—Varasdates
A.D. 210 to A.D. 393

Roman Legions Spread
Boxing to Africa,
Europe, and England

Discovery of America 1492

James Figg—Jack Broughton—Jack Slack
Tom Johnson—Jack Jackson—Tom Cribb
John L. Sullivan—James J. Corbett
James J. Jeffries—Jack Johnson
Jack Dempsey

Joe Louis—Rocky Marciano

Muhammad Ali

For the first time, ten countries on every continent share eleven titles!
A fight in Zaire is seen in Australia, England, Argentina, and the United States

3. Graph of the History and Development of Boxing

The Saga of the Fist

1 • Origins, Early History, and First Golden Age of Boxing

The Saga of the Fist is the story of the human fist. As the poet, Maurice Maeterlinck, once shrewdly observed, the fist is the only weapon organically adapted to the sensibilities, the resistance, the offensive and defensive structure of our body.

If you desire to check this, just clench your fist and (very gently) hit yourself in the eye with it. You will find that the position of the bones over and under your eye combined with your nose may allow you to get a black eye but will not permit the blow to reach your brain. If you try to hit a man on the Adam's apple or in the neck from the front, a blow which might prove fatal, you will find his chin is usually in the way. The ribs protect the heart and lungs from injury just as the intestines and stomach are protected by the abdominal muscles. Each kidney is protected by the last rib and hip bone and can be reached only partially by a blow with the fist. Try to get your fist into this opening and you will see it is a tight fit.

To circumvent nature, we have, unknown to Mr. Maeterlinck, but well known to the less literary Mr. Tunney, the thumb for the eye and the kidney-cut with the back of the hand. Mr. Tunney learned these improvements when he took a licking from the less literary Mr. Greb, an unorthodox boxer from Pittsburgh, Pennsylvania.

The most recent research on boxing shows that the sport had already made progress in 1800 B.C. in Crete. However, the history of the fist without doubt goes back considerably farther. Combative use of the fist was known in prehistoric times. We must use our imagination in beginning the saga of the fist in the days when dinosaurs and cave-men roamed the earth. In fact, there is every reason to believe that the fist was used in the early days either as a major or supplementary weapon by man prior to the stone age and prior to the advent of the club, sword, or knife.

Man is probably the most naked, the most fragile, and the most unprotected being in creation. Compare him with one of the lower forms of animal life. The insect, for example, is formidably equipped for attack. If you doubt that, think of the last time you were stung by a hornet or bee. Like the most modern tank or plane, many insects have their own armor-plating for defense. Think also of the strength of the ant which can lift a thousand times the weight of its body. Consider the cockroach and its strength and abilities in comparison to its size. It can run, swim, and even fly as well as fight. Man cannot match this.

Go to the zoo and look at the bear, lion or tiger. Observe their teeth and claws and the muscles be-

3A. Indian lion reaching for the throat of a Bengal tiger (20th Century-Fox)

hind these, as well as the speed, form, perfect co-ordination and deadliness of their playful clawing and biting. Note the defensive nature of their thick fur and hard leathery skin, and the difficulty of reaching vital organs such as the jugular vein or heart. A fight between an India lion and a Bengal tiger would make any heavyweight world title fight a very tame affair. Look over the rhinoceros or elephant; no glandular freaks, like Primo Carnera, but coordinated and muscular creatures with almost armor-plated skins for defense. Even the poor fish, small or large, has it all over man in offensive and defensive equipment. It has scales for armor, together with speed of motion, a strong tail and teeth, none of which we can boast in relative proportion. Not even Johnny Weismuller or Mark Spitz could defeat a fish in his native habitat, except in the movies.

On the Chagres River I once shot at a cayman or crocodile with a powerful Springfield army rifle at almost point-blank range, but the bullet merely glanced off the animal's armor-plated back. My pet macaw in Panama could gnaw through a baseball bat in a few hours; yet a tough steak can give us humans a jaw ache.

By comparison with animals, man's gelatinous state is close to primitive protoplasm. Only our skeleton, while none too strong, has any solidity, but our spine, admittedly the center of our skeleton, is an ill-set group of vertebrae. Even the very bones of the human spine are not safe from nature's afflictions.

After being adjudged by doctors and medical boards disabled by an accident in line of duty in World War II, which caused or activated arthritis of the spine, the Surgeon General of the Army reversed the findings in writing because in his opinion I had arthritis before I entered the Army because I had my nose broken several times in my boxing career in a previous Army service twenty years before. I am not an animal expert, but I doubt if animals are subject to arthritis, especially as a result of such nonsequitur thinking. However a Review Board in the face of expert testimony and X rays upset the reversal.

In order to return to the logic of nature, our only means of attack provided by our own bodies is the fist. Therefore, were mankind to follow the laws of nature, the fist is to man what horns are to the bull, claws and teeth to the lion and tiger. In fact, a wiser human race might well forbid any other weapon of combat and be better off.

The science of using the fist concerns agility, co-ordination, muscular strength, and resistance to pain. With respect to the latter and our utter lack of defense, we may be considered to be a cross between the frog and the sheep. We bleed like a sheep but are as vulnerable and thin-skinned as the frog. Offensively the kick of a horse and the bite of most animals are mechanically and anatomically perfect. Instinct has taught these animals to use their natural weapons with perfection. On the other hand, strangely enough, man does not come naturally by his skill with the fist.

Perhaps this is the reason why man alone resorts to what might be called artificial means of defense and offense, while other animals use as weapons only those given them by nature because they are instinctively adept in their use. However, in the case of man, while it would seem that his fist is his natural weapon, nevertheless the development of its use is a conscious one and therefore of tremendous interest aside from boxing as a sport. The primitive man or athletically uneducated man does not naturally hit with his clenched hand. Instead, he relies on rushing, grasping the throat, gouging the eyes, hair-pulling, biting, use of the feet and knees, or resorts to the club, knife, or any other object with offensive capabilities.

When I was Police and Prison Officer at Governor's Island, New York, one of the dangerously insane prisoners at Castle William escaped and showed up in my office. He rushed at me, and when he reached me, although I hit him on the chin with my fist, he instinctively grabbed for my throat with both hands and tried to choke me to death.

So that, while the fist is the principal weapon organically given to man by nature, he does not learn to use it instinctively.

The story of the fist goes farther back in the history of man than is recorded. One day, before the Stone Age, and even before man had developed the use of bones of prehistoric animals as clubs or weapons, he came face to face with a saw-toothed tiger in a defile, with nothing to protect him but his bare hands. Necessity always being the mother of invention, it is probable that the man quickly grasped two stones, one in each hand, and desperately struck at the big cat. The first blows of this primitive boxing were swings similar to Angel Firpo's overhand flail-like blow which knocked Jack Dempsey out of the ring at Yankee Stadium in our modern era.

The jump from conjecture and the fist of prehistoric man to the first records of boxing is a dark and tremendous one. The first evidence of boxing as a sport is found in certain Egyptian hieroglyphics dating from approximately 4000 B.C. The hieroglyphics show that a form of boxing was practiced by the soldiers of the Pharaohs in that period. The few facts that have come to light seem to indicate that boxing was then a crude form of sport or combat engaged in with the help of a primitive cestus.

The "cestus," later identified with the cruel loaded and spiked hand-piece or metal knuckle used by boxers in Roman times, originally consisted only of wrappings of leather thongs, bark, or primitive cloth around the fist, hands, and forearms. These wrappings protected the bones in the hands and arms of the wearer from being broken by the impact of the blow and also increased the blow's effectiveness. A form of this original cestus exists today. Boxers, before putting on their gloves, tape their hands and wrists with cotton gauze and adhesive tape for the same purpose that the Egyptians did six thousand years ago. The Egyptians and Greeks used leather wrappings as both soft and hard boxing gloves for centuries before the introduction of the Roman cestus. This bloody weapon was an adaptation of the ancient Etruscan murmex. The loaded cestus may originally have been an invention of some shrewd manager, or second, as a secret weapon for his boxer. The unsuspecting opponent fell an easy victim to the "sneak" use of lead or other heavy metal in the wrappings. From then on it was a contest to see who could invent further additions of metal, spikes, barbs and the like to assure victory or to make contests more exciting, bloodier, and deadlier. Possibly the difference in the cestus came about in order to distinguish the amateur from the professional. We do know, however, that the loaded cestus was never used in Olympic or amateur contests, even in the days of the Romans.

But returning to the ancient Egyptians: while it must be admitted that the beginnings of boxing are cloudy, we do have sufficient records to give us more

than a sketchy picture of the time. According to the Greek historian, Herodotus, who had access to more ancient Egyptian records than we do today, the Egyptians participated in "games comprising every form of contest practiced by the Greeks and offered animals, cloaks, and skins as prizes." This is corroborated by the hieroglyphic findings, and by boxing murals unearthed in the tombs of the Pharaohs.

There is evidence in the boxing murals of Egypt of 6000 years ago that contests and competitions in the earliest boxing were conducted in squared or circular arenas perhaps resulting in the first reference to "the ring." Perhaps our giving the "bird" to a contestant arose from some old custom of awarding to a poor competitor a fowl while the victor got a coveted cow or ox.

In any case, Herodotus referred to "a period covering the reign of 350 kings, and of these there were eighteen Ethiopians." Egypt and Ethiopia were seemingly tied together in those days, and long before Rameses II ruled both Egypt and Ethiopia, perhaps as far back as 8000 B.C., or 10,000 years ago, boxing was introduced into Egypt from Ethiopia. Some evidence in what is now modern Ethiopia, Kenya, and Tanzania, according to anthropologists, indicates that primitive man may go back over two million years ago with Africa as the cradle of mankind so the use of the fist may go back to the African hominids.

While we have no absolute proof, this is an interesting possibility, for it would mean that the black race, so prominent and adept in the sport today, comes by its prowess not only as a result of an effort to overcome handicaps and injustices, but because it is a sport innately suited to its racial characteristics and one which it originated.

From Egypt and Ethiopia boxing spread. A stone slab relief of about 3000 B.C., found in Bagdad, shows boxers with leather-taped hands. Historical research has established the fact that Egypt developed a large navy and overseas commerce and that the Aegean Sea to the north became also an Egyptian lake. It is not difficult to see, when one looks at a map, that the channels of trade, civilization and, in fact, "world" supremacy, would naturally pass from Egypt to the island of Crete and thence to Greece. Boxing also followed this route.

Statues, friezes, and murals showing boxing scenes and boxers have been found in ancient Crete. Within the past seventy years archeologists have unearthed proof of the existence of large amphitheatres with special boxes for seating the king and his royal entourage. There is evidence to show that women attended the early boxing shows which were held in these amphitheatres. This feminine interest in the sport was not permitted in Greece until the games of Hellenistic times and was not sanctioned again by society until the Dempsey-Carpentier fight.

Crete, as a nation, enjoyed spectator sports. In the great city of Knossos, during the period 2000 B.C. to 1200 B.C., interest in boxing and other sports was at its height. Palaces, great theatres, and amphitheatres have been unearthed showing arenas devoted to bullbaiting or bullfighting, rodeos, boxing, and dancing. In fact, the connection of the fist with dancing, practiced by some of our present-day boxers, probably has its historical explanation here.

There is also incontestable evidence that boxing and rodeos followed each other in the Minoan circuses of Crete. Paintings show not only boxing in the ancient counterpart of the Madison Square Garden, but also rodeos in which men and women performed somersaults over the backs of charging bulls, or wrestled calves.

Unfortunately we cannot find any evidence that boxing champions of those days should be considered in our selection of the greatest champions of all times. In addition to the progress since that time of the science of boxing, skeletons in graves and other evidence prove that the Minoan or early Crete boxer was too small to worry about. He was never taller than five feet four inches and was very small-boned.

When boxing moved from Crete to Greece, we find our first real world's heavyweight champions, Theseus, Pollux, and Odysseus, otherwise known as Ulysses. The word "heavyweight" is used advisedly, for there were no weight classifications in boxing among the ancients, and "good big men," generally speaking, were the champions.

Greek mythology and Greek legend, so dear to some of us and so confusing to most of us, are based primarily on historical fact, and boxing has an important place in this mythology and legend because it was so important to the ancient Greeks. For instance, Theseus, one of the first heavyweight boxing champions, is no longer merely a legendary character, but has stepped into the pages of history. According to the legend dealt with in American literature by Nathaniel Hawthorne, the favorite son of the King of Knossos, Crete, had been killed by the Greeks during a foray on the mainland. For this outrage the king exacted from the offending Greek city, Athens, a specified number of youths and maidens to be sent annually to Knossos as sacrifices to the minotaur—a monster, half man, half bull. It was reported that they were held captives pending the day of the festival, in great underground chambers within the heart of the palace accessible only by a maze of corridors, a labyrinth through which no stranger had ever found his way out. Then according to the legend came Theseus, a prince with a punch, who had distinguished himself in local fisticuffs, who volunteered to go along as one of the hostages. Ariadne, the daughter of the King of Knossos, fell in love with Theseus and gave him a spool of thread and a sword. With the sword he killed the minotaur and with the ·spool of thread which he had been careful to unwind when taken into the labyrinth, he led himself and his fellow hostages to freedom.

Now that sounds like a fairy tale. However, you may yourself have heard an ex-boxer recount the story of a fight he lost or won twenty years before. In-

4. Bull-grappling scene; contemporary wall-painting from Knossos, 1200 B.C. (Library of Congress)

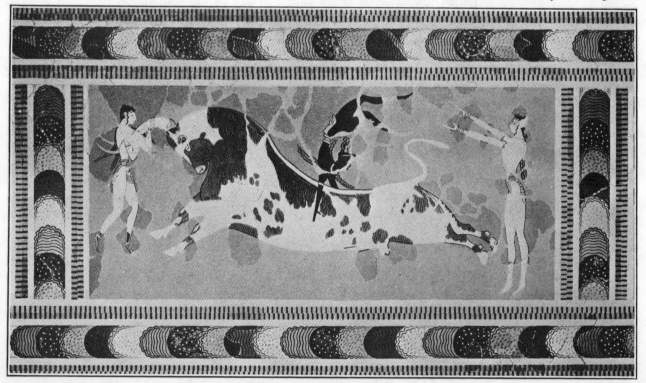

variably his opponent of yesteryear has grown in his imagination and often is transformed in later telling to a giant, a terror, half man, half bull, who just managed to beat him by a whisker or whom he heroically overcame. Mythology and legend are, after all, the stories of man relayed by word of mouth over hundreds of years and then often recorded by poets. That should explain much.

There was of course no actual minotaur. It is probable that on account of the death of his son, and for winning a war, the king of Knossos wanted some forced labor. Consequently, many of the best young men and young women of Greece had to be delivered to Knossos each year. Some of these were undoubtedly placed as prisoners in the intricate underground passages unearthed in modern times by the excavations of the scientist, Dr. Evans. Following the custom of the times, these hostages were sometimes used in circuses to fight bulls or men or to supply other entertainment, and either were killed, retained as slaves or assimilated by the Minoans of Crete. The so-called labyrinth, underground passageways and galleries, the quarters for the prisoners and the stables for the bulls they fought, have all been found.

So when we read in mythology about Castor's twin brother, Pollux, an even earlier boxer than Theseus, we may be really looking over the record, or what remains of the record, of the first world's heavyweight champion. His outstanding recorded fight was with a bully named Amycus who compelled all strangers that came to his country to box with him. Amycus was a killer and he made an end of all strangers in this way. To make the story short, Pollux fought him and "killed him with a blow on the elbow." So here is our first but rather uncertain champion. We feel sure that here, too, time has twisted the facts. The blow that killed Pollux's opponent was either *with* the elbow on which was affixed a lead, iron, or bronze instrument or gimmick or, since boxing in those days was a free swinging affair, Pollux with a bronze knuckle swung his right as Amycus swung his left, and landed one to Amycus's *heart* after grazing the latter's left elbow. According to another account, Amycus was not killed, but merely cured of his inhospitable treatment of strangers.

Odysseus, alias Ulysses, hero of the Trojan wars and of Homer's epic poem, was unbeatable with his fists. He is accepted today as an historical, as well as a legendary character. There is more to support his record than any of his predecessors and therefore I prefer to give you as our first world's heavyweight boxing champion: Odysseus. With this selection I will describe one of his fights.

Many boxing statisticians are interested in the shortest major fight in ring history, usually accorded to Jack Dempsey's knockout of Fred Fulton in eighteen seconds in 1918 at Harrison, New Jersey. However, this is not correct if Homer is to be believed. Odysseus knocked out Irus in a real boxing bout which must have lasted less than five seconds. The bout started quickly; Odysseus threw a right "roundhouse" to Irus's chin, Irus fell like a "poled ox" and the fight was over. As Homer described it, "though it was a light blow, yet Irus's jaw was smashed and blood rushed from his mouth . . . as he lay unconscious on the marble floor." It is difficult to give the exact date of this, but it was probably about 1185 B.C. or well over 3,000 years ago.

For those of us who like dates to pin down our facts, here are a few in the early annals of boxing. Pollux probably lived before 1500 B.C. Theseus, who escaped from Crete, did most of his heavy punching in 1250 B.C. Heracles, one of the mightiest boxers of pre-Homeric times, was a contemporary of Theseus. The Trojan wars came about a half century later and lasted from 1194 B.C. to 1184 B.C. Homer's *Iliad* covers fifty-two days in the tenth year of the war and his *Odyssey* tells of the return of Odysseus, the war hero. The first recorded date after this in the history of boxing is 776 B.C., the first recorded Olympiad.

The golden era of boxing in antiquity was during the Olympic era. Evidence shows that there is hardly

5. Theseus; drawing by Agna Enters from First Person Plural

anything today that is new when compared with the sport then. Boxers at that time had boxing gloves of leather which they kept in good condition by rubbing animal fat on them. The gloves were, generally speaking, used for the same purpose that gloves are used for today. There were different types of gloves for different uses, such as we have today: training gloves and fighting gloves. Due to the fact that the technique of boxing was not as far advanced as it is today, the fist and arm were used by the Greeks more like a club or hammer than like a ram, spear, or piston, as they are today, so that instead of having the present small wrist-pad or guard, ancient Greek gloves extended up, on the arm, sometimes to the elbow. Even the light striking bag and the heavy punching bag are not new. In the fifth century B.C., boxers trained in gymnasiums similar to Stillman's gym in New York City, in the 1940s . . . and more recently to Bobby Gleason's in lower Manhattan, and used punching bags made of leather and canvas filled with fig-seeds and sand.

Bobby Gleason was voted the James J. Walker award for long and meritorious service to boxing by the boxing writers. Walker was the debonair boxing (New York City) mayor who brought back legal boxing to New York State. Gleason has been around fisticuffs since 1908. As a sixteen-year-old bantamweight, he fought fifteen round fights for $15, providing the promoter did not run out with the receipts. Bobby fought on barges off Yonkers and in the backyards of bars in Greenwich Village. But at eighty-two Bobby runs a 1975 training emporium for boxers . . . very similar to those in Greece over 2,500 years ago.

Within recent years boxers in training had adopted a special headgear, or headguard of padded leather, to protect their foreheads from being cut over the eyes and to prevent cauliflower ears. Even this was not unknown to Hellenic boxers, who wore a leather cap called *amphotide*, for the same purpose. Even mouthpieces were used, only they were not made of rubber like those of today, but were made of leather.

There were, nevertheless, some major differences between boxing then and boxing now. In those days there were no rounds or rest periods, nor were there any weight divisions. In addition, life and limb were not held so dear, and men were often killed in those ancient bouts. The ancients believed in the full application of the adage "may the best man win." Boxing contests lasted until one of the men was knocked so cold he could not continue, or until either one or both fighters were so exhausted they were unable to stand up.

Considering some of the peculiar decisions rendered under modern boxing rules, one sometimes wonders whether or not the ancients had the better system.

What follower of boxing, for example, has forgotten such peculiar decisions as the one which enabled Philadelphia Jack O'Brien to win a fight against Stanley Ketchel in 1907 while he was at the time lying outstretched in the middle of the ring, colder than a kippered herring? There have been times when the final bell saved a fight for the more clever boxer, but not necessarily "the better man." This argument is not meant as an attack on present-day boxing which puts a premium on skill and science, and improves and develops the game. This is as it should be. However, it is a controversial point in which any close follower of the game will be interested. There are, after all, excellent reasons behind the rules of the ancient Greeks who, it will be remembered, were sportsmen also.

The Greeks had some unfair rules, too. For instance, it appears that if, after hours of fighting, both boxers were too exhausted to continue, lots were drawn and each was given the privilege of getting a free punch at the other, like a free throw in basketball. Perhaps this ancient practice gave us our modern

6. Greek Boxers; sixth century B.C. (British Museum)

fight term "draw" for an inconclusive decision. Naturally the boxer fortunate enough to win "the draw" and get the first punch had a tremendous advantage.

Boxing was one of the main events in the Olympics, of which the date of origin has not been accurately established. All that is known to modern researchers is that the Olympic games probably were begun about 1000 B.C., or more probably according to archaeological findings at Olympia, in 1253 B.C., temporarily abandoned, and then revived, and first recorded in 776 B.C. In the revival, boxing was not featured as a regular championship event until the twenty-third Olympiad, 688 B.C., when Onamastus won the championship, and established the first boxing rules. In these early games, the contestants were exclusively

Greeks, but by 146 B.C. the Romans had begun to participate. The games continued until the Greco-Roman rivalry, aided and worsened by government take overs, degenerated into so many brawls, especially in the boxing contests, that Emperor Theodosius abolished the games in A.D. 394. Over fifteen hundred years later, in 1896, the Olympic games were revived at Athens and have continued at four-year intervals ever since, except for the war years 1916, 1940, and 1944. The ancient Greeks, however, did not let war interfere with their games, much to the astonishment of Xerxes when he learned that Theagenes, the greatest boxer of the ancients, was being crowned victor at Olympia while the fate of Greece was being decided on the battlefield of Thermopylae.

Boxing contests in the ancient Olympics featured the cestus, the Grecian boxing glove. As has been previously mentioned, this was not loaded with metals or spikes like its later Roman counterpart, but was made of heavy leather thongs wrapped around the hand and arm, with a hard thick leather surface over the knuckles. In addition to the regular boxing contests, the Greek Olympic games included a rough-and-tumble contest called the "pancratium" in which wrestling as well as boxing was allowed. There were similar events for boys, with about the same rules.

Olympia, where the Olympics were held, was not a city but a plain in the district of *Pisatis*. Here magnificent temples were erected to the gods, as well as gymnasiums, amphitheatres, and other structures necessary for the games. Just outside the temple enclosure was the stadium, 750 feet long and 125 feet wide, where the boxing was held. Nearby, in the sacred grove of Altis, grew the wild olive trees whose leaves provided coveted crowns for the champions. In the four great games the victors were also awarded a palm branch, and our expressions "winning the crown" or "getting the palm" evidently date back to those days.

Boxers, as well as all other participants at the Olympics, were expected to train for ten months in advance and no one "with a police record" or "impure" by Greek standards could compete. The athletic uniform of Olympic contestants was complete nudity. No women were allowed at the Olympics even as spectators in the beginning on penalty of being thrown off a nearby rocky cliff. Later, however, this rule was changed, and eventually girls' events were actually included, in the games.

Politicians had not yet figured the graft that could be gotten by requiring boxers to wear standard trunks or standard protectors, purchasable only from one merchant or manufacturer. Special protectors for the genital organs were known and were used in Crete. Several were found in the ruins of the Knossos am-

7. Boxing scenes, fifth century B.C. (British Museum)

phitheatre, since World War II. However, hitting below the waist was a foul and not countenanced by the Greeks. This rule was observed so carefully in Greece that no protectors were worn at the great games.

The winners of each of the events at the Olympics were announced by a herald who proclaimed the victorious entry's name, his father's name, and the name of the city or country from which he came, and each victor was then privileged to erect a statue of himself in the sacred Altis.

There were other games during the Golden Age of boxing in Greece, though none so famous as the Olympics. However, the boxing events were just as popular and just as closely contested at the Pythian, Nemean and Isthmian games. After 573 B.C., in every four-year span, the Olympics were held in July or August of the first year, both the Isthmian games and the Nemean games in the summer or spring of every second and fourth years, and the Pythian games in August of every third year, or a total of six championships in the four "great games" every four years. According to the records, the various games, including all preliminaries, semifinals and finals in all events usually lasted five days.

Since the winners in all these contests were virtually certain to be subsidized or supported by their city-state or country for the rest of their lives, and since most competitors had their expenses paid by their sponsors or city-states, contestants were attracted from every corner of the Greek and Roman empires so that at no time in the world's history was a consistent winner more truly entitled to the name, "World's Champion."

When one examines such records as remain, and sees the startling accomplishments and consistency of championship performance of some of the ancient boxers, one wonders why more has not been said and written about them. For instance, a boxer named Tisander won four Olympic boxing championships covering a span of more than twelve years.

In the chapter on the development of boxing as an art and science, we will see how the technical progress of the sport might give the modern pugilist an advantage over the boxer of antiquity. However, based only on cunning, experience, endurance, power, killer instinct, speed, agility, and strength, it is very questionable if the great boxers of ancient Greece could have been beaten by the best of today. How, for instance, does Joe Louis's record compare with that of the man who in twenty years won 1,400 championships, each representing many fights in series of eliminations, often involving as many as ten fights in a single day and who is reported to have killed over eight hundred men with his fist and knocked out many more? This is the record of Theagenes of Thasos. Even if this were a tenfold exaggeration, it still leaves a challenging record.

Theagenes is believed to have been born in Thrace about 505 B.C. At the age of nine he is said to have carried away a huge bronze statue which stood in a square in his city, simply because he took a childish fancy to it. Instead of being punished, he was made to return it before witnesses to its place and thereupon became famous for his tremendous strength.

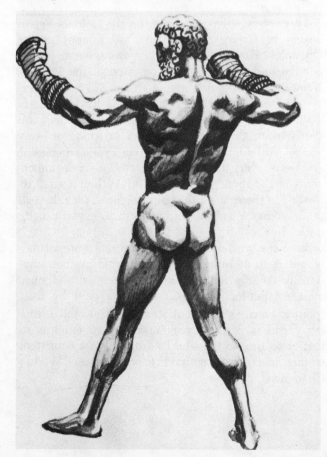

Upon coming of age, he began competing both in boxing and the pancratium and, when older, in long distance running. He won twenty-five or thirty major championships in boxing and as many more in the pancratium, some concurrently in the same games, and had placed upon his head about 1,400 olive wreaths during his lifetime.

To prove further his championship caliber, Theagenes defeated another of the greatest boxers of ancient Greece. This boxer, Euthymus, by name, had won many boxing championships including the 74th Olympics, and probably would have had a greater niche in the history of boxing if he had not been contemporary with Theagenes. In the 75th Olympics, Theagenes decided he wanted to win both the boxing and the pancratium and so entered both events. The two greats met in the boxing final. Theagenes won, but was so badly cut up by Euthymus that, while he had also qualified for the final in the pancratium, he had to forfeit the final bout in this event and, consequently the championship. Euthymus was not entered in the pancratium.

The officials took a very arbitrary view of the situation, probably out of love for Euthymus who was the older champion. They ruled that if Theagenes had been able to defeat Euthymus and also win the pancratium, he would have been a competitor worthy of the best Greek tradition. However, the judges felt that in depriving Euthymus of his title but in having then to default in the pancratium final, Theagenes had shown a flaw in his character by biting off more than he could chew. So they fined him, claiming he had spoiled the Olympic show and wronged Euthymus by being too greedy in wanting two titles. Part of his fine had to be paid to the Olympic gods and part to Euthymus.

Theagenes paid his Olympic fine, but settled his debt to Euthymus by not entering the boxing event in the next or 76th Olympics. As a result, of course, Euthymus won, although he couldn't really be considered boxing chompion. Theagenes won the pancratium and at a later Olympiad, probably the 77th, won the double victory. Only one other boxer ever accomplished this—Cleitomachus, of whom we shall hear later.

The fame of Theagenes on earth seemed to have been reechoed in the halls on Mt. Olympus for, according to the legend, the gods vindicated by death a slight to his memory by the hand of man. When Theagenes died, one of his jealous enemies flogged his bronze statue, and as if in retribution, the statue fell and killed him. The family of the dead man then prosecuted and convicted the statue for murder, and following traditional Greek punishment for crimes of this nature, the Thracians dropped it to the bottom of the sea. Later, after a great drought and upon the ad-

7A. Theagenes, Undefeated World Champion 484–468 B.C.

vice of the Delphic oracle, the statue was recovered by fishermen with nets, and set back where it had been. Thus Theagenes became almost a god, and for centuries his statues were considered cure-alls, especially for the injuries of athletes. Some of the greatest artists and poets of his time immortalized him in sculpture and poetry, but wars, earthquakes, time and man have destroyed most of these portraits of him.

Boxing in general, and Theagenes in particular, are mentioned in the extant writings of Pausanias, Oenomaus, Dio Chrysostom, and Lucian, but we regret that there was no Paul Gallico, Grantland Rice, Nat Fleischer, Nat Loubet, or Red Smith in Olympic times to describe his style.

Next in line for fistic immortality are Cleitomachus, Glaucus of Carystus, Polydamus of Scotussa, and Milo of Croton. Although they won their crowns some 2,100 years before modern boxing got its start in the early eighteenth century, these champions should definitely be classed with the best of the modern eras Figg and Broughton; Sullivan and Jeffries; Dempsey, Louis and Marciano.

Milo of Croton was more of a wrestler than a boxer, although he fought in accordance with the custom of the day and showed equal abilities in wrestling, boxing, and the pancratium. He evidently preferred wrestling, but there is little doubt that he could have built up a record in boxing second only to Theagenes's had he had the latter's killer instinct.

When a boy, Milo won the boy's wrestling championship at the Olympic, Pythian and other games. Later he won many boxing championships and six men's wrestling Olympic championships, which made him world's wrestling champion for twenty-four consecutive years. While more modest and less confident competitors waited to retain famous sculptors to reproduce their likeness until *after* being crowned champion, not so with Milo. This cocky gentleman arrived at the games with his statue already on his shoulder and bore it triumphantly in the processional and inaugural ceremonies. His faith in himself was justified, however, and the end of the five-day contest found him placing his victory statue in the sacred Altis with unprecedented regularity.

Milo was a showman and delighted his public. In this respect he was the Max Baer of his time, though unlike Baer, he always made good his boasts.

Milo's strength was fabulous. When a small boy, he began carrying a young calf on his shoulder and continued every day thereafter until the calf had become a full-grown bull.

He performed all manner of tricks to confuse his enemies, amuse his friends and attract publicity. One of these was to grasp a pomegranate and to challenge anyone to take it away from him. Not only was it impossible to do so, but his powerful

8. Home of boxing in its first Golden Age— Olympia, Greece (Library of Congress)

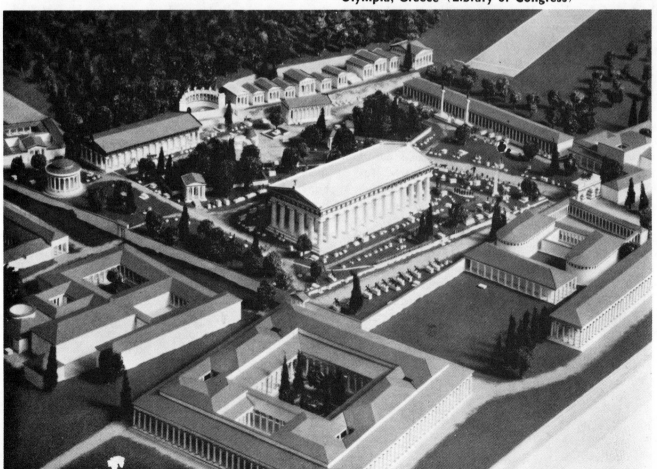

grip was so controlled that the fruit was never crushed or damaged in any way. He could stand on a greased quoit (discus) and make a fool of anyone who tried to rush or push him off. This is reminiscent of Young Griffo's trick, performed in the late nineteenth century, of standing on a handkerchief and daring anyone to hit him or make him move off it. Another popular feat of Milo's consisted of having a cord tied around his head, holding his breath and making the veins in his head swell to a point where the cord broke. But Milo's tricks and own confidence in his strength proved his undoing in the end. He tried to replace a wedge in a tree trunk with his hand, became hopelessly entrapped in the aperture and was eaten by wild animals.

Glaucus of Carystus was a farm boy. One day, according to the legend, while he was working with his father, the ploughshare fell out of the plough. He fitted it into place, using his bare hand as a hammer. His father, on seeing this, decided his son should become a boxer and entered him in the Olympics.

The story goes that in spite of his inexperience and lack of boxing knowledge, Glaucus got through the preliminaries by virtue of sheer strength and his good right hand. However, he took lots of punishment and in the finals was so faint from exhaustion and loss of blood that it looked as though he were through. Fortunately for him, it was not then illegal to coach from the sidelines, and his father shouted from the gallery: "Remember the ploughshare!" and Sonny came through with a quick knockout.

After this, Glaucus made a thorough study of the art and science of boxing as it was understood in those days and took very little further punishment as a great champion for many years. His boxing style was considered so fine that statues of him in sparring or "on guard" positions were made. His acquired science, plus an apparently unusual natural punch, earned him in the course of his career several Olympic, two Pythian, eight Nemean, and eight Isthmian boxing championships as well as hundreds of minor championships. He was known as an aggressive fighter who never stopped until he had killed, or knocked out his opponent, and he can be definitely considered the Jack Dempsey of the early era of the fist.

Polydamas, who lived about 380 B.C., while certainly not in a class with Theagenes, Glaucus, Cleitomachus, or even poor Euthymus, was, like Milo, very colorful and the subject of great contemporary ballyhoo and publicity.

While he was a boxer and pancratic performer, who won many championships in addition to several Olympics, he is more famous for his accomplishments outside the realm of boxing.

He was the giant of the Hellenic amphitheatres—an Olympian Primo Carnera. To be exact, he was 6 feet 8 inches tall, weighed 300 pounds and topped other champions, even the greatest, in size. Our other four champions of that period varied from 6 feet to 6 feet 4 inches and from 190 to 235 pounds. Incidentally, the means by which we have been able to figure out the measurements of these fighters is interesting. In many cases the victory statues had at their base the actual imprint of the athlete's foot: a sort of an Olympian Grauman's Chinese Theatre. While the imprint of a movie star's hands or feet in Hollywood may tell generations to come their stature in the field of the cinema, the imprints of the Olympic athletes' feet, next to their perfectly proportioned statues, allow us, centuries later, to figure out rather closely their height, size, and weight. Also the Greek measurements of some have come down to us in *cubits* and *fingers*: 18.25 inches and 0.7 inches respectively.

Polydamas with his tremendous size, weight, and strength did some phenomenal things, if we can believe the original sources. He could stop a chariot drawn by three horses by holding on to the back of it. In a battle royal against three men, he killed all three. In various exhibitions he pulled a bull's leg off and killed a lion with his bare hands.

As in the case of Milo, overconfidence caused Polydamas's death. He and some friends were in a cave when a cave-in started. The others ran out, but Polydamas tried to hold the roof up and perished when the hill fell in on him.

Next we come to Cleitomachus, who was neither colorful nor a performer of spectacular stunts, but in the ring or in the stadium he was second only to Theagenes. He was the only other man to win both the boxing and pancratium crowns at the same Olympics—the 141st, 216 B.C. But boxing was his specialty and, like Theagenes, he was undefeated in hundreds of championships over many years. Unfortunately, however, his competitive career overlapped that of one of the greatest wrestlers of all time, Caprus, who also competed in the pancratium event. It was during the 142nd Olympics. Caprus had won the wrestling championship, and Cleitomachus had already started in his boxing elimination contests. At this point Cleitomachus made a request unprecedented in the Olympic records. It was for permission to compete in the pancratium first before the boxing competitions, where contestants were usually badly cut up, in order to have a better chance to retain both his titles.

We get some idea of his importance as a competitor when we learn that the games were rescheduled to meet his request. The two men met in the pancratium finals, but the wrestler won, not the boxer, and the contest did not match the drama or ferocity of the Theagenes-Euthymus boxing final in the 75th Olympiad. However, Cleitomachus went on to retain his boxing crown, and has come down through the ages a challenger worthy of any one of our best heavyweights. He is the only ancient champion whose statue has come down to us by a famous contemporary sculptor. It was found in a building construction excavation in Rome. It is one of the few Greek Olympian records not destroyed by the Romans when they overran Greece and were jealous of Greek culture.

Let us now examine the irregularities, if any, which existed in boxing in those days. Apollonius, a boxer from Alexandria, Egypt, was very late in arriving for one of the major games, but he and his handlers demanded that he be allowed either to enter the last stages of the tournament or fight the winner. They claimed he had been delayed by an act of the gods; his ship had been held up by the winds. When refused the right of entry, he attacked the winner, and as a matter of fact, gave him a beating. Official investigations followed and revealed that Apollonius had not been delayed by bad winds, but by "trade" winds. He had been picking up some loose change in boxing championships at the Ionian games, which delayed his arrival at Olympia where he intended to add further to his fortune. A heavy fine dented his profits for the year, although neither he nor his manager was suspended. This should suggest an idea that might be tried in modern boxing.

Paul Gallico, the former sportswriter who once braved the punches of Jack Dempsey to be able to tell his readers what it was really like to be jolted into insensibility by the Manassa Mauler, in his *Farewell to Sport,* gives a vivid description of a painting to prove that boxing started in Etruria and that boxers in those days practiced the finger-in-the-eye technique of some unorthodox fighters of today. The latter or technical aspect will be treated later, but on origin, Paul goes on to intimate that the boxers of Etruria antedate the Greeks and gives the impression that boxing originated in Etruria. This sadly enough for Gallico is very doubtful. I respect Paul as a boxing expert though his fencing, based on our N.Y.A.C. workouts, needs improvement.

Boxing was, in fact, brought both to Rome and to Etruria by the Trojans and Greeks when Aeneas and others migrated there after 1174 B.C., prior even to the founding of Rome in 753 B.C. One of the historical mysteries of boxing ties Etruria and Greece with the early development of Roman boxing and, we

fear, with one of its most bloody and deadly aspects. This mystery was at one time as interesting as anyone might expect to find in the books of Erle Stanley Gardner, who, by the way, was a boxing devotee. For many years archeologists were puzzled over strange ornamental articles they found in ancient tombs in Greece, Etruria, and Rome. At first they believed they were snaffles, curbs, or bits for horses, spear throwers, or the like. It was not until 1879 that Dr. D.G. Brinton, professor of archeology at the University of Pennsylvania, identified them as the Greek murmex worn on the cestus and referred to in contemporary records. Several years later he proved his claim by finding an old statue in the Louvre, of a Greek boxer wearing them.

The murmex, *myrmex,* or *myrmekes,* called by the early Greeks "limb piercers," were the most terrible weapons ever intended for use on the fist. They were bronze, spurlike instruments which the pugilist of early Rome and Etruria strapped to his cestus in order to make the blow of his fist potentially fatal. So heavy was the punch of the ancients that many of the murmex have broken or bent points.

Considerable study seems to indicate that while boxing regulations in the Hellenic period, and at most of the Olympics, countenanced the hard leather cestus which sometimes proved fatal, they *never* permitted the murmex or the loaded, or Roman cestus which could not help but prove fatal.

9. Cleitomachus, heavyweight boxing champion of the world, 225–215 B.C. (Library of Congress)

With the advent of the Greco-Roman civilization and its brutal wars of conquest, boxing became more cruel and deadly, and the murmex or more brutal cestus came into use, especially by the gladiators or slaves in spectacles and circuses, while the more conservative cestus was retained for purely athletic competitions.

There is no doubt that the murmex is more closely identified with Roman rather than Greek boxing, although it was used before the true Hellenic and Olympic period but was not used in Greece thereafter. It was revived later by the Etruscans and the Romans who made boxing more brutal, and adapted it to gladiatorial spectacles with death as its logical conclusion.

Lucillius, a first-century A.D. poet, wrote a little jingle:

Your head! Appollophanes has become a sieve.
From the straight and oblique holes made by the
    myrmex.

In A.D. 500, a Greek poet left a description of the gym at Byzantium and of a boxer who "grew furious whirling in his hand the limb-piercing myrmekes."

In other words, from the beginning of gladiatorial fights about 264 B.C. to about A.D. 500, boxing as a sport, together with its development as an art and science, went into decline and finally disappeared.

The first of the Roman gladiatorial spectacles which have become so notorious was staged at the funeral of Junius Brutus. Originally held as a ceremony for the honored dead, they later became public spectacles promoted by emperors, governors, and political demagogues for the entertainment of the masses. Slaves, prisoners of war, and criminals were forced to participate in these entertainments which were as lavish as they were cruel.

Gladiatorial contests brought about the development of schools for gladiators, operated by men (*leudi*) who were particularly experienced and tough, in many cases former contestants themselves. The professional gladiators and their trainers had no standing in the social life of the country. On the other hand, the owners of these stables of fighters (*lanista*) were usually noblemen or citizens of importance and their interest in this dubious racket was not considered in bad taste.

The gladiatorial boxer led a pampered and closely guarded, but dangerous and brutal life. He was fed the best food, trained with unremitting regularity, granted no personal freedom, and forced to risk his life—or at best horrible disfigurement—at each contest. He was subject to the whim of his master, who might decide at any time to match him against a lion or tiger. No wonder Spartacus, possibly one of the greatest of the gladiators, led a revolt and almost succeeded. With his band of gladiator followers, he suc-

10. Sorrentino pugilist, A.D. second century—Coblanus of Aphrodisias

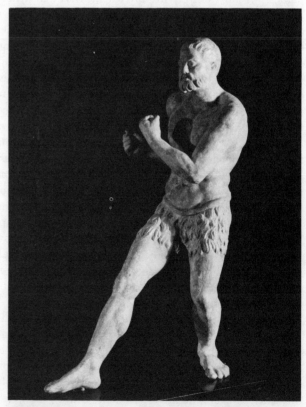

11. Barbarian boxer, Hellenistic Period—second century B.C.

ceeded in staving off the Roman army until he was finally defeated and killed. Had he been successful he might well have been emperor, and a worthy one at that, because he was a brave, shrewd and fair leader.

During these years we find few gladiatorial boxing champions. There was little skill involved; the first man hit was usually the loser. If a boxing champion became too good, he might be thrown into the main bout against a gorilla, a tiger, or a lion, so that many an outstanding boxer when offered the wooden sword and the freedom it symbolized accepted his retirement with understandable speed.

It must be remembered that the Olympic boxing contests continued right through this period and, as a matter of fact, up to A.D. 393 when Theodosius terminated the games after the 291st Olympiad. They had become the object of quarrels and bitterness between the Greek and Roman competitors. The latter were always jealous of Greek victors. There was a war at hand, for the Huns were pressing too far into the great Roman Empire. In addition, the gladiatorial boxer overshadowed the athletic boxer, who by contrast took on the appearance of a weakling.

However, while they lasted, the Olympic games were conducted with a certain respect for their ancient tradition. Cheating and bribery were rarely tolerated, boxing was conducted only with the leather cestus, and the rules were relaxed in only a few cases. But both the morale and incentive were missing. The Romans had instituted professional games of a similar sort all over the empire, and an athlete could make a fortune just following the circuit. Not too many Olympic champions of this period have come down to us and this is evidently due to the jealousy of the Romans who were not too anxious to preserve the victories of their foreign rivals. We do know that these contests were held at Olympia because the lists of the administrators between the years 36 B.C. and A.D. 265 are extant, and other records bring us up to the year when they were officially outlawed. The takeovers of Olympic teams by governments for national honors spelled the end of the games as they threaten to do again, now.

Three champions who look up at us from the books of the historians are Marcus Tullius of Apamea, who in about the second century A.D. described himself as "the first boxer from all time"; a certain Aurelius Helix who evidently survived many gladiatorial spectacles and won both the boxing and pancratium in all-Roman competition; and a certain Varasdates, an Armenian prince, who closes the list of Olympic winners as boxing champion in the last ancient Olympic contest. A Thracian strong man and soldier, Caius Verus Maximin, boxed, wrestled, and bullied himself to become Emperor of Rome from A.D. 215 to 238.

We find rising above the clamor of all the Roman and Greek-Roman games and gladiatorial spectacles, several sane voices of protest. The loudest probably came from Emperor Agrippa. He warned that the increased taxes necessary to subsidize this ridiculous array of athletes might better be spent in a way that would benefit the people more directly. He advised that all competitors, including boxers, who won a victory in minor games no longer be given maintenance for life as had been the custom, but that this award be reserved for the victors in the Olympic, Pythian, and Roman games. In this way he believed money would be saved and the quality of competition improved, for only outstanding athletes would then be encouraged to enter sports as a profession, while the rest would find other occupations more profitable to their communities. In other words, the great Agrippa did not want stumble-bums either stalking each other in the arena or walking on each other's heels in the bread line.

12. Roman boxer, Pompeii, second century B.C.

We also know that the great Marcus Aurelius, Emperor in A.D. 176, was averse to bloodshed for purposes of entertainment. As a result, in his time all gladiators competed like athletes without risking their lives, and all weapons were dulled or equipped with pads or buttons like our modern fencing foils. During the period the use of the murmex or Roman cestus was barred, and only very lightly leaded cestus were used by the boxers.

When scientists uncovered the city of Pompeii and knocked away the lava that had buried it for centuries, they found a number of things of considerable interest to the followers of boxing. On the outer walls of some of the buildings were posters still wonderfully preserved. One of them read,

"THE GLADIATORIAL TROUPE OF SUETTIUS CURUIS, THE AEDILE, WILL FIGHT AT POMPEII ON THE LAST DAY OF MAY. THERE WILL BE A CHASE OF FIELD BEASTS, AND AWNINGS TO PROTECT SPECTATORS FROM THE SUN."

The Colosseum where boxing contests were held in Pompeii from about 300 B.C. to A.D. 63, when it was destroyed by the eruption of Vesuvius, was impressive. It was 430 feet by 335 feet and had a seating capacity of over 10,000 spectators. Many of the seats were protected by permanent awnings, and there was an unusual frame by which a tremendous awning could be pulled over the entire stadium. The seats were numbered and corresponding tickets were issued, but whether or not there were ticket speculators in those days is an unanswered question. On the very last day of Pompeii there was a particularly good show at the amphitheatre which was crowded to capacity. Every ticketholder got his money's worth, for most of the spectators were able to escape when the great volcano erupted, while persons caught in the city itself perished. So perhaps, thanks to the antiquity of boxing, many a fight fan is here today—descendants of those original 10,000 spectators at the Pompeii Colosseum. The Theatre of Marcellus, where boxing was sometimes held and which also was destroyed, seated over 30,000.

Two contributions, if they can be considered such, that have come down to us from the Romans are the custom surrounding ownership of a fighter or the dividing up of such ownership, and the use of professional trainers and seconds.

Rich men, consuls, senators, and generals of Rome owned shares in gladiatorial luminaries just as many big businessmen and prominent people today own shares in boxers. Former Assistant Secretary of State Braden, Al Jolson, Frank Sinatra and many a stockbroker have all owned a fighter or two; not to mention James Norris and the St. Louis businessmen who owned or once owned at least a part of Cassius Clay.

Perhaps because horses, animals, and gladiators used in gladiatorial contests were often quartered together, the Romans also gave us our quaint term of "stable" for a group of fighters owned by one manager or investor or several of these.

But there is one custom we unfortunately failed to adopt. It is the use of the Roman *tessera*, a four-sided bone or ivory tablet hung about the neck of the gladiatorial boxer which identified him by name, owner's name, the place and date where he was first tested or licensed, and the then current consul's or ruler's name. Translated in terms of the modern prize ring, some of the advantages are obvious. Above is a sketch of a tessera found in some Roman ruins, while alongside is its modern counterpart if we adhered to Roman rule.

When Braddock entered the ring to lose his title to Louis, a tessera would have shown whether he were the chattel of Joe Gould, Owney Madden, or possibly Mike Jacobs, if, as rumored, Braddock had a new owner.

The contests and the games of the Egyptians, Minoans, Greeks, and Romans go back for thousands of years and the tradition of our modern prize ring was undeniably thrashed out by the fists of these ancients. As the wind scatters the seed, the Roman legions carried the sport of boxing all over the then-known world, even to a remote little island off the northern coast of Europe. As far as the history of boxing is concerned, this last is interesting, for while we have no positive proof of a connection, twelve centuries later a new chapter in the saga of the fist was to open suddenly and unexpectedly in England—this same little island, visited by the Romans.

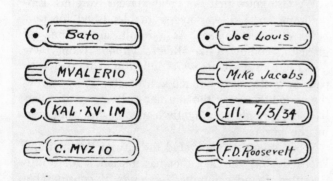

13. Tessera worn by boxers. Left: found in ruins; Right: modern counterpart

2 • The Rebirth of Boxing and the Bare-Fist Era

The period when boxing had disappeared, from A.D. 500 to A.D. 1700, was a tough one, with dictatorships, no political or religious freedom, and bloody wars of conquest. Records in Italy disclose the fact that a monk of Siena, at the beginning of the thirteenth century, taught boxing and arranged amateur tournaments among his congregation. However, while boxing sponsored by the Church enjoyed some temporary local favor, it was lost in the shuffle of the wars and the strife of this confused period. Man was further handicapped during this era by ignorance, disease, poverty, and the slowest means of communication for the largest world, comparatively speaking, of any time in history.

The eighteenth century dawned in England not too differently than in other civilized countries of that time. Men are very much alike in spite of differences in language and the span of centuries.

The advances and regressions of races, nations, art, science, and sports are usually assigned dates and ascribed to decisive battles, great men, or discoveries, although the fate of mankind could as well have been attributed to a deformity, a flood, a discovery, an accident, a whim or a hunch. Progress, according to many, travels like a pretzel. What sidetracks progress or what sidetracked boxing can be explained in dozens of different ways; what impels progress or what brought back boxing after a thousand years is equally controversial.

Man is essentially filled with bounce or rebound. This resilience has conquered many of the difficulties into which races, countries, or individuals including boxers have got themselves.

England had, at the beginning of the eighteenth century, what other countries at the time lacked: a form of government similar to that of Egypt, Crete, Greece, and Rome, which permitted athletics to be freely and nobly participated in. Therefore it was not surprising to find our old friend, the fist, reappearing. When an Englishman of this period wanted to battle or argue out a point, he drew a ring on the ground around himself and invited his opponent to fight it out and "may the best man win." Here in the ring he threw off his tight-fitting embroidered waistcoat, his dainty shoes, his silk stockings, his lace shirt, his feathered hat, and embroidered jabot and went to work unencumbered by the artificial sartorial trappings inherited from his forefathers.

English historians believe that John Broughton, the father of modern boxing, was as important to English history as any one of the decisive battles between fleets or armies. A punch on the jaw was exactly what the Englishmen needed at this time to shed their powdered wigs and bad influences, and develop again the innate courage and manhood necessary to take them and their American cousins through the next tough centuries. It is interesting to note that even before 1650 Milton, the blind poet, in his *Treatise on Education,* recommended boxing for boys not only as an excellent athletic exercise, but as a character builder.

If anyone challenges the importance of Broughton to English history and to humanity, let him remember that Jack Broughton, the boxer, is buried in Westminster Abbey with the greatest kings, soldiers, and poets of the British Empire.

But now let us study the influences behind the reappearance of the clenched fist. In the seventeenth century fencing had become a very necessary accomplishment, and rapier fencing was taught to gentlemen by foreign "cavalier" masters, while people of lesser quality dealt with fencing masters of more plebeian background. These later specialized in the backsword, in single-stick, and also in boxing. They staged exhibition contests both to advertise their trade and to collect money through contributions, gifts or prizes. These stage fights were soon called "prize fights," later to be identified exclusively with boxing, since these masters of the sword were also instructors in the "gentler" art of self-defense. This was the origin both of our current "prizefights" and of our reference to the "gentle art" of boxing, a fist being considered gentle in comparison to steel.

While the rapier was more deadly and more continental, the English people as a whole preferred the national backsword. It was perfect for gory exhibitions, usually without being too dangerous, and Englishmen loved the exhausting slash and parry of a hot backsword contest.

In 1662 Samuel Pepys relates in his diary:

I came and saw my first prizefight . . . between one Mathews who beat at all weapons and one Westwicke who was cut several times both in the head and legs . . . all over blood . . . I felt one of the swords, and found it to be very little if at all blunter on the edge than the common swords . . . strange to see what a deal of money is flung to them both between every bout.

To show how the technique of fencing applied itself naturally to the development of the new sport of boxing, the following is enlightening. In 1692 a manual on fencing was published and gained wide circulation but its general rules were also applicable to boxing.

Rule I was; "Whatever you do, let it always be done calmly, and without passion, and precipitation, but still with all vigour and briskness imaginable, your Judgement not failing to Direct, Order and Govern you as to both."

This instruction was correct for either contest. Furthermore, the positions of "on guard" were very similar except that in boxing the left arm and left leg were forward, while in fencing the sword or right hand and the right or sword leg were forward. In the case of a lefthanded contestant in either sport, a change around was required.

Some of the fencing masters or prizefighters competed not only with backsword, sword and dagger, sword and buckler, but boxed with their bare fists. One of the leading prizefighters of that day was a Mr. Johnson, uncle of Dr. Samuel Johnson.

An old poster, with handbills to match, advertised an entertainment with the manly arts of foil play, backsword, cudgelling, and boxing, as follows:

"Delforce, the finished Cudgeller, will exhibit his uncommon feats with the single stick; and who challenges any man in the kingdom to enter the lists with him for a broken head or belly full.

"Buckhorse and several other pugilists will show the art of boxing.

"To conclude with a grand parade by the valiant Figg who will exhibit his knowledge in various combats with the foil, backsword, cudgel and fist.

"Vivat Rex."

James Figg came just before Jack Broughton and was known as the "Atlas of the Sword" throughout England. His interest in the new sport soon made him famous, and in 1719 he became the first (heavyweight) boxing champion in modern history. He was famous for his almost uncanny judgment of *time and distance*, then called *time and measure*. Figg was not only the boxing champion but the leading teacher and the dominant authority in fistic matters for many years. It was his ruling that required contestants to continue battling until there was a definite winner and loser. No rest periods were allowed. These rules were not changed until 1743, when Broughton made radical changes to give the sport more finesse and science.

James Figg's business cards and some of the posters advertising his bouts were drawn by Hogarth, one of England's more famous artists. According to English records, Figg beat all comers with his fists. The only reason why he was not known as world's champion was that, while he would have been only too glad to accommodate all comers in boxing, he was rather conservative with respect to his fencing, and feared that the European masters and experts, who occasionally journeyed to England, might drive a rapier through his belly if he claimed to be world's champion. However, in boxing he challenged all, and was believed to be invincible.

Once, outside a booth at Southwark Fair, he demonstrated his dexterity as a cudgel expert, fencer, and boxer by taking on all comers. In one of Hogarth's most celebrated pictures, King George II is seen at a prizefight laughing heartily at the ease with which Figg is disposing of an opponent.

By 1735 boxing had become sufficiently popular and Figg sufficiently prosperous for him to undertake the construction of an amphitheater. He was undisputed boxing champion from 1719 to 1730, defeating his leading challenger Ned Sutton three times. Figg was six feet one inch in height, weighed 185 pounds and, though illiterate, had a pleasing personality and attracted the "swells" to his amphitheater. These often included Sir Robert Walpole, Jonathan Swift, and Alexander Pope.

As far back as this early period, many literary figures as well as the newspapers pointed out what we all know today: a good boxer is nimble on his feet, does not slouch, has complete control of his muscles, is coordinated, quick of eye, mentally alert, and decisive. It was also rediscovered that boxing develops the faculty for self-control and that once a man loses his temper, he loses his head.

14. James Figg

Jeffrey Farnol, author of *The Amateur Gentleman*, the greatest modern romance about boxing, pointed out that boxing particularly suited the Englishman's temperament as a means of settling personal differences.

Scorning all treacherous feud and deadly strife,
The dark Stiletto and the deadly knife,
We boast a science sprung from manly pride,
Linked with true courage and to health allied,
A noble pastime, void of vain pretense,
The fine, old English art of self-defence.

Although the rebirth of boxing in England was attended with enthusiasm, the infant almost succumbed again because of bad company. Boxing, single-stick, and fencing were often taught to the gentry in establishments frequently devoted to other and less athletic pursuits. In fact, houses of call sometimes had their prizefighter owner, bouncer, or bar-keep double in brass by teaching the sports of cudgelling, fencing, and boxing as well as attending to their regular duties in the establishment.

However, boxing by its sheer power of entertainment, plus the spirit, quality, and color of its contestants, pulled itself up by the bootstraps.

Let us see how this was done, or preferably let us learn about the boxers and sponsors who did it. For without the progress through this crucial period accomplished by the British, boxing might again have died for another 1200 years.

Probably the one man who did the most to establish the position of boxing and whom many statesmen and historians consider one of the important men of English history is Jack Broughton, father of modern boxing.

In sharp contrast to James Figg, his predecessor, Jack Broughton, a former yeoman of the guard of George II, was cultured, well-educated, intelligent, and polite. An expert fencer, broadsword and single-stick fighter, and boxer, he erected an amphitheater in Hanway Yard, Tottenham-Court-Road, in 1742, for instruction in the art of self-defense and the promotion of prizefights. The year after his amphitheater was built, he drew up and published the first boxing rules:

"For the better regulation of the Amphitheater approved of by the gentlemen, and agreed to by the Pugilists.

"1. That a square of a yard be chalked in the middle of the stage; and every fresh set-to after a fall, or being parted from the rails, each second is to bring his man to the side of the square, and place him opposite to the other, and till they are fairly set to at the lines, it shall not be lawful for one to strike the other.

"2. That, in order to prevent any disputes, the time a man lies after a fall, if the second does not bring his man to the side of the square within the space of a half a minute, he shall be deemed a beaten man.

"3. That in every main battle, no person whatever shall be upon the stage, except the principals and their seconds; the same rule to be observed in by-battles, except that in the latter, Mr. Broughton is allowed to be upon the stage to keep decorum, and to assist gentlemen in getting to their places, provided always he does not interfere in the battle; and whoever presumes to interfere in the battle and whoever presumes to infringe these rules, to be turned immediately out of the house. Everybody is to quit the stage as soon as the champions are stripped, before they set-to.

Within the illustration:

Will.

Hogarth f

James Figg

Master of y Noble Science of Defence
on y right hand in Oxford Road
near Adam & Eve court. teaches Gentle
-men y use of y small. backsword. &
Quarterstaff. at home & abroad

15. James Figg's business card (N.Y. Athletic Club)

"4. That no champion be deemed beaten, unless he fails coming up to the line in the limited time; or that his own second declares him beaten. No second is allowed to ask his man's adversary any question, or advise him to give out.

"5. That in by-battles the winning man to have two-thirds of the money given, which shall be publicly divided upon the stage, notwithstanding any private agreement to the contrary.

"6. That to prevent disputes in every main battle, the principles shall, on coming on the stage, choose from amongst the gentlemen present, two umpires, who shall absolutely decide all disputes that may arise about the battle; and if the two umpires cannot agree, the said umpires to choose a third who is to determine it.

"7. That no person is to hit his adversary when he is down, or seize him by the hair, the breeches, or any part below the waist; a man on his knees to be reckoned down."

It is too bad that modern boxing cannot be guided by rules as simple as these. Regulation No. 5, regarding the public division of prize money with reference to possible private and confidential side deals, would be beneficial if applied today. Things were dealt with much more simply then, even to calling the "ring" the "square," which is certainly more accurate. Why a thing that is obviously square should now be called a "ring" probably is due to the fact that for generations men had traced a circle on the ground within which to settle an argument either with swords, sticks, or fists. Possibly it went even further back to the Roman days when the challenger threw his bloody cestus into the ring—a round arena. One thing certain is that the history of boxing is most certainly encompassed in squared rings of one kind or another.

The publicity, ballyhoo, and advertisement of a boxer's prowess were carried on in those days in quite a modern manner. While perhaps not as obvious, the lack of diffidence or modesty current today was present in earlier years. The so-called grudge fight, so often the last resource of publicity men and promoters to stimulate interest today, thrived in those days also. The challenge which was publicly posted was equivalent to the publicity release of today. Here is the wording of an actual Broughton Amphitheater poster:

Whereas I, John Francis, Commonly known by the name of the Jumping Soldier, who have always had the reputation of a good fellow, and have fought several bruisers in the street, etc., nor am I ashamed to mount the stage when my manhood is called in question by an Irish braggadocio, whom I fought some time ago, in a by-battle, for twelve minutes, and though I had not the success due to my courage and ability in the art of boxing, I now invite him to fight me for two guineas at the time and place abovementioned, where I doubt not, I shall give him the truth of a good beating.

John Francis

The old English effort to stimulate a grudge fight, however, pales when compared with Max Baer's more daring and modern version. When Max and Primo Carnera were being weighed in for the world's heavyweight boxing championship at the New York State Athletic Commission, Baer walked over to the big Italian and started pulling tufts of hair from Primo's chest, coyly intoning:

"Love me! Love me not! . . ."

The result was almost fatal, not to Baer, who ducked, but to the late General John J. Phelan, New York State Boxing Commissioner, who was present for the official weighing-in pictures. Baer gleefully announced to the press that he had "beaten Carnera to a mental pulp." This, of course, made good copy along the grudge-fight slant and you cannot blame the press and the public for enjoying it. More recently, the antics and comments of Cassius Clay, aka Muhammad Ali, have amused or annoyed the public as well as his opponents who have frequently not been able to catch up with him.

Several times in early English boxing one of the contestants would publicly invite a doctor or two to Broughton's Arena to be present in case he seriously injured his opponent. The modern counterpart of this trick turned up in 1935 when Ancil Hoffman, Max Baer's manager, and the Madison Square Garden Corporation insisted on having an ambulance ready for Braddock at the Baer-Braddock world's heavyweight championship bout in which Baer was a ten-to-one favorite. As it turned out, however, the only persons who needed an ambulance after that fight were those who had bet on Baer.

But now back to the eighteenth century and Broughton, who became undisputed champion in 1734. This gentleman boxer was unfortunate in having as his sponsor the powerful Duke of Cumberland, known in Scotland as the "Butcher." John Broughton fought with unvarying success and made much money for his sponsor until 1750 when, fat and forty-six years old, he became an easy mark for Jack Slack, a tough hard-hitting 5 feet 8 inches 196 pounder. Slack blinded Broughton with a terrific punch, but His Grace the "Butcher" who accused Broughton of bribery, withdrew his support, and forced the amphitheater to close. Little is known about Slack ex-

16. Jack Broughton, from an old print

cept that he was an expert fencer and a master with the broadsword. More fame surrounds his grandsons, Jem and Tom Belcher, who fifty years later brought pugilistic honor and a scientifically improved game to the ring.

Broughton's greatest contribution to modern boxing was also a major factor in developing the British and indirectly the American combative spirit which was to assert itself successfully through three world wars. This was his invention of the modern boxing glove. The story is told that Broughton, in studying the Olympic type of cestus on a Greek statue, suddenly wondered if the leather band or doughnut effect could be replaced by soft padding inserted in a glove. If this story is correct, then our modern glove is merely a copy of the Greek Olympic hard glove.

Although gloves were discovered, or rediscovered, in this period, they were only used for sparring, training and especially for instruction, while prizefights continued to be fought with bare knuckles.

When Broughton lost to Slack and the Duke of Cumberland turned against him, a shadow fell across the sport. The Duke, bitter over his betting losses of $50,000, went around England claiming he had been robbed. This old familiar cry was echoed in our day when Joe Jacobs, after the Sharkey-Schmeling fight, griped into the microphone his famous "Geezus, we wuz robbed!" Cumberland even caused Parliament to declare prizefights illegal, and many of the English gentry, or "fancy" as they were called, withdrew their support from the game.

Although boxing was under a cloud and therefore badly handicapped, a number of colorful, if not great champions stood out in this period. The first of these was Peter Corcoran, a 6 feet 7 inch, 260 pound Irishman, who won his championship with a single punch on 18 May 1771, at Epsom in Derby Week. Captain J. O'Kelly, Corcoran's sponsor and backer, a wealthy racehorse operator, won about $200,000 on this fight. Corcoran had a terrific wallop and in the next six years he fought about twenty men, stopping most of them with his first clean punch. He lost his title in 1776 by being out of condition.

The next great champion who stood up against all comers was Tom Johnson, also known as Tom Jackling, a former stevedore and weightlifter, who started fighting at the age of thirty-three. He made his professional debut by winning the title in 1783 by a ko. He was 5 feet 10 inches and weighed 200 pounds; fought more than most bare-knuckle champions; and reigned supreme until 1791, a long tenure as champion. Johnson had supreme confidence in himself and was a born gambler. He probably made

17. "Romany" Jem Mace, the Father of Australian boxing

more money betting on himself than did any other pugilist. He retired in 1789 and within one year lost every dime he had through gambling—but not on himself. In 1791, poverty forced him back into the ring only to be knocked out by Big Ben Brain. Incidentally, the latter died that same year, the only heavyweight champion ever to die training for a fight.

Johnson's most famous fight was with Isaac Perrins, a giant choir singer, who was 6 feet 4 inches tall and weighed 238 pounds. This fight lasted sixty-two rounds, with Johnson retaining his title and winning over $75,000 in bets on himself. Later Perrins was killed in attempting to rescue some people from a fire.

The next champion who came along put boxing in a position it had never enjoyed before. It became a sport second only to fox hunting among the male aristocracy.

This man, Gentleman Jack Jackson, was the only amateur heavyweight to win the professional title until Gentleman Jim Corbett came along in the United States one hundred years later. Jackson was a college youth, in fact, a graduate in medicine and the son of a prominent builder and contractor. At college he had been a great athlete, track man, and weightlifter. He stood 5 feet 11 inches and for most of his life maintained a constant weight of 197 pounds.

35

17A. Gentleman Jack Jackson, world and English heavyweight champion 1791–1800. First two-handed scientific boxer in modern times and first college graduate (in medicine); friend of kings and sartorial leader who inspired The Amateur Gentleman

Jackson, the only college graduate ever to win the heavyweight crown, first entered the ring in 1788 at the age of nineteen. It was in a fight brought about by a bravado spirit on the part of the college youth. Bill Fewterell, his antagonist, was a giant of a man and a local bully. Jackson's friends were all there, including the Prince of Wales, to cheer him on, although they were not too hopeful of his success. In one hour and forty-seven minutes, however, he stepped out of the ring the victor, intent on testing his newly found boxing abilities again. He successfully fought several other prizefighters during this year, among them the French Hercules, and the following year met George Ingleston, the brewer, six feet tall and a terrific hitter. Jackson floored him in the first round but later fell, breaking his ankle. He asked to be allowed to continue, strapped to a chair, but his opponent liked Jackson for his courage and refused to continue under the circumstances.

He did not return to the ring until 1759 when, by popular demand and at the request of his friends, he fought Daniel Mendoza, the uncrowned heavyweight champion. Mendoza, a Spanish Jew was considered a foreigner by the English. Although Mendoza was a four-to-one favorite, Jackson beat him easily, knocking him out in eleven minutes.

18. Humphries-Mendoza, 29 September 1790 (N.Y. Athletic Club)

Jackson then retired and opened a school for boxing where the Prince of Wales, later George IV, Lord Byron, and the leading figures in society took lessons in the art of boxing and sparred with each other. Jackson, by royal command, gave boxing exhibitions at the palace for the Czar of Russia, the King of Prussia and other distinguished visitors. He was actually, if not officially, champion from 1791 to 1800.

He was the link between the sporting world and its royal patrons. It was a full-time job and kept several servants at his London town house busy answering the door, receiving notes of good wishes, and sending replies two days before a fight.

Naturally, with a champion and representative of Jackson's type, boxing prospered. In addition, the four closely fought Humphries-Mendoza fights in this period helped increase the general interest. They were the subject of discussion all over the British Empire.

Mendoza, the final winner, opened a boxing school in the Old Lyceum Theatre in the Strand. His lessons were very expensive, his school well patronized, and he knocked the heads of noble lords and right honorables about at will. The most fashionable theatres during this period featured boxing exhibitions because of its social following.

Although Mendoza, champion of England, brought renewed interest to the game by his great skill and strength, Humphries was equally responsible for the recovery of boxing. He was a gentleman, Beau Brummell, and a friend of the then Prince of Wales. However, as contestants and factors in the progress of the game, they have to be placed after Jackson.

19. Gentleman Jackson's school, from an old print

During this period boxing was beginning to spread to Wales, Scotland, and Ireland. This fact is important in the saga of the fist, for it was later that the Scots and particularly the Irish, dissatisfied with their lot in the British Isles came to America, bringing with them the English sport. They contributed to the development of the art and science of boxing as well as to its rise as an industry in the entertainment field. Its tremendous mass appeal in the United States was to result in the second golden era of the fist.

Mendoza went to Scotland in 1795 and acted as a recruiting sergeant for some Scottish regiments, instructing recruits, on the side, in fencing and boxing. Although there is no evidence that he was successful in spreading interest in boxing, yet the Scots did not dislike using their fists to settle arguments. In 1797 the leaders of two rival Glasgow gangs, Jim Naylor and Jimmie Quinn, were feuding. A promoter arranged for them to meet under prizefight rules for $500 each side. It is too bad Tex Rickard or Mike

Jacobs never could get our gang leaders in Chicago or New York to settle their difficulties in this way, with the numbers racket or the taxi monopoly to the winner. The Naylor-Quinn fight attracted great crowds and the police. Stakes and the ring were pulled up six times just ahead of the police while the fight was going on. Quinn finally gave up, with Naylor an exhausted winner. The publicity and notoriety of this engagement, however, awakened interest in local boxing.

English boxing was at its zenith from about 1785 to 1825, due mainly to the excellence of its fighters. Daniel Mendoza was this period's counterpart of Bob Fitzsimmons, a natural middleweight whose punching power and science licked all the heavyweights of his time save one—Jackson.

In the ring Jackson distinguished himself as probably the first really two-handed scientific fighter of modern boxing. Unlike others up to that time, but like Jack Dempsey later, his left and right were equally potent. Outside the ring Jackson was known among other things for his sartorial perfection. He probably inspired *The Amateur Gentleman*, the greatest romantic story ever written around boxing.

Strangely enough, although there was no question that Gentleman Jackson was the first and greatest scientific boxer of his time and too much for Mendoza, a reported winner of a coast-to-coast radio quiz program involving a $64,000 award claimed the answer was in favor of Mendoza and was, it is believed, awarded the prize notwithstanding the incorrect answer. Eddie Eagan, Chairman of the New York State Athletic Commission at the time, admitted that there had been an error notwithstanding his inadvertently voiced but incorrect concurrence on the program. I contacted the reported and well-known individual winner, a lady doctor, to confirm the controversial answer and the award of the prize for an incorrect answer, however, the winner did not want to discuss the matter. Later the program became highly controversial and was discontinued.

Here we must stop a moment and look with the historian's eye at both Broughton and Gentleman Jackson, for they played a part in the development of American boxing and the current golden era. Boxing in America did not really come into its own until more than a century after its rebirth in England. The first definite bid by America for pugilistic honors was made in 1810 by Tom Molyneux, a black ex-slave. This was almost a century after Figg.

Since we have the records, we are able to be more definite in tracing the path of boxing from England to America than in tracing the saga of the fist from Egypt to Crete and from Crete to Greece and from Greece to Rome. We already know that both the Scots and particularly the Irish emigrated from the British Isles to America and were to a great degree responsible for supplying the impetus boxing needed in America in the latter part of the nineteenth century. But boxing was present in America before that.

What brought it over, and how? Strangely enough, the custom of clenching the fist in America was not originated by low-brows or ruffians. The origin of boxing in America was on the highest level.

In the early days of our colonial history the wealthy aristocracy of America was in the South. The blue-blooded landed gentry with extensive estates and slaves were especially numerous in Virginia, which was then a state rather elastic in size encompassing a lot of territory south of the Mason and Dixon line.

No family who took itself seriously, and these all did, considered its children had acquired the proper polish unless they were educated in England or had at least visited there and exchanged pinches of snuff with the nobility and gentry of the motherland.

These youngsters went to prizefights and were taught boxing in the fast and fashionable company of which they were part. They received instruction from Broughton, and later from Gentleman Jackson, the idols of social England.

Naturally, when these young dandies returned home they had to show off all they had learned abroad, so they boxed against each other. However, since distances between plantations were great and they could hardly use their fathers or sisters as sparring partners, they turned to their personal young slaves. Rivalries sprang up between the young masters' pupils and later between the various plantations' slave champions. More money was won on wagers on fights than on horses. Outstanding boxer-slaves, after earning fortunes in bets for their masters, were given their freedom and moved away from the South so they could ply their fistic trade to better financial advantage for themselves.

Strange as it may seem, this is the exact story behind the spread of boxing from England to America, according to the evidence of history.

For instance, Tom Molyneux, Tom Molyneux's father, and Tom Molnyeux's grandfather were famous boxing slaves in Virginia before Tom Molyneux, as a freeman, came to England to challenge the English champion in the early nineteenth century. A most extraordinary fact is that the great great nephew of this challenger, Tom Molyneux, was John Henry Lewis, light heavyweight champion of the world in 1935.

It is small wonder that the black is effective with his fists today when you consider that boxing probably started in Ethiopia ten thousand years ago, and that later boxing was to become his last resort as a means of escape from slavery, and later from discrimination.

So during the latter part of the eighteenth century destiny was working toward the transfer of boxing supremacy to America. The Irish, Scots, and Jews in England, all discriminated against for religious reasons, were migrating to America and bringing with them their boxing knowledge.

It is to be noted especially during this period that the English, who are by nature a conservative race, consistently referred to their boxing champions as champions of England, just as the Greeks and Romans referred to their victors as champions. However, as soon as Americans took up boxing and introduced a broader view of things, they started the "World's Championship" designation. There is no doubt, however, that Figg, Broughton, Jackson, and the other English champions, as well as the famous Roman and Greek boxers, were by right "World Champions" in its fullest meaning. Certainly Cribb who beat Molyneux, and Sayers who later drew with the American,

Heenan, were world's champions. So our cousins, the English, are not only responsible for the rebirth of boxing, but also monopolized the world's boxing championships from the latter part of the seventeenth century to the latter part of the nineteenth.

As has already been said, the beginning of the nineteenth century saw the height of boxing in England. After Jackson, the exploits, careers, and fights of Dutch Sam, the Star of the East; Tom and Jem Belcher; the Guardsman, Noah James; and others brought further glory and interest to the sport.

Dutch Sam, born Samuel Elias, was a White Chapel Jew who, by means of his fighting, pulled himself out of poverty and obscurity. Although beaten only twice in heavyweight competition, he was a small man, 5 feet 6 inches tall and weighed about 131 pounds. He was one of the most terrific hitters of all time and, according to no less an authority than Pierce Egan, he was compared with two of the greatest: "Gully never struck with more force, nor Cribb more heavily."

Jem Belcher, champion from 1800 to 1804, is the only known son or grandson of a heavyweight champion to follow the tradition of his forebears in the prizering. He was the grandson of Jack Slack, champion from 1750 to 1760. Tom Belcher, Jem's brother, also fought hard to win the title and there was talk of the two brothers fighting for the championship, although they were so inseparable that it is a question whether they would have ever agreed to it.

The American prize ring never quite matched this family's attainments. In 1816 Jacob Hyer, because he was the first white American to box professionally, was recognized as American Champion over the few existing fighters. In 1847 his son, Tom Hyer, became a real American champion, defending his title against Country McCloskey in a 101-round fight and challenging Perry, the English champion, for a world championship match. In 1923, Bob Fitzsimmons' son tried to follow in the footsteps of his dad, but failed, and in 1934, Max and Buddy Baer, like Jem and Tom Belcher, were in line for a possible family bout for the world's title.

After Belcher came one of the few champions who retired undefeated. His name was Henry Pierce, but he was known as "The Game Chicken." At the turn of the century, this popular champion, who at the risk of his life once rescued a girl from a burning house, defeated all opponents, only to die of consumption in 1809 at the age of thirty-one. Perhaps the many two-or-three-hour battles he fought to exhaustion, according to the custom of the times, resulted in his contracting this ailment and in his early death.

His only defeat, if it can be considered such, was in an exhibition bout held in a debtor's prison with a young unknown named John Gully. However, the two met again in a championship bout and Pierce won in the fifty-ninth round when Gully's friends physically prevented him from continuing the battle.

The story of Pierce's exhibition bout with Gully brings up a cntroversial issue often discussed among fight fans, sportswriters, newspaper men and the public. Can a champion, especially a heavyweight champion, where there is no weight limit issue, lose his title by being knocked out or beaten by an unknown in an exhibition bout?

This interesting question first arose in the saga of the ring at the beginning of the nineteenth century. One hundred years later it came up again when James J. Jeffries, world's heavyweight champion, was beaten by unknown Jack Munroe in an exhibition bout in Butte, Montana.

In 1805 the champion of England, "The Game Chicken," Henry Pierce, was persuaded to visit a prison to box for the entertainment of its inmates. One of the prisoners was a young butcher boy who was fairly good with his "dukes" and whom Pierce knew. An exhibition bout was arranged between the two. The champion thought that an engagement of this sort would particularly please the prisoners, and make him and his exhibition more popular.

To the surprise of all, Gully, who was in prison because he had impatient creditors, proceeded to give the champion a going over, and at the end of the exhibition there was not much doubt as to who had won.

It was the custom in those days to imprison all who could not pay their debts. Today it is almost the reverse, and who knows but the time may come when creditors will be imprisoned and their belongings divided among their irate debtors. However, the peculiar customs of Gully's time were to his advantage for it was all part of the social pattern that landed him in jail, released him, and later enabled him to become wealthy and powerful.

John Gully, after his surprising display of fighting ability, was immediately bought out of prison by a group of gamblers who paid all his debts. They planned to manage and own him as a fighter, but did not fare as well as they had expected, for Gully proceeded to buy himself back. Now, sometimes, a fighter, like theatrical or opera stars, is owned and managed by one individual who, in order to obtain money, spread the risk or for other reasons will sell shares of him to others. It was once reported that Primo Carnera and Lily Pons were each cut into twenty-two "pieces." In this case however, Gully reversed the modern procedure, bought himself back piece by piece and became his own manager.

Gully successfully managed himself, built a huge fortune, and became a member of Parliament. If he had been living today, however, certain State Boxing Commissions in the United States would have prevented him from managing himself. Every boxer must have a manager in order to obtain a license to fight in many states, while in other states, if a fighter has no manager, the commissions recommend, suggest or urge him to get one. Modern boxing custom appears to be not always to the fighter's advantage in spite of the progress boxing has made in other ways.

Anyway, Gully could and did own himself and manage himself. Although he lost to Pierce in the fifty-ninth round of an official championship affair, Gully prospered as a fighter.

In 1807 Pierce, because of ill health, retired and Gully became champion, although he refused to consider himself such while Pierce lived.

Probably Gully's most famous fight in defense of the title he refused to "wear" was with the "Smiling Giant," Big Bob Gregson, 6 feet 2 inches tall, weighing 210 pounds. Gully was 5 feet 11½ inches and weighed 189 pounds. This was a bloody and hard-

20. Old painting by Gericault in French museum; Boxers 1810—Cribb-Molyneaux

fought battle, but Gully won by a clean knockout in the thirty-sixth round.

The poor butcher boy, John Gully from Bristol, had three ambitions: first, to be boxing champion; second, to win the Derby; and third, to become a member of Parliament. In 1807 he became champion, saved his ring earnings, invested them in successful tavern and inn operations, pyramided his profits, and, like Mr. Louis B. Mayer, bought racehorses and maintained a very successful stable. After a few bitter disappointments, he realized his second ambition when his colors crossed the finish line on a Derby winner, and finally in 1832 he was elected to Parliament where he served for several terms. Gully died in 1863 at the age of ninety leaving a fortune and a beautiful estate to his heirs—the hero of the most famous rags-to-riches story in English boxing history.

When John Gully retired, Tom Cribb, the "Black Diamond," assumed the title. He will always be known for his tremendous popularity and his luck. His unusual good fortune was evident throughout his entire life. He had come to London at the age of thirteen from Ireland and worked as a coal

heaver, thus gaining his nickname. He became champion of England during one of Britain's crucial periods, when she was bearing the worse blows of another would-be world conqueror in an earlier world war. At Waterloo, however, England saved her empire and in consequence, boxing. Perhaps Waterloo was not won on the cricket fields but in the prizering or "P.R." as it was commonly called.

This period and the career of Cribb is distinguished by the famous Cribb-Molyneux fights that marked in many ways a turning-point in the story of the fist.

Tom Molyneux, a former slave from America, had worked his way across the Atlantic to seek his fortune in the English prize ring. He had confidence in his fistic prowess and believed he could beat Tom Cribb. After he had proved his abilities in some preliminary fights, the first Molyneux-Cribb fight took place on 10 December 1810, at Copthall Common, Essex, in the open air. Cribb had a two-inch height advantage, but Molyneux had a greater reach and weighed 196 pounds—eight pounds more than Cribb. While Cribb was considered to have the advantage in experience and skill, it must be remembered that Molyneux had boxed from an early age, although the calibre of his competition could not, of course, compare with the calibre of Cribb's. Neither man was in good physical condition, Cribb being probably the worse off.

At first the fight was all Molyneux's. This resulted in the partisan crowd, ring followers, and seconds, getting out of hand. The prospect that one who was both a foreigner and a black might win the championship of England was too much for the crowd and there occurred an unsportsmanlike incident, comparatively rare in the story of English boxing, that hurt the game for many years. Having failed to stop Molyneux by repeated foul blows and by biting his thumb to the bone, Cribb and his supporters resorted to another device. Between the twenty-third and twenty-fourth rounds, Cribb being too far gone to "come to scratch," his seconds created a diversion by claiming that Molyneux had lead weights in his hands. During the long argument that ensued, Cribb rested and completely recovered, which was the purpose of the delay, while Molyneux, used to hot climates, was thoroughly chilled and his muscles stiffened by the dampness and cold of a British December day. When the fight was resumed, Cribb began to catch up and finally knocked Molyneux out in the fortieth round. Even the British sportswriters declared that Molyneux should have been awarded the fight at the beginning of the twenty-fourth round when Cribb could not resume the match.

Naturally there was a rematch, and nine months later Cribb and Molyneux met to settle the question that had been bothering the sporting world. However, while Molyneux had been sticking close to the rum bottle, Cribb had been training with the first modern trainer of boxers, Captain Barclay, and was in excellent shape. Molyneux had a weakness for chicken. When he climbed into the ring for his second fight with Cribb, he had just put away a huge chicken pot-pie, a whole apple pie, and a tankard of port ale. Under these circumstances the outcome of the fight was a foregone conclusion, although Molyneux showed skill, courage, and determination before being knocked out in the eleventh round before a record crowd of 40,000.

It was the first important fight in the story of boxing or the Saga of the Fist where a white man exploited the now century-and-a-half old claim that the black race can take more punishment about the head than about the body. Cribb concentrated his attack during most of the fight on Molyneux's body, although in the end, he finally broke Molyneux's jaw and knocked him out with blows to the head and jaw.

The Cribb-Molyneux fights, unfortunately started the career of the fist on a decline. Fights where the ringside crowd could not be controlled, where unfair tactics were used, where pockets were picked and heads bashed in, and where the police might arrive at any time and arrest everyone, discouraged attendance by boxing fans. The wealthy and titled classes lost interest and withdrew their sponsorship. Pugilists and members of the boxing fraternity were blamed for a crime wave that followed.

During this period of decline, however, it must be admitted that Tom Cribb, at least, was a fighting champion worthy of the name. He did his best to encourage the sport, and continued to challenge contenders for the title for the next eleven years without avail, until in 1822 at the age of forty-one he retired.

During the Cribb period and thereafter in spite of the adverse circumstances described above, certain progress was made in the game. Stands or raised seats were adopted for the first time at Tom Spring's battle at Worcester with an Irish contender named Jack Langan. These stands seated 4,000 at $2.50 a person and were filled to capacity; 22,000 standees also viewed the fight. Spring, born Thomas Winter, knocked out Langan in the seventy-seventh round and received about $27,000. Tom Spring, by the way, was the first heavyweight champion with a really educated left hand. He is often compared with Jim Corbett. Although he had no punching power, he wore his opponents down by keeping his left hand in their faces or stomachs from the beginning to the end of every fight.

The period of decline lasted from about 1820 until the appearance of Tom Sayers, about forty years later. During this drab period one colorful fighter did appear and won the heavyweight title—William Thompson, known as Bendigo. He weighed only 165 pounds, but won many tough battles with bigger men. He retired to become an evangelist, and later was ordained a methodist minister.

When boxing speeded up its forward movement with the appearance of Sayers, it marked the last great period of English boxing before the sport and its control and development passed to America.

Tom Sayers was "a great little man." He was a natural middleweight who had been a butcher at Pimlico, Brighton, and whose father had been a bookmaker. For calm, cold courage, and ring craft, there have been few to surpass him. He had baffling speed, judged by the accounts of those who saw him, which overcame his shortcomings in height, weight, and strength. He defeated William Perry, the Tipton Slasher, in 1857, for the title, giving away four inches in height and about fifty-two pounds in weight.

While England was enjoying another progressive chapter in boxing history, in the middle of the nineteenth century the popularity of the clenched fist in America had spread from the plantations of Virginia and from the Scotch-Irish and Jewish immigrants of New York, even to far distant California.

John C. Heenan of Benicia, California, had fallen heir to the American championship when John Morrissey retired. As Heenan was 6 feet 2 inches tall and weighed over 200 pounds, fight fans in America believed that here was the man to go to England and defeat little Tom Sayers and bring back a true world's championship to the United States.

The result was, therefore, the first international heavyweight championship actually publicized and billed as such. Correspondents were sent to cover it and many fans decided to go to Europe to see it. Actually however, the same thing had happened fifty years before when Cribb and Molyneux fought.

The Sayers-Heenan fight, as we shall see, was not conclusive in establishing a world's championship, but it did establish a very definite and significant milestone in the Saga of the Ring. It actually did as much for boxing, especially in its international aspect, as anything ever did. In addition, it illustrated how athletic competition, even in professional boxing, could bring two nations and their peoples together.

The fight was held at Farnborough, England, on 17 April 1860, before 2,500 distinguished spectators. Sayers was small, while Heenan had a build which artists claimed was classic. The contrast was impressive. During the fight, Heenan knocked Sayers down twenty-five times and Sayers practically closed both Heenan's eyes with his sharpshooter punches. Before

the end, Sayers was completely exhausted and Heenan was completely blind. After two hours and twenty minutes the police broke up the fight and the referee declared it a draw. The championship belt was given to Sayers as the defending champion. In a gesture of good sportsmanship, Sayers offered half of it to Heenan who, not to be outdone, refused to accept it. The two fighters became friends, and so did the partisan American and English spectators.

Two more English champions must be mentioned. Jem Mace, the "Swaffham Gypsy" who owned the Red Lion Tavern, played the violin, and is said to have been responsible for Jeffrey Farnol turning writer, was, notwithstanding these extracurricular activities, a great boxing champion. Tom King, whose most important wins were over Jem Mace and John Heenan, became one of England's greatest scullers, a successful racing stable operator, and a very wealthy man. After he retired, Mace was generally recognized as champion from 1865 to 1868. He was the last champion of the world under London Prize Ring rules.

Jem Mace, as if to prove his gypsy blood, was the first English champion to travel abroad to defend his title. He journeyed to the United States, Canada, and Australia. In Australia he established a boxing school and is thought of as the father of Australian boxing. Boxing is very popular there—and who can tell but that another century may see the control and development of the sport pass to the nation "down under."

After the retirement of Mace, boxing in England lost ground, although John Sholto Douglas, eighth Marquis of Queensberry, introduced a new set of rules for the ring, sponsored amateur tournaments, and insisted on the use of gloves. His rules included many changes, particularly the elimination of wrestling and holding, and designated ten seconds as the time allowed a floored fighter to recover.

In 1839 when Deaf Burke, the reigning British champion, came to America on a barnstorming tour, he found little competition and poor pickings. Boxing did not really start in the United States until about 1850, and unfortunately it had no wealthy patrons to carry it through its infancy, such as the early British ring enjoyed. Prizefighting was outlawed for many years in the States and some of the bare-knuckle fighters actually were criminals. Neither fact helped its social progress. But the powerful appeal of boxing has never failed to assert itself.

It took the gloved fist, however, to put boxing over in America. When John L. Sullivan, the bare-knuckle champion, became a fighter under the Marquis of Queensberry rules, boxing entered the United States golden era of the game.

The so-called first champions of America are rather debatable, so no exact chronology of the sport in this period is possible. Suffice it to say that Molyneux, Jacob Hyer, Yankee Sullivan (James Ambrose)—an escaped convict from Australia—Tom Hyer, John Morrissey, John C. Heenan, Mike McCoole, Tom Allen, Joe Goss, Paddy Ryan, to name a few, were the best of the early fighters in America.

The United States really took over the control and development of boxing when John L. Sullivan, the "Boston Strong Boy," stiffened Paddy Ryan in nine rounds at Mississippi City, 7 February 1882. John L. was the last of the bare-knuckle champions, a title which he held to his death.

John Lawrence Sullivan was an Irish-American born in Boston in 1858. His best fighting weight was about 196, but he was only 5 feet 10 inches tall. Like many fighters, he first enjoyed a reputation as a strong man. According to writers of his time, he was a great burly, slugging fighter with bull-like tactics, mighty fists, and little science. He was good-natured, generous, conceited, blustering, and extremely popular. In fact, many claim that no fighter ever captured the hearts of the general public to the same extent as "The Boston Strong Boy." His championship was the most important thing in the world to him, with hard liquor and women combined running a close second. His affair with Ann Livingston, a hefty armful according to contemporary pictures, lasted for years. She gave up a career as burlesque queen, followed him to England dressed as a boy, ignoring both convention and Sullivan's wife in Boston. But there is no saint like a reformed sinner, and when Sullivan turned over a new leaf, he became a teetotaller and a lecturer for the Women's Christian Temperance Union.

Sullivan's career was a milestone in the history of boxing. As we have seen, he was the last of the bare-knuckle fighters and the first champion of the padded-glove era. He lived by the rules of the old school, where he had received his pugilistic upbringing, and trained according to the dictates of his desire for liquor and bright lights. In the fight with Paddy Ryan that made him champion, Sullivan was in good physical condition, but three years later when they met in a return bout, he was fat and dissipated. Amazingly enough, this condition did not seem to impair his punch. The police stepped in and ended the fight in the first round, after he had landed a blow on Ryan's jaw that would have killed an ox.

Promoters were trying constantly to convince Sullivan that he could make a fortune in other fields, and there is little question that, had he not loved fighting more, his name would be found today in Baseball's Hall of Fame. He played football in an exhibition to help Boston College break into the game, and he took a successful swing at the theatre, where no less a person than William Brady said he did a more than adequate job of entertaining his audience on the other side of the footlights.

Just as there was a "white hope" campaign in the days of Jack Johnson and in the forties a search for a contender to meet Joe Louis, a "beat John L" campaign was started in his day sponsored particularly by Richard K. Fox, publisher of the pink *Police Gazette*, favorite of the barber shop literati. "Pink" of course, referred to the color of the paper this publication was printed on, and not to its political orientation.

Sullivan had a reputation in the ring that terrified many of his opponents. Men who fought him seemed mesmerized like some of Joe Louis' challengers. Often opponents had actually to be hired to get into the ring with him. The story goes that when one of these gave up and ran out of the ring before the fight was over, Sullivan glared at the audience and shouted: "My name is John L. Sullivan. I can lick any sonofabitch in the house. Does anyone here want to take me up on that?" No story of John L.'s career is complete without this key to the old champion's character.

Sullivan's most important challenger for his title was Charlie Mitchell, the English 160-pound middleweight, who knew all the tricks of the game. They fought in the old Madison Square Garden in 1883. Mitchell's cunning and skill made Sullivan look foolish at first, and he even knocked the great man down with a first round punch. He was finally all but overcome by the champion's bull-like rushes and flurry of pounding fists before the police stopped the bout.

Sullivan's temperament was willful. He played the game according to his own rules, and he took full advantage of the fact that few dared to disagree with him. It was impossible to anticipate how he would act. On the night of his return fight with Charlie Mitchell, Sullivan climbed into the ring too drunk to fight, announced the fact regretfully to his audience and promptly retired. He got away with it. On another occasion, after seven rounds with Dominick McCaffrey, he quit the ring, declaring he just did not want to fight any more. Yet, in a battle with Patsy Cardiff he fractured one of the bones in his right arm, kept the fact to himself, and continued a stiff fight against the younger, capable man until it was stopped, a draw.

Losing the championship to Corbett was probably the most desperate moment in Sullivan's life. He fought a grim and frantic battle. It cannot be denied that the great Sullivan could take it as well as dish it out. In spite of his unsportsmanlike refusal to shake the admiring Corbett's hand before the fight began, he came through with a remark at the end of the contest that put him right back on the pedestal. "I fought once too often and if I had to get licked, I'm glad

it was by an American. Yours truly, John L. Sullivan." When he chose to be, John L was charming and his appeal seemed to be more than just local. In England in 1887 he had to have special body guards to protect him from the admiring throngs, and even the Prince of Wales saw one of his matches and asked to have him presented at court. When the Prince met Sullivan, he confided to the great John L. that his son was a regular slugger.

While in England, Sullivan tried to meet Charlie Mitchell again, but fighting was outlawed there, and so they fought at the country estate of Baron Rothschild at Chantilly, France. Sullivan desired to beat Mitchell because he personally hated him, and because he believed that, if he did, he would have a claim to the world's championship. He was not in good condition, weighed 216, much of it fat, to Mitchell's 168. The fight lasted for three hours, thirty-nine rounds, when rain and the officials stopped it, and called it a draw. Charlie Mitchell was not England's official champion at the time, so Sullivan's idea with respect to the world's championship does not appear to have been very reasonable. However, tough little Charlie did win the English heavyweight title from Jem Mace in 1890 and when James J. Corbett fought and beat him in Jacksonville, Florida, three years later, the world's heavyweight title was officially at stake for the first time.

Upon his return to America, John L heard the news of the arrival of the Australian heavyweight champion, black Peter Jackson, who had beaten George Godfrey so efficiently he was finding it impossible to get another match. Using the color line as an excuse, Sullivan ducked the fight.

While Sullivan was reluctant to risk his title, he was finally forced to accept the challenge of Jake Kilrain. His condition at that time made training imperative, and there was little time to get him into shape. There was only one man in America who could do it: William Muldoon, the wrestler and weightlifter who was also a fanatic on conditioning. Sullivan feared and respected him. For $10,000 Muldoon took a job which was finally accomplished only by locking the champion up and putting him on a water diet.

The famous Jake Kilrain-Sullivan fight was fought on 8 July 1889, in Richburg, Mississippi. The spectators were seated in stands that came right down to the ring. This cut off all circulation of air. The sun shone brilliantly during the entire contest and the day was one of the most blistering ever experienced in a section accustomed to heat. The temperature at ringside was 108°. After three hours or seventy-five rounds of mauling and sweltering, a physician from the New York Athletic Club told Donovan, one of Kilrain's seconds, that if Jake con-

22. John L. Sullivan-Jake Kilrain fight

tinued he would die. Mike Donovan, who had seen two men killed in the ring, tossed in the sponge. Charlie Mitchell, Sullivan's jinx, also was in Kilrain's corner but even his knowledge of John L's weaknesses could not stop the decision from going to him. Actually both men fought each other to exhaustion, although the Boston Strong Boy's native strength plus Muldoon's training carried the day.

After the fight, Muldoon, who was then wrestling champion, and Sullivan planned a trip through the States in a combination exhibition and challenging tour. But Sullivan went on a binge, and Muldoon, deciding that he could not handle John L on a tour, abandoned it. He teamed up with Kilrain in 1890 after having downed Strangler Lewis. A feud between Sullivan and Muldoon began about this time and negotiations for a fight between the two were widely discussed. Muldoon had boxed as well as wrestled and speculation ran high with respect to a boxing or rough-and-tumble contest between the two. However, the two men never met in the ring and seven years later became friends again. Muldoon later was one of the first Athletic Commissioners of New York State and the dissenting member of the 1930 New York State Athletic Commission which voted Max Schmeling "Heavyweight Championship of the World." Muldoon contended that winning on Sharkey's foul did not make Schmeling the best heavyweight in the world.

About 1889 there appeared a young former amateur boxer from the Olympic Club in San Francisco who had just turned professional, and who seemed to be making quite a reputation for himself. James J. Corbett, the first of the present line of boxers who had had no experience in bare-knuckle contests, was a tall, thin youth, weighing around 165 pounds. He was proving himself to be a dazzling fighter, clever, and fast. He originated the theory that "you can't be beat if you can't be hit." His weaving, dodging, sparring tactics were at first looked upon with dis-

favor by the old-timers used to toe-to-toe slugging.

On his way to the championship bout, Corbett had the good fortune to meet worthwhile challengers and to put them away in such a manner as to leave little doubt of his abilities. He fought a six-round exhibition with gloves against Jake Kilrain in New Orleans, Louisiana, and jabbed and hooked him to a pulp without even getting his hair disarranged. He knocked out Dominick McCaffrey whom Kilrain was afraid to touch, and in 1891 he fought Peter Jackson, the black man who was so dangerous that John L had refused to meet him. In this bout Jackson, the Australian champion, had thirty-six pounds advantage and the experience of many more fights. While he was of the old school, he used a powerful one-two punch in various combinations which made him a tricky adversary. Corbett dodged, slipped, ducked, sidestepped and in this way avoided Jackson's punches, but the fight soon developed into a fierce endurance contest which was finally stopped by the referee, Hiram Cook, at the end of the sixty-first round. It was declared a draw and all bets were called off. For four hours Peter Jackson had held off one of the greatest and cleverest boxers of all time. For sixty-one rounds young Corbett had successfully withstood one of the most powerful and experienced fighters of his time.

Next on Corbett's list of pre-championship fights was a contest with none other than the Champion himself.

John L. Sullivan was at this time barnstorming in a play "Honest Hearts and Willing Hands," and shortly after the Corbett-Jackson fight he reached San Francisco. A charity affair was being arranged at the Opera House, and Sullivan had been prevailed upon to give a boxing exhibition as a leading attraction. Corbett eagerly volunteered as the other contestant; Sullivan accepted, but specified that they must appear on stage in evening clothes, for it was not his intention to get in the ring in boxing togs and risk his reputation against this little-known fighter. It was a fortunate opportunity for the younger fighter, as in this exhibition he was able to study at first hand the technique of the great man who he was to knock out the following year.

In 1891 another event should be noted. In New Orleans, Robert Fitzsimmons, a clumsily built fighter developed by Jem Mace in faraway Australia, won the middleweight title from Jack Dempsey, the Nonpareil. This was an important event in boxing because it pushed Fitzsimmons up into the heavyweight class and on the road toward the championship title. This fight also ended the career of one of the greatest fighters of any weight anywhere in the world. Dempsey, the Great, the Nonpareil, a mere

23. A very rare photograph—the earliest-known ring pose, taken of Sullivan when he was about nineteen-years-old.

The fight was a perfect demonstration of the old technique versus the new. For the first few rounds, Sullivan did all the rushing and threw all the punches. Corbett was an illusive, moving target that infuriated the champion and caused the audience to scream accusingly—"Get in there and fight." These were tactics the crowd was not used to, nor did they realize until later that something new was being added to pugilism. After the seventeenth round, the result of the fight was no longer in doubt, and in the twenty-first the end came; John L was counted out, and Corbett was champion.

John L never crawled through the ropes as a contestant again. He was beaten, not because he had lost his punch, but because he could not find his man. The new game was too fast. However, if the strength, speed, hitting power, fighting instinct, and ring ferocity of Sullivan had been developed in the school of modern boxing, and were he around today, he would be a dangerous challenger to any champion.

John L's popularity never faded, and it is because of him that boxing in America gained the patronage it so badly needed to make it the sport now followed by millions. In addition, it was John L Sullivan who voluntarily adopted the Marquis of

consumptive shadow of his former self, fought on to defeat, as men sat about the ringside with tears coursing down their cheeks in unashamed emotion.

About this time Sullivan found himself once again in a position where the cries of his challengers were becoming much too audible. Charlie Mitchell, his bête noire, Frank Slavin, Peter Jackson, and Corbett each wanted a try at the title. Sullivan had been dodging a fight since his contest with Kilrain three years before. He could no longer get away with it, so he issued a statement that he would accept a bout with any one of his challengers except Jackson, for a purse of $25,000, and a side bet of $10,000, winner take all, the fight to be fought with five-ounce gloves and conducted under Queensberry rules. The first to raise the side bet, issue the formal challenge, and post his wager, was Corbett. The Olympic Club of New Orleans, in conjunction with the Bohemian Club of New York, put up the purse, and the Crescent City got the star bout.

Sullivan weighed 224 pounds, mostly fat that had been trained down; Corbett, 186, all of it coordinated muscle. The challenger was also eight years younger than the champion.

24. Sullivan at the age of twenty

Queensberry's rules and gloves and in this way was largely responsible for the American padded glove, golden era of boxing. He made the following significant announcement ushering in a new chapter in the saga of sock:

The London rules allow too much leeway for the rowdy element to indulge in their practices. Such mean tricks as spiking, biting, gouging, concealing snuff in one's mouth to blind an opponent, strangling, butting with the head, falling down without being struck, scratching with the nails, kicking, falling on an antagonist with the knees, the using of stones and resin, are impossible under the Queensberry Rules. Fighting under the new rules before gentlemen is a pleasure.

3 • The Padded-Glove Era

Although most official records state that John L. Sullivan was the last and undefeated world's bare-knuckle champion and James J. Corbett the first world's champion under the Marquis of Queensberry rules with padded gloves and three-minute rounds, this, like many statements concerning the saga of the fist, is technically incorrect.

John L. Sullivan actually was the first world's champion with padded gloves as well as the last bare-knuckle champion. On 29 August 1885, in Cincinnati, Ohio, Sullivan and Dominick McCaffrey fought for the Marquis of Queensberry championship of the world using padded gloves and with three-minute rounds. Billy Tait was referee, and Sullivan was billed and introduced just as he was in New Orleans on 7 September 1892, when he fought Corbett, as the "Present World's Heavyweight Champion." Although this particular fight started a controversy that time and old records have not solved, there is no question that Sullivan retained his official title. The fight was scheduled for "*six rounds or to a finish.*" A contemporary expert, J. S. McCormack, stated that Sullivan actually koed McCaffrey in the third round but time was improperly called and McCaffrey was revived by his seconds for the next round. At the end of six rounds, Sullivan decided to continue perhaps in an effort to "finish" his opponent, but at the end of the seventh round, infuriated by the fact that McCaffrey could not be "finished," he quit amidst much confusion. The seventh round was unrecorded and the referee disappeared. Two days later both the referee and the newspapers all agreed that Sullivan had "won." In any case, as the fight was a six-round no-decision affair, and Sullivan was not knocked out but, in fact, won the newspaper decision, there seems to be no reason why Sullivan should not be considered the first padded-glove champion. Anyway, as the first bare-fist champion to adopt the Marquis of Queensberry rules, he legitimately became champion under the new rules. Otherwise Corbett's own title, and the championship right down to the present is not clear.

However, James J. Corbett did usher in the new era of the padded glove. Not only was he the first heavyweight to win his title with gloves, but his style also marked the end of the old era and the beginning of the new in fistiana. John L. Sullivan based his entire strategy on offensive tactics and hitting power. Corbett first introduced into championship competition defensive tactics, and the principle that a man cannot be defeated if he cannot be hit.

Corbett knocked out Charlie Mitchell of England in 1894, a feat the great John L could not perform. When Corbett knocked out Mitchell, the world's championship was first established with clear formal title rather than by mere public acceptance or by assumption. For Charlie Mitchell was champion of England and Europe and considered world's champion.

Next, Corbett knocked out a Peter Courtney at Orange, New Jersey, mainly for the production of the first fight picture for Edison's kinetoscope. Thomas Edison was personally present at this first "filming" of a motion picture of a championship fight.

Bob Fitzsimmons, the tall middleweight with stilts for legs and the shoulders and arms of a heavyweight blacksmith, was Corbett's leading challenger. On St.

24A. Charlie Mitchell, claimant of the English title, who made several attempts, unsuccessfully however, to win the American championship.

25. 1897: An artist's idealized conception of Jim Corbett and Bob Fitzsimmons shortly before their bout for the championship at Carson City, Nevada. The famous Richard K. Fox belt appears in the background. (Police Gazette)

Patrick's Day, 1897, Corbett and Fitzsimmons met in Carson City, Nevada, for a purse of $15,000 and a side bet of $5,000. A western sheriff frisked the spectators and checked the 400 guns he obtained. He refused to take any chances in case the crowd got too excited. Fitzsimmons weighed 156½ pounds, Corbett 185.

Although Corbett gave the flat-footed Fitz a boxing lesson in the early rounds and knocked him down for a count of nine in the sixth, Fitz's terrific blows began to tell on him. In the fourteenth, a lefthand drive to the solar plexus did the trick and there was a new champion—a champion incidentally who at eighteen had been taught the English art of self-defense in Australia by none other than "Romany" Jem Mace. Although sportswriters discussed the "new" and "mysterious" solar-plexus punch, actually it was just a belt to the breadbasket taught Fitzsimmons by Jem Mace and a direct heritage from good old Jack Broughton's left to the stomach.

Fitzsimmons did not fight again for two years, pre-

ferring to pick up all the money he could without risk by barnstorming with a theatrical troupe as champion. While he was doing whis, Corbett was challenging him to another bout, and a burly young man, James J. Jeffries, was accumulating a reputation. Fitzsimmons having popularized the remark, "the bigger they are, the harder they fall," agreed to fight Jeffries, a tremendously large but slow-moving fighter, who had once been a sparring partner to Corbett. Fitz thought that this slow-moving mastodon would be made to order for him.

He did not know about the famous Jeffries crouch, and when he met it he could not solve it. Jeffries was a giant who weighed, trained-down to a "shadow," 220 pounds. He was as strong as a bull, but not as fast. William A. Brady, his manager, who had originally hired him as sparring partner for his first champion, James J. Corbett, decided that he had to improve Jeffries's boxing if he could not improve his speed. He hired Tommy Ryan, a former great middleweight champion, to work with the "Boilermaker," as Jeffries was sometimes called.

In a gym bout one day Ryan, with heavy gloves, was punching Jeff's face with a barrage of fists, and throwing a few extra ones to his stomach without getting a return, when suddenly Jeff dropped into a sort of a leaning forward crouch with his huge left hand

26. J. J. Jeffries vs. Tom Sharkey, twenty-five rounds at Coney Island, New York in 1899.

27. James J. Jeffries

extending sideward and forward from his body—his long arm almost straight—with the result that Ryan could no longer reach him by straight punches, swings, or rushes. Jeff then gave him short but powerful love-taps from his almost fully extended battering-ram left arm.

Ryan realized that Jeff finally had found a natural style that compensated for his slowness: one which would utilize his tremendous reach, height, and strength. And so the Jeffries crouch, which was to carry its creator to a championship and a great pugilistic career, was born. Jeff who was a natural left-hand puncher, was so big and powerful that his blows from an almost extended left did not have to travel more than a few inches to be damaging. He was immediately put to work on the heavy bag, beating a tattoo with his long left in preparation for its riveter-like action on the faces of smaller and faster men who would try to get past it.

So when Fitzsimmons picked out Jeffries as a slow target, he was right—but the target could never be reached. Fitz tried every trick and threw his best Sunday punches, but he could not keep Jeff's long left out of his face and stomach. The youth, weight, and strength of the challenger finally resulted in a knockout victory for Jeffries in the eleventh.

The Jeffries-Fitzsimmons fight was the second regular heavyweight championship battle filmed by motion pictures, the first having been that of the Corbett-Fitzsimmons bout at Carson City. For some reason, most of the Jeffries-Fitzsimmons films were ruined, and the two boxers were brought back at a later date to try to recreate their fight. Here for the first and last time a world's heavyweight championship was refought unofficially for the movies. Later, as we shall see, the reverse happened when Carnera and Baer fought a fight for the movies before their championship battle. However, the Jeffries-Fitzsimmons movie retake was not too successful, and it was obvious that the pictures were not those of the actual battle.

Jeffries at twenty-four, with years of hunting and fishing and outdoor life behind him, and possessed of one of the greatest physiques any champion has ever had, then proceeded to lick everybody in sight. He fought and knocked out Corbett in the twenty-third round. This proved to be an unusual fight. For twenty-two rounds Corbett piled up a safe lead on points. He apparently·solved the Jeffries crouch and avoided Jeffries' rivetlike left, but in the twenty-third round, according to Corbett's own account, he miscalculated the nearness of the ropes which caught him across the back as Jeff stepped forward and popped his short riveterlike left from an almost extended arm to Corbett's chin. Corbett came-to shortly thereafter, sitting in his corner with his seconds working over him. It was this Jeffries fight, three years after Corbett lost to Fitzsimmons, that made Gentleman Jim more popular than he had ever been as champion. Corbett had come, in truth, within the thickness of a rope of regaining his title. Only the rope had stopped him from getting out of the way of Jeffries' lefthand punch in the twenty-third round. The fight scheduled for twenty-five rounds would have gone to Corbett on points if he had finished.

Jeffries as a fighting champion fought everyone in sight. In fact, public demand even dug up Bob Fitzsimmons again. They fought in 1902. Fitzsimmons was then forty years old, but in fair shape and still had terrific punching power. For four rounds Fitz gave Jeffries an unmerciful beating, but in the fifth Jeffries caught him with that left hand and turned the tide of the battle. In the eighth, Jeffries landed two more terrific lefts—one to the jaw and one to the stomach—and down on his hands and knees dropped Fitzsimmons. Once more a former heavyweight champion had failed to come back.

Bill Brady, Jeffries' manager, actually had a hard time getting suitable opponents for the champion, whose absolute superiority over the field was so great that he ran out of challengers. By 1904 Jeffries found himself in the same position as Sullivan, Dempsey, Louis, and Marciano at their best. Jeffries, however, did not have a boxing-conscious Latin-America to barnstorm, or million-dollar gates to tide him over the dull periods between fights. In 1905, discouraged at the lack of worthwhile opponents, the poverty of the gates, and purses obtainable for fighting palookas, and disappointed, too, because he never quite captured the tumultuous wave of popularity enjoyed by another great champion, John L. Sullivan, Jeffries retired to his California farm. He named Marvin Hart, the winner of the Hart-Jack Root bout he had refereed, the new champion. Of course no one took either the retirement or the appointed champion seriously.

In 1906 Hart lost his questionable and unrecognized championship to a Canadian, Tommy Burns.

Burns (Noah Brusso) weighed less than 175 pounds but proceeded in the next two years to take on the best men in America, Australia, England, and Ireland, and beat them all. After achieving thirteen consecutive victories against as many opponents he went to San Francisco in 1906 and fought the clever boxer and light heavyweight champion, Philadelphia Jack O'Brien, to a draw. Burns later wiped out this only blemish on his record by beating O'Brien in a return fight. That left only one man to fight.

This man was Jack Johnson, a huge black from Galveston, Texas, who had an impressive record of successive wins and who had challenged Burns consistently. In fact, the big black man had followed Burns from America to Canada, from Canada to England, then from England to Australia.

In Australia, where the sports writers remembered how Peter Jackson, their black fighter, had been sidetracked from a championship fight with John L. Sullivan and James J. Corbett, Johnson secured help. As a result, a Johnson-Burns fight took place 26 December 1908, at Rushcutter Bay near Sydney, in a wooden stadium reminiscent of the one later constructed on Boyles' Thirty Acres. The day before—Christmas—Santa Claus evidently forgot to put anything in the Burns sock, because Johnson beat him so badly that the police had to stop the fight in the fourteenth round.

It is interesting to note that once more in a championship contest a white man attempted to defeat a black man by subjecting him to a body attack. After being knocked down by Johnson's first punch Burns worked almost exclusively on Johnson's body for seven rounds. However, according to witnesses, this body punishment had no effect on Johnson who, from the seventh round on, toyed with Burns and cut his face to pieces. This fight, filmed for silent pictures, included dialogue, but no radio or talking picture company could possibly have reproduced it for public consumption since the contestants for the championship hurled insults and profanity at each other during the entire fight with even more abandon than their fists.

Now, for the first time in the modern history of boxing, a black was the recognized world's champion. Unfortunately, Johnson was an ignorant, willful, happy-go-lucky man, who brought no credit either to boxing or to his race. He offended both blacks and whites by living with white women, and finally was indicted on a Federal morals charge and had to flee the country. He became an outcast and a man without a country.

But before all this happened, a vociferous portion of the public insisted that Jeffries, still the official champion according to many, come out from retirement and lick Johnson. Tex Rickard, sensing the popular demand for a Jeffries-Johnson fight, was instrumental in persuading the former champion to return to the ring. This marked the entrance of Rickard, the Barnum of boxing, into the sport, who was later to build the million-dollar gates of the roaring twenties.

At last Jeffries agreed to reenter the ring and started to work off the accumulated fat of five years. Although the thirty-five-year-old giant finally got down to 227 pounds, his zip and spark were gone. Rickard arranged, promoted (in conjunction with Jack Gleason of San Francisco), and refereed the fight at Reno, Nevada, on 4 July 1910. A majority of fight fans were pulling for Jeffries, but that was not enough to bring him victory. A perfectly conditioned 208-pound Johnson toyed with pugilism's "old man of the mountain" and knocked him out in the fifteenth round.

Johnson never again fought in the United States. As a result of his unpopularity, a frantic "white hope" search followed the defeat of Jeffries, but to no avail. The only fighter who probably could have extended Johnson was Sam Langford, the Boston Tar Baby, but he also was black, and no promoter was interested in such a bout. Nor indeed, was Johnson. Johnson knew too much about Langford's skill and punch, because he had just managed to shade him in a fifteen-round decision in 1906.

All the white hopes fizzled out in the ring with Johnson. Gunboat Smith, Frank Moran, Carl Morris, and others fell in the ring as well as by the wayside of the fistic path. Finally a six-foot-seven, Wild West show giant who weighed over 250 pounds, named Jess Willard, began to attract attention.

Johnson in exile, financially flat, and physically softened by high living, was lured into a fight with Willard, to be held in Havana, Cuba. Money, of course, was Johnson's main problem and his sole reason for taking the fight. He needed plenty of it, and quickly, and many people believed he accepted an offer of an additional amount to lose the fight.

Anyway, while Johnson took the earlier rounds, Willard's great strength seemed to overwhelm the champion who finally took the count in the twenty-sixth round, more exhausted and battered than knocked out. Johnson always maintained that this fight was fixed and that he "took a dive." Photographs of the knockout do reveal a most questionable position for a man whose reflexes were supposed to be beyond control, since he appeared to be protecting his eyes from the sun with his extended arm. It is doubtful if a helplessly battered fighter would trouble to shade his eyes against any strong light while semiconscious or unconscious on a ring floor.

The news of Willard's victory was glad tidings for fight fans and boxing circles everywhere. Johnson

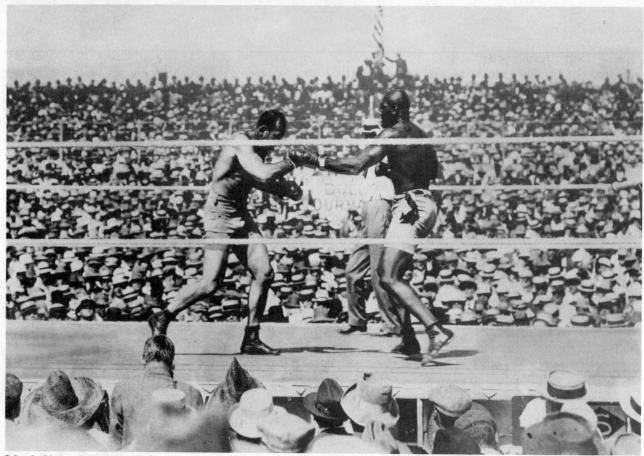

28. Jeffries-Johnson fight

had alienated the public by his immoral living habits, his flight from the law, his deportment in the ring, and his long abstinence from his chosen business—that is, training and fighting. Many blacks before him had earned the respect of sport followers—Peter Jackson and George Dixon, for instance. However, under the circumstances people of all races turned favorably toward the new champion.

The new title-holder was very much like Primo Carnera, a later giant who won the championship by virtue of his bulk. Willard like Carnera, had size and strength but little ring ability and his personality lacked the ingredient called "color."

In a drab, dull, "no-decision" affair at the old Madison Square Garden, Willard took on Frank Moran and his favorite "Mary Ann" righthand punch for ten rounds. Willard, whose only title risk was to go to sleep with Mary Ann (Moran's round house right) just covered up. Moran was out-reached and out-weighed by Willard whose clumsy left hand held him off and left Moran pawing and swinging at the air. The newspaper decision went to Willard, but the public's decision on the dull match was "thumbs down," and no one would promote another fight with Willard as the defending champion. As a result, Willard toured with "The 101 Ranch" Wild West show and did not fight again for more than three years.

29. Jess Willard eliminates Jack Johnson as heavyweight champion at Havana, Cuba, 5 April 1915.

The most important boxing event after that was a fight in Boston in 1917 between black Sam Langford, who had seen his best days and had been unable to arrange a bout with Jack Johnson, and Fred Fulton, a big powerful white fighter who, although he was a beautiful boxer, lacked a "fighting heart." Fulton certainly looked like a champion in this fight however, and beat Langford so badly that the referee stopped the fight in the seventh round.

A new heavyweight from the West, named Jack Dempsey after the "Nonpareil," began at this time to show his fistic wares. The story goes that when one of William Harrison Dempsey's earlier managers went to a fortune-teller, he was advised to change Dempsey's fighting name to Jack after the Nonpareil because the stars showed that fighters had to have "J" for an initial to become a world's champion. While others deny this story, claiming that William Dempsey's nickname had always been Jack,

"J" in any case became one of his initials—and it worked. During the single year 1918, the Manassa Mauler scored eighteen knockouts. Among his victims were Jim Flynn, the Pueblo fireman, a Colorado neighbor of Dempsey's and the only man who ever knocked him out; also Bill Brennan, Fred Fulton, Battling Levinsky, Carl Morris, and Gunboat Smith —all extremely tough competitors.

In the meantime, rumor had it that Willard's oil wells in the Southwest were paying him dividends and there was no compulsion for him to fight for financial consideration. But the public clamor could not be stopped. They wanted a Willard-Dempsey match and they wanted a fighting champion.

Tex Rickard's siren voice again asserted itself. He sought out and sold Willard the idea of grabbing some quick money. A championship bout was signed for 4 July 1919 and Jack Dempsey, who once rode the brake-rods, was on his way to the most phenomenal career in the saga of the fist. Horatio Alger never wrote a more fantastic "rags-to-riches" story.

Jess Willard came into the ring at Toledo at 240 pounds, a pale, reasonably well-trained, apathetic champion with no great love either for boxing or for his title. Jack Dempsey, his body almost black from sunburn, heavily bearded, a superbly trained athlete, fairly danced on his toes in anticipation and eagerness for the championship contest.

If there was ever a doubt about the outcome, it was settled after the first minute. The champion led with a long left jab three times in succession, and three times Jack slipped inside and under, and let go with a barrage of punches. These blows of Dempsey's however, were not just fast-thrown punches without body follow-through. A left hook to Willard's stomach with everything behind it, would cock Dempsey's body for a right, then would come the right, and then a left to the jaw. Every instant confirmed the fact that Dempsey, like Broughton and Gentleman Jackson before him, was a two-handed fighter and had a knockout wallop in either hand. In fact, although the lethal quality of Dempsey's right is conceded, many people to this day believe his left was more murderous than his right.

After that first minute, the fight degenerated into a massacre. Before the first round was over, the heavyweight champion of the world had been knocked down seven times for varying counts. It is interesting to conjecture what difference the application of Marquis of Queensberry, London Prize Ring, or Broughton rules would have made in the outcome. Had they been in effect, each knockdown would have been the end of a round, and Willard would have had a chance to recover. Even as it was, the bell ending the first round saved Willard from a knockout.

The story is told that Dempsey and his cunning manager, dapper Jack Kearns, bet all the money they had or could borrow at ten-to-one odds that Dempsey would win in one round. They were able to put up $10,000, and therefore stood to win $100,000. Knowledge of this bet is, no doubt, one of the reasons why Dempsey was later accused of having plaster-of-Paris in his gauze-and-tape bandages which, when wet, would have hardened into a sort of Roman cestus or hard plaster knuckle. A dissatisfied handler started the rumor but later recanted. There was never any evidence to substantiate this, and other fights showed that Dempsey did not need plaster-of-Paris either to win or to knock out the toughest of opponents.

The astonishing part about the betting story is that Dempsey and Kearns almost collected. After seven knockdowns, Willard was being counted out when the bell rang ending the first round, but, in the din, it was not heard. A later version of what happened was that, with time running out and referee tolling the knockout, some interested party rang the bell several financially important seconds ahead of time. An "ear-witness" claimed that the bell sounded at the exact moment the referee was counting "ten."

Be that as it may, no one at the time heard the bell, not even Ollie Peccord the referee, who counted Willard out. Dempsey and Kearns left the ring thinking they had won their bets, and most of the milling crowd started out. After much confusion and considerable time which accrued to Willard's advantage, Dempsey and Kearns were called back and the contest was resumed.

Naturally the fight after that was anticlimactic. Dempsey was "punched out," and Willard was "punched in." A right uppercut by Willard, his favorite blow, hurt Dempsey, but at the end of the third round Willard stumbled back to his corner and fell into his seat. His jaw was broken, his cheekbone split, his nose flattened, one ear was cut and bleeding, and the white skin over his body showed large red bruises. His seconds wisely threw a towel into the center of the ring in acknowledgment of defeat. Toledo witnessed one of the worst beatings a champion ever received, and the start of the reign of one of the greatest heavyweight champions of modern times.

Promoter Tex Rickard and Manager Kearns saw in Dempsey a fighter and a colorful personality capable of building a tremendous gate and worldwide interest in boxing. Unfortunately, Dempsey was accused of being a draft-dodger in World War I, and it took many years to convince the public to the contrary. In fairness to the young Dempsey, it should be recalled that during those early years in his boxing career, Jack Kearns was his absolute boss. Kearns was the one who, by agreement, made the decisions. He controlled the young fighter, and he was adamant in having his way because, after all, Dempsey was an important property. Dempsey on the other hand was, at the time, no more than a fighting automaton who had to split every dollar he made in the ring with Kearns. So when Kearns told Dempsey to go to work in the shipyards instead of in the army, the young fighter naturally obeyed.

After World War I Dempsey, for a while at least, was not a popular champion even though he never let the fight fans down. He continued to bowl over all opposition with startling speed and dynamic knockouts. A never-ceasing two-handed attack and a killer instinct seemed to be his order of the day, and even in training it is said that Dempsey never pulled a punch.

During this period there arose a black shadow in the person of black Harry Wills to challenge the titleholder. Everyone agrees that Dempsey would gladly have fought Wills and, as it afterward transpired, would easily have beaten him, but politicians and the fight public blocked the match. While Wills was at one time Dempsey's logical challenger and a man of good reputation, the unsavory memory of Jack Johnson was still too fresh in the minds of the public, so that this match, though signed up twice, never came off.

By 1921 Dempsey had run out of competition just as James J. Jeffries had in 1904, Joe Louis in 1947, and Rocky Marciano in 1956. However, Tex Rickard accomplished the impossible, and virtually manufactured a logical contender and a good one, at least as far as the box office was concerned.

In 1920, Georges Carpentier, a handsome Frenchman, came to try his luck in America. Carpentier had started boxing as a boy and, in fact, had fought in practically every weight category as he grew from boyhood to manhood. He was a fast, experienced boxer with a lightninglike, if not exactly lethal, right hand. His disadvantages lay in his small size and in his lack of experience with heavyweights as tough as those in America. He averaged only 165 to 172 pounds, and this weight was evenly distributed over his body which denied him the hitting power of Fitzsimmons, who had thin legs, but the shoulders of a blacksmith.

However, for all his obvious shortcomings as a heavyweight challenger, Carpentier was an urbane, sophisticated, romantic, and debonair Frenchman with an excellent record in the army of the country which had borne the brunt of World War I. Rickard and Kearns saw the age-old recipe for success at the box office: a romantic hero against a snarling and bearded villain. Here began the golden age of boxing. Up until then only one fight had attracted over $400,000 at

the gate—the Dempsey-Willard fight. Since then, up to 1948, twenty-one fights have gone over that figure, and eight of them over a million dollars, of which five are traceable to Dempsey's popularity. The remaining three "million dollar gates" arose from the appeal of another dynamic puncher, Joe Louis. Of course with the advent of radio broadcasting, television, closed circuit audiences, and the worldwide spread of boxing, we have a new ball game after 1949.

The Dempsey-Carpentier fight, in its time a promoter's and manager's dream, was held in Jersey City on 2 July 1921. It made ring history in more ways than one. It was the first truly international world's championship in the padded-glove boxing era and it was the first fight to gross over one million dollars. (According to some records, it grossed $1,626,580, according to others, $1,789,238).

A special wooden stadium designed to hold 100,000 spectators was built for the contest at Boyle's Thirty Acres, and when fight time came every seat was filled. Following his usual custom, Dempsey entered the ring with several days' growth of beard and well tanned from outdoor training. Carpentier, by contrast, was white and dapper.

For the uninitiated, it was worth noting here that a few days' growth of beard provides good protection against cuts and abrasions caused by punches delivered with the inside of the glove where the laces are. This is called "heeling" and may be accidental or intentional. Another precaution which is occasionally taken, but not officially allowed, is to apply vaseline or grease strategically along the eyebrows and down the side of the face. This application is difficult for an official to distinguish from perspiration. Often the forehead or brows are cut open by a punch or by an inadvertent butt of the opponent's head and bleeding will ensue. The vaseline, the eyebrows and the beard help direct the flow of blood down the sides of the face away from the eyes. A little blood in the eye could blind a fighter just long enough to enable his opponent to land a KO punch.

In any case, the hirsute and dark Mr. Dempsey was the villain and Mr. Carpentier the debonair war hero. The crowd was at first for the French challenger and against their own champion, a reaction as old as mass psychology. A Greek audience, over two thousand years before (141st Olympic, 216 B.C.) had cheered for Aristonikos, the romantic and handsome Egyptian, and not for their own Greek Olympic Champion, the hirsute Mr. Cleitomachus. The outcome, however, was the same in both cases: Cleitomachus punched his way to victory, and Jack Dempsey knocked out his challenger in such a way as to win the lasting admiration of the crowd. The villain

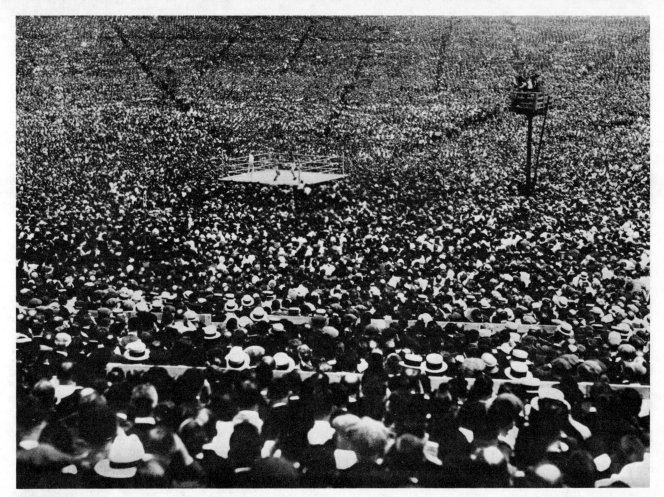

30. Dempsey-Carpentier fight; first million-dollar gate.

became the hero, while the former hero merely became the victim.

From the first round, Dempsey had forced the fighting. Many people believe that if Carpentier had elected to box at long range with Dempsey, he might have had a better chance. Instead, he chose to trade punches with the heavier and more powerful champion. Carpentier did land a terrific right hand on Dempsey's jaw in the first round, but the round was otherwise all Dempsey's who concentrated on short powerful inside jolts to the Frenchman's body.

In the second round Dempsey subjected the Frenchman to the now-proverbial Dempsey attack, a tattoo of punches from all angles to the head and body. Carpentier boxed well, avoided many of Dempsey's blows and in the middle of the round landed one of his famous lightning rights on the side of Dempsey's cheek. Dempsey staggered, clinched, and slowed up, but soon started to punish Carpentier's midsection again and finally knocked him through the ropes as the round ended.

Dempsey, fully recovered, charged out of his corner at the beginning of the third round. His punches were now being delivered at the rate of about five to Carpentier's one, and carried more snap and

weight in the bargain. It was easy to see that the body punishment Georges had been subjected to was beginning to tell on him. Again Carpentier managed to land a clean right hand on Dempsey's face, but it did far less damage than in previous rounds. Carpentier was actually holding on at the finish of this round.

Dempsey's first or second punch in the fourth round knocked Carpentier down for a count of nine. As the Frenchman arose, Dempsey rushed in and ended the fight with a crashing right to George's jaw. Carpentier was actually unconscious for four minutes from that last punch, according to one of his seconds.

In the semifinals that same night one James J. Tunney, known as Gene, showed his fistic wares. After his fight, he dressed quickly and took a seat to watch the main bout. It is interesting to note in the light of Dempsey's fortune teller's advice that in the semifinals of the Baer-Carnera world's championship, a James J. Braddock was one of the participants. Both James Js were destined to dethrone, at a later date, the winners of the main bouts in question and become world champions.

For the next two years, while ex-Marine Tunney,

31. Jack Dempsey in his prime, ready for a movie appearance. (Courtesy of Jack Dempsey)

the semifinalist, kept fighting up the ladder, Dempsey, the champion, could find no major opponents. Then Jack Kearns closed a deal which has been talked about more than the resulting fight.

The town of Shelby, Montana, was then a rising Western community with ambitious citizens. A group of amateur promoters believed that Shelby could be "put on the map" by staging a world's heavyweight boxing championship there between Jack Dempsey and Tommy Gibbons. The contender was a thirty-four-year-old light heavyweight whose main claim to fame was his masterful boxing. These Shelby businessmen were not as innocent as they have often been represented. Hadn't Rickard made a fortune for Goldfield, Nevada, with a championship fight? It appears likely that they intended to make their collective fortunes from the real estate boom and the expansion of industry that the fight and Dempsey would bring them.

Kearns and Dempsey were risking the championship, which was more than just a meal ticket, whether they fought in Shelby, New York, or Timbuctoo. As a result, Kearns demanded by contract and collected a $200,000 advance to be supplemented by an additional $100,000 to be taken from the gate receipts and paid to him while the fight was in progress. Kearns insisted on payment to the last penny in cash, so that when Dempsey and he left after the fight, they, or more properly speaking the amateur promoters, had succeeded in eliminating the town from even the largest-scale map. The promoters thought of everything except getting enough people to attend the fight.

As a result the small town, heavily mortgaged, received a knockout punch. Several banks failed due to the difference between the guaranteed purses and the income from the sale of seats.

The fight itself, on 4 July 1923, was dull and developed into a contest between a fighter intent on knocking out his opponent, and an experienced and canny boxer determined, not necessarily to win, but to stay the limit and avoid a knockout. The fact that Dempsey won in spite of a two-year layoff was a tribute to his condition and boxing ability. Gibbons, the defeated challenger, quit boxing and later became sheriff of St. Paul, Minnesota.

The Gibbons fight did demonstrate, however, that Dempsey was at his best with big, slow-moving targets like Willard or flashy one-punch fighters like Carpentier who would swap punches with him. Against an experienced and astute counter-puncher with determination, patience, a good defense, and some weight as well as speed, the Dempsey style was vulnerable. Tunney, whose ring cunning has never been questioned, knew this, and so went to Florida to gain extra weight and strength. He studied Dempsey's style and even became Dempsey's sparring partner to perfect his plans. Here we see a parallel to the way Corbett stalked John L. Sullivan.

While Tunney plotted, another foreign fighter literally forced his way through all opposition to become Dempsey's No. 1 challenger. His name was Luis Angel Firpo, the "Wild Bull of the Pampas." He stood 6 feet 3 inches and weighed 220 pounds before a meal. With seventy-four straight victories in South America to his credit, he first appeared here in 1922. Captain Tom Sheridan, the pugilistic, cauliflower-eared sea captain, who was a tough man with his fists, boxed with Firpo on his ship and labeled his cargo "fistic dynamite." Firpo knew little about boxing and used his right hand like a club. However, it eventually landed, and when it did, it produced the desired result. In addition, his style was so unorthodox that the experienced or able boxer could not figure out how to handle him. After knocking out a few unknowns, he knocked out old ring-wise Bill Brennan and big Jess Willard who up to that time was making a successful comeback campaign.

Tex Rickard immediately saw the possibilities of another million-dollar gate and the colorful implications of an international match between the "Manassa Mauler," now the fair-haired boy of America, and the "Wild Bull of the Pampas" from the Argentine. The ballyhoo started.

However, this time Rickard had plenty of trouble, for Firpo was hard to handle and refused to let anybody manage or advise him. The Wild Bull was as difficult out of the ring as he was in it. He refused to train, and ate gigantic meals sometimes consuming as much as three steaks, all the trimmings, and a gallon of ice cream for lunch. He fired his American trainer, Jimmy de Forrest, a skillful conditioner who many believe could have coached Firpo to the championship. His workouts were so ridiculous they finally had to be conducted in private. With no particular interest in training, Firpo was probably the worst looking tyro ever to invade MacLevy's training gym in the old Madison Square Garden.

Firpo had a peculiar and fatalistic viewpoint on everything—especially his boxing career. He refused to train because he sincerely believed that his success lay in his natural and unorthodox style, and that his unusual strength and phenomenal right hand would carry him farther than any attention to technique or training. Who knows? Perhaps he was right, for his bull-like rushes, lionlike heart, and clublike right, without any coaching, training, or improvement came very near to upsetting Dempsey and winning the championship for him. Had he acquired a defense and caution, been slowed up by newly acquired knowledge and attempted to box and shorten his punches, he might have become no more than just another lumbering heavyweight.

I boxed with Firpo in training and often talked with him, and I feel that I may know more about his ideas and boxing psychology than many newspapermen. Once when I had feinted Firpo into a corner of the ring with orthodox boxing tactics, I saw him cross his feet to turn and walk out of the corner. This, of course, was a signal to catch him off balance, step in, and let go with lefts and rights to the body and chin as his guard came down. Since a man whose legs are crossed is not supposed to be able to hit or at least hit hard, I was not worrying about drawing or catching any punches. However, I was wrong, for Firpo threw an overhead right hand just like a club and hit me partly on top of the head and partly on the back of my neck, and even though he had heavy training gloves on, I felt like a tack being driven through the floor.

Luis Angel had a failing which did not make him popular with the hangers-on of boxing. According to many, he was the stingiest man that ever laced on a glove.

There are many stories told about poor foreign heavyweights like Primo Carnera who come to this country, fight for purses totalling hundreds of thousands of dollars, yet go back to their native land penniless, after being cleaned out by the smart boxing mob. The Wild Bull was not one of these.

I will bet anybody any amount of money anywhere that no one ever got even a thin penny out of Mr. Firpo. Every dollar ever paid to Firpo stuck to him. In addition, most of his spare waking hours in the United States were spent figuring out ways and means to use his name to obtain the necessities of life without recourse to his bank roll. The main reason he used me as a sparring partner was because, as an amateur training for the Olympics, I could not accept any pay.

He got his clothes, shoes, and hats by autographing pictures or boxing gloves for show windows. He gave a well-known trainer and second ten dollars for attending him in his fight with Willard when he himself had received $100,000 for the fight. In the circumstances, a hundred-dollar bill would not have been generous. The best-known story around the old Madison Square Garden regarding Firpo's stinginess was the one about his hat which he had worn the entire two years that he was in this country. It was a robber this time who, annoyed at Firpo for his parsimony, decided to wound the Wild Bull where it hurt most. So one day, just before Firpo was about to leave the country, this man ran up to Firpo on the street, grabbed his hat, scurried across the street and stuffed it down a sewer. Needless to say, Senor Firpo let out a roar, tossed his huge head of unruly black hair and lit out down the street after the one person who had hurt him more than Dempsey ever did in the ring. Fortunately for the homicide squad, he never caught the offender who, I am told, was apprehensive of Firpo's return and the possibility that the story about the elephant's memory applies to Argentine bulls as well. From that day on, Firpo never wore a hat

I think that Firpo had more intelligence than he is often given credit for and that he had determined that he would or would not win on what he had, and that getting rid of his unorthodox—but natural—style would not help. I believe the fight proved he

32. Luis Angel Firpo. (Courtesy of Firpo)

was right. We should respect Firpo notwithstanding his penny-pinching, for he came to this country for one purpose, to make a fortune, and this he accomplished. There never has been a more straight-forward, never-say-die fellow than Luis Angel. He knew what he wanted, and he went after it, without cutting corners or making any circuitous approaches.

But he lost his main objective, the world's championship by a victory against Dempsey at the New York Polo Grounds on 14 September 1923. On the day of the fight, eighty-five thousand people stormed the entrances and many were injured in the rush for seats. It was the second million-dollar gate and the most incredible fight in the entire saga of sock. Nothing ever surpassed it for action and thrills per second. There was never a dull moment. Two of the greatest hitters of all time abandoned science, and boxing rules and literally almost batted each other's brains out.

At ringside, Dempsey weighed 193; Firpo, 221. At the very outset, Dempsey went down for no count, caught by Firpo's right in the usual Dempsey rush at the first bell. Immediately afterward, Firpo went down for a count of "three" from Dempsey's left to the head. As Firpo got up, Dempsey dropped him again for a count of "two" and again Firpo got up to be floored by Dempsey's left to the body for "three." When Firpo jumped up again, Dempsey's right to the jaw stretched him out for a full count of "nine." But Firpo arose again and this time went down from a left to the body for "two," followed by another knockdown for a count of "six." When Firpo got up from this one, he rushed Dempsey, clubbed away at him and knocked Dempsey out of the ring with a right.

At this point, all accounts of what happened are garbled because of the chaos and confusion that ensued. I was at the ringside behind Firpo's corner myself but cannot do any better reporting than anyone else. I don't know what happened because I was too excited.

Some claim Dempsey was out of the ring and in no condition to proceed. For perhaps ten seconds the referee was so confused he forgot to start a count. However, under the rules at that time, I do not believe he would have been justified in starting a count until Dempsey was in the ring or actually unable to get back.

As it was, Dempsey was hoisted into the ring by the willing hands of the newspapermen who acted in self-defense, for otherwise a 193-pound weight would have fallen on them and their typewriters. Hype Igoe, a sports reporter, who was a close witness, said that Dempsey was not dazed but grabbed one of the ropes and with the help of the press pulled himself back into the ring, saying as he did "allez-oop." Igoe further stated that he believed Dempsey had been out of the ring less than ten seconds. All I can add is that while I believe Dempsey was out of the ring more than ten seconds, he had fallen out and was not actually knocked out of it. In other words, I believe it was a matter of balance and that the rush and clublike blow of Firpo's combined with a loose top rope catapulted him out of the ring; Firpo's punch did not land on any vital spot and Dempsey was not hurt.

As soon as Dempsey had got back into the ring, he rushed Firpo and landed a right hand as the bell rang, ending the most exciting round in the story of boxing.

When the second round started, Dempsey tore out of his corner and, landing three rights, dropped the Argentine for a count of "four." When Firpo arose, he tried to close and clinch, but Dempsey hit him with a left on the jaw followed by a right to the chin. Firpo fell again and this time was still out at "ten."

There is no doubt, as the motion pictures of the fight will attest, that Dempsey often hit Firpo before he had gotten off the floor, stood over him, and never retired to a neutral corner. Referee John Gallagher was as helpless as if he had been in the ring with a tiger and a bull.

It was undoubtedly Dempsey's strategy in this fight that caused Tunney and his handlers prior to the second Dempsey-Tunney fight to insist on the "neutral corner" rule and to call nationwide attention to it by the famous incident that occurred. This rule provides that after a knockdown, the fighter who delivered the knockdown blow must go to the farthest neutral corner of the ring from the prostrate boxer before the timekeeper begins his count. It was Dempsey's failure to observe this rule that cost him the championship when he fought Tunney the second time.

The Firpo fight was a turning point in Dempsey's career. From then on he began to "get soft" in many ways, according to those nearest him. He had his nose straightened, went on the stage, made a movie, sailed to Europe, and relaxed his daily training. He did not fight again for over three years. During this time Wills, his black challenger, had pretty well proved he was no match for Dempsey by his poor performance against Bartley Madden and Luis Firpo. The only really rising heavyweight was Gene Tunney, who during the same period knocked out Georges Carpentier, Tommy Gibbons, and Bartley Madden.

Firpo, the Wild Bull of the Pampas, is much too colorful a figure ever to be forgotten. The man who walked across the Andes on foot to his first fight got the best of the smart American fight crowd. He returned to his home in Argentina without the championship, but with his pockets full of gold and an untarnished reputation. After abandoning boxing, he entered commercial competition finally as a real estate operator and made another fortune. According to Argentine newspapers, he was worth approximately two million dollars and owned about 40,000 acres of land in the pampas. He probably was the richest exprofessional pugilist in the world. He lived quietly and comfortably and was respected by all. I visited him in Argentina in 1950 where he was interested in my fencing against the Argentine duelling sword champion at a special gala exhibition. He insisted on our being photographed together at his home, a marble replica of a French town house.

Notwithstanding many delays after the Firpo fight, Tex Rickard finally had a Dempsey-Tunney fight under contract, but as the New York State Boxing Commission would not let him stage it in New York City, he took it to Philadelphia and the Sesquicentennial Stadium. Here on the night of 14 September 1926, 130,000 people assembled expecting to see the greatest modern American champion knock out the overgrown Marine light heavyweight.

During his training, Dempsey had been worried by process servers, his exmanager and all kinds of legal troubles. When he weighed in for the fight, he looked worried and scaled 190 pounds, less than his fighting weight had been in years. At the last minute the legal complications became so great that

Rickard discussed calling off or postponing the fight.

Tunney, on the other hand, appeared to be in perfect shape, and it was known he had carefully planned the fight and had supreme confidence in himself.

Notwithstanding all this, Dempsey was an odds-on favorite. No one could believe that the conqueror of Willard, Brennan, Carpentier, Gibbons, and Firpo could lose. It was reminiscent of the public's faith in the invincibility of John L. Sullivan when he met Corbett a generation before.

Just before the fight, it rained and the ring canvas was wet and slippery. It was the first time it had rained at a Rickard-promoted fight, and it was the first time a Rickard favorite lost. Shortly after the fight started it became increasingly clear what was going to happen. The champion's repertoire of punches was rusty. In addition, Tunney boxed beautifully and his strategic plan and tactical moves were letter-perfect. Even the Dempsey followers could only hope that Jack would find an opening for one of his famous punches and land with it. Only once did Dempsey appear to have a chance, and that was when he landed on Tunney's "Adam's apple" in the fourth round. At the end of ten rounds, Dempsey's face was badly chopped up, while Tunney had taken little or no punishment. The decision soon became a foregone conclusion and a great champion had lost his crown.

A few days after the upset a young heavyweight named Jack Sharkey defeated Harry Wills, and Rickard then matched Sharkey and Dempsey to determine which was to challenge Tunney's crown. This fight was staged at Yankee Stadium in New York City before 75,000 people on 21 July 1927. Sharkey had all the better of the fight until the seventh round, but in a now famous "bonehead beef," Sharkey was knocked out while appealing to the referee about an alleged low punch by Dempsey.

The fight started much argument but generally speaking, everyone was happy and satisfied that Dempsey had earned a return match with Tunney. Would he be the first and only ex-heavyweight champion to regain his title?

Tex Rickard promoted this one too, although politics had stepped in to grab some of the boxing gold and the law made it necessary for Tex to act as assistant to a Chicago promoter, so that native sons could participate. The fight was limited by Illinois law to ten rounds, and the Illinois Boxing Commission ruled that in this fight if a boxer were knocked down, his opponent must retire to a neutral corner before the referee could begin the count in accordance with the new regulation. This rule became the crux of a controversy people are still arguing about.

33. Millionaire Louis Angel Firpo, the Wild Bull of the Pampas, at his home in Buenos Aires in 1950 with the author who was one of his sparring partners for his fight with Dempsey in 1923.

The fight was held in Soldier Field in Chicago. Jimmy Barry, once a great bantamweight champion of the world, was the referee. More than 100,000 people were on hand—most of them hoping to see an old precedent broken and Dempsey win his title back. For the first seven rounds, it was almost a replica of their first Philadelphia fight. Then suddenly in the seventh round, it happened. An old-time flurry of punches by Dempsey, and Tunney, battered and glassy-eyed, lay on the floor in a corner of the ring. The timekeeper began his count, but Dempsey stood in the corner about a yard away. Referee Barry motioned to Dempsey to go to a neutral corner but the latter hesitated. Finally Barry led him to a neutral corner and, returning to the side of the prostrate Tunney, began his count over again. At "six" Tunney got to his knee and at "nine," Tunney arose and began to back-pedal around the ring with quick sliding steps. Dempsey pursued him, but being unable to catch Gene, he stopped and made a motion exactly like the one John L had made at Corbett when the latter had refused to "mix it" with him. Both gestures were futile. Tunney weathered the seventh, and from then on, fighting cautiously, he proceeded to outbox the former champion. Dempsey had failed, as all had failed before him to regain the heavyweight title.

Although the battle was over, arguments were just beginning. Estimates of the length of time Tunney was actually on the floor vary from fourteen to twenty-six seconds. That the famous long count was "long," there can be no question, but that the long count was fair cannot be disproved. Some of the wiser and older fans felt that Barry, after leading the ex-champion to a farther corner, should have picked up the timekeeper's count at the point he had left off instead of beginning all over. In any case, this fight with its long count proved to be the first and the last two-million-dollar ringside or physical gate: $2,650,000. Tunney incidentally received the highest pay a professional athlete had ever attained—$990,000 for thirty minutes—more than the late Mr. Louis B. Mayer, the highest priced executive in the world, at that time received for one year's salary, bonus and all, or more than General Marshall probably made in his entire career as Chief of Staff of the Army of the United States in World War II and as Secretary of State in the postwar period.

Tunney defended his title only once after the long count. He fought Tom Heeney 21 July 1928, a big Australian plugger, and defeated him easily. However, the Golden Age was at least for a time in a period of suspension—or perhaps Tunney was not the crowd magnet that Dempsey had been for the Madison Square Garden Corporation that promoted this fight, lost $200,000, although the take was almost $700,000. Less than a month later, Gene Tunney announced his retirement and became the first modern world's heavyweight champion, up to that time, to retire his title. In sixty-eight fights he had lost only once—to Harry Greb. Tunney subsequently married into society, invested his money well, became a Commander in the Navy physical training program in World War II and is respected by all.

Tunney, incidentally, is reportedly another rare millionaire expugilist, but one who has had some parental trouble. His son, however, is a United States Senator and like so many second-generation monied politicians is a liberal and a believer in expanding government control. Young Tunney was responsible for the introduction of a Senate Bill, S-3500, "The Amateur Athletic Act of 1974," which would have the United States government take over all amateur athletics and the control and management of all U.S. Olympic teams. Many believe that young Tunney is helping the NCAA break up the AAU control over many sports; however, the result, if the bill becomes law, might be the barring of U.S. athletes from the 1976 Olympic Games. The International Olympic Committee has sanctioned our present controlling organizations for some eighty years, including the AAU's control over amateur boxing, a sport the NCAA gave up. Senator Barry Goldwater, Congressmen, F. Edward Hebert, William J.B. Dorn, and Bob Mathias, a two-time Olympic gold medalist, are all reportedly against the Tunney Bill. It has been re-introduced but may, it is hoped, leave sports and United States Olympic teams out of government and political control and even more important unsupported by government financing!

Dempsey, like Tunney, was a Commander in World War II but in the U. S. Coast Guard. Dempsey, like Tunney, was director of a physical training program. At Okinawa, Dempsey saw action while on a world trip to inspect the Coast Guard physical training program and its results in the field. He slipped ashore with the attack, disappeared and could not be traced by Navy brass for half a day. Naturally this little incident created considerable attention and a rumor spread in the United States that Dempsey had been killed. The day after President Roosevelt died, a sign in the window of Dempsey's restaurant read, "Closed because of the death of our President." The fight mob and thousands of passers-by, knowing Dempsey was in the Pacific with the fleet, drew the wrong conclusion and the rumor spread like wild fire. For two days the switchboards of the Federal Communications Commission, War and Navy Departments, were flooded with phone calls, cables, and telegrams asking about Dempsey. The rumor became so serious that Dempsey's business manager, Max

34. At Jack Dempsey's—Left to right: Ed Ahlquist, Stockholm boxing promoter and manager; Elis Ask of Finland, featherweight champion of Europe and contender for world title; Jack Flynn, former amateur champion; and Jack Dempsey, sponsor of Ask's trip to the United States. In the background is James Montgomery Flagg's famous painting of the Dempsey-Willard fight. (Courtesy of Einar Thulin)

Waxman, phoned me in Washington to get the Navy to determine the accuracy of the report.

Commander Dempsey was decorated for his World War II service. In addition to his regular duties, he went on frequent inspection tours for morale purposes all over the world and on many barnstorming tours throughout the United States for bond sales. According to a spokesman in the U. S. Treasury Department, Jack Dempsey may have influenced the purchase of one billion dollars worth of Government bonds.

One of the greatest and most colorful champions Dempsey is today the most popular and best-known sports figure in the world. For years he attracted crowds into the fights he refereed from Montreal and Mexico to Manila and into his restaurant on Broadway in New York City. He successfully promoted a number of big outdoor matches including the Schmeling-Baer fight and attracted the best pugilistic talent. He sponsored Max Baer and helped him to the World's Championship and once had three World's Championship prospects as proteges: middleweight Laurent Dauthuille of France (nontitle victor over champion Jake LaMotta), featherweight Elis Ask of Finland, and flyweight Pascual Perez of the Argentine, world's Olympic champion in 1948, all first contacted by the author. Dempsey's New York restaurant, a boxing tourist's Mecca, was closed in late 1974 based on a reportedly exorbitant demand for increased rent by a corporate landlord who had just recently purchased a Park Avenue building for over seven million dollars. It was rumored that the ownership was a covered foreign source and that the principal was none other than the British royal family. The U.S. dollar appeared to have been evaluated as safer than the British pound. Efforts by Dempsey's daughter and by a friendly private detective agency

35. Dempsey landing with the United States Coast Guard at Okinawa two hours after initial attack. (Courtesy of the United States Coast Guard)

36. Jack Dempsey and his Finnish protege, Elis Ask, featherweight champion of Europe and challenger of Willie Pep. (Courtesy of Einar Thulin)

(the latter unknown to Dempsey) were too late to influence any compromise.

The story of Tunney presents a remarkable display of force of character and will to succeed, qualities Tunney claims he developed in military service to his country. Unlike several outstanding boxing champions, Tunney answered the call of duty and had battle experience in World War I and also served in World War II. However, when he first enlisted in the Marines, he had only mediocre original physical gifts. The Tennyson quote on the title page of Tunney's book "Arms for Living" sums up Gene's philosophy:

"Made weak by time and fate but strong in will,
To strive, to seek, to find and not to yield."

The retirement of Tunney threw the heavyweight situation into confusion. It ushered in a decline in fistic talent which was not over until the advent of Joe Louis in 1937. A contest for a successor to Tunney's crown began. A long drawnout series of eliminations wound up with the Jack Sharkey versus Max Schmeling fight on 12 June 1930. Sharkey, the garrulous gob from Boston with the temperament of an artist, was already known for both his good and bad fights. Max Schmeling was a young German newcomer of "pure Aryan stock," later to become a favorite of Hitler. He looked like Dempsey, could absorb punishment, had a good inside right hand, but was not too good a boxer at the outset. The battle between Sharkey and Schmeling was fairly even until the fourth round, when it ended in complete confusion with Schmeling lying on the floor claiming a foul, and Sharkey crying and wringing his gloved hands.

The confusion was so great that Referee Crowley did not render his decision until after the bell beginning the fifth round had sounded. He then declared Schmeling the winner by a foul. On 18 June 1930, the New York State Athletic Commission awarded the heavyweight title to the foreigner, and under strange circumstances, for the title went to a contestant who was lying on the floor at the end of the bout. The coincidence of this unsatisfactory outcome with the financial depression which began at this time led to a reduced interest in the sport.

In January 1931, the new champion made matters worse by embarrassing the Commission that had been more than fair to him. He refused to sign for a return fight with Sharkey, and the Commission then declared the title vacant. Nothing daunted, Schmeling then fought and ko'd Young Stribling. This fight also lost money for the promoters. Schmeling and Sharkey finally met on 21 June 1932, in the Long Island Bowl in New York. Jack Sharkey won in a dull fight and the title was again in American hands.

At this point another challenger appeared on the scene in the person of Primo Carnera, Italian circus giant and wrestler. Carnera was 6 feet 6 inches tall and weighed 270 pounds. His position in the heavyweight world was so well established, following a series of twenty-two easy knockouts which had been arranged for him by his sponsors, that by 1933 he was the logical contender and was signed to fight Sharkey in the Bowl on 28 June 1933. Jack Sharkey, now past his prime, succumbed easily to the giant's righthand uppercut, the old weapon of Jess Willard, a giant of other years. Once more the American crown was in the hands of a foreigner, once more the champion was a giant, but also once more the boxing championship had attracted neither top flight talent nor big money.

The financial life story of Primo Carnera is just the opposite of Luis Angel Firpo's. Whereas Firpo took nearly every penny he made back to Argentina with him, Carnera was "picked to the bone." Everyone admits he took nothing back with him to Italy but his own disillusioned self. Even for the championship title fight that Carnera lost to Max Baer, Carnera's managers, the fight promoters, and their friends got all of his earnings.

Many newspaper men and fight fans have maintained that the uppercut with which Carnera knocked out Sharkey was a shadow (or nonexistent) punch, a new development in the fistic art. Carnera appeared surprised and utterly bewildered while Sharkey was being counted out. There is absolutely no evidence for the suspicion that Sharkey "took a dive," but there are those who feel that, unknown to Carnera, many of his other opponents had lost "at the threatening requests" of his backers. In any case, few will disagree with the statement that neither Sharkey nor Carnera was worthy of holding the same title once held by Dempsey, Jeffries, and Sullivan.

Next on the pugilistic horizon appeared a young man who seemed to have everything necessary for a great champion, including what the box office calls "color." He should have gone far, but unfortunately did not.

Max Adelbert Baer of Livermore, California, had the physique of the classic Greek boxer. He stood 6 feet 2 inches and weighed about 205 pounds. No man ever came to the ring with better natural equipment. He could take all kinds of punishment and had, in the bargain, a killing right hand. This statement can be taken literally because he had in fact killed two men in the ring—one almost instantly and another who died of a cerebral hemorrhage following a later fight.

Baer was fast and had great native intelligence. He also had a strange streak of cruelty in his personality which made him a "killer" at times. Most of the time, however, he was primarily a happy-go-lucky extrovert. The press enjoyed him, he was a delight to his tailor, he was sought after by photographers, night-club owners opened their doors to him, and women "cooed" when his name was mentioned. His good looks, easy spending habits, and entertaining ways attracted all types of feminine admirers and he responded in kind.

Max just would not train; he would not learn his trade and could not concentrate on anything for long. But even with all his foibles, his looping right hand was an efficient compensator. After knocking out Max Schmeling on 8 June 1933, in a fight promoted by Jack Dempsey, he became Carnera's leading challenger.

Carnera and Baer met for the championship title at the Long Island Bowl on 14 June 1934. This fight was at least the most colorful and exciting event since the second Dempsey-Tunney fight. The sport seemed to be improving financially too, for the gate was quite respectable and amounted approximately to $447,600.

Carnera weighed 260 pounds; Baer, 205. Baer never looked better as he scored repeatedly with his right on the side of Carnera's face. In the clinches Baer also dominated the champion and on several occasions wrestled the former wrestling behemoth all over the ring. In eleven rounds Carnera was felled twelve times and finally signaled that he could not continue, just as referee Arthur Donovan was about to stop the fight.

For a year Baer did nothing but fight in exhibitions and appear in vaudeville, movies, and on the radio. He could act quite effectively and took direction well, especially from those who had won his confidence and friendship. He could sing and dance a little and was a natural showman. Unfortunately for his boxing, he became very much in demand as an entertainer, which further convinced him that it was not necessary for him to work too hard at his principal trade. For a three-minute performance on a single radio program in early 1935, he received $3,500 and all round-trip expenses from California to New York for three people. His coast-to-coast radio program series which did not even disturb his training schedules and was broadcast directly from his training camp at Asbury Park, together with other radio and theatrical engagements, grossed him over $250,000. I should know as I handled all of Baer's broadcasting and ancillary rights.

When the summer of 1935 arrived, Baer and his manager, not particularly anxious to help the Madison Square Garden and Jacobs retain their stranglehold on boxing, cast about for some way out. But all worthwhile opponents were also Jacobs chattels. However, since the big money in radio and pictures for Baer appeared to be tied up with the publicity of another big fight, he signed to meet James J. Braddock on 13 June 1935, in the Long Island Bowl, by now an accepted jinx for all champions. The Gillette contract for a thirteen-week series and the fight broadcast rights and options for renewals and a motion picture were pivotal!

This match appeared on the surface to promise little in the way of a contest. Considerable thumping and ballyhoo failed to arouse much interest. The odds in favor of Baer were ten to one. The publicity men even circulated a report that Baer was sure to injure Braddock seriously and that an ambulance was being made ready to take Braddock away after the fight. The attendance was only 35,000, the gate a paltry $169,000. The outcome of the fight was a great upset and the only putative patients for the ambulance were the promoters, the spectators, and the gamblers who had bet on Baer.

The fight is difficult to describe. Actually nothing happened in the first eight rounds except that Braddock kept circling to Baer's left to make it impossible for Baer to hit him with a right hand. Baer responded to these tactics by fooling around, hitching up his pants, and clowning. Had he properly learned his trade, he could have jabbed and hooked Braddock silly with his left, since it must be remembered that Braddock was no speed demon. The next seven rounds were a repetition of the first eight, except that too much night life had robbed Baer of his speed afoot, and his punches of their snap. He tried hard in these rounds but could never get going. Braddock, on the other hand, began to score with left jabs and "one-twos," following each offensive action by falling into a clinch where he handled Baer surprisingly well. Anyone could see that boxing was certainly in the doldrums, judging from this bout, although there is no intention here of discrediting Braddock who used his head and his boxing superiority to win the title.

Prior to the Braddock fight, fight managers and promoters had begun to hear of a fighter in the Middle West who was destined for ring greatness. They knew that this fighter was a ring natural, a lazy, gliding, effortless performer with maximum effectiveness and minimum waste motion.

The new sensation was Joe Louis Barrow, a black garage mechanic who fought under the name of Joe Louis. As an amateur, Louis had won the national light heavyweight championship. As a professional, in less than two years he had won twenty-four out of twenty-four bouts, eighteen of them by kos. In 1935 he wound up fighting the best of the talent, and knocked out both Primo Carnera and Max Baer without drawing a hard breath.

Joe Louis, even seen through contemporary eyes too often prone to look to the past for great fighters, was definitely one of the finest fighters in the history of boxing. Let us quickly review some of his important fights.

On 25 June 1935, Joe faced the giant Primo Carnera in New York. Although Primo was five and a half inches taller and sixty pounds heavier, Joe chopped him down, especially with left hooks, until by the sixth round Carnera was helpless, unable either to hold his hands up or to straighten his back because of the great body punishment he had received; his face was beaten to a pulp and his mouth and lips badly cut. Louis showed an easy, relaxed style, delivering lightning left hooks, and two-handed attacks to the body. He displayed in addition nice pacing and unusual ability to handle a much bigger and heavier man in the clinches.

37. Confusion: Godoy wants to continue after referee Billy Cavanagh has stopped bout with Joe Louis. (Wide World)

In his battle with Max Baer, I believe that, unknown to most people, Louis worked harder for a longer time than in many of his other bouts. He hit Baer harder and more often than he did almost any opponent before or after. I was watching Louis' corner for Baer and feel safe in saying that Louis must have hooked his left to Baer's chin over 200 times in less than four rounds. It was Baer's plan, worked out before the fight with Jack Dempsey and others, to come out of his corner and sling leather without ceasing from the sound of the first gong. Max promised to do so, but either did not, or could not, follow these instructions. Instead, he tried to box Louis with a long left lead in a quarter crouch keeping his chin well under his left shoulder. This technique, of course, would give Baer a chance to throw his looping right if he saw an opening and would protect him from Louis' right hand and avoid too much body punishment. But as it transpired, it made him vulnerable to Louis' best weapon, a lightning left hook. As Louis would step back, Baer would follow; Louis would at that instant beat Baer's hand down with his right, step inside, and hook his left to Baer's chin. Baer would then usually break backwards or sideways, but if he failed to do this Louis would follow his left hook with a right to the body or with more left hooks. If

38. 24 September 1935—Joe Louis KOs Max Baer in the fourth round at Yankee Stadium. Arthur Donovan was the referee, and it was Baer's first KO of his career.

Baer threw his right, Louis would jab with his left, or merely close, and Baer's right would go over his neck and left shoulder. These maneuvers were repeated many times but always with the same result. Louis would land one, two, or three left hooks to Baer's chin or perhaps lefts and rights with no return.

Baer tried to box, but could not get anywhere, and he was finally knocked down and counted out. The best punch landed by Baer was a right hand after a bell ending a round. Many people criticize Baer for taking a count when he probably could have gotten up only to be beaten further. Remember, however, that even the Greeks and the Romans permitted a boxer to admit defeat by holding up his forefinger. One of the earliest pictures of a boxing contest in the sixth century B.C. shows a fallen boxer holding up his hand fore finger extended in acknowledgment of defeat.

Baer, after reading some criticism about his unwillingness to continue after being battered to a pulp, remarked:

"I'll bet very few persons in the crowd would worry about me twenty years from now if I were blind and standing on a street corner with a tin cup because I had needlessly taken more punishment for their entertainment."

After knocking out the heretofore indestructible "Bounding Basque," Paolino Uzcudun, Louis became widely known as the "Brown Bomber." In 1936 the fight world could think of nothing but the championship fight between Louis and Braddock, and the general opinion was that the Brown Bomber would win and that the championship would again go to a man worthy of the title.

Max Schmeling, another ex-champion, however, wanted a crack at Louis. The German had studied movies of Louis' fights and had come to the conclu-

sion that he could beat him. According to a report, Schmeling believed Louis was often open to an inside right hand punch which happened to be Max's best stock in trade. So on 19 June 1936, Schmeling at the age of thirty met Louis who was then twenty-two. Schmeling weighed 195; Louis, 201. Again fight fans were to be treated to a surprising upset, but one which would at the same time show the real class of the Brown Bomber.

Unlike most of Louis' opponents, who had been almost hynotized with fear when face to face with this implacable heavyweight, Schmeling was not afraid. In fact, the German was apparently certain he would win, although no one believed this. For three rounds Louis outboxed Schmeling. During these rounds Max tried inside rights, especially when Louis threw wide left hooks, but none of them landed. At the beginning of the fourth round however, Max made Louis do all the leading instead of the countering, which was Joe's forte. Immediately following one of Louis' jabs, Max hit him on the chin with his right. Joe came in quickly and started to throw a left hook; Max stepped inside with a solid right to Joe's chin and Joe dropped to his knees. He jumped up at the count of two, proving that he lacked experience as to what to do when on the receiving end of a punch. Louis fought that round out, but he was evidently hurt so badly that he never recovered and Schmeling never gave him a chance to recover.

Thereafter Max kept feeding Louis right hands with startling regularity, usually when Louis led and always when Louis started a left hook. Finally in the twelfth round Louis was knocked out. He proved in this fight that he had plenty of courage but that he had "come along" too fast.

Two months later Joe Louis fought Jack Sharkey and knocked him out in the third round. Schmeling went back to Germany and was subsequently signed by the Garden to fight Braddock for the title, but fortunately the fight never came off, because if the German had won the title, he would have disappeared with it into Nazi Germany.

39. Schmeling KOs Louis (Wide World)

Joe Louis in the meantime continued on his comeback trail. He defeated everyone he met and finally was matched to fight Braddock for the world's championship on June 22, 1937. Almost everyone believed that Louis would beat Braddock with ease. No one believed it would be an exciting fight. In both respects they were wrong. Some boxing experts I have talked to do say that they could never understand the strategy of the fight. According to some, if Braddock had boxed carefully and defensively, as he had against Baer, and had refused to lead to Louis, while it might well have made a drab and dull fight from the spectators' standpoint, he might have had a chance to retain his title and certainly would not have had to take the enormous amount of punishment he did. These experts claimed that Braddock only invited disaster when he elected to carry the fight to Louis who was the greatest "counter-puncher" in history.

Yet, that is exactly what Braddock, an experienced and veteran boxer, did. Why? Did Louis, as many great competitors do, make Braddock fight the wrong kind of a fight or did Braddock believe that Louis had prepared himself for the defensive type of strategy and that taking the offensive would confuse him? Did he believe that in spite of his age he should gamble on his good right hand and a lucky punch, notwithstanding the prospect of certain defeat and severe punishment should he fail to put that ko punch over? Or did certain interests believe that the boxing industry needed a slam-bang fight with a knockout victory to bring it out of the doldrums?

Probably no one will ever know. However, what is often reported is that both men were guaranteed a return fight if they desired one, whatever the outcome, and that someone guaranteed ten percent of all the money earned by Joe Louis during his lifetime to Braddock and Joe Gould, his manager, if Louis won the title. We must remember that Braddock was penniless when he became world's champion and was unable to make any money as champion, so that any deal which enabled him to make honestly the maximum amount of money while risking his title is excusable. It is generally conceded that Braddock was "broke" when he fought the fight that had made him champion. That the Louis-Braddock fight was a bloody one and that Braddock was fairly as well as badly beaten, there can be no question. Braddock fought like a champion and lost like one, but many believe the strategy he employed made him an easier victim.

Unlike many champions, Louis was willing to defend his title against Tommy Farr of England only two months after he had won it. Farr, a Welshman, gave Louis a tough fifteen rounds.

40. Louis-Mauriello (Press Association Inc.)

While Farr had no punch, he demonstrated again what Schmeling and Walcott and (in reverse) Braddock had shown—namely, that Louis was at his best when his opponent carried the fight to him, led to him and exchanged punches with him. Farr made Louis do most of the leading in fifteen rounds and sometimes outboxed him, but was not rugged enough, or hard-hitting enough, to affect the ultimate decision. Louis outpunched him and wore him down. In addition, Louis was the aggressor throughout, Farr being content to avoid being knocked out.

But the opponent Louis wanted to fight more than any other was Max Schmeling, the man who had humiliated him. On 22 June 1938, the return engagement of Schmeling and Louis took place at Yankee Stadium.

The gate was a fat one and went over the million mark: $1,015,096. This was a grudge fight if there ever was one. Germany and Hitler had insulted the black race at the Berlin Olympics in 1936. Max Schmeling had made derogatory remarks about blacks and black fighters and to add injury to insult he had knocked out Louis in their previous encounters. Max, for his part, would have loved to grab the title and take it back to Germany as proof of Aryan superiority.

Joe Louis was an acknowledged slow starter, and like many great athletes warmed up slowly, but he started quickly that night. Why? Because he and his board of strategy had determined that he should start fast. In order to do this, he had shadow-boxed a couple of rounds in his dressing room before making his trip to the ring where he appeared wrapped in towels, sweater, and bathrobe.

When the bell clanged, Joe shot two-thirds of the way across the ring. Herr Schmeling threw his right, the usual sedative for this opponent, but it did not land. Instead, he received a flurry of rights and lefts that practically pitched him backward. The flurry continued. The spectators rose in a body and stood on their chairs. The seating arrangements, by the way, were bad and many a fan with a "ringside seat" found himself a half mile from this point in an arena with all the seats on the same level.

At the finish, which came two minutes after the start, Louis hit the German with a left to the pit of the stomach that turned him around, and followed with a right that seemed to hook Max to the top rope. There he hung, supported by his chin and right shoulder. His pupils went up, his eyes remained open in a glassy stare. His mouth opened and a half groan, half cry emerged that could be heard by all in the press rows on that side of the ring. Schmeling was through. Louis had won. The German was removed to a hospital immediately after the fight and was carried on a stretcher aboard ship for Germany. However, he recovered sufficiently in the course of time to become a paratrooper, and to participate in the German conquest of Crete from the British where, ironically, boxing had thrived some four thousand years before.

After the Schmeling fight, Joe Louis discovered he was in such a high income tax bracket that if he fought any more that year his purses would go to the government. So, because of the income tax, Louis did not fight again in 1938. In 1939, he knocked out his friend, John Henry Lewis, in one round; Jack Roper in one round; Tony Galento in four rounds; and Bobby Pastor in eleven rounds. In 1940 and 1941 he maintained his pace. In fact, in 1941 he established a record by risking his title nine times. Billy Conn showed up the best of any of his opponents and was actually leading Louis on points when he was knocked out in the thirteenth round. In 1942 Joe Louis, like millions of others, was inducted into the army. The army permitted him to fight twice professionally while in the service, once against Buddy Baer and once against "Jock" Whitney's ex-chauffeur, Abe Simon, both of whom he put away handily. A Louis-Conn championship fight for Army Relief had also been arranged by Mike Jacobs and had originally been approved by the Secretary of War, but later the approval was withdrawn. Louis was honorably discharged 1 October 1945—147 days after VE day—after boxing exhibitions for soldiers all over the world.

41. Louis KOs Buddy Baer (Press Association Inc.)

On 19 June 1946, Louis defended his title against Billy Conn for the second time before a "million-dollar gate" crowd at Yankee Stadium in New York City. This time, however, Conn never had a chance, and was knocked out in the eighth round. On 18 September 1946, the heavyweight champion knocked out Tami Mauriello after slightly more than two minutes of the first round had elapsed.

However, after defending his title a total of twenty-three times, the young black, who had left a share-cropper's farm to become one of the greatest heavyweight champions of all time, began to show the wear and tear of age. His performances began to indicate that he was ripe to be defeated by a courageous and confident boxer with a good right hand who could force Louis to do the leading. Throughout his career Louis showed that his best role was as a counter-puncher and that when his opponents did not lead to him his efficiency was greatly impaired.

On 5 December 1947, Jersey Joe Walcott, a veteran black heavyweight from Camden, New Jersey, in the opinion of many out-boxed, out-maneuvered and out-fought the champion. According to the official record and score of the bout, Louis was knocked down twice—in the first round for a count of two, and in the fourth round for a count of seven—and was out-pointed by the Eagan system (developed by Eddie Eagan and the basis of the N.Y. Athletic Commission's current rules on the officiating of bouts.) thirty-seven to thirty-two. However, the officials awarded the fight to Louis and did not elect to take advantage of the Eagan rule which permits a loser on rounds to be awarded the fight if he has in their opinion won and if his point score is greater. Judge Marty Monroe gave Louis nine rounds, Walcott six; Louis eleven points, Walcott ten. Judge Frank Forbes gave Louis eight rounds, Walcott six and one even; Louis nine points, Walcott twelve. Referee Ruby Goldstein gave Walcott seven, Louis six, even two; Louis twelve points, Walcott fifteen.

In all fairness to Louis, it must be admitted that the defensive tactics of Walcott degenerated in the latter rounds and especially in the last, in an effort to keep out of reach by running backwards and that if Louis had not kept after him there might have been no fight. Since Louis was champion, it was technically difficult to take his title away because he was not able to catch his opponent. However, the boxing world realized that the long and almost unprecedented career of Louis was drawing to an end, and that the Louis of 1948 was no longer the Louis of 1937.

On 25 June 1948, a return Louis-Walcott fight took place at Yankee Stadium. The gate for this (Louis's twenty-fifth) defense of the title was $841,739.

While the fight started out to become a replica of the first fight with Walcott's defensive tactics being too much for Louis, the hitting power of one of the greatest of modern champions finally asserted itself. Louis caught up with Walcott and knocked him out in the eleventh round.

However, it was again evident that Louis was slipping and that the great leveler—age—was about to claim another victim as soon as it received the help of some youthful collaborator. While many friends advised Louis to retire undefeated, his financial needs, alleged to be great notwithstanding the fact that he had received almost five million dollars of gross income in the course of his fistic career, prompted him to continue. Mike Jacobs, it was reported, also urged him on, for Jacobs without Louis was like Rickard without Dempsey.

On 1 March 1949, Joe Louis announced his retirement and the abandonment of his world's Heavyweight Championship and at the same time announced the formation of a new organization to promote boxing called The International Boxing Club, in which Louis himself, Arthur M. Wirtz, and James Norris were to be the principal officers. Louis also announced that he had under contract to that organization the four leading heavyweights, and further, that two of these—Ezzard Charles and Joe Walcott—would fight for his vacated World's Heavyweight Championship. The winner of the Charles-Walcott fight would then fight the victor of a Savold-Lesnevich bout.

42. Louis KOs Billy Conn (Press Association Inc.)

The resignation of Louis and recognition of the Charles-Walcott engagement as a World's Championship fight was authorized by the National Boxing Association and its president, Abe J. Greene. Colonel Edward Eagan and the New York State Athletic Commission on the other hand, did not approve the right of Louis to sign up the four best men in the heavyweight division for the championship. Perhaps Jacobs contended that, because he had controlled the championship through Louis for so many years, he alone had the right to name a successor or run the fights to establish a successor.

In any case, the result of Louis' move offered a really new situation in the story of boxing. While the whole boxing world was in favor of Louis' trying to capitalize on his championship and looked forward to a change in the alleged Jacobs' monopoly, yet many well-informed followers of the sport believed that first, Joe Louis undeniably one of the greatest champions of all times, would nevertheless not necessarily prove to be a Rickard or a Jacobs as a promoter; second, the partners of Louis could not contribute the experience, acumen, and flair for promotion necessary for a successful undertaking or for the future of Boxing.

As an aftermath of this situation, boxing could again have two champions with the N.B.A. recognizing one champion and the N. Y. State Commission recognizing another. However, in the past public opinion or actual ring tests have favored the N.B.A. The cases of Angott-Jenkins, Lesnevich-Mauriello, Zale-Abrams, Ortiz-Salica, Ike Williams-Bob Montgomery all proved Colonel Eagan and the N. Y. State Boxing Commission wrong. In each instance the first named was the N.B.A. nominee and he won out over the N. Y. State Champion.

The first concrete result of the formation of the new promotion combine and the retirement of Joe Louis was the Ezzard Charles-Jersey Joe Walcott "title" fight at Comisky Park in Chicago. Twenty-five thousand three hundred and ninety-two persons paid $246,546 to see what Nat Fleischer referred to as a "dance of the mediocrity." Walcott could have won by taking a few chances and throwing a few more punches, but he did not, so for the third time this finished fistic craftsman sometimes with "the heart of a sparring partner" could not come through. A Bruce Woodcock-Lee Savold match in London also became a factor in the so-called championship picture. Joe Maxim, N.B.A. American light-heavy champion, managed by Jack Kearns and supported by independent promoter Sam Becker of Cincinnati, appeared to be the most serious challenger of the new "title" holder. However, Octopus, Inc., which was the name given by the newspapers to the new

merger of the Joe Louis combine with the Jacobs empire, the Madison Square Garden, and the Tournament of Champions, next put on an Ezzard Charles-Gus Lesnevich "world's championship" fight at Yankee Stadium. This fight was also won by Ezzard Charles, but disproved rather than proved the appeal or abilities of a manufactured champion still not recognized by the New York State Boxing Commission. All that could be said was that perhaps Ezzard Charles was the best active heavyweight in a world grown unusually short of any good heavyweights other than the retired Joe Louis.

43. Quartet of American Champions: Dempsey, Tunney, Louis, and Braddock. (Ring Magazine)

No one in any weight class actually held and defended a championship in the "Gloved Fist Era," which started in 1888, as long as did Joe Louis. When Joe Louis announced his retirement as world's champion, he had completed a reign of almost twelve years. The closest rivals for this record are John L. Sullivan, who held the title only for ten years and seven months, and Johnny Kilbane, who held the featherweight championship for eleven years, three months, and eleven days, but who, for the last five years of that period, rarely defended his title. In the entire modern era of boxing, including the bare-fist era, Louis ranks third in length of tenure of any championship. For only two men held a world or major championship longer—Jack Broughton, the "Father of Boxing," for sixteen years, and Tom Cribb, the "Black Diamond," for thirteen years. Figg, the first modern bare-fist champion, is credited with an eleven-year reign. All four of these champions were heavyweights. Jack McAuliffe, the "Napoleon of the Prize Ring," held the American lightweight championship for approximately eleven years before retiring undefeated in 1896.

44. Joe Louis, world's heavyweight champion 1937–1949 (Ring Magazine)

Joe Louis, born Joseph Barrow, had therefore established an outstanding mark in the history of the sport and must go down in its records ranked with the greatest heavyweight champions of all time—Theagenes and Cleitomachus of the ancient Greek era; Figg, Broughton, and Cribb of the English barefist epoch; John L. Sullivan, James J. Jeffries, and Jack Dempsey of the American period—a period Louis terminated.

Joe Louis, as far as the year 1949 is concerned, marks the end of the American or padded-glove golden era in boxing and the formal beginning of the broadcasting and monopoly era. This period marked a decline in the sport, and was a dangerous time where boxing, in spite of a vicious and illegal monopoly, just managed to survive. However, this dangerous period resulted, as we shall see, in a strong upturn where boxing spread on an unprecedented worldwide basis aided by man's scientific inventions of television and satellite relay.

In order to include the development in the new "broadcasting" expansion of boxing, which is also a part of the story of boxing and the saga of the fist, we must include the following earlier statistical and historical data:

(1) First world's championship broadcast by radio; Dempsey-Carpentier, 2 July 1921.
(2) First world's championship broadcast tied in with a weekly radio broadcast dramatic series starring Max Baer, one of the participants—Baer-Carnera, 14 June 1934.
(3) First theater closed circuit TV broadcast—Boon-Danahar, 23 February 1939 (London).
(4) First major fight televised from Madison Square Garden—Nova-Baer, 4 April 1941.
(5) First TV broadcast of a world's heavyweight championship—Louis-Walcott, 5 December 1947.
(6) First theater closed circuit world's championship TV broadcast—Louis-Savold, 15 June 1951 (United States) Eight theaters in six cities.
(7) First international theater closed circuit TV broadcast; Marciano-Moore, 21 September 1955 (limited).
(8) An early closed circuit theater broadcast with exact records—Robinson-Basilio, 25 March 1958 for middleweight title 174 outlets, 364,870 persons, paid receipts of $1,410,000 (Actual audience approximately 18,000 with gate of $350,000).

These of course were merely a beginning in the combination of boxing with broadcasting and were before the astronomical increase in worldwide installations and interest.

4 • The Broadcasting and Monopoly Era – Outside the Ring 1949-1961

The history of modern boxing entered into a new era but, like all eras in history, its beginning and end are sometimes difficult to define. The story of the modern sport of boxing also had become more complicated, with millions of dollars involved and with championship fights described and heard and, later, with further inventions, both seen and heard over the entire world within a fraction of a second. So there are now two different stories to tell—one about the square rings and the haymakers (the fights and the fighters), and the other story about the promoters, managers, and the persons who battled and won or lost control of a sport that later became big business, involving over ten million dollars in the take of a single boxing contest; and also where mere physical ringside audiences or "gates" were very secondary to the huge number of "paying" television viewers.

Although this chapter may appear to duplicate chapter three and chapter five, which deal with the world heavyweight title fights up to 1949 and then from 1949 to 1961 respectively, this chapter presents the other side in the story of boxing that no longer can be ignored, and because of its world aspect, its financial promotion, and its tax complications, contributes to a vital phase of boxing history. It presents the story not of boxers and boxing, but of outside the ring intrigues, maneuvers, and contacts, and contracts between promoters and managers, and between moochers and gangsters. Violations of state and federal laws and an ever-increasing underworld influence managed practically to take over boxing, and almost ruined boxing in a strange era where

only the United States government and the law saved boxing from a resulting monopoly based on conspiracy and extortion, which would have meant the final extinction of the sport.

So, if there is some repetition it will be because the same boxers and fights are covered, but actually they were minor episodes as compared with the behind-the-scene struggle of the sport to survive—a struggle in which the author is proud to have played a very small part to save the sport. Chapters five, six, and seven will, on the other hand, concern themselves with the fights and fighters during this era. The saga of the fist's passage from its modern golden age or padded-glove era (from 1888 to approximately 1949), to the broadcasting or monopoly age (1949 –1962), that almost killed boxing, is introduced by Joe Louis being forced to abandon a sick and partially paralyzed Mike Jacobs, an effective but deservedly unpopular tyrant, for what would turn out to be worse—namely, the control of James Dougan Norris, the International Boxing Club and a proven group of conspirators and extortionists.

In 1933, however, the preliminary groundwork began to usher in the monopoly age. Mike Jacobs was organizing the Twentieth Century Sporting Club with three well-known Hearst newspaper men under the guise or original objective of promoting boxing shows for Mrs. William Randolph Hearst's Free Milk Fund for babies. They were Edward Frayne, sports editor of the *New York American*, Wilston "Bill" Farnsworth, sports editor of the *New York Journal*, and Damon Runyon, Hearst columnist for thirty years. Jacobs, a most successful ticket speculator on

71

Broadway, was known to have been chosen by Tex Rickard to help him but only in ticket promotion and sales; however on Rickard's death, his ticket man, Jacobs, became interested in boxing as a promoter as well as a ticket agent. Jacobs was soon challenging Madison Square Garden's monopolistic hold on boxing, inherited from Tex Rickard. Outwardly, Mrs. Hearst's Free Milk Fund was a charity affair but, in reality, was a cover for a group of hungry, dog-eat-dog opportunists.

Actually, the Twentieth Century Sporting Club was organized when the so-called Hearst Milk Fund group started an attack on the Garden and on James J. Johnston the Garden's fight promoter, a personable man known as the "boy bandit" along Broadway, although his boyhood was far behind him. He chose to criticize Jacobs, Frayne, Farnsworth, and Runyon as money-hungry moochers. The result was that the Hearst press soon went on the offensive to attack Johnson as an inept promoter and the Garden as a selfish, big business enterprise. In 1933, Colonel John Reed Kilpatrick, president of the Garden, informed the Milk Fund group that the next Garden rental would be increased. The Heart press accused the Garden of being indifferent to helpless and starving babies.

Laying philanthropy aside, Jacobs joined the rebellion, for he had helped Tex Rickard run boxing to lofty million-dollar gates. The plotters met secretly in the Forest Hotel on West 49th Street, off Broadway, opposite Jacobs' Ticket Brokerage Emporium. The stock was held one hundred percent in Jacobs' name as none of the others wanted their financial involvement to be known. Only Frayne, however, was sharp enough to demand a letter of agreement from Jacobs to prove his participation. Farnsworth and Runyon took Jacobs' word only, which they lived to regret; thus, the plotters started to bring down the monoply only to replace it with another and far-worse monopoly in the promotion of boxing, previously beneficially initiated and controlled by Rickard. However, just as Jack Dempsey had proven to be Rickard's ace card, Mike Jacobs, shortly after the beginning of the combine described above, acquired the inside ace promotion card in the person of a so far unknown young black heavyweight, Joe Louis. With the help of the Hearst trio's editorial influence plus, it is reported, the help of certain underworld characters, Jacobs not only acquired Louis as a chattel, but became the owner and sole principal of the Twentieth Century Sporting Club. Thus, quite unnoticed, Jacobs began to gain a monopoly, which was bad enough, but was to lead to an even worse one.

The Madison Square Garden did not go into a panic at this time as it did not realize it was about to be underpinned and superceeded. Even though Louis had become the exclusive property of Mike Jacobs and his press partners, and Jacobs had a connection in boxing promotion with the Garden, he already planned to take the play away from the Madison Square Garden, which was busy promoting the Max Baer-James J. Braddock title fight for 13 June 1935. The strange part about this fight was that for the first time an ancillary right, namely broadcasting (not TV as yet, but radio) made the fight possible. In other words, the new era, that of monopoly and radio broadcasting, had begun in a preliminary way. Neither the Madison Square Garden nor its terms could possibly have interested Max Baer and his manager, Ancil Hoffman, but Baer's coast-to-coast series "Taxi" (produced and promoted by the author in which Baer played a "tough taxi driver who preferred blondes"), tied in with the world's heavyweight Baer-Carnera fight and the broadcast of this title fight. They both were sponsored by Goodrich, and had attracted Baer's ambition to be an actor, as did Baer's starring role in a major motion picture *The Prizefighter and the Lady*. These were so successful that the Baer-Braddock fight was sold in connection with the broadcast the fight tied in with another radio coast-to-coast series to Gillette with Baer as "Lucky Smith—"the private detective with a wallop who preferred action to theory," and a contract for another picture based on Baer's radio vehicle. The author was the producer and manager of Baer's broadcasting entertainment and advertising activities. Although the Baer-Braddock fight is covered in the chapter on the ring and the ring's actors, it marked, in this chapter, the end of the Madison Square Garden's ascendency of control of boxing developed by Tex Rickard, and marked the beginning of the Mike Jacobs' monopoly, which was tighter, more dangerous, and more questionable. The Baer-Braddock fight, as far as its promoter was concerned (the Madison Square Garden), was a financial failure. Although Baer made out all right financially, because of his ancillary activities, the fight staged in the old Madison Square Garden Bowl in Long Island City only drew $205,366, and was a listless fight in which the ten to one underdog, Braddock, outfoxed and outboxed Baer, being most careful to move away from Baer's looping right hand for fifteen rounds. Baer lost close to $500,000 after the fight in broadcasting and motion picture options (held through the author) alone.

Less than two weeks later Jacobs matched Louis against Primo Carnero, world's boxing champion (before Baer) in a Twentieth Century Sporting Club fight sponsored by the Hearst charity Fund connection and even aided by Mayor LaGuardia. The bout at Yankee Stadium drew $328,655, thereby outdrawing the Garden's world championship fight and immediately elevating Joe Louis, and with him Mike Jacobs, to fistic ascendency.

Three months later, Jacobs matched Louis with Baer, another exchampion, at Yankee Stadium. Louis was now known as the "Brown Bomber." As part of the deal, the author of this book acquired from Mike Jacobs the radio broadcast rights to the fight, which he sold to General Motors. The fight, which only lasted four rounds, saw Baer knocked out after taking more punishment than Louis ever meted out to any other opponent. Jacobs' till rang up over a million dollars notwithstanding the economic blight at that time.

Jacobs now started to plot for the final acquisition of an all-out monopoly based on the possession of the greatest lever, namely, the world's heavyweight championship. Braddock, the titleholder, was under contract to Madison Square Garden and managed by Joe Gould, although it was rumored that Owney Madden, a prohibition character, had a sizable piece of the champion which he acquired by loans. Another unconfirmed report was that through loans Jacobs actually owned Braddock and Gould. Madison Square Garden had matched Braddock to fight Max Schmelling at Madison Square Garden for 3 June 1937; however, this did not stop Mike Jacobs. Jacobs had found out that there was a bug in the Garden's contract. He convinced Braddock and Gould, and perhaps others, that there was more to be gained and a far better gate and ancillary rights to a Braddock-Louis fight. As a final clincher to get the Braddock-Louis championship fight on the line, Jacobs guaranteed Braddock and his manager, Joe Gould, in addition to a purse of $320,000, a bonus—namely, ten percent of Louis' earnings for a period of ten years. This was widely reported but never confirmed. Another version was that the ten percent was to come from Louis' purses for his fights for a period of ten years. Jacobs, who personally liked Max Baer, told the author, who was involved in Baer's management, that the agreement was that in the event Braddock lost his title, he would give Braddock and Gould ten percent of his (Jacobs) profits on all Louis fights for up to ten years. This sounds more reasonable.

The author, who had had some past business contact with Braddock and Gould in broadcasting, tried, years later, to find out, especially from Gould, if Jacobs had made good or had welched on his promise. Rumors along "Jacobs' Beach" (the Broadway area around Jacobs' ticket agency) was that Jacobs had reneged on his confidential bonus agreement. The

only answer obtained by the author was that Jacobs had paid nominal amounts, allegedly representing ten percent of his profits on some twenty-three Louis fights beginning with the Farr fight. But Gould implied that he had no possible way of auditing Jacobs' alleged profits based on alleged costs and alleged deductions as well as on claims, collections, and receipts, and also, on the important interpretation of "before or after" taxes. In addition, the war unfortunately cut into the boxing business and influenced tte bonus agreement in the fact that Louis' normal fight schedule was interfered with by his military service in World War II. The impression that Gould indicated was that he had been "taken" by Jacobs' cunning as there was no way in which Braddock and he could take any legal action since the agreement was a confidential one and there was no way to check out what Jacobs claimed was ten percent of his profits. This arrangement was, of course, typical of the type of deals Jacobs was famous for and in keeping with his legal steal of Braddock's contract with the Madison Square Garden to defend his title.

A very reliable and authentic book on the world heavyweight championships, copyrighted in 1974, which claims some knowledge of the Gould-Jacobs deal, refers to a ten-year take of Braddock and Gould, totalling $150,000. Of course, this means an average of $15,000 a year, which is obviously ridiculous when compared with Jacobs' gross of ten mil-

August 30 1935

National Broadcasting Company Inc
30 Rockefeller Plaza
New York N Y

Jean V Grombach Inc
115 West 57th Street
New York N Y

Gentlemen:

The undersigned, The Chase National Bank of the City of New York, Forty-fifth Street Branch, acknowledges the receipt from National Broadcasting Company Inc. of its certified check in the sum of $27,500 to the order of Jean V Grombach Inc. on The Chase National Bank of the City of New York, Rockefeller Centre Branch, which the undersigned agrees to hold in escrow in accordance with the following:

1 - In the event that the boxing contest between Max Baer and Joe Louis takes place on September 24 1935, on or about 10:05 P.M. Daylight Saving Time, or at an earlier hour if the time is advanced because of inclement weather conditions, or in the event that the contest is postponed and takes place in accordance with the above on the postponed date but not after October 28 1935, then the undersigned unconditionally agrees to deliver said certified check to Jean V Grombach Inc., or order, at the conclusion of the contest;

2 - Should the contest fail to take place in accordance with the above, then the undersigned unconditionally agrees to deliver said certified check to the National Broadcasting Company Inc. at the above address.

The undersigned will exact no charges for the services to be performed by it in connection with the above.

Very truly yours,

THE CHASE NATIONAL BANK OF THE CITY OF NEW YORK
Forty-fifth Street Branch

By _____ (L.S.)
Assistant Trust Officer

45. Letter of agreement indicating the author's possession and sale of the Baer-Louis-Mike Jacobs' promoted fight broadcast in 1935.

lion dollars on Louis fights. In the author's opinion, Jacobs welched on Braddock and Gould but did it in such a way that it could not be legally questioned; however the purses alone of Louis on his fights for the ten-year period in question totalled $2,547,107.74, according to actual records. Based on these figures and those of the gates and ancillary rights, ten percent of Jacobs' profits could never have dwindled to $15,000 per year or a total of $150,000.

Although Jacobs had succeeded in signing up the Braddock-Louis fight, the Madison Square Garden immediately sought an injunction in Federal court to prevent it. However the deaf, but not dumb, cousin and lawyer of Mike Jacobs, Sol Strauss, had found a slip in the contract. While Braddock and Gould had guaranteed Braddock's services to the Garden when he signed the Max Baer contract, the contract had failed to set any time limit on Braddock's indenture! On this technicality, Judge Guy L. Fake (his real name!) denied, on 14 May 1937, the Garden's application for an injunction. Several weeks later, the District Court of Appeals upheld this decision. Braddock was now free to be knocked out legally by Louis, and the rather loose monopoly of Tex Rickard and the Madison Square Garden was definitely ended to be replaced by an even closer monopoly of Mike Jacobs. Much later, Jacobs would be superceded by the worse monopoly of all—that of the International Boxing Club and James Norris and his associates, as we shall see—but not without the physical help of Joe Louis who, in turn, abandoned his benefactor, Mike Jacobs, when the latter became terminally ill and partially paralyzed. In all fairness to Joe Louis, whose honesty, sportsmanship, and ethics have never been questioned, it must be stated that Mike Jacobs, or "Uncle" Mike as he was to Louis, announced publicly that he had only one wish and ambition, namely, to recover his health and boxing be damned. He admitted he could no longer take care of Louis' interests. But that was years later after the Jacobs' monopoly, and we are getting ahead of ourselves, for long before Jacobs had obtained complete control in this ever-changing double-cross game, he had to first get rid of the Hearst triplets.

In this, once more, a happy circumstance was in Jacobs' favor.

In 1937, the Hearst organization merged its *New York Journal* with the *New York American*, Farnsworth was out of a job, and Frayne was named sports editor of the *Journal-American*. On Saturday, 13 August 1938, an article in the *New York World Telegram* announced in a headline: "Mike Jacobs admits Hearst writers share in boxing swag." The article went on to explain that in closing a new five-year

contract between the Twentieth Century Club and the Madison Square Garden, Jacobs wound up paying to one of the Hearst group $25,000 for his twenty-five percent interest in the Twentieth Century Sporting Club after the partners reportedly drew down their share of the Louis-Schmeling return bout. The Hearst Milk Triplets were now out of the running. This left Jacobs sole "survivor" and "king" of boxing promotion, but only as long as Joe Louis continued to take orders and be all but managed in name by Jacobs.

During the next ten years and through World War II, Jacobs prospered as a ruthless and arrogant dictator of boxing—probably unequalled in the long history of boxing. From 1937 to 1947 he promoted sixty-one world championship fights and more than 1,500 others. His promotions with Louis only added up to over ten million dollars, and during his thirteen years as a promoter, he sold over ten million tickets worth over thirty million dollars. He was frequently accused of having some connection and cooperative relationship with the underworld—specifically with Owney Madden, Frank Carbo, Frank Palermo, and others—but at least he was smart enough, cunning enough, and tough enough to have a pretty tight control of things and observed pretty close security with respect to agreements and contracts, especially off-the-record ones. It was the ten years of the Jacobs monopoly that built up the underworld power and influence that was to assert itself in a monopoly that succeeded Jacobs through the innocent and indirect cooperation of Louis, Norris, and others.

The story of boxing, therefore, cannot at this stage be complete without leaving the square ring, as we are doing in this chapter, and turning our attention to the crosses and double-crosses of the principals of boxing in control and in management. It was because of the evermore vicious and more illegal conduct of boxing, with conspiracy and extortion, that contributed to the end of the golden age of boxing (1888–1949). This last was aided and brought to its zenith by the benevolent semimonopoly of Tex Rickard and his Madison Square Garden setup, who did not try to swallow up everything and refused any underworld infiltration or penetration.

The Jacobs monopoly was dependent solely on Jacobs; with Jacobs weakened by terminal illness and partially paralyzed, and with the desertion of Louis (who was used as a pawn by the new, incoming group), a new group, the International Boxing Club (IBC), headed by the millionaire operator, Jim Norris, with Louis allegedly a partner, came into being. (Joe Louis allegedly was promised a full partnership with Jim Norris and his associates, Arthur Wirtz and Truman Gibson.) Norris and Wirtz owned the Chicago Stadium, the Detroit Olympia, and the St. Louis Arena; they also had a major investment in the Cincinnati Garden, leases on the Omaha Coliseum and the Indianapolis Arena, and thirty-eight percent of the Madison Square Garden stock, most of this last owned by Norris and his father, who were also co-owners of the Detroit Red Wings. Part of the deal was Louis' contracts for the services of the four top heavyweight contenders to result in a championship tournament when Louis would retire, also prearranged. The key to the deal was reportedly a cash payment of $100,000 plus a guaranteed salary of $10,000 per year for ten years, and twelve percent of the IBC stock to a penniless Joe Louis who reportedly owed the IRS over a million dollars. Louis' original arrangement, as set up by Truman Gibson, was reported as fifty-one percent of IBC stock, $250,000 in cash, and $20,000 per year salary.

Of course, when Norris and Wirtz completed their negotiations to finance the plan for the exclusive control of the heavyweight championship, if not of boxing, the asking price was considerably cut.

The deal was very secretly closed, but rumors reached the Twentieth Century Sporting Club, which still had a two year lease on boxing in the Madison Square Garden. Jacobs, kingpin of both the Twentieth Century Sporting Club and boxing at the Madison Square Garden, and banker, friend, and benefactor of Louis, would not believe that Louis had deserted him. However, when informed by Louis and Gibson in person his only comment was "If you are retiring as a champ, I'm going to quit too!"

However, according to many sources, Madison Square Garden with its two-year contract with Mike Jacobs, and Mike Jacobs with a contract of unknown value on the services of Joe Louis, joined with the IBC and Norton who owned a major share of the Madison Square Garden stock. As an indirect result, the renegotiation left Louis with his very reduced terms. So the ace card in the boxing game had been topped by a joker—a joker picturing many wolves! Later, the IBC bought out the Tournament of Champions (an organization that is dealt with in more detail later, and that had gained control of the world's middleweight title) from CBS and the Music Corporation of America. Larry Lowman, notwithstanding his experience in the OSS as one of the CBS principals in their many interests, could not or would not match wits with the IBC combine and its clandestine allies. Thus, a bigger and more powerful monopoly had replaced that of Mike Jacobs, and the monopoly era had begun.

In other words, before Louis officially resigned his championship and retired, he and the coconspirators had signed up the top challengers to exclusive agreements. However, Louis never became a real or true partner or copromoter or principal of IBC, nor did he collect any proper direct participation in IBC's over all profits according to reliable sources.

However, there is no question that the underworld had an ever-increasing voice in the fight game during this period, both in the Jacobs era and even more so when the IBC gained control of the sport. No other world champion, incidentally, had tried to retain the heavyweight crown by signing the leading contenders before his official retirement and thereby controlling the title in retirement. But with the help of Gibson, Norris, and the IBC, this unusual gambit was successful.

During the Mike Jacobs days and even more so with IBC in control, and during the period designated in this book as the broadcasting and monopoly period in the history of boxing, the underworld and Frank Carbo, a top underworld character, had great influence if not control. Carbo had unquestioned contact with Mike Jacobs and even moreso later with Jim Norris and Al Weill, IBC's matchmaker, and the Madison Square Garden management under IBC's control. Carbo's arrogance had been great even in the Jacob's days when he held court in the Forest Hotel on West 49th Street. Carbo's police record (B95838 with the N.Y. Police Department) began at age twelve with some seventeen arrests—five for murder. To further indicate the relationship between Carbo and Norris, Carbo's girl friend, later his wife, Viola Masters, was given a job by Norris with the Neville Advertising Agency and Cameo Enterprises, spinoffs of IBC, handling broadcast rights and fight pictures. Later, Norris testified that he had employed her to help his good relationship with boxers and their managers. Mrs. Carbo was reportedly paid approximately $41,000 in not more than three years.

Other underworld characters had great interests and influences in boxing. Among them were Eddie Coco, Frank Blinky Palermo, and Felix Bocchicchio.

On 4 December 1952, Jim Norris' father died at the age of seventy-five. This was a great shock to Norris who loved and respected his father. His father's death seemed to make Norris conscience stricken and that is when he made his famous offer to J. Edgar Hoover to take over the IBC and run it legitimately without underworld interference or influence. The definite contract offered was $100,000 per year for a minimum of ten years, or one million dollars. Hoover rejected the offer, but recounted it to the author requesting the author's reaction through

Hoover's deputy, Mickey Ladd, with whom the author had been closely connected in espionage and counter-espionage as a colonel in Army intelligence during World War II. Hoover was amused by the Norris offer as it seemed like a cry for help from Norris and for a confrontation with Frank Carbo, Palermo, et al who were evidently actually running the IBC.

Of course, this period was characterized by ever-rising revenues from radio broadcasting and the beginning of TV broadcasting, as exemplified by the TV and radio rights to the second Walcott-Marciano fight in the Chicago Stadium on 15 May 1958. This fight and its broadcast lasted less than three minutes. Nevertheless, Norris received $300,000 for this three-minute broadcast. The fact that Walcott, a challenger, who lasted less than one round, received a $250,000 guarantee with his manager, Felix Bocchicchio, while Marciano, the world's champion, managed by the cunning Al Weill with years of experience as both manager and matchmaker, received only $166,000, could only be attributed to Carbo's having set up the deal. Nothing else could explain Weill being taken with Marciano as the real victim.

Things began to leak out or become unearthed in various places proving that the underworld had much more than occasional influences on prizefights. For instance, an investigation by Governor Knight of California into boxing revealed the fact that Al Weill had seemingly received an unreported under the table $10,000 in connection with the Marciano-Cockell fight in California in 1955. Shortly after this revelation, Marciano announced his retirement and, according to reports, the Marciano-Weill relationship was at an end. Many cases of extortion, threats, and assaults that surrounded the management and promotion of professional boxing began to come to light.

Finally, the situation became so bad that the United States government, the Department of Justice, and the FBI began to look into professional boxing's obvious and illegal monopoly. In 1953, IBC was already a defendant to a Federal antitrust prosecution in the United States District Court, Southern District of New York. The defendants were IBC of New York, IBC of Illinois, the Madison Square Garden Corp., James D. Norris, and Arthur Wirtz.

In February of 1953, the author, as reported in the press, was a witness for the Department of Justice, and was not only able to testify, but to support his testimony with documentary proof. In order to get an IBC promoted world's middleweight championship fight with Jake LaMotta for Laurent Dauthuille of France, whom he comanaged, the author had to guarantee to IBC a return bout or Dauthuille's future services supported by a personal $25,000 bond!

The contract the author submitted in court had been held out by IBC until the author insisted, at the last minute, it be delivered to him, or Dauthuille would not show at ringside. However, Justice Noonan, although monopoly had been proven, decided that the Supreme Court had granted boxing immunity from antitrust action when it ruled, in 1953, that major league baseball was not adjudged as interstate commerce. The Department of Justice appealed to the Supreme Court to reverse this decision which it did on 31 January 1955.

Shortly thereafter, the United States government began further antimonopoly prosecution, and although the IBC issued a statement to allay the fears of the sponsors of the Wednesday night and Friday night broadcasts of bouts, the days of the IBC monopoly were numbered. At the second trial, strangely enough, notwithstanding excellent prosecution witnesses and past evidence for the government, many persons present at the trial believed that the strongest testimony against the IBC and the Madison Square Garden Corporation was that of General Kilpatrick's file of letters and his diary. A government attorney reading a back issue of the *New Yorker* magazine came across the fact that the general was an habitual diarist and recordkeeper. The government attorneys found that General Kilpatrick's file did indeed seal the government case against Jim Norris and his boxing empire.

When Norris was on the stand he was faced with explaining and confirming General Kilpatrick's memos. Altogether, the IBC and its Madison Square Garden and its non-boxing fighters had a very bad day. Truman Gibson, a lawyer, tried to establish that the Joe Louis deal had nothing to do with the later organization of IBC, or several IBC's, or the amalgamation with the Madison Square Garden. But here again Gibson was cross-examined based on General Kilpatrick's diary and its excerpts, and although objected to, were ruled admissible by Judge Sylvester J. Ryan. Kilpatrick's diary proved beyond any doubt a conspiracy in restraint of trade. The ruling of the Court in March 1957 confirmed by the Supreme Court of the United States on 12 January 1958, called for a complete "divestment, dissolution and divorcement" of the IBC Complex, Madison Square Garden Corp., James Norris, and Arthur Wirtz, and even fingered Truman Gibson. Shortly thereafter, Norris suffered a coronary attack and was inactive for months.

As if Norris and Company had not been punished enough during the trial in 1956, Rocky Marciano, world's heavyweight champion, managed by Al Weill and therefore an IBC property, announced his retirement from the ring. Marciano did not consider that he had any right to sign up the leading con-

DEPARTMENT OF JUSTICE

ANTITRUST DIVISION

UNITED STATES COURT HOUSE
FOLEY SQUARE
NEW YORK 7, N. Y.

April 14, 1953.

Mr. John V. Grombach
113 West 57th Street
New York 19, N. Y.

      Re: U.S. v. International Boxing Club, Inc.
                        et al.

Dear Mr. Grombach:

      In response to your recent request we enclose herewith a photostatic copy of each of two contracts submitted by you on the occasion of your appearance before the Grand Jury last year. Both contracts are between Jacob La Motta and Laurent Dauthuille and both are dated August 14, 1950.

      We are unable to return the original contracts to you at this time since they have been marked as grand jury exhibits. However, if it is necessary that you require them in legal proceedings, we can arrange to make them available to you for a short period of time in the event that photostatic copies are not acceptable.

46. A letter from the United States Department of Justice confirming author's submission of a world's championship boxing match contract, the major evidence in the antimonopoly case against the IBC.

      Sincerely yours,

      EDWARD P. HODGES
      Acting Assistant Attorney General

      By *Richard B. O'Donnell*

      RICHARD B. O'DONNELL
      Chief, New York Office

Enclosures - 2

---

tenders and both retire and sell his title. Al Weill tried to convince him to use his title to continue the IBC monopoly and make further profits, but evidently the Marciano-Weill relationship was at an end, and in addition, the lawyers of the IBC and the Madison Square Garden Corporation were afraid that any such move would make them criminally liable in the face of the antitrust case and its probable final decision. Because of the trial and the position it placed IBC, since the second trial was especially based on an exclusive monopoly of world heavyweight champions or contenders, IBC was check-mated! In this case, the leading heavyweight contenders were Archie Moore, Floyd Patterson, and Hurricane Jackson. All Norris could do, according to reliable sources, was to loan a furrier named Lippy Breidthart $10,000 to buy Hurricane Jackson's contract. To add to Norris' woes, Gus D'Amato, Patterson's manager, was violently opposed to the IBC and its power. When Patterson easily won a twelve-round decision over Hurricane Jackson and when Patterson ko'd Moore in the sixth round, D'Amato

then made clear that he would not do business with IBC or Norris. This signified that boxing was about to enter into a new era.

Only the racketeers, Carbo, and his associates, had to be dealt with. This the United States goverment also took care of, although Carbo was very much in evidence in 1957 to 1959. Among other developments dug up by New York State authorities was the meeting between Norris and Carbo at fight manager Hymie Wallman's apartment at 225 West 86th Street. Detectives tailed Weill and Frank Carbo to the same hotel on the night of the Basilio-Robinson fight on 15 April 1958. Norris resigned as President of IBC because of reasons of health, and Truman Gibson was named as president to succeed Norris. Frank Carbo was indicted by New York State as an undercover and unlicensed manager, but he could not be found to be arrested.

In the meantime, forced by the Supreme Court's divestment ruling on 12 January 1959, the Graham Paige Corporation paid the Norris-Wirtz interests in the Garden close to $4,000,000 for approximately a forty percent ownership. IBC became NBE; National Boxing Enterprises. On 20 March 1959, Harry Markson as Managing Director of Boxing, of Madison Square Garden (of NBE) wrote a letter to Joe Louis stating that due to a United States Supreme Court ruling against IBC the Garden et al could no longer pay him any salary, although Louis might become associated with the NBE and perhaps sometime in the future the Garden might be able to use his services again if it could do so without breaking any law.

In July 1959, Norris, accompanied by Gibson, met with Rosensohn, a new promoter responsible for bringing the Swedish heavyweight Johansson to the United States. A plan for a promotional combine of Norris, Rosensohn, Jack Solomon of London, Edwin Alquist, Johansson's advisor, and Swedish boxing promotor, and Johansson himself was discussed. Rosensohn was to be president and receive a salary of $100,000 per year for five years. Of course, Norris had to be careful of any world plan because the only place where he could operate legally in the boxing business was at the Chicago Stadium. However, Rosensohn was financially involved with Salerno and Velella who were not in good standing and with backgrounds to which Wirtz objected, so Norris, Gibson, and the IBC withdrew from any further association with the world promotion plan. Young Rosensohn did not know what a dog-eat-dog struggle faced any would-be boxing promoter. Squeezed by Salerno and Velella, abandoned by Norris and the IBC, he read a *Life* magazine article that turned out to be a violent attack on him by Johannson who stated he would never fight for any Norris, Rosensohn, Gibson, Velella, and Salerno combine as promoters. The sole asset left to Rosensohn was the contract for a return bout between Johansson and Patterson. Cornered from all sides and lacking finances, he sold out to a group put together by attorney Roy M. Cohn who also, evidently, could not survive or swim in the dangerous rapids of professional boxing, or did not want to be, although he was offered help through his friend, the newspaper columnist, George Sokolsky. So Rosensohn was merely a spectator when Patterson ко'd Johannson and won his title back. Rosensohn, when last heard of, was selling dry cleaning equipment. The boxing jungle had been too much for him.

But now to the last act of the broadcast and monopoly period. Frank Carbo had finally been found and arrested and was out on bail on his New York State indictment. He was a patient at Johns Hopkins hospital in very bad health. Suddenly on the night of 22 September 1959, the FBI went into action. Truman Gibson, a respected black lawyer, who had put together the Louis-IBC deal, was arrested at his home in Chicago by the FBI who clapped handcuffs on him and shut him up in the city jail. Frank Carbo was arrested while in bed at the Johns Hopkins hospital in Baltimore and jailed irrespective of his poor health. Frank Palermo was hauled in by the FBI in Philadelphia, and Sica and Dragna were handcuffed by the G-men in Los Angeles. The FBI had made all five arrests in less time than a ten-round fight and only two rounds' time separated Carbo's arrest in Baltimore from Truman Gibson's in Chicago. The charges based on a Federal Grand Jury indictment by the Southern District of California in Los Angeles, involved conspiracy to violate Federal law, extortion, and conspiracy. The charges, of course, involved the IBC-Norris setup and its fights. Carbo, already indicted in New York State, was also in trouble with the IRS for the recovery of $750,000 in unpaid income taxes.

Even after Carbo's arrest and release on bail, the New York and New Jersey police recorded a secret meeting between Carbo, out on a $100,000 bail, and Norris at the Newark Airport on 1 October 1959.

On 30 November 1959 Frank Carbo, a diabetic with bad kidneys and an erratic heart, white-haired, well-dressed, and distinguished-looking, but apparently in very poor health, stood before Judge John A. Muller. Carbo had pleaded guilty to some of the New York State charges. After a long tirade against the prisoner by Prosecutor Scotti and the judge, the judge's sentence, mindful of the prisoner's poor health, was two years out of a possible maximum sentence of three, to be served at the Riker's Island Penitentiary. The judge summed up his opinion by telling Carbo that Carbo's wish was evidently a definite command in the boxing world . . . that Carbo had supreme but improper and illegal influence in the fight game and that Carbo had no doubt made an incalculable fortune.

However, this was only the beginning. On 21 February 1961, Frank Carbo, Frank Blinkey Palermo, Joe Sica, Louis Dragna, and Truman Gibson went on trial before Judge Ernest Tolin in Los Angeles. This was the United States government case and the prosecutor was Alvin H. Goldstein, Jr., as the government prosecutor. Judge Tolin on the prosecutor's motion cancelled bail for all involved, then changed his mind about Gibson and ordered his release on bail. None of the others had their bail reinstated. An application for Gibson's case to be separated had been made but denied. There were ten volumes of testimony. Gibson, Palermo, Dragna, and Sica testified; Carbo remained silent. Only Gibson introduced character witnesses. Judge Tolin's charge to the jury was very long but all inclusive. On 30 May 1959, the jury returned its verdict. All the defendants were found guilty. Judge Tolin set 20 June to hear all motions before sentencing. Gibson was still the only one out on bail. On 11 June, Judge Tolin died suddenly. Judge Boldt of the Western District of Washington was named to handle the case, which resulted in all the defendants asking for new trials. All the motions were denied, however.

On 2 December 1961, after denying all motions made by the defense attorneys, the following sentences were announced:

Carbo	25 years in prison and $10,000 fine
Palermo	15 years in prison and $10,000 fine
Gibson	5 years suspended sentence and $10,000 fine
Sica	20 years in prison and $10,000 fine
Dragna	5 years in prison and $ 5,000 fine

All except Carbo were released on bail, while Carbo was incarcerated in Alcatraz prison in San Francisco Bay.

Needless to say, Jim Norris was very saddened by the results—especially with respect to Carbo and Gibson with whom he had close contact. He had paid most of Gibson's legal fees including the greater part of some $60,000 apparently extorted by a Sidney Brin, who came up with some forged papers to prove supposedly that the Department of Justice was to dismiss the indictment against Gibson. Gibson was criticized by the government in this last matter and Mr. Brin wound up in the federal penitentiary. On 13 February 1963, the Court of Appeals in San Francisco, in a very detailed and long opinion, confirmed the convictions of Carbo, Palermo, and Gibson, reversed the conviction and sentence of Dragna, and confirmed only two of the three counts against Sica with no change in his sentence.

Truman Gibson, who was a principal with Joe Louis in making possible the IBC monopoly and who distinctly, and perhaps unfairly, suffered from his association with the IBC, was reported to have complained that neither he nor Louis had ever received the promised profits from the now-shielded splitup IBC operations.

Thus ended the monopoly and broadcasting period of boxing at the end of 1961. The next era of boxing can only be labelled the Worldwide and Television Era, where a fight in Zaire, Africa, or in Manila in the Philippines, is seen and heard within a fraction of a second in London, Paris, New York, Buenos Aires, Tokyo, and Cape Town, and where boxing is indeed worldwide. To prove further that boxing has entered a worldwide era, out of the eleven weight classifications as of this day of writing, the titles are distributed among nine countries: United States—2; Argentina—1; South Korea—1; Nicaragua—1; Mexico—3 (15 October 1975).

The following chapters will cover the fights and the fighters and the story of the squared ring while boxing was, in a way, held back by the monopolies and conspiracies and the many promoter and management conflicts that could not be omitted or ignored in any history of the sport. The following chapters will also continue to tell the extraordinary story of the sport and its relation with art, literature, theater, government, and its great actors and its technical development.

5 • The Broadcasting and Monopoly Era Inside the Ring 1949-1961

So notwithstanding Jim Norris, the IBC, and Frank Carbo, all who really wished to help boxing as well as themselves, boxing survived. In fact, the sport exploded very quietly into the next historical period —namely, the worldwide and television era with boxing matches and championships deployed on a global basis for the first time. We are now in this era. No longer are spectators in six figures and total takes in U.S. dollars in the very low seven figures; actual spectators are of no great consequence today because the television audience is in seven and eight figures, and gross receipts in U.S. dollars are in eight figures. Thus, another survival, or perhaps we should say another revival, of prizefighting through the centuries has been accomplished and, as always, accompanied by at least comparative freedom, democracy, culture, civilization, and the free enterprise system, but helped by man's inventions and even his harnessing of faraway satellites. It is to be noted that the Communist world does not permit professional sports of any kind. Once more, as in the Dark Ages, the possible disappearance of boxing may be accompanied by dictatorships of one kind or another.

As this chapter will indicate, boxing per se, and the sport and its disciples—namely, its history as far as the actual participants are concerned—hardly mirrored its decline, monopoly, and inept management. In fact, this rather shabby period in control and operations produced, nonetheless, one of the greatest heavyweight champions of all time.

It also will be noted that while the broadcasting and monopoly period, as far as the rings, the fights, and the boxers are concerned, ends closer to 1956 than 1961, while the same period in management and in the important monopoly and underworld control was definitely ended only when Carbo, his associates, and Gibson were convicted of conspiracy and extortion relating to monopoly, which was in 1961.

The reason for this apparent inconsistency in historical periods is because monopoly or its continuation was not legally and officially ended until the divestiture, dissolution, divestment, and conviction of all the elements of IBC. However, as far as fights and fighting are concerned, when Floyd Patterson was recognized as the world champion in November 1956, it ended IBC's control of the world's heavyweight championship, the most sought-after diadem of the ring.

The specific reason for the beginning of freedom for boxers and their managers in 1956 rather than in 1961 (when IBC was completely kayoed) was because in 1956 both Floyd Patterson and his manager, Gus D'Amato, after winning the title by a KO of Archie Moore, announced they would not negotiate with or fight for IBC or Jim Norris. Actually, they cut their noses to spite their faces, for beyond eight exhibition matches and three title defenses from 1956 to 1960; a KO against Tommy Jackson, whom Patterson had beaten before; a KO against Peter Rademacher, an amateur fresh from a heavyweight Olympic title; a KO over Rod Harris; a KO of Brian London and the loss of the title to Ingemar Johansson by a surprising KO in the third round; they did not produce the financial results the IBC could have obtained. Patterson's take of a total of a million dollars for five title fights hardly compares with the well over a million dollars to Gene Tunney for his single Dempsey fight promoted by Tex Rickard or, more recently, the reported five million dollars to both Muhammad Ali and George Foreman for their world closed-circuit TV extravaganza in Zaire.

The "inside the ring" story of the world heavyweight title of the monopoly period from 1949 to the retirement of Marciano in 1956, and the fringe period to 1961 when Floyd Patterson became the heavyweight king, can now be told. The heavyweight class, needless to say, was as busy or busier than ever. A retrospective review, strangely enough, indicates that several performers considered average or below average now appear to have been far better than contemporary judgement allowed.

The first champion after Joe Louis, and the Louis reign of almost twelve years (1937 to 1949), was Ezzard Charles. In retrospect, he was an accomplished boxer, an outstanding athlete, and a heavy puncher. He won two national AAU amateur championships as a middleweight. He was, however, handicapped by being too modest, mild, and lacking the initiative of Joe Louis, without of course the latter's talent. In the words of the 1949 edition of this book (and repeated in an earlier chapter), Charles was described as being "only the best in the world grown unusually short of great heavyweights other than the retired Joe Louis." However, let us look back on the record. First, Ezzard Charles won a formal tournament legally or illegally controlled by a combine of Joe Louis with a group of hungry promoters. He won recognition by defeating Jersey Joe Walcott who certainly gave Louis quite a battle in December 1947. Then Charles ko'd the former light heavyweight champion Gus Lesnevich in eight rounds; ko'd Pat Valentino in eight rounds, Freddy Beshore in fourteen rounds, and actually beat an aging Joe Louis; then ko'd Nick Barone and Lee Oma; decisioned Walcott again and beat Joey Maxim, a cunning boxer—not bad for an underrated champion!

Although Charles made over $750,000 in thirteen title fights and well over a million dollars altogether, he wound up absolutely broke and seriously ill with lateral sclerosis of the spine. In 1974 he was reported paralyzed from the waist down, a wheel chair, and welfare or charity case, and died penniless in 1975.

Jersey Joe Walcott, who followed Charles, had many points in common with Jim Braddock. Both were from New Jersey, both were highly moral and religious, both turned to boxing to support their families, both became disillusioned and quit boxing, both were well past the top athletic age when they won the title. Jersey Joe was the oldest titleholder

47. Ezzard Charles, world's heavyweight champion, 1950–51. (Ring Magazine)

in modern boxing without benefit of any birth certificate. When he ko'd Charles after being beaten twice by him, he was probably more surprised than anyone else. To indicate how religious Arnold Cream (Walcott's real name) really was, after winning the title he stated, "I want to thank God for helping me win. I want to tell the young folks what it means to have God on their side." Felix Bocchicchio, notwithstanding his police record and being a handicap to Walcott, after the days of Norris and Carbo, saved Walcott and his family from poverty and hunger. Bocchicchio encouraged and financed Walcott for another and proper try and was responsible for Walcott's comeback and for Walcott finally winning the world heavyweight title.

When Jersey Joe fought Joe Louis on 5 December 1947, he was given practically no chance to win, yet most everyone agreed he deserved the decision although Louis was given the decision by the two judges against the referee's vote. But six months later, Louis ko'd Jersey Joe in round eleven and while Walcott did not deserve a shot at Charles' title, Charles decided to give Jersey Joe another shot. Walcott ko'd Charles in round seven and stalled the rematch for almost a year with Walcott winning on points over fifteen rounds.

Walcott and Marciano did much to bring back the boxing business on 23 September 1952. Previous to the fight, Walcott was compared with Satchel Paige, an ageless athlete. The fight was labelled "great" by all the oldtimers and experts. After twelve rounds of superior boxing by Jersey Joe who was

48. Rocky Marciano KOs Louis in the eighth round of their fight. (Marciano Estate)

49. World's heavyweight champion, Rocky Marciano, one of the greatest champions in modern boxing: 43 KOs, 6 wins, and 0 losses. (Courtesy of Mary Anne Marciano)

Best to you
Rocky Marciano

ahead on points, in the first half minute in round thirteen Marciano nailed Jersey Joe with a right hand as Jersey Joe was propped against the ropes. A picture caught the knockout blow and projects its power. The return match was anticlimactic and, according to some, tarnished Jersey Joe's reputation as he went out in total disgrace. A right upper cut from Marciano in the first round knocked Jersey Joe to the floor where he sat dazed and, without any effort to get up, was counted out. In 1971, Walcott was elected sheriff of Camden County in New Jersey and is a respected and financially independent citizen in his community, doing extracurricular work for the youth in his neighborhood.

The story of the next world champion is very dramatic, a rags to riches tale and one covering one of the very few boxers who never lost a fight and retired undefeated, and refused two offers of a million dollars or more guarantees to return to the ring. It is also the story of a boxer discovered through his Army service in World War II, rather than the story of some top boxer who avoided military service to their country because in their limited judgement their country was wrong or they believed themselves above ordinary citizens. Marciano saw combat service overseas with an amphibious unit. It is also a sad story, for undefeated champion Marciano was killed in a rather senseless accident followed after several years by the death of his wife and the mysterious disappearance or loss of what was estimated to be a large fortune. His son and daughter will have no real share in the millions he made. It is also the story of a dedicated, never-say-die, superbly self-disciplined athlete with many physical handicaps. Only Gene Tunney equalled the quite unannounced confidence, discipline, and insurmountable will-to-win of Marciano, although Marciano's physical equipment was far inferior to Tunney's. Tunney was six feet one-half inch tall, Marciano five feet ten inches tall. Tunney weighed 196 pounds against Marciano's 184. Tunney's reach was seventy-seven inches while Marciano's was sixty-eight inches, a nine-inch difference of great importance.

Rocky Marciano, born Rocco Frances Marchegiano, the "Brockton Blockbuster" was born 1 September 1923 in Brockton, Massachusetts. He started boxing early, although originally was more interested in baseball. In high school he was a star in football and baseball. He was a good enough catcher to have a tryout and a listing with the Chicago Cubs. He particularly became interested in boxing in the Army and he first showed at a professional training gym in Tacoma, Washington while still in the Army. His personality, his gutter-type swarming offense, and his terrific punching power resembled those of Jack

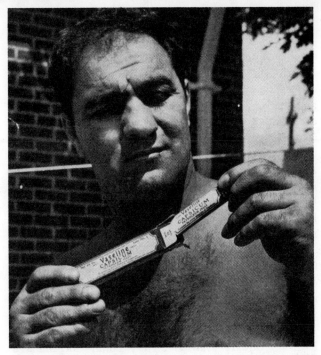

50. Picture of Marciano with tube of salve that almost blinded him temporarily in his fight with Walcott, reportedly spread on Walcott's gloves by his manager. (Curtis Publishing Company, with permission from Mary Anne Marciano)

Dempsey, Mickey Walker, and Stanley Ketchel. His first appearance in the record book is as heavyweight on the Fort Lewis United States Army boxing team. He went to the National AAU Junior Championships in Portland, Oregon where he knocked out four opponents in two nights, but broke his hand and could not continue. Marciano may well have been the hardest hitter in the game. His punches even on the arms of an opponent rendered them numb and of little use. He scored forty-three knockouts and six wins in forty-nine fights without a single loss or draw! He won the title by a KO over Jersey Joe Walcott on 23 September 1952 and retired, undefeated, on 27 April 1956. In 1958, Jim Norris offered him a guaranteed $1,000,000 to fight Patterson and later in 1958 a highly responsible Kentucky financial group offered him a guarantee of $1,250,000 in return for one single fight. The author offered him a broadcast and advertising contract for a little part-time work in 1960. All these offers were turned down because, according to Marciano's own statements, he had enough money for himself and his family for their lifetimes and he was making plenty of money and improving his fortune in an easy way where he was his own boss for the first time. As his management under Al Weill, who became an absolute dictator, had worn thin at the end and when all contact and friendship had ended, this last statement was very understandable. In fact, it seemed that Al Weill never missed a chance to degrade or humiliate his boxer as if jealous of his popularity, for Weill had few friends and no admirers. It is reported that Marciano's conscience bothered him as an outstanding and compassionate person with regard to his abandonment of his original manager, trainer and coach, Gene Caggiano of Brockton, Massachusetts. A gentlemen's agreement had been made—namely, that if Rocky ever turned professional, Gene would be his manager for all the time, effort, and help given Rocky. This agreement was even confirmed in writing, but without benefit of counsel and later ruled technically of no value.

When sent by friends to New York City and to Charley Goldman, famous trainer and coach of boxers, who had already trained four world champions and had four hundred fights as a bantamweight, he was introduced to Al Weill, the pirate manager of Broadway. Weill, even though as matchmaker for the Madison Square Garden legally could not manage boxers according to New York State law, he nevertheless became Rocky's manager, later assigning his stepson as official manager and then later picking up Marciano's management officially after resigning as matchmaker. This was when he was certain that he would make more money as Marciano's manager than as matchmaker for the Garden. Caggiano sued Weill and Marciano, but the friendly agreement, preposed without legal counsel, was of no value. However, in making an investigation of this matter in 1974, it would appear that Marciano's conscience and his loyalty to oldtime friends had caused him to pay Caggiano on a highly confidential basis some secret compensation or gift to make up for having shifted to Al Weill—probably because of assurances that only he, Weill, could pilot him to the championship and that Caggiano would be more of a hindrance than a help in the boxing industry in its monopoly era. It must be remembered that Weill had close contact with Carbo, IBC, and with the group that definitely controlled boxing at that time. Caggiano, when contacted in 1974, while refusing to talk, projected no bitterness or animosity toward Marciano or the Marciano family, but was highly and properly critical of Al Weill and his lack of any ethics and of the IBC monopoly.

According to some sources, the only time Marciano faltered and was almost checked in his extraordinary career was in his first championship Walcott fight because Al Weill, in lieu of Charley Goldman, issued the coaching directions in the corner between rounds. Charley helped Rocky through forty-one fights without a defeat and was an accepted "corner" brain or strategist, while Weill's cunning was as a negotiator and an excellent cigar smoker, never having boxed a round in his life, and no ring

51. Rocky and Barbara Marciano—they waited three years for manager Al Weill to approve their marriage. "Wives hurt fighters," said Weill. "When it's right for you to marry, I'll tell you." (Courtesy of Mary Anne Marciano)

strategist. But with his boxer fighting for the greatest of all titles in boxing, Weill had the swelled head and tried to take command in Rocky's corner between rounds. There was even a report that some of the underworld characters at ringside who had bet on Marciano between the ninth and tenth rounds informed Weill to let Goldman take over for, if Marciano lost, it would be Weill's fault. In any case, Marciano overcame all by one punch to the "whiskers" in the thirteenth round and Jersey Joe was counted out. Al Weill once told the author that he had no boxing experience and little boxing knowledge except to be able to judge what contrasting styles would result in great fights or "stinkeroos!"

However, the death of Rocky in an airplane accident on 31 August 1969, and the death of his wife from cancer in 1974 and the resulting inheritance information, introduced a mysterious and still unsolved question. Marciano made over $4,000,000 as a boxer in less than eight years and according to his own statement had plenty of money for his family and made good money after retirement. He and his family were not high livers, on the contrary, were very frugal. He owned property both in New Jersey and Florida with the former estimated as worth $400,000, and Mrs. Marciano was awarded $50,000 for the accidental death of Rocky, yet the estate of Mrs. Marciano at her death—namely the Marciano estate—was reportedly worth only $150,000 including the real estate. The explanation supplied by his daughter was that her father had never treated money as being important, but that he had a bizarre habit, like that attributed to W.C. Fields, namely, to hide money, stocks, and bonds. However, Marciano's caches were not in savings accounts and safe deposit boxes under aliases and different names as those of W.C. Fields, but in bags or boxes containing cash and negotiable valuables buried in the ground—a custom of French and Italian farmers. Some of the caches have been found but have yielded very little.

But, Mary Ann Marciano stated, "My father was dedicated to his friends and many took advantage of him by having him sign guarantees or notes or mortgages or making him merely a partner or principal of some commercial or financial project." "For instance," his daughter continued,

"my mother's major problem, which may well have undermined her health after my father's death, was a claim of over $1,500,000 arising from my father's association or relationship as a principal with a major business project. While I do not know the details, I know it took years to settle and even though a settlement was made for less than the original claim, it was in seven figures or close to it."

In fact, Marciano's death is itself typical of his devotion to friends. The story as told was that Marciano on a business trip to Chicago was to return home to Florida from Chicago in time to be at a party for his and his wife's birthday—by a coincidence one day apart—namely, on 1 September. He had already purchased his commercial airline tickets. A friend however appealed to him to put in an appearance at a "shindig" in Des Moines, Iowa as a favor. When Marciano explained his family birthday party in Florida and his planned commercial plane return home, the friend offered to fly Marciano in a private or rented plane to Des Moines and then to take him from there to Fort Lauderdale, Florida. So Marciano turned in his airline tickets in Chicago and proceeded in a single engine Cessna 172 to fly to Des Moines for a short stopover for the friend. However, on the night of 31 August 1969 in a heavy fog the plane cracked up very near Newton, Iowa killing pilot Glenn Betz, age thirty-seven, Marciano's friend, Frank Farrell, age twenty-three, and Rocky Marciano. In a claim and lawsuit, Marciano's widow was granted and received $50,000, an unusually conservative amount for the life of someone who had made at least $4,000,000 in eight years.

It took several months and the help of the United States Air Force to finally get the thirty-three-page report on Marciano's fatal airplane accident on 31 August 1969, together with statements of witnesses and experts and maps and charts. A summary of the National Transportation Board was released on 10 October 1969. It states that the tragedy of the accident, in addition to the loss of a nationally known and respected sports champion, was the tragedy of other similar accidents, namely, that it could have been prevented. The board found that the pilot had attempted operations exceeding his experience ability level by continued Visual Flight Rule (VFR) into adverse weather conditions. A very low ceiling and a dark night were cited as contributing factors. The pilot was not qualified for instrument weather flight with a total flying time of 231 hours, 107 in Cessna 172 type aircraft and only thirty-five hours at night. In other words, the flight should not have been made.

A last minute, unconfirmed flash on the strange evaporation of the Marciano estate is that a Florida lawyer charged the sick Marciano widow for "straightening out the estate" a fee possibly up into six figures . . . more than remains for the two orphaned Marciano children. According to a further report, someone connected with the Marciano family and estate are now (1975) requesting a detailed accounting including all financial records, which according to IRS rules must be available for seven years or well before Rocky's death on 31 August 1969. All tax records before that should also be available if requested by the Marciano estate. This may clear up the matter of what happened to Marciano's seven-digit earnings, and might be an interesting item in the story of boxing.

So in death, as in life, Marciano gave for his friends without regard to his own interests. As expressed by the famous late New York Times sports columnist, Arthur Daley, Marciano was: "A man of gentleness, kindness compassion and affability . . . who brought dignity to the championship he held with such modest graciousness." However, the rather mysterious evaporation or disappearance of an estate reported and confirmed to have been over several million dollars is a sad but not unusual epilogue in a boxing champion's life in the saga of the fist.

After Rocky Marciano retired and after a series of eliminations featuring Hurricane Jackson, Archie Moore, Joey Maxim, and Floyd Patterson, the latter (who was an Olympic gold medalist in the middleweight class in 1952) won and was recognized as the new champion. Notwithstanding his very difficult manager and a nonsensational peek-a-boo style, Patterson's abilities and punch ко'd Archie Moore, Jackson, Pete Rademacher, Roy Harris, Brian London only to be surprised by Ingemar Johansson, a Swedish import by a ко in three rounds in New York city. However on 20 June, 1960, Patterson became the first heavyweight ever to regain his title by a ко over Johansson in the fifth round and, for good measure, doing it again in Miami in the sixth round. Then Patterson ко'd Tom McNeeley in Toronto. But on 25 September 1962, he was knocked out by Sonny Liston to the great surprise of the whole boxing world. The first part of Patterson's career up to the first loss of his title, in the opinion of most boxing fans, was a poorly managed one. D'Amato, Patterson's manager, got off on the wrong track fighting the monopoly when he could have knocked off all kinds of second-rate opponents with championship receipts including the sale of ancillary rights—radio, television and closed circuit. Then D'Amato could have abandoned the IBC and demanded his own terms. This was the opinion expressed by many experts including Jack Dempsey; however Patterson is reported currently in excellent financial shape due to the second part of his career and the regaining of his title. He now raises horses on his own farm and is a successful boxing broadcaster.

During this semi-active period of the IBC, James Norris and Truman Gibson on one level, and on another level a new promoter named Rosensohn, who brought Johansson to the United States but was reportedly financed by questionable sources, failed to tie up either Patterson or Johansson. As far as Johansson, he was better in fianace than in the ring and managed himself out of any obligation to Eddie Ahlquist, his Swedish manager and promoter, moved to Switzerland reportedly to avoid Swedish taxes, and is said to be very successful in business.

Johansson was the Swedish heavyweight representative at the 1952 Olympic Games at Helsinki. He went to the finals but lost to Ed Sanders of the United States by disqualification at the beginning of the second round when he refused to continue. Ed Sanders, a great prospect, was accidentally killed in a professional fight a year later. Johansson's amateur record included eleven losses. His record as a professional was seventeen коs, nine decisions and two losses, both by being ко'd by Patterson and both for the world title. He retired from the ring in 1967 at age thirty-one.

After Floyd Patterson lost his title to Sonny Liston an unusual result manifested itself in the appeal of the return match—perhaps because Patterson was the first heavyweight to have already recaptured his crown or perhaps because Liston was unknown but had been built up as almost a Neanderthal man fresh from jails. In any case, the second Patterson-Liston fight in Las Vegas, Nevada, drew gross receipts of $4,747,690.50 with Patterson and D'Amato collecting almost a million and a half dollars—more than they had received for all of Patterson's championship fights up to his loss to Johansson.

51A. Floyd Patterson, the first heavyweight ever to regain title as Heavyweight Champion of the World (**Courtesy**, Ring Magazine)

Sonny Liston can be labelled as the hard-luck champion of all time. However, this hard luck did not prevent him from knocking out Patterson in a return bout in short order. Sonny Liston's first knockout of Floyd Patterson was two minutes, six seconds of the first round, and in his second fight two minutes and ten seconds in the first round. Sonny Liston was probably one of the most illiterate top performers in modern boxing. He was a mental deficient, hardly able to read and write. He spent years in the penitentiary and was always attracted by and associated with criminals and hoodlums. His judgement of right and wrong was all distorted according to experts, yet Liston was highly sophisticated in keeping secrets. No one ever found out who, if anyone, was his manager or who owned any piece of him. Liston had a record of nineteen arrests and served two prison terms. He was born on a small cotton farm near Little Rock, Arkansas and had twenty-four brothers and sisters. Sonny once confessed that the first time he ever had three square meals a day was when he was in jail. As a great puncher, he scored seven коs and seven wins between 1953 and 1956, then retired or was incarcerated, and then had a record of sixteen коs and three wins from 1958 to 1962. After his second fight with Patterson he went on an exhibition tour in Europe, after which he lost his title to Cassius Clay in Chicago by not coming out from his corner in the seventh round. Many gamblers and gossips questioned this one.

In this connection, it is interesting to remind the reader that on 14 December 1960 at Senator Kefauver's Committee Hearings on Crime, Frank Carbo on the stand and under oath was asked by Senator Kefauver:

"Do you share by virtue of an undisclosed contract on the fight purses of Charles Sonny Liston?"

Carbo replied:

"I respectfully decline to answer the question on the grounds that I cannot be compelled to be a witness against myself."

Nothing more could be obtained from the witness, Carbo, who may well have had some connection with Liston's wins and losses under orders from the underworld . . . or else? According to at least one sports writer, no one will ever know the story of why Liston refused to come out for the seventh round against Cassius Clay or for Liston's "splash" at the very beginning of his return match with Clay . . . except, of course, if Clay is what he claims—"the greatest."

Liston continued to box after losing his title, first in another fight with Clay where he was ko'd in the first round. From 1965 through 1970, his record was fourteen kos, one win, one loss by a ko. To seal the sad story of Liston he was found dead in bed by his wife in his home in Las Vegas, Nevada. He had been dead a week before being found on 5 January 1971. In death he had turned to a view he knew best—lying on his side—closely facing a wall!

This brings us to the end of the monopoly era or a little beyond, insofar as the story of its boxers and of the happenings in the squared ring. The ever-changing history of the fist and boxing and its actors

51B. Sonny Liston, the hard-luck heavyweight champion of all time (Courtesy, Ring Magazine)

now fall into our present extraordinary worldwide and television era. The best proof of this is the fact that eleven official titles (October 1975) are deployed over eight countries. In this era, boxers, championships, competitions, and spectators are no longer limited to one or more countries, but to the entire world from Grant Land and the Lincoln Sea to the Palmer Archipelago and the Weddell Sea—from Severnaya Zemlya and the Laptev Sea to and including Wilkes Land.

6 • The Worldwide and Television Era Both In and Out of the Ring

Now we come to probably the most controversial, strange, and most unbelievable character in the history of prizefighting from the resuscitation of boxing in England around 1700 to our present era and probably beyond to the year 2000—namely Cassius Clay, who KO'd the huge, overrated bad man, with tremendous hands measuring over fifteen and one half inches, Sonny Liston. This new champion's conduct, often bordering on that of a psychopathic case, his outbursts similar to someone who had lost his marbles, and also his self-confidence and incessant talk (mostly about himself), amused some people, but rubbed most people the wrong way. Clay reportedly began boxing at the age of twelve, won the Golden Gloves championship of the city of Louisville, Kentucky, and in 1957 already told everyone he was going to win the 1960 Olympic light heavyweight championship—which he did.

Soon a syndicate of Louisville businessmen decided to take over Clay. They advanced him $400 per month and a fifty-fifty split, later changed to sixty for Clay and forty for themselves. He was, according to Angelo Dundee, who was retained to train and coach him, dedicated, hardworking, and highly disciplined with respect to training, even though he could never control his tongue. In his first three years as a professional boxer, he won nineteen fights. A turning point in Clay's career was meeting a young Muslim minister, Samuel X. Saxon, who was selling subscriptions to a newspaper, "Muhammad Speaks," in Miami. Cassius began going to meetings and visited the sect leader, Elijah Muhammad. Then when Clay started shrieking and talking too much, aided

by a confidant and adviser, Drew Bundini Brown, many boxing fans and writers began to turn against him. When Clay announced his membership to the antiwhite Black Muslims and took on the alias of Muhammad Ali, conferred on him by Elijah Muhammad, the press and newspapers accepted the new name but it was never (so far as known) legally established. There was, as a result of this, certainly no rise in popularity, yet more people turned out at his fights, and his appeal increased. However, many persons contend that large proportions of the persons who paid to see him fight either directly or by TV close circuit paid to see Ali beaten . . . not to see him win.

In 1963 he flunked a preinduction mental examination and was classified 1-Y, but in February 1966 without a reexamination he was reclassified 1-A. No doubt proper authorities decided that any man that won the world's heavyweight boxing championship in 1964 and had defended the title in seventeen fights and exhibitions and could talk as much and as intelligently and ad lib poetry, was capable of some type of military service or even combat service that all citizens, rich or poor, black or white, owed their country. Even conscientious objectors on religious grounds were drafted on a limited duty basis. The Lewis Ayres case in World War I was remembered where Ayres had refused to bear arms because of his religious beliefs, but served in the Medical Corps and earned a battlefield decoration for courage in combat, evacuating the wounded. However, Cassius Clay, alias Muhammad Ali, refused service on the grounds that he was a Muslim minister and war was against his religion. On 9 May 1967, he was indicted in Houston, Texas by a Federal Grand Jury for refusing service and the New York State Commission and the World Boxing Association deprived him of his title. Clay was also banned from boxing in the United States. As cruel as this may seem it was considered deserved by all those who answered the call to service and the parents and families of those who were drafted—much less those killed . . . even if in an unpopular war.

Strangely enough, Clay's popularity declined as rapidly as his boxing skills improved. His fast tongue got him into worse trouble when he stated he had no quarrel with the Vietcong, guilty of untold cruelty and a murderous war against civilians of every age and sex, and that the taxes from his fights alone paid salaries for 200,000 soldiers a year. Although tried and sentenced to five years in prison and $10,000 fine, due to costly appeals, Clay was never jailed. Many efforts were made to promote a Clay fight in the United States. To indicate the extent to which promoters tried to promote a Clay fight, one was even planned to be held in a 747 Boeing jumbo jet trainer with only 250 seats for $1,000 per seat, and to be beamed via closed circuit TV and video tape to the entire world. It was to be like the old days when boxing was illegal, so fights were frequently held on barges in rivers or harbors or secretly run off in forests. No sanction, permit, license, or taxes could apply to a location not on United States soil or in any state, but thousands of feet in the air. However the plan, handicapped by approaching winter weather, did not get off the ground!

Finally, for no special reason or no formal decision with his drawing power enhanced a thousandfold because of his forty-three months of exile from the squared ring, Ali sounded like the old but younger Cassius Clay, namely, Clay was still a champion, a showman, and a public relations stirrer-upper. According to Ali's promoters, over a half million people followed his first fight after his exile in over two hundred theaters and arenas in the United States. This first fight of the new period in his career was against Jerry Quarry in Atlanta, Georgia on 26 October 1970. Ali ko'd Quarry in the third round. Naturally, the next natural fight was to match Ali with the then-recognized heavyweight champion, Joe Frazier, also a former Olympic champion. [To avoid confusion, here are the Olympic backgrounds of recent pro champions: World Olympic gold medalists-Floyd Patterson, 1952, Middleweight;] Cassius Clay, 1960, Light Heavyweight; Joe Frazier, 1964, Heavyweight; George Foreman, 1968, Heavyweight. T. Stevenson from Cuba, 1972 Heavyweight champion. (Stevenson, being from a Communist country, is not allowed to box professionally.)

However, in order to be ready after his long lay-off, after Quarry, Clay took on Oscar Bonavena, Argentine and South American champion with a record of thirty-six kos, nine wins and five losses. In a very close fight, Ali ko'd a very difficult opponent in the fifteenth round. The Bonavena fight was a close call and certainly did not support Ali's claims of super speed, super boxing ability, and any super punching power. In fact Ali's performance was very mediocre in this fight. Then, finally, on 8 March 1971, Ali and Frazier met in a fight promoted by a brand-new character who refused to describe himself as a promoter. Frazier, in the meantime, as the new champion had met and soundly beat all contenders. Frazier was frequently compared to Marciano as highly dedicated in his training and an explosive puncher. Frazier was a dropout in the ninth grade, a hard worker on his father's small farm near Beauford, South Carolina, who weighed over 230 pounds and had eleven sisters and brothers. Frazier's philosophy expressed in words of one syllable was that he was not interested in being champion to help blacks, nor was he an Uncle Tom, nor did he have any ideologies, religions, or causes. "Hell," explained Frazier, "my cause is me!"

The story behind the promotion of the Ali-Frazier fight is extraordinary. A young theatrical agent, formerly with MCA (Music Corporation of America) and then on his own when MCA was broken up by an antimonopoly suit; with an unusual brand of salesmanship, brought his own agency to the point where it did some $30 million worth of business per year. This man was Jerry Perenchio and he had never had any contact or connection with boxing whatsoever. He was in London selling his stable of theatrical and movie stars when his friend, Frank Fried of Chicago, called him to tell him he had been talking to Herbert Muhammad, the Black Muslim who was Ali's manager of record.

"Ali wants to fight Frazier!"

"Could Perenchio organize and promote the fight?" Fried asked.

Perenchio assured Fried that he could and flew to New York immediately. A group had already bid a million dollars for the fight. Perenchio decided to promote the fight positively and offered $5 million, plus a million and a half or fifty percent of the profits for a rematch. He met with the two fighters and their lawyers. He offered to put up $250,000 of his own money to seal the deal. But the guarantee was not considered sufficient, and also, both parties desired a site to be fixed and arranged—either the Houston Astrodome or the Madison Square Garden. Perenchio was about to leave and give up when Frazier's manager, Hank Durham, confidentially suggested he should make a pitch to the Madison Square

Garden under its new ownership and management. Perenchio rushed to New York and to the Garden and caught Alvin Cooper, executive vice president, still at work, and in ten minutes a deal had been concluded whereby the Garden would put up half a million dollars against a percentage, leaving four and a half million dollars to be raised by Perenchio. Jerry flew back to Los Angeles on Christmas Eve. The next day he contacted a man he had met once, Jack Kent Cooke, owner of the Los Angeles basketball Lakers and part owner of the Washington football Redskins. Cooke wanted too much money for his help and insisted the fight be held in the Los Angeles Forum. However, Perenchio with the threat of no deal being consummated, finally convinced Cooke on the Garden and accepting only fifty percent of the profits.

As soon as the fight definitely was signed up and secure and the entire $5 million guarantee to the Garden duly paid, Ali began his talk, blank verse, and frothing at the mouth. It was welcome to the promoters, for it seemed to stir up publicity and ticket purchases. Most experts picked Frazier to win by a ko. Ali actually screamed over and over again that he was the greatest, the fastest, the most gifted heavyweight who ever breathed on the face of the earth and he could not possibly lose to an amateur like the 1964 Olympic champion when they met in 1971 at the Madison Square Garden. Astrologists however all picked Frazier, although they admitted both were Capricorns born five days short of two years apart, which caused some difficulty in selecting a winner according to the stars—especially on 8 March 1971.

Astrology or not, the twenty-seven-year-old Frazier, weighing 205½ pounds and twenty-nine-year-old Ali, weighing 215 pounds, fought a very close battle for nine rounds. Then, in the tenth round, Frazier began to turn the bout around, winning the tenth round and almost ko'd Ali in the eleventh round. Ali was in deep trouble as he just made his corner at the end of the eleventh round. The crowd of almost twenty thousand were screaming and yelling in anticipation of Ali's being knocked out. Frazier continued to punish Ali in the twelfth and thirteenth rounds. Then, unexpectedly, and almost unbelievably, Ali came back and may have even won the fourteenth round, but perhaps because the fourteenth round took too much out of him, at the very beginning of the fifteenth round, Frazier landed a short but heavy punch and Ali went down. The crowd was wild. The self-claimed "greatest" was about to be counted out. However, Ali got up at the count of four and took the referee's required eight count. Thereafter, Frazier landed several solid body and head punches without return. As the final bell rang, Ali was reeling around the ring without much control of his rubbery legs or almost useless arms, with glazed eyes and an open mouth. Ali had been definitely defeated in his fortieth professional fight.

Incidentally, Clay, aka Ali, won in a way a far more important victory when the Supreme Court of the United States in an interesting decision overruled the lower court in their conviction of Clay and the sentence of two years in jail for avoidance of service. Evidently, this was based on the legality that a Muslim minister could refuse military service of any kind.

Some of Muhammad Ali's or Cassius Clay's scenes or what some doctors describe as "self induced hysteria" were unusual to say the least. Bud Schulberg, one of the greatest admirers of Ali, admits that at Miami Beach, minutes before the Liston fight, Jesse Abramson, an experienced sportswriter, was shocked at the weighin and believed the fight should be postponed because of Ali's unbelievable performance which boiled his blood pressure to a count of 200. Observers were convinced that Ali's next step would be in a psychopathic ward.

Elijah Muhammad had bestowed the name of Cassius X on Clay and then later the Islamic name of Muhammad Ali, but according to some sources later suspended Ali from the Muslim Order in 1969, although he was reinstated. However Herbert Muhammad, son of Elijah, became manager of Ali.

According to Ali's messianic visions, his heart allegedly belongs to Allah and the Third World. But unlike George Foreman, Ali has been reported only recently as discussing contributing from his millions of dollars money for the starving hundreds of thousands of Muslims and citizens of the Third World. According to the New York Times of 29 June 1974, George Foreman discussed with Undersecretary of the United Nations, F. Bradford Morse, that he would have liked to make a contribution to the Sahalian drought involving possibly 100,000 dead. Certainly Ali as a Muslim minister should become more interested in saving Muslim lives and reducing his taxes than owning many automobiles. A statement from some authoritative financial source that it received a large contribution to Muslim charity from Ali could do much for Ali's popularity. All of the various spellings of Muhammad or Mohammed, etc. are all variations based on the name of the Prophet of Islam who incidentally conquered, by military force, Khaibar and Mecca. Strangely enough there are other Muhammad Alis; one is listed in most Who's Whos who as a professor of mathematics and literature, philosopher, and a cabinet member and minister of the Royal Court was once Prime Minister in 1953 of the Afghan government. He is known throughout the world for his book "The Afghans,"

52. Muhammad Ali, aka Cassius Clay, world's heavyweight champion from 1964–67, and from 1974 to the release of this book. He was one of the first three champions during the worldwide and television era, therefore the athlete who will have made probably the most money in his lifetime, not only in boxing but in any and all other sports—probably over twenty million dollars. (Ring Magazine)

which is about Afghanistan—an important Muslim country of Central Asia. It is ruled by Islamic law and Islam is the principal religion mostly of the Sunni sect.

From his ring record alone, Muhammad Ali or Cassius Clay has an impressive record. He won the title when Liston failed to answer the bell for the seventh round and in a rematch, ко'd Liston in a minute or a minute and forty-two seconds of the first round. Then Clay ко'd Floyd Patterson in the twelfth round; Henry Cooper in the sixth round; Brian London in the third round; Karl Mildenberger in the twelfth round; Cleveland Williams in the third round; defeated Ernie Terrell by a fifteen-round decision; Zorry Folley by a ко in the seventh round; before being suspended for refusing to be drafted in May 1967 when his title was officially taken away from him by the various boxing bodies. After an elimination, Joe Frazier was declared world champion, although official recognition by all bodies was only on 16 February 1970 when he knocked out Jimmy Ellis.

Then came the fight between Frazier and Ali already described in which Frazier retained his title. After two ко́s in defense of his title, Frazier was ко'd in the second round in Kingston, Jamaica by George Foreman. This was 22 January 1973. Foreman defended his title successfully by a one round ко of José Roman in Tokyo on 7 September 1973. In June 1974 Foreman ко'd Ken Norton in a brief two-round defense of his title in Caracas, Venezuela. Norton was the man who broke Ali's jaw in their first twelve-round fight, with Ali the loser, on 31 March 1973. In the second match with Norton, Ali won a twelve-round split decision. However, it took Foreman only two rounds to complete the destruction and knockout of Norton. Although Video Techniques, Inc. lost money on the Foreman-Norton title fight and its closed circuit promotion, they came back in connection with Don King of Cleveland (Don King Productions) and foreign financial support—reported to be English, Belgian and Swiss mining interests with a stake in Zaire, probably headed or solicited by the other announced principal, namely, John Daly of London and his Hemdale Leisure Corporation—to promote a Foreman-Ali fight in faraway Zaire, which reportedly required an $11 million investment or guarantee. This promotion combine, it will be noted, did not include Jack Kent Cooke of California whose guarantee of $4 million for the Ali-Frazier fight was pivotal. He evidently was pushed out or did not like the associates he would be forced to work with, perhaps because of Don King's reported police record. Don King, incidentally, is the man credited with organizing and

53. John Daly, President of the Hemdale Leisure Corporation of London, generally credited with having financed or arranged the finances of the first truly world-seen heavyweight championship of the world between Muhammad Ali and George Foreman. As the guarantee totaled over eleven million dollars and the receipts, over twenty million dollars, Rickard, Jacobs, and Norris were small-time in comparison. (Courtesy of the Hemdale Leisure Corporation)

53A. Don King, co-promoter of the Zaire fight and promoter of the Manila title fight—first real worldwide feature of TV satellite coverage. (Don King Productions)

putting over the Zaire promotion based on a $5 million purse to each of the two fighters, namely the $11 million financing by John Daly of London.

A strange story is behind Foreman's avoidance of fighting in the United States. It is reported that Foreman and Saddler, his manager or adviser, sold so many "pieces" of Foreman for eating-money, that they are beset with creditors and investors bearing written notes and had to evade United States court orders. The American embargo may have been lifted by some of the $5 million guaranteed and reported to have been paid to Foreman for his late 1974 Zaire defense against Ali.

The final closed-circuit gate from Kinshasa (once Leopoldville) in Zaire (once the Belgian Congo), may have broken the paper record of the gross take of over $20 million set by Ali and Joe Frazier in their world championship fight. Video Techniques, Inc. also promised a *liagniappe*, a word better known in Louisiana and Jamaica than in Zaire, of another million for a Foreman-Ali rematch agreement.

As usual, some mystery surrounds this promotion because of the absence of Jerry Perenchio, Jack Kent Cooke, and the Madison Square Garden Corporation who evidently did not even try to bid for perhaps the first true worldwide boxing championship. Mike Burke, who failed in his batting average, according to many, in the direction of the New York baseball Giants for CBS, was reportedly the Garden's boxing executive. Not even his OSS clandestine worldwide experience made him interested in any offshore promotion of tremendous international interest in boxing. According to Don King, the Garden was approached, but did not want any piece of the action.

Foreman is a great puncher, which may have been his downfall for it is believed he may not have trained to go a fast fifteen rounds with Ali. His record may have deluded him into thinking that he would not have to fight many rounds. He underrated Ali's boxing ability and speed, and believed that he could catch up with Ali in a few rounds. On the other hand if he listened to his trainer—cunning Archie Moore—he would have known better. Even before the fight, the United States was stunned and punch-drunk from the money binge at a time when finances and business were very bad. Yet, on the sound and light waves relayed by satellite, TV heavyweight title boxing gross receipts make even the gross take of the second Dempsey-Tunney fight look puny indeed. Can we now prophesize $30 million gross receipts for a championship boxing contest before the year 2000?

The Ali-Frazier fight number two (unfortunately not for the title since Foreman had already ko'd and shorn Frazier from his crown) was a record-breaker according to the issued financial reports, which are more certain than those of offshore fights because all financial aspects are reviewed and checked by city, state, and federal tax people in the United States. Although there were only 20,748 fans in the Garden, the largest nontitle indoor gate of $1,053,688, with the help of closed circuit TV, and of close to a million and a half closed-circuit audience made the gross receipts 18 million dollars. This, incidentally, proved the tremendous drawing power of Muhammad Ali, aka Cassius Clay. No matter if Ali is a freak to many people, he is truly "the greatest" as an attraction for crowds from New York City to Jakarta. Ali has proven a powerful stimulus, which has benefitted boxing notwithstanding his taunting talk and his draft avoidance. Even after Frazier lost his title to Foreman, the Ali-Frazier fight number two still produced thousands of closed-circuit locations and a gross of approximately 18 million dollars. Even his reported dedication as a Muslim minister to preach the teachings of Elijah Muhammad when he retires is beginning to be believed. He, unlike Marciano, seems certain that his wife and their children will be well taken care of for the rest of their lifetimes by his estate. He believes he would like to develop new and young boxers but adds, "But can the world be ready for another Ali . . . (but) I will never forsake boxing!"

The fight that made the Zaire world championship fight possible was the Ali-Frazier fight number two on 20 January 1974, a twelve not a fifteen rounder. Although an interesting fight, neither contestant equalled their past performances, especially Frazier. He could not hit as hard as before and could not even come near to putting Ali away. Neither man boxed as well as in past showings. Although the official decision was unanimous, Perez's (the referee) decision in favor of Ali was by 6-5-1 rounds, which is mighty close. However, thousands left the Garden convinced that Frazier had won. Even such oldtime experts as Sam Taub gave Frazier a 9-3 score. The fight as we already know picked up enough "moola" to give both Frazier and Ali over $3 million dollars apiece.

One great advantage that Ali had was the expert advice he received in his corner. Advised as usual by Angelo Dundee, Ali started punching to the body and always finished fast for the last minute of each round —an old but very impressive trick to influence the judges. There is no question that in the opposite corner Frazier was handicapped by the absence of his manager, ring adviser, and strategist, Hank Durham, who had died of a heart attack in September 1973. He had been in Frazier's corner when Frazier beat and almost KO'd Ali in the fifteenth round in their first fight.

As to the Zaire fight for the world's title, it seems that Foreman was unable to put Ali away and ran out of gas as he evidently had not trained for a fifteen-round fight, nor even for a ten-round bout.

The Foreman-Ali fight at Zaire, can be summed up easily as a complete change of tactics caused by a natural development for Ali who has been around for fourteen years and has definitely lost some of his speed, illustrated in his last two fights. Ali was intent in fighting with his back to the ropes, his feet flat, at a forty-five degree angle with the upper part of his body and his head the target zone, actually removed from his opponent's punches. Yet, this astute tactical maneuver gave him inside punching room. It is doubtful whether Ali can get away with this same tactical plan again. However, it worked beautifully and completely confused Foreman who suffered a KO at 2:58 of the eighth round. The one mystery is that Foreman's seconds—two ringwise exchampions, Archie Moore and Sandy Saddler—did not advise Foreman

54. Joe Frazier, world's heavyweight champion from 1970–1973—one of the first three champions during the worldwide and television era, therefore will break many records for total receipts.
(Ring Magazine)

to assume the defensive even if it had produced a poor fight and refused to fight Ali's fight and force Ali to come out from playing the ropes and insist on making Ali do some leading—also to concentrate on the lower part of Ali's body, the nearest target, when Ali played the ropes. As it is, many ringside observers believe Foreman was in control until the fifth round. Actually, Foreman played himself out, aided by the heat of the very early morning and the mucid tropical dampness. While there was much enthusiasm for Ali in being only the second man in boxing his-

tory to ever win back the heavyweight title, some of the comments were caustic with regard to Ali's constant claims of being "the greatest." Many experts commented that Jack Dempsey, Joe Louis, or Rocky Marciano in their prime could have taken Ali out at his best . . . and in a few rounds; however none of them could have outtalked the self-styled Muhammed Ali.

The latest gimmicks in the ever-increasing, so-called ancillary rights in the boxing industry or professional sport in the non-Communist world, are fur-

55. George Foreman—world's heavyweight champion from 1973-74—one of the first three champions during the worldwide and television era, therefore will break many records for total receipts. (Ring Magazine)

ther uses of the motion picture or video tape of a fight. There is first the original relay by closed circuit to one thousand to ten thousand stadiums and theatres all over the world by television-relayed by satellite. Hundreds of thousands of spectators may see these showings for paid admissions. Then, later, comes broadcasts from film or tape on tens of thousands of commercial or government TV stations to the millions of TV sets in homes, hotels, bars, and offices often sponsored, used and paid for by advertisers. Then, also now there are showings to passengers on board transcontinental or transoceanic airplane flights as jets traveling faster than sound entertain their passengers. TWA was responsible for one of these first major and extraordinary showings on some of their routes—showings of the Zaire fight. Naturally, in order to accomplish their commercial purpose, these broadcasts had to be advertised and TWA did it in full pages of the New York Times and the Wall Street Journal. Needless to say, this all cost a lot of money with the Zaire promoters, and it is assumed that Muhammad Ali is collecting. However, when an effort was made to further promote TWA and world championship fights and all the principals of the Zaire fight listed in the ad, the permission to include the ad (with credits to all) as an illustration in this book could not be obtained immediately. But with the effective help of Murray Goodman, top P. R. man for the last big fights, the unusual "ad" is herewith reproduced.

The financial reports on the Zaire fight were very difficult to get and even more difficult to evaluate. One source, that should be considered reliable, has the following breakdown:

Total Receipts	$19,000,000
Total Costs	13,000,000
Gross profits	
(to be divided)	6,000,000

Participation:

Fighters (each)	$ 5,000,000
Total	10,000,000
Don King Productions	900,000 or 15%
Video Techniques, Inc.	900,000 or 15%
Hemdale Leisure	1,200,000 or 20%
Zaire Government	600,000 or 10%
Risnelia Investments	2,400,000 or 40%

Yet another source, just as reliable, states that the Zaire government and Risnelia Investment Co., to-

gether, lost approximately seven million dollars, although the fighters got ten million dollars and the operational elements, namely Don King Productions, Video Techniques, Inc., and Hemdale Leisure, grossed some two million dollars with some bills still unpaid. All that can be said is that as of the writing of this book, all possible contacts and means were used to try to get more and surer details, and that these figures represent the best estimates that the author could obtain.

After Zaire, with its contradictory financial reports, it was obvious that the best fight with the greatest potential was an Ali-Frazier number three for the world's heavyweight championship. It also was apparent at the time that Don King, with the experience behind him and with the help of a TV technical organization, a mass promotion and public relations man, and the close racial affinity with the two black principals, should be the logical promoter. It was also apparent that a lot of towns or, more properly speaking, countries, felt that a worldwide TV event with millions of TV spectators was worth

TWA Exclusive.
Right now you can see Muhammad Ali upset George Foreman on most non-stops from California to Chicago & East Coast.

56. Newest ancillary right and use. After worldwide-televised boxing matches to audiences all over the world, movies are distributed and shown on airplanes traveling through space and properly advertised for travelers. Example: Wall Street Journal ad of Foreman-Ali fight showing on flight. (Courtesy of TWA)

almost a national investment or certainly a loan or stake that might result, in addition to the promotion and publicity, in a financial profit. So there were bidders for a great fistic attraction. It is doubtful, however, if the countries involved keep losing money, that many more suckers will fall for what is perhaps a worldwide, more modern, more scientific reproduction of the famous Kerns-Dempsey-Gibbons-Shelby fiasco that broke a town and its banks in sponsoring a world heavyweight title fight.

So with Ali, Frazier, and Foreman attached sentimentally to Don King and the promise of more millions and unbelievable guarantees, the next top boxing promotion was practically assured, notwithstanding the persistent reports that the Zaire fight actually lost seven million dollars and that the Madison Square Garden, the old home of boxing, was in poor financial shape. The Garden's financial status was projected further by the fact that reportedly the Garden had received offers from an Arab oil bank or from Don King, supported by an Arab oil bank to sell the Garden for thirty-six million dollars without, of course, including the office building. The report went on to say that the offer had been turned down and that the part of the Garden involved in the sale cost over sixty million dollars to build and the Garden would never consider any offer of less than fifty million. Later, the New York State Off-Track Betting Corporation reportedly was purchasing the Madison Square Garden arena but this also fell through; however, in any case, the Philippine government and the city of Manila, no doubt because of the great interest and background in boxing in the Philippines, evidently put up the money for the Ali-Frazier fight Number three as a presentation of Don King who controls boxing by virtue of his abilities, experience, and a sentimental hold on the three or four top heavyweight fighters of the world—all blacks.

Tex Rickard had a small, not very richly furnished office in the old Madison Square Garden. Mike Jacobs had a small, almost barren office in his ticket emporium in the Broadway area, and later did not do much better with respect to his office in the Garden setup. Jim Norris had a host of offices in several cities but conducted most of his boxing business through others or from hotel suites on his frequent trips. However, Don King, current emperor of boxing, has a penthouse suite above the Rainbow Grill at Rockefeller Center with a breathtaking view of New York City and the harbor and even the Westchester horizon, sixty-seven stories above a near bankrupt city. A LeRoy Neiman portrait of Ali hangs above and behind King's desk, as well it might, since King is, to all intents and purposes, the manager of Muhammad Ali. Just as Tex Rickard sold Jack Dempsey, and Mike Jacobs sold Joe Louis,

and rather shakily through Al Weill, Rocky Marciano, Don King is in full charge of the sale of Ali. The ceiling of Don King's penthouse is fifteen feet high and the rent $85,000 per year—a tax deduction, no doubt, in promoter King's world boxing adventures. Don King is reported, at least in personal interviews, to admit being a former numbers man and a former convict for an accidental manslaughter, which real story builds great sympathy for him. King is also reported as a frequent user of quotes due to his voluminous reading and self-education. Because of the unbelievable eight-digit figures of the fights he promotes, King is very careful to explain that half of all fight grosses goes to the government, or perhaps he should state governments. For it would certainly appear that foreign governments are involved in financing his fights in one way or another and must cut in on them. He admits that through governments he has promoted Ali fights in Zaire, Malaysia, and the Philippines with Saudi Arabia suggested as next in line. Most peculiar is the absence of any offers by King or by Ali to become interested in contributions to the millions of starving blacks and Muslims that, of course, would be tax free and also be a powerful and most convincing support to Ali's claimed Muslim priesthood. Since King has the great advantage of having a racial affinity to Ali, as well as to Frazier and Foreman, and must also have a great feeling for the starving peoples of Africa, many persons have mentioned the extraordinary promotion possibilities in the unselfish generosity of persons like King and Ali, the latter who can make five million dollars for an hour's work.

The first, formal, almost exclusive Don King production was the Ali-Frazier fight for the world's heavyweight championship at Manila in the Philippines. Don King must be given full credit for this fight, which might well have broken many records—especially on total number of spectators or, more properly speaking, viewers. It was a well-promoted fight that turned out to be a fierce, top-notch, cruel, but sensational battle by two outstanding professional fistic gladiators.

The fight, labelled "The Saga of a Lifetime," for no special reason, soon was popularly called "The Thrilla of Manila" and "The Thrilla of Gorillas in Manila," and there is no question or dissent in calling the resulting fight a great one. Two well-trained super athletes and combination boxers and hitters went at each other in the ring. Although Frazier's second and new manager refused to let him come out for the fifteenth round, thus giving Ali the fight at the end of the fourteenth round, it was evident that Frazier was badly hurt at the end of the fourteenth and that Frazier's right eye was closed and almost useless; however, there was little to choose between the two men until the fourteenth round. Ali was generally credited with the first, second, third, fourth, eighth, twelfth, and thirteenth, while Frazier was given the fifth, sixth, seventh, ninth, tenth, and eleventh. Of course, Ali won the fourteenth round by a large margin. Some boxing experts believe that *if* Frazier had been seconded by the late Hank Durham, his former manager and second, he would have beaten Ali as he did in the Ali-Frazier fight Number two. Frazier would have paced himself better, some experts believe; however, as the French often say, "With the word *if,* one could put Paris in a bottle." One thing is certain for those who seek to rate Ali in the history of boxing, namely, that the margin of victory between Ali and Frazier, and Ali and Norton in five fights, and some of Ali's other close fights do not compare with the margin of victory and showings of Dempsey, Louis, or Marciano over their challengers in their prime. So while Ali is without question the most controversial, the greatest salesman of himself in boxing, the greatest talker, and the greatest moneymaker (due to TV worldwide coverage), his standing as a top fighter of modern history remains in considerable doubt. In the opinion of a leading boxing writer, Ali is less impressive in victory with time but may well retire as undefeated world's champion for, according to the latest word, he will fight Foreman again for one more worldwide TV defense and then retire with a "bundle." To sum up—an informal poll of experts, in which the author concurs, shows Jack Dempsey, Joe Louis, and Rocky Marciano as the greatest in the last seventy-five years or more.

To summarize today's situation as this book goes to press, the current worldwide and TV era, from 1961 to, we hope, the year 1980 at least, might well become the greatest golden age of boxing—greater than the ancient Greek period, 500–200 B.C., and the United States golden era of the padded glove, 1880–1949. There is no question, however, as in every other period, its performers will usually be of antecedents or have backgrounds involving downtrodden and discriminated-against people. Also, the improvement in diet, training, form, equipment, experience, technique, etc. has improved performance. Unlike the past, however, the sport of boxing has now become such tremendous business as to need government financial support and also, in contrast to the past, boxing is worldwide with the world reduced in size by the fraction of a second's flight of sight and sound.

On the other hand, the financial figures of all kinds in present-day boxing are believed by many to be figures just thought up by someone and only suggested by the true facts. As a result of all but dismissing the New York State Athletic Commission and losing its confidence in boxing, the New York State authorities in Albany almost lost their leverage in the boxing industry and are hardly in the current boxing picture; however the entire boxing financial picture is not too attractive, notwithstanding all the large figures and tremendous number of digits. If the Zaire fight did result in the loss of nearly seven million dollars (this according to the lastest reliable sources), it may discourage further overseas fights with no change in the tax picture in New York State, and the results will seriously handicap boxing in its oldest and most profitable home.

There is bound to be a recession in boxing as there in the general economic world. The ridiculous guarantees, five million dollars paid each to Foreman and Ali for a low-grade fight, cannot be overcome even by the far better and outstanding fight between Ali and Frazier. There is no question but that top heavyweight boxers are now overpaid and that the world that wants screened showings, and closed-circuit theaters are paying unreasonable prices for their tickets. So, while we may indeed be in a new golden era of boxing for the time being, perhaps around the corner no one will pay to see a boxing burlesque such as the George Foreman circus in Toronto, Canada. Here Foreman opposed five boxing burlesquers, limited to three rounds each, with not one of the five even going through the routine of being knocked out. Each of the five received $7500 for their bizarre fistic performance, while Foreman pocketed (allegedly) $100,000. The Canadian Boxing Authority and ABC bought this shabby bill of goods and a shrieking Ali was at ringside. The only positive fact in this case was that the promoter did not claim any profits. Needless to say this promotion did not help boxing.

According to publicity releases, the live gate at Manila was very close to two million dollars, yet twelve hours before fight time, the 25,567 seat coliseum had not been sold out according to the Philippine Games and Amusement Board. The tickets ranged from $4 to $330, although, in an earlier publicity release, the prices had been listed as from $4 to $220. Assuming the paid gate, as claimed, was twenty thousand, an alleged financial gate of two million dollars would mean that every one of the twenty thousand had paid an average of $100 per seat, which is very doubtful indeed. At the Madison Square Garden, 20,129 persons paid over $400,000 to see the TV worldwide title fight and a live feature that proved a dull, one-sided heavyweight match won by Mike Quarry over Mike Rossman. The gross world receipts were reportedly $20,000,000, then later reduced to $18,000,000.

In Manila, although Don King had brought over three top referees—Henry Gibbs from England, Zack Clayton from Philadelphia, and Jay Edson from Phoenix, Arizona, representing a cost of over $6000—the bout was judged and refereed, as it should have been, by Filipinos in a country with a well-established background in boxing. It would, of course, be interesting to get the actual amounts of money collected for taxes by the State of New York and the State of New Jersey (where Ali resides), and the taxes collected by the bankrupt city of New York from the Manila fight; that is, at its Garden and Coliseum versions. It is, of course, the exorbitant New York State and New York City taxes that are responsible for the exodus of boxing from the City and State of New York. The geese that lay golden eggs have indeed been chased overseas!

The New York State Athletic Commission, with a new lease of life as of August 1975, with James A. Farley Jr. as the new Chairman (the son of James A. Farley who held the same job from February 1924 to February 1933), welcomed the inquiries of the author and gave permission for the reproduction of the commission's rules that appear in the appendix of this book and promised to find figures on the TV showings of the Ali-Frazier fight in New York, just as the same commission cooperated with previous queries and editions. An official of the New York State Athletic Commission was reported at Manila, but in no official capacity and his trip was not paid for by the New York taxpayer.

Among the curious and inexplicable things about the extraordinary Cassius Marcellus Clay, aka Muhammad Ali, is that no boxing champion has inspired so many books during his active fighting career, much less while still champion. There are already quite a number of books about Ali and/or his fights. In fact, publishing experts cannot understand how competing book producers can expect so many books on Ali to all make money, especially after a prospective "bestseller" book, an alleged sensational exposé of fixed fights on an international scale, *Weigh-In*, flopped miserably, although surprisingly escaping any libel suit. Yet top writers have been attracted by the strange appeal of Muhammad Ali as the subject of a book, evidently with the very quick approval of publishers. Among the first was Bud Schulberg of *The Harder They Fall* fame in a book called *Loser and Still Champion, Muhammad Ali*, which follows the transformation of "Cassius the Caterpillar into Muhammad the Butterfly" and how the super ego, militant, antiwar, and antiwhite black Muslim became almost an American folk hero. Many remarked at the similarity of the exaggerated self-esteem of both the author and his subject. Then came another book by another "greatest," namely, *The Fight* by Norman "Marilyn" Mailer. Mailer makes an interesting remark in his book, which is mighty close to once more exhibiting Cassius Clay's constant controversial nature: "A victory for Ali would also be a victory for Islam." Yet history can support the fact that Moslem or Muslim countries were the last to give up slavery and slave traffic of blacks from Africa, in fact, long after slavery and slave traffic were ended in Europe and America. Islam, like Christianity, accepted slavery for a long time and it became a standard institution in Muslim lands. Even the Prophet, according to history, had slave girls in his harem. Arab slave traffic from Africa was common, so much so that the white world held the Berlin Conference in 1885 that produced the Berlin Act, which bound the Moslem potentates to act against slave traffic. So here again we see the extraordinary trend or quality of Ali's controversial nature or his adherence to controversy. Even Muhammad Ali's name and its spelling is interesting. All references and historical records in English in the United States and Britain refer to and spell the name of the Prophet—a half dozen sultans of the Ottoman Empire from 1413 to 1922, several pashas of Egypt, Islam or Muslim religious leaders, the Shah of Persia (1906), the king of Afghanistan in the early 1930s, the present Shah of Iran, and the current president of Egypt—as "Mohammed." However, we come to Ali and his clan who spell it Muhammad. It is not contended that this is wrong (it is a Turkish version or spelling), merely that, as usual, Ali seemingly always departs into the realm of controversy and seems always to attract added attention by being controversial.

Of course so many books have already been published or will be published about Ali that no attempt to list them all will be made in this nine-thousand year history of boxing.

Wilfred John Joseph Sheed, author of *The Hack*, wrote a book on the heavyweight boxing champion called *Muhammad Ali* and, last but not least, the overwhelming self-esteem of Ali led him to tell his own story in an autobiography entitled (according to his own appraisal of himself) *The Greatest*, with an assist from Richard Durham, former editor of *Muhammad Speaks*, who is given due credit. These books and others were priced from 95¢ (paperback) to $10.95. The three pre-publication printings of the last of these at this writing, *The Greatest*, published by Random House at $10.95 was 175,000 copies. This meant that the publisher's estimate of the minimum domestic "gate" of this book was close to $2,000,000. This again proves that Ali is, indeed, the world's heavyweight boxing champion in salesmanship.

In fact, Muhammad Ali, in an introduction to Peter Heller's *In This Corner*, admits his extraordinary qualities or controversial attractiveness. He sums it up: "I am the only one. There's nobody but me." He therefore rates an important place in any book on boxing!

To prove further the mystic attraction of Muhammad Ali, he appeared at the October 1975 Frankfurt Book Fair with the Random House staff and was the major and record attraction, protected by green-uniformed German police from hardened book-trade professionals, grown men and women who wanted to see or touch him or solicit his autograph. A German publishing firm paid $200,000 for the German rights to his book and Random House announced a half million dollars collected so far from subsidiary and foreign rights. Even Red China and Panama attended the fair for the first time, possibly also to meet Ali. Ali, not to be outdone by a literary surrounding, told the press: "I predict that this will be the greatest book ever and it will sell more than any other book in history." He confirmed that the story was based on 140 tapes by him over a six-year period.

In contrast, Jack Dempsey, probably in his prime the greatest boxing champion of modern times, and also a world celebrity in his time, told a very different story to Bob Considine and Bill Slocum in 1960 at age sixty-four. A more modest, down-to-earth, gentle, and self-critical book of a mature man who suffered many disastrous private emotional setbacks, was never told to two more sympathetic, admiring, and straight-forward writers. In fact, in reading the book, one gets the idea that perhaps Ali, notwithstanding his phenomenal success and his unbelievable financial earnings, suffers from a deep-rooted inferiority complex, covered up by an exaggerated supreme superiority psychosis or eidonic hysteria. If so, his good fortune and his worthiness, with maturity, will no doubt make him a credit to the long history of his sport and of his convictions.

The Random House book referred to (*My Own Story* by "the greatest," Muhammed Ali, with Richard Durham) seems overwritten, with nineteen pages of a dialogue between Ali and Frazier, and also with discussions on sex and its already well-known relation to athletic performances. There is also every effort to explain, rationalize, or excuse Ali's white racial hostility and his refusal to serve his country in any capacity when called on in a draft of all able-bodied and mentally normal persons of a certain age group. Further, there is an effort to denounce discrimination of the black race, along with the Arab Muslim world and the Vietcong. His anger at failing the mental examination for the draft also seemed unnecessary. Ali's dislike for his "slave name" of Cassius Marcellus Clay is again strangely controversial if not contradictory, for we find that in history the Caucasian Marcellus Clay lived from 1810 to 1903 and was, without a doubt, one of the most important abolitionists and champions of antislavery in the United States. A man whose father served in the War of 1812, himself served in the Mexican War as a captain, and his opposition to slavery cost him many an election, both

in state government and perhaps the chance to become president. It also caused him to engage in many duels, and when he published an antislavery newspaper called "The True American," his office and his press were destroyed by a mob that might well have destroyed him if they had caught him. This Cassius Marcellus Clay was sent by President Lincoln as our minister to Russia, a job he held for some seven years. So here, also, Ali's antagonism against one of the greatest fighters for the emancipation of blacks makes him again "the greatest" in the art of controversy and contradiction, which strangely serves him so well, for it always spells attention, publicity and most important, "box office!"

However, Ali is perfectly honest in his admission of losses and close calls in his fights with contemporary fighters. We learn that our subject lost two "pro" fights—one close to being a K.O. victim and fought two fights so close that at least half of the experts questioned the decision: Ali was possibly saved from being K.O.d by Henry Cooper, by the presence of mind of his trainer and second, and by a split boxing glove resulting in an extra minute between rounds, after Ali was on the floor at the end of a round. Ali won 161 out of 167 fights as an amateur, suffering a technical K.O. by an amateur (Kent Green) and losses to both Jimmy Ellis and Tony Madigan of Australia, although in his book, Ali reports Madigan as being from Argentina. Of course, in all fairness, these two defeats were wiped out later by victories. This is most interesting, however, because it shows that while Ali failed to win six fights in the amateurs and lost two in professional boxing with three close decisions—thirty-nine K.O.s and fifteen wins—this hardly can compare with the records of Rocky Marciano, with forty-three K.O.s, six wins by decision, with no losses or no draws either as a professional or as an amateur; or with Gene Tunney, with forty-one K.O.s, fifteen wins, and one loss by decision (both Marciano and Tunney retired as world champions); or even with Jack Dempsey, whose record from the time he had enough to eat until he was over the hill, from 1918 to 1927, includes forty-five K.O.s, nine wins by decision, three losses (two to Tunney after Dempsey's prime); or with Joe Louis, with fifty-four K.O.s, fourteen wins by decision, one loss, and two losses by K.O. (one of these by Schmeling was reversed in a sensational manner, and one was by Marciano when Louis was over the hill). Therefore, from the standpoint of boxing, Ali cannot be referred to as "the greatest."

However, with respect to being a world figure—due in part to the television age and his extraordinary and unusual personality that won him a tremendous following, and, most important, his earnings of $31,251,115 (according to his book only up to and including his 30 September 1975 fight in Manila), which by far exceeds the total earnings of any two past athletes in the entire history of the world of sports—there is no question that Ali is '"the greatest!" Even the tax problems of his fights have been simplified but are "the greatest!"

Based on a change in New York State tax laws, brought about by Governor Carey and Commissioner Jim Farley, Jr., New York State taxes in boxing shall now be only applicable on the gates, attendances, etc., of fights or closed-circuit presentations in the confines of New York City and New York State; while all other earnings from close-circuit presentations and ancillary rights outside of New York State shall not be taxable by or accountable to New York State. This change makes the return of boxing and world championship fights possible for New York State and New York City, which will bring millions of dollars, not only in taxes, but in the flow of tourists and fight fans and spenders to the city and the state. It also, of course, will bring back the potential of Madison Square Garden Corporation and Madison Square Garden and Yankee Stadium and other proper and major sites for boxing for large "gates."

However, there is still another handicap to be removed to return boxing to its old and probably proper home: that is to correct a hardship and an unfair and improper miscarriage of justice based strangely enough on a legal decision of a United States Court. In other words, if Don King of New York, John Daley of London, or Luna Park of Buenos Aires want to sign up Ali, Norton, Foreman, or Carlos Monzon to a legal contract to perform for them in a title fight or several title fights anywhere in the world or in New York City, it is perfectly legal for them to execute such protective business arrangements. But the Madison Square Garden cannot meet them on an equal basis, for if the Madison Square Garden Corporation wants to sign up a world's boxing championship and/or a current or potential champion for several bouts, they may be guilty of a violation of a United States Court decision by Judge Sylvester J. Ryan of the United States District Court, 7th District of New York, who ruled, after a long trial, that the IBC (International Boxing Club) of New York and Illinois, and the Madison Square Garden Corporation and Jim Norris and Arthur Wirtz, et al, as co-defendants, had engaged in a conspiracy in restraint of trade and had made a monopoly of the promotion of world boxing championships in the United States, in violation of the Sherman Act. However, the Garden is no longer in the IBC empire (also called the "octopus") that the decision referred to. The "octopus" of interlocking boxing interests disappeared by the ruling referred to above. In fact, the "octopus" empire,

as a result of the court's decision, was forced into "Divestiture, Dissolution and Divorcement." The Madison Square Garden Corporation is no longer an arm of the huge "octopus" (i.e., the IBC) and no longer a combine or part of a combine of various elements, stadiums, corporations, and persons involved in the boxing game for promoting world boxing championships and other boxing contests, and no longer part of a monopolistic structure. In other words, all other promoters, whether individual or corporate, can approach the boxing-promotion industry with an advantage over Mike Burke and the Madison Square Garden Corporation because of Judge Ryan's ruling. Manifestly, this is an unplanned miscarriage of justice. As a matter of fact, the most important stockholder of the Madison Square Garden Corporation today is Gulf and Western, with thirty-eight percent of the stock, and this owner is far from the boxing game and involved in many industries, in fact is one of the largest conglomerates in the world, with no monopoly in any of their various endeavors.

Other current major owners of Madison Square Garden Corporation stock are private persons or organizations with no relation to monopolies and, in many cases, with little relation to boxing. Even the underworld element that had become part of the "octopus" by accident or design, willfully or innocently was eliminated by another court decision on conspiracy and extortion, and several individuals were sentenced to terms of up to twenty-five years in jail. So that this situation may be altered and properly cleared up, the Madison Square Garden Boxing, Inc. has petitioned the United States Department of Justice to lift the restraint or handicap described. So perhaps with patience the Garden will no longer be discriminated against because of its past relationship, and some normalcy may return to boxing; and the importance of physical gates will return, supplemented of course by TV and closed-circuit coverage, but will not tend toward the promotion of comparatively less controlled fights in faraway places essentially for TV closed-circuit audiences and often for the promotion of little-known countries and towns. For instance, Don King in mid-1975 was reported in the press as flying to Kuwait, where he was offered a package of three Ali fights in one year against Frazier, Norton, and Foreman. The asking price was allegedly $30 to $50 million, but a Philippine national sponsored fight followed. Both the Zaire and the Philippine fights were reportedly costly to their government sponsors.

In the ring, Ali fought in the following world-televised Don King-related fights: 21 February 1976, Pierre Koopman of Belgium at San Juan, Puerto Rico, in which Ali k.o.d Koopman in the fifth round; 30 April 1976, Jimmy Young of the United States, at

Landover, Maryland, a very close one with an unknown and generally considered not first-class fighter, but Ali got the decision; 24 May 1976, Richard Dunn of England, at Munich, Germany, in which Ali won by a к.о. in the fifth round. In the meantime, George Foreman к.о.d Joe Frazier to become again a challenger for the heavyweight title. Last, but not least, was the fight of 28 September 1976. It took place in the newly renovated Yankee Stadium and was promoted by the Madison Square Garden Corporation and Michael Burke, thus breaking with the black-supremacy promotion of Don King that had been in effect for some years (although Don King was alleged to have both Ali and Norton under contract). Ali was guaranteed six million dollars and fifty percent of the take over twelve million. It featured a third fight between Ali and Norton (each had won one of their previous fights). It was first reported that a compromise or arrangement had been made with Don King in lieu of any legal or court action. However, later, legal sources reported that the Don King contracts or agreements with both Ali and Norton were of no legal value and that the Garden had properly resisted any efforts to pressure them into any settlement or payment. As far as Don King's reported hold on George Foreman, the winner of the 28 September fight, being the champion, will be the real and final key to the challenger he will meet next, which would seem to give the Garden an advantage, although there is little question that George Foreman would be the natural opponent for the winner.

The fight proved an unusual one with several expected events but several surprises.

The expected was a cheap three-ring circus "thrown" at the formal physical examination of both fighters at Grossinger's, the site of Norton's training installation. Ali arrived with a fifteen-car caravan of his royal entourage, like some Arab sheik, in contrast to Jim Farley, the New York State Athletic Commissioner and Dr. Harry Kleiman, the New York State Athletic Commission doctor, both of whom arrived in one single car. Ali then went into one of his tantrums of shrieking and almost insanely violent shadow boxing, with unfavorable talk about Norton—once more representing himself or acting like some kind of a freak, in fact so much so as to almost unnerve the commissioner and the commission's doctor. Only Ken Norton remained cool and collected. Even when one of the Ali circus members took a cat out of a bag and shoved it toward Norton, who is known to dislike cats, Norton did not break up. A little later, however, Ali sat down and began actually sobbing and crying and exclaiming that he would be talking to Norton all during their fight. Norton kept quiet through most of this strange but usual Ali show and had one telling remark: "This

should be good tor the box office"—showing considerable judgement and cool.

The third Ali-Norton fight on Tuesday, 28 September, was a surprise in many ways. First, it was the first outdoor fight in New York City since 1959—seventeen years! Second, the paid attendance was approximately 30,000, instead of the heralded 40,000, but did not include perhaps a thousand gate crashers. The gate of course did not come anywhere near the record gate of 2,658,660 of the 27 September 1927 Tunney-Dempsey No. 2 fight at Soldier's Field, after forty-nine years, almost to the very day. However, with the closed circuit, this may have been the biggest local boxing haul ever. But because of the worldwide network of closed-circuit coverage, it will be some time before the final confirmed figure can be obtained. This figure, however, will probably be far more accurate than the figures that were given out for the Zaire and Manila fights. Ali's contract calls for fifty percent of all receipts over $12 million. As it stands, Ali will receive $6 million, and Norton reportedly will be paid $1.5 million. This will leave a little pin money for the Garden and for Mike Burke, whose performance as the master strategist, including the difficult handling of the complex and unpredictable Ali, was especially commendable. A few boxing buffs, however, believe that Burke should get a haircut! However, one not so pleasant surprise was the fight itself. It was a bore. For fifteen rounds Ali could not hurt Norton, and for fifteen rounds Norton could not catch Ali. All the leading, the fighting, the punching was done by Norton, while Ali danced, wiggled, took on the role of a cheerleader, shuffled, ran, rope-a-doped, and went into an impenetrable shell. He evidently mesmerized the officials that all this was worthy of points. Ali received the official, unanimous vote of the three officials by the margin of one round. Many believe that the fifty-four-degree temperature at ringside may have frozen or chilled the reason of both the judges and the referee. Most of the spectators, whether at ringside or via closed circuit, believe that Norton won. A sportswriter asked twenty-two fellow writers at the fight for their opinion, and only four gave the fight to Ali. An experienced former professional-boxing official scored the fight 8-5-2 in favor of Norton.

The fight, according to many, dispelled any claim of Ali's greatness, and many felt that Ali should retire, for he is definitely over the hill according to this performance and, following all the past "greatest," has worn down with time. A typical newspaper headline on 29 September read: "Ali's decision is a unanimous dud." Several boxing experts called attention to the fact that Dempsey, Marciano, and Louis had no contemporary Norton with which to go thirty-nine rounds and three fights, with no certain results. Only one of the three fights was decisive, and that went to Norton. In contrast, both of Ali's wins by decision were questionable. As usual, and as further demonstrated in this latest fight, Ali is the "greatest," but only as an actor and crowd pleaser in the ring—so much so that many experts believe that when Ali does bow out of boxing, the sport will suffer a serious financial deflation.

CURRENT WORLD TITLEHOLDERS
(from Ring Magazine—January 1977

Heavyweight	—	Muhammed Ali,* U. S.
Light Heavyweight	—	Victor Galindez, Argentina
Middleweight	—	Carlos Munzon, Argentina
Junior Middleweight	—	Miguel Angel Castellini, Argentina
Welterweight	—	Carlos Palomino, U. S.
Junior Welterweight	—	Wilfredo Benitez, Puerto Rico
Lightweight	—	Roberto Duran, Panama
Junior Lightweight	—	Samuel Serrano, Puerto Rico
Featherweight	—	Alexis Arguello, Nicaragua
Bantamweight	—	Alfonso Zamara, Mexico
Flyweight	—	Miguel Canto, Mexico

SUMMARY: U.S.A. 2; Argentina 3; Puerto Rico 3; Mexico 2; Nicaragua 1.

* "The Ring" magazine, following its policy and precedent, does not yet accept Ali's retirement, at least for another 60 days after which it will recognize the winner of a fight between George Foreman and Ken Norton.

7 • Development of Weight Classifications and Their Outstanding Performers

While heavyweights have naturally taken the spotlight in the history of the fist, and were usually the champions before the creation of weight classifications, they are not by any means the only actors on the boxing stage. In the first eras of boxing in Egypt, Crete, Greece, and Rome, there were no weight categories, which made it hard for the small man and gave boxing over to the heavyweights. When boxing was revived in England, the heavyweights again controlled the sport. There was only one class and the best man was the one who could lick any man of any size or weight. Naturally, no matter how good some 135 pound lightweight might be, or how tough, if he met in a squared arena an equally good man who weighed 195 pounds, the result seldom varied. The heavyweight won.

In addition, when boxing started again in England there was very little interest in watching small men fight, for the game at that time, and the public interest in it, was concentrated on brawn and weight, muscle and punch, blood and guts, rather than on speed and skill. Later, as people began to appreciate the science in the noble art, matches began to be made among fighters who conformed to the same general size or weight.

While on the subject of the science and art of boxing, let us determine once and for all why boxing is *both* a science and an art. Science, according to the dictionary, is "an exact and systematic classification of knowledge concerning some subject or group of subjects, any department of knowledge in which the results of investigation (or experience) has been systematized." Art, the dictionary describes as "the skillful and systematic arrangement or adaptation of means for the attainment of some end, the practical application of knowledge through natural ability, skill, dexterity, facility, power, craft, cunning." Applied to boxing, we can readily see that its accepted and general basic principles—the stance, punches, the methods of advancing and retreating, feints, counters, parries, slipping, ducking, dodging, and rolling—have, through years of progress, been evolved into almost an exact science, and as such constitute the science of boxing. However, the accomplishment and adaptation by the individual of the principles of this science constitute an art and may only be called the art of boxing.

A painter studies the principles of painting technique—how to mix his pigments and his oils; how to put paint on his brushes; how to use his brushes and canvases. He may have an extensive knowledge of the science of painting or be the best-informed man in the world on painting, paints, and painters, yet be unable to apply that information to produce a picture that would even gain attention in an amateur show. Knowledge and information belong to "science" and can be acquired; the application of this knowledge and information is "art." Without genius or temperament, no painter can be a real master. Without genius, called instinct in the prize ring, no pugilist can become a champion boxer or fighter. That is why we must always refer to both the art and science of boxing.

As interest in the art and science of boxing progressed, it naturally led to the assortment of boxers by size. For unlike the painters who do not work on each other, science and art in a boxer were of no avail, if a good little man had to dispatch a good big man. At first the assortment fell into three general groups: "large," "medium" and "small." A "small" man was called a "lightweight" because he did not weigh much. This class originally covered anyone from tough little jockeys who had eaten themselves off their horses' backs, to husky young men with small frames, and included men weighing from 95 to 140 pounds. The earliest lightweights fought in the preliminaries put on before the fights the fans had really come to see—the main engagement between the big men. Small men were not taken seriously, and depended for their support entirely on the generosity of the crowd when the hat was passed around. However, many an overweight jockey became a horse owner from the proceeds of the prize-fight collection for the "lightweights."

Although the lightweight division as it is today has little connection with this early development in the sorting out of boxers by weight, it is, by virtue of the original start made, the oldest class division after the heavyweight class. It became more or less an official division in England in 1746, and comprised every modern classification from flyweight to middleweight. As early as 1867 a battle for the "lightweight championship" was billed in the United States between Tom Chandler and Dooney Harriss. Chandler won in twenty-three rounds.

The medium-sized man—or the so-called "middleweight"—became, in point of chronological origin, the third weight category. Originally the English considered as "middleweights" all men too heavy to fight the "lightweights" but not big enough to take on the "heavies." While some middleweights stayed in their own class, many, after success and experience in their class, would take a shot at more money and glory by entering competition in the heaviest class. Many of the bare-knuckle heavyweights of England first gained prestige in the prize ring as outstanding middleweights. In America, Bob Fitzsimmons, a middleweight, won the world's heavyweight title.

For many years there was no effort made to subdivide boxers beyond small, medium, and large, or lightweight, middleweight, and heavyweight classifications. Very little attention was paid to an official championship in any but the heavyweight class. There was no recognized champion title bout in the lighter classes until the nineteenth century. Then, as boxing began to enjoy more popularity, recognition of the smaller men began, and public interest demanded that lightweight and middleweight championships be featured.

Because of this new interest in the lighter classes,

more men who could never have become heavyweights began boxing, and soon there was a natural demand for more classes in order to have better matches. In 1792 some English boxers began to call themselves "welters." "Welter" was an English horse-racing term and referred to an impost carried by a horse in a handicap race. A "welter" weighed "ten stone" or 140 pounds. The first welterweight champion was Paddington Tom Jones who weighed 145 pounds and from 1792 to 1795 defeated all comers anywhere near his weight. After he passed from the scene, this weight division disappeared until about 1815, and even then it did not gain much recognition. In the United States it was not until after the Civil War that this weight class was recognized and not until the late eighties that it became established, mainly through the efforts of one Paddy Duffy. It is interesting to note that when Jack Dempsey the Nonpareil won his middleweight title, he actually was a welterweight. Can you blame our forefathers for being confused about boxing weight classes? Prior to about 1910 weight classes and weights were by no means clearly defined.

Before we plunge into too many confusing statistics, let us stop and summarize. Originally boxers were either heavyweights (over 140 pounds) or lightweights (under 140 pounds); then they were either heavyweights (over 170), middleweights (156-170), or lightweights (below 156). Next, as interest in boxing increased, came heavies (over 170), middles (156-170), welters (135-156), and lights (under 135). Then came more classifications, especially in the lighter classes. In 1879 or 1880 "Ike" Weir, the Belfast Spider, being much too light for the lightweights, but a colorful and outstanding fighter, became known as the champion of the "feathers." For many years, "featherweight" was the only class under "lightweight" and included anything from 100 to 130 pounds. Eventually 126 pounds became the featherweight limit. Here also popular demand on

57. Wolgast-Rivers fight, Los Angeles, 4 July 1912.

the part of both spectators and fighters led to the development of more classes, for it was found that differences in weight among smaller men are much more important than among heavier men. A man of 165, for instance, can hit almost as hard and sometimes harder than a man of 185 and is usually faster. However, there is no great difference in speed and a tremendous difference in strength and hitting power in the twenty-pound difference in weight between a man of 110 pounds and a man of 130 pounds. The result was the eventual creation of the bantamweight and flyweight classes. The "bantams," or little chickens, were first officially labeled in 1885, although there were "bantams" in England as far back as 1856. Due to the fact that this division was as elastic as a rubber band for many years, it is difficult to be too definite with respect to its history or its first champions. For instance, its top limit was once 105 pounds, then 112, then 116, and now 118. The "flys" were the last lighter weight division to be recognized. This division got its name from the fact that its exponents are not only small, but as fast and buzzingly busy as the insect. This weight division began in England where men are often short on size and weight but long on "guts." Originally the top limit was 108 pounds, but American influence raised it to 112 pounds.

In the meantime another weight division, one often referred to as the least necessary, was developed in the United States in 1903. In fact, its origin immediately touched off a boxing controversy. Since we do not want to become involved in too many controversies, we shall merely state that one of the following fights ushered in the light heavyweight class: Bob Fitzsimmons vs. George Gardner, 25 November 1903; Jack Root vs. George Gardner, 4 July 1903; Kid McCoy vs. Jack Root, 22 April 1903. From its origin to the present time, the weight limits of this class have always been the same: from 161 to 175 pounds. It will be noted that this weight division is the only one of the eight standard and currently recognized divisions that originated in the United States.

There has been discussion and definite indication of the possibility of establishing further weight classes. Some sports writers and promoters years ago tried to split the heavyweight class into heavyweights (176 to 190) and dreadnaughts (191 and over). This effort failed, and it is extremely doubtful if it will ever be justified, for there is no great difference between a good man weighing 180 and another good man weighing 240. They can both deliver knockout punches, absorb punches, and move around nearly as fast as lighter men.

A paperweight class with a maximum limit of 105 pounds actually existed around 1910, especially in England, and may be revived. Here there is a definite

justification for the classification. No boxer weighing less than 105 pounds should have to box a man weighing 112 pounds, for seven pounds in this category is a tremendous advantage.

Due to the impossibility of accurate and complete coverage of the story of all the championships in all the weight divisions, we will attempt to cover the history of each class by touching on the most important incidents only. The most important fighters and fights from the standpoint of what these contributed to the game will be described.

LIGHT-HEAVYWEIGHT CLASS

Most of the early light heavies fought as heavyweights. The first great light heavyweight was Philadelphia Jack O'Brien. He was a cagey and clever boxer, a wily fox in the ring and held the title from 1904 to 1907. He lost it by a hairline twenty-round decision to Tommy Burns who, by the way, never bothered with the light heavyweight title, but turned heavyweight. Then came Battling Levinsky, the man who made "no-decision" fights famous. A "no-decision" fight was a popular pastime for boxers just prior to the roaring twenties and consisted in a champion fighting an unofficial championship bout, with all the

58. Henry Armstrong, only man ever to hold three world championships. (Wide World)

trimmings, except that there was no decision unless one or the other boxer was knocked out. Therefore, the only way the champion could be separated from his title was by a knockout.

Battling Levinsky, a tough, rough gentleman, won the championship in 1916 from Jack Dillon in a "no-decision" bout in which the impossible (a knockout) happened. Levinsky continued with no-decision bouts, but was never caught napping. He fought no-decision bouts all over the country until he almost wore himself out. Then in 1920, when Tex Rickard had to build up Georges Carpentier, Levinsky was brought out of the semiretirement of the "no-decision" circuit and pitted against the French champion. Georges Carpentier knocked him out in the fourth round and the title again meant something. Georges was still light-heavyweight champion when he fought Dempsey for the heavyweight crown. In 1922 this weight division gave the boxing world a shock when Carpentier in his own arena and with his adoring Parisians looking on was stiffened in the sixth round by Battling Siki, a former Senegalese soldier who had learned to box in the French Army.

Siki was a peculiar pug but a colorful one. He insisted on strolling along the Paris boulevards with a pet lion in tow and also developed a passion for snakes. In 1923 the French, who are famous for subtlety in accomplishing their objectives, packed him off to Ireland to fight Mike McTigue on St. Patrick's day. Siki lost his title. McTigue, probably one of the toughest men to nail with a right hand, finally lost his title to lefthanded Paul Berlenbach, the "Astoria Assassin," in 1925.

Berlenbach was a former Olympic wrestler and amateur boxing competitor for the New York Athletic Club. NYAC trainer Dan Hickey with great patience developed this southpaw into a boxer with a paralyzing lefthand shift. He had a colorful career but succumbed to the clever, hard-hitting Jack Delaney. When Delaney left the division to fight in the heavyweight division, there were a few years of confusion. Then Tommy Loughran became undisputed champion and in a still famous fight with Leo Lomski, came back from two nine-count knockdowns in the first round to retain his title. Loughran then followed most of the other good light heavies into the heavy class in quest of the "golden fleece." Leo Lomski, known as "the Aberdeen Assassin" because of his powerful right hand punch, died in November 1975. He will be remembered as one of the most ruggedly handsome boxers of his time and of the Friday night fights at the old Garden. He lost only eighteen out of 275 fights and his earnings topped $275,000. Before he died in Aberdeen, Washington, his life-long home, he remarked that when he earned dollars, they were real dollars, not inflated bucks.

The next definite champion was Maxie Rosenbloom, who is the perfect example of "cuteness" in the ring—cuteness having nothing to do with blond curls or blue ribbons, but with canny, wily, and shrewd generalship, and boxing. Maxie was such a light puncher and such a slapper with the open glove that he was dubbed by the newspapers "Maxie the Slapsie" or "Slapsie Maxie." He nevertheless kept the title from 1930 to 1934. Many fans went to see him fight for the same reason that they went to see Leach Cross—hoping someone would come along who would solve his defensive slapping style and knock him cold. No one did.

In 1934 Bob Olin, a "college man" and Wall Street stock salesman, defeated Rosenbloom, but lost the title about a year later to John Henry Lewis, a black young man from Missouri. The story of how Olin became a professional fighter is unusual. A fight manager tried to convince him to turn pro. The manager guaranteed he would make him light heavyweight champion in five years. Olin accepted, and won the championship six years later.

John Henry Lewis resigned his title to enter the heavyweight class in 1938. Billy Conn of Pittsburgh, another good champion in this division left it to gain the questionable privilege of being knocked out twice by Joe Louis for the heavyweight title. In 1943 Gus Lesnevich was confirmed as champion, although he had actually been No. 1 man in the division since 1941. His quick knockout victories over Melio Bettina and Billy Fox—the latter in 1948—established Lesnevich's position as well as a new record, for no one ever held the light heavyweight title as long. In late 1948, however, Lesnevich was defeated by age and Freddie Mills, a mediocre Britisher.

In 1949 Guiseppe Antonio Berardinelli, a new light heavyweight, trained, coached, and managed by no less than Jack Kearns, original manager of Jack Dempsey, finally defeated Gus Lesnevich in a fifteen-round bout in Cincinnati for the American light heavyweight title. Early in 1950, he also won the world's championship by stopping Freddy Mills in ten rounds in London, England. Do not be surprised, for Guiseppe's boxing name was Joey Maxim. Maxim is famous for making Ray Robinson quit in a fourteen-round KO. However after 116 fights in eight years at age thirty-seven, Maxim lost to Archie Moore on points in a fifteen-round bout in Ogden, Utah in 1952. Later, this opened up a controversy resulting from Archie Moore's refusal to defend his title when ordered, although Moore was still recognized by every boxing board except the N.B.A. Moore was a great performer who took on all the top heavyweights and retained the light heavyweight title for over ten years. He fought 230 times in twenty-nine years. He was deservingly admired and respected.

However in February 1962, New York withdrew its recognition of Moore also, and when Harold Johnson beat Doug Jones of New York in fifteen rounds in Philadelphia, Johnson was given international recognition as the new light heavyweight champion. He lost it, however, the next year in 1963 to Willie Pastrano on a fifteen-round decision in Las Vegas, Nevada. Pastrano kept the title for a couple of years, but in 1965, was knocked out by José Torres in New York City in the ninth round. In 1966, Torres and Dick Tiger of Nigeria fought in Madison Square Garden in a title match and Tiger, at 167 pounds, defeated Torres at 175 pounds via a unanimous fifteen-round decision. Bob Foster of Washington, D.C. in 1968 took the title away from Dick Tiger, by a knockout in the fourth round in Madison Square Garden. Bob Foster has continued to hold the light heavyweight title since that time, defending it frequently and always winning. Foster suffered two KOS, both when he invaded the heavyweight class; once for the world's heavyweight championship when he was knocked out by Joe Frazier in the second round, and once in 1972 when he was knocked out by Muhammad Ali in the eighth round. Bob Foster, incidentally, is one of the current champions, (1975) together with Carlos Monzon, who are outstanding, and only age will catch up with them.

In the days when promoting big fights was a profession, and called for specific and special skills and experience, a match would have been arranged between Bob Foster and Carlos Monzon of Argentina, the present middleweight king. But in the days of worldwide closed-circuit fight promotion, typical promoters today only gather money around them, connect with a specialist in managing relations with movie theaters and arenas for closed circuit TV and a technical TV organization and they are in business but as amateur or tyro fistic promoters. So without a Rickard or a Jacobs or even a Norris and his IBC, a light heavyweight vs middleweight encounter between these two outstanding stars in their respective division but with Monzon coming in probably heavier, undoubtedly would be arranged. Before the tax wall against fight promotions and the exorbitant taxes levied against promoters and boxers in New York City and New York State it would have filled the garden and done well on closed-circuit TV to the rest of the world; however, after 1975, perhaps these two great champions may be over the (age) hill!

As almost a postscript to the above and in time for the updating of this book because of delays in publication, Bob Foster, feeling himself handicapped by age, retired. The two leading candidates for the title are John Conteh of Great Britain, the WBC choice, and Victor Galindez of Argentina, the WBA selection.

MIDDLEWEIGHT CLASS

The middleweight class, strangely enough, has been the weight division with the greatest hitters, the cleverest boxers and toughest contestants of any in modern times. Mike Donovan and Jack Dempsey, "the Nonpareil," were among the greatest boxers of all time. Fitzsimmons and Stanley Ketchel could hit harder than most heavyweights. Harry Greb and Mickey Walker were pretty "tough hombres" with or without gloves, in or out of the ring.

Mike Donovan defeated the best men of his weight and over for many years, both with bare fists and gloves. It is interesting to note that Mike Donovan taught Teddy Roosevelt how to box and retired to become boxing coach at the New York Athletic Club. He sired Arthur Donovan, top referee, and also boxing coach of the NYAC. Arthur Donovan's son, Mike's grandson, was an all-pro football player with the championship Baltimore Colts. Upon Mike's retirement in 1882, his successor was Jack Dempsey who also fought both with bare and with gloved fists. For almost ten years, 1881 to 1891, the original Dempsey was unbeatable. In many ways he is considered the most extraordinary boxer in the epic of the ring. He actually was a welterweight in many of his battles. "The Nonpareil," as he was called, continued to display a profile fit for the movies notwithstanding his many gruelling fights. This great personality inspired the poem which is to boxing what "Casey at the Bat" is to baseball. This poem written by his lawyer may be found in the appendix.

Bob Fitzsimmons, the Australian blacksmith, was so powerful a hitter that he soon abandoned the middleweight class and successfully moved to the heavyweight class. Stanley Ketchel, the Michigan assassin, was never a boxer, but few men, even heavyweights, could stand up under his whirlwind attack or his dynamic punching. In his first thirty-nine fights, he knocked out thirty-five men. He even knocked Jack Johnson down with a single punch on the whiskers, though Johnson outweighed him by at least forty pounds. In 1919, while still champion, Ketchel was shot and killed in a brawl over a girl by a man who evidently did not want to trade punches with him.

For difficult competitors in or out of the ring, we give you Harry Greb and Mickey Walker. Harry Greb, the Pittsburgh windmill, was an unorthodox fighter who sometimes did not follow the rules, never trained but swarmed all over his opponent from

59. Jack Dempsey, the Nonpareil.

60. Jack Dempsey, probably the greatest boxer pound for pound in modern history.

start to finish. He threw more leather from more angles than any two other boxers, and he never stopped and never tired.

He is the only man who ever beat Tunney, and he made Jack Dempsey look very bad in a number of training sessions. Few fighters ever landed a solid punch on Greb, and few fighters ever were permitted to do any leading or follow any preconceived plan in any round of a bout with this dauntless exponent of perpetual motion. He burned the candle at both ends, yet fought more than 500 bouts and was knocked out only once, and that time when he first started in 1913. He was middleweight champion from 1923 to 1926. Mickey Walker, the Rumson Toy Bull Dog, was also as tough as they come. To prove it, although a welterweight, he invaded the middleweight, light heavy, and heavyweight divisions. Walker was a good boxer but also a fighter and a puncher. Like Greb, he liked a good time and loved to fight even in the street and without gloves. Greb and Walker fought in the ring in New York on 2 July 1925, for the middleweight championship. Walker never got a chance to let a punch go and Greb won every round. Later the two men fought an informal continuation of their championship bout in the Silver Slipper, a night club along Broadway, bare-fisted and without benefit of ring, rounds, ropes, or rules. No one knows the results of that one. Walker is now a promising artist in oil painting although in poor health at age seventy-five.

No other weight classification, not even the heavyweight class, can claim on an all-time basis any greater boxers than Jack Dempsey the Nonpareil, and Mike Donovan; any greater hitters than Bob Fitzsimmons and Stanley Ketchel; any tougher competitors than Harry Greb and Mickey Walker. No other weight classification can claim as many great competitors in the ten-year period from 1940 to 1950, namely, Tony Zale, Jake LaMotta, Steve Belloise, Laurent Dauthuille, Sugar Robinson, Marcel Cerdan and Rocky Graziano. In Europe Tiberio Mitri and Randy Turpin were considered every bit as good.

61. World's middleweight championship, 7 September 1908. Billy Papke, covered with blood, KOs Stanley Ketchel with James J. Jeffries as referee. On 26 November 1908, Ketchel KOed Papke.

This extraordinary class has had many stars through the years. Tommy Ryan, Kid McCoy, Billy Papke, George Chip, Al McCoy, and Mike O'Dowd seem to indicate that, in the old days, most of the best big little men were Irish. Johnny Wilson and Tiger Flowers were both "southpaw" champions who worried Greb. Then came Marcel Thil, a bald Frenchman, who coveted and claimed the world's championship from 1932 to 1938 but was deprived of technically holding the undisputed championship by the New York Boxing Commission.

Any old-timer still remembers another great middleweight, a black fighter named Jeff Clark, the "old Joplin ghost," who was a marvel. Although never more than a middleweight, he rarely fought in his own weight class but defeated men like Sam Langford, Joe Jeannette, and Harry Wills. Jimmy Bronson, one of the greatest fight managers, places Clark as the best fighter he ever managed, with Bobby Garcia, the Mexican Indian featherweight next, and Bob Martin, his AEF World War I heavyweight champion, as the hardest hitter he ever knew, and Jack Zivic as the fighter easiest to manage.

After the voluntary retirement of Walker from this class in 1931, there was frequent uncertainty as to who held the championship, with the N.B.A. and New York State often recognizing different champions. However, in 1941 Tony Zale, by defeating George Abrams, straightened out the championship succession.

Graziano, the first postwar middleweight champion, might have equalled the greats of this unusual division. Certainly the terrific fight put on by Tony Zale, prewar champion, and Graziano on 27 September 1946 will long be remembered. A rematch was, of course, scheduled. While the second bout was not as exciting as the first, Graziano reversed Zale's KO victory in the first fight and won the middleweight title. This bout drew $422,918 establishing many records. It hit a new high for the middleweight class and both the champion and challenger received more money than ever obtained by any fighters in a middleweight bout.

The discrimination against Rocky Graziano as a middleweight champion and the fact that he was barred in some states even though he was a world's champion, because of his military record, is difficult to figure out. According to reports, Graziano was convicted of absence without leave in wartime and received his full punishment for this offense. Desertion calls for the death sentence or long imprisonment and means that a soldier either leaves his post under fire or absents himself from the Army for the purpose of permanently hiding himself under another identity from further military service, or through cowardice abandons his companions in a moment or situation of dire necessity. Absence without leave means that a man just skips out because he has hit his sergeant or captain in a moment of temper, is tired of peeling potatoes on KP duty, or is homesick for mother, the white lights, or a girl friend. Graziano, whose judgment is questionable, just took French leave. There is no report that he jumped ship, or was avoiding combat duty or H hour. It is hard to believe that our modern society should have helped in ending Graziano's boxing career, after he had officially and actually received his punishment for his mistake.

A further interesting twist on the Graziano story is the fact that Sugar Robinson, World's Welterweight Champion, who was not barred anywhere after World War II and was even a major participant in a one-minute knockout fight sponsored by the American Legion, has a peculiar military record.

According to a story often repeated in the Army, Robinson, a pet of Mike Jacobs, was, unlike Graziano, no soldier in the ranks or bad boy doing KP in an Army mess. Robinson was a sergeant member of the Joe Louis troupe of boxers who barnstormed all over the world entertaining the GIs in comparative comfort. However, when it came time to leave the United States, Robinson reneged and, just like Graziano, went AWOL with probably less cause and more permanent purpose. He even lost a fight by technical knockout to some MPs later in his flight. However, here, according to the story, Uncle Mike and others stepped in, and Robinson born Walker Smith, after his arrest was placed in Army hospitals for observation.

According to Army sources, Walker Smith, Jr. (ASN 832813544) had the charge of desertion dropped for an "honorable" discharge on 3 June 1944 under "AR 615–366" for "constitutional psy-

chopathic state . . . mental deficiency . . . mental age 10 years and 6 months . . . and failure to pass the EEG test." Of course as one of the greatest boxers of our time, Sugar Ray's intelligence, ring cunning, and ability to communicate makes this medical report unbelieveable, especially the failure to pass the EEG test when Robinson was examined by many boxing commission medicos and passed many required EEG tests both before and after his Army service. The failure to pass the Army EEG test and the diagnosis as stated above would seem to be an error either arranged or accidental. If accidental it could well be due to lack of experience on the part of the wartime lower level Army medical specialist involved, whose foreign qualifications and experience were very controversial and who, by the way, had legally changed his name very late in 1942. In all fairness to Robinson his story in his book as told to Dave Anderson and published by Viking Press, is that he suffered complete amnesia as a result of falling down his barrack stairway after tripping on some laundry bags and he evidently did not remember ever stating he would not go with the boxing troupe, jumping ship, going AWOL, being arrested by MPs, and his many interrogations, examinations, and hearings, etc., etc. Another reasonable conclusion is that the Army Medical examiners and various boards of officers and the reviewing authorities believed that no matter what the facts, Sugar Ray would represent too great a morale, public-relations, and security problem for a wartime Army and should be helped in an avoidance of service. However, boxing should have given Graziano the same unusual break it gave Robinson and many believed the punishment, discrimination, and treatment given Graziano injured his morale as a great fighter, even though he was later reinstated.

Born Rocco Bardella, Rocky was a character who

62. Zale down, Graziano up, second round, 27 September 1946. (Press Association Inc.)

63. Graziano down, Zale up, sixth round, 27 September 1946 (Press Association Inc.)

64. Marcel Cerdan cuts Abrams eye, 6 December 1946

"until age twenty-five was locked up or running wild" and who hated the world and the Army, but finally "knocked the hate out of himself." His extraordinary story of how a New York hoodlum wound up as a legitimate and friendly guy is told in his book *Somebody Up There Likes Me*, written with Roland Barber. As honestly admitted in his story Rocky, private unassigned 32201881 received a "dishonorable" discharge and prison at hard labor for one year.

Although barred in New York State, a Zale-Graziano deciding match was signed, approved by the National Boxing Association and scheduled for early June 1948. It was held in Jersey City. The gate was $335,646 and Zale won by a third-round knockout and recovered his world's title. There are few boxers with the "crowd appeal" of Graziano. Although a middleweight, Graziano grossed over $100,000 three times in the Garden against Red Cochrane, Harold Green, Sonny Horne; almost $200,000

65. LaMotta KOs Dauthuille with thirteen seconds to go in the fifteenth round (9/13/50), otherwise he would have lost the decision and the world's middleweight championship. The contract of this fight produced by the author, Dauthuille's manager, for the Department of Justice, proved IBC's monopoly.

66. Jake La Motta takes his defeat by Laurent Dauthuille in Montreal, Canada. (The Forum)

against Marty Servo; and drew well over a million dollars in three fights with Zale. To prove further his appeal, it is interesting to note that the greatly advertised international match for the world's championship between Zale and Cerdan which followed the last Zale-Graziano fight only grossed $242,000. The passing of Graziano from the boxing scene at his physical peak is a tragic story, reminiscent of Les Darcy the great Australian middleweight, accused of being a slacker in World War I, who died of pneumonia and a broken heart in his prime.

The Zale-Cerdan championship fight was not sensational. There were no knockdowns but Cerdan proceeded with a relentless methodical and careful wearing down process which finally left Zale exhausted and defenseless at the end of the eleventh round. Zale fell to his knees as the bell rang and was unable to continue when the twelfth round opened. Cerdan, at thirty-four, showed up unusually well. As usual this is one class never short of outstanding challengers and Cerdan found almost ten men who appeared on their record to be dangerous opponents.

Cerdan handpicked his opponent for his first title defense, but as is often the case caught a tartar in Jake LaMotta. After he had absorbed a bad beat-

66A. Jake LaMotta after his defeat by Dauthuille in Montreal talking to Ed Strangler Lewis. (The Forum)

113

ing, the Frenchmans' seconds refused to permit Cerdan to come out for the tenth round. The middleweight class more than any other buzzed with topnotch competition. Ray Robinson, welterweight champion, became a contender by stopping Steve Belloise before over a $100,000 worth of ticket stub holders . . . LaMotta, Cerdan, Graziano, Fusari, Gavilan, and Castallani were all put to work by Octopus, Inc. In Montreal, Canada, Laurent Dauthuille, who defeated and almost knocked out Jake LaMotta just before he became champion, and koed Johnny Greco before a bigger crowd than that which attended the world's heavyweight Charles-Lesnevich fight at Yankee Stadium in New York. Later, in a world title defense, LaMotta knocked out Dauthuille in the last seconds of the fifteenth round after being

67. "Sugar" Ray Robinson, world's welterweight champion and five times middleweight champion, 1951–58. (Ring Magazine)

way behind on points. It was the contract of this fight, supplied by Dauthuille's manager (the author), that was a pivotal piece of evidence in the Department of Justice's monopoly case against the IBC.

Ray Robinson, the welterweight king in February 1951, took on and knocked out Jake LaMotta in thirteen rounds to win the middleweight title in Chicago, Illinois. In July of 1951, Randy Turpin defeated Ray Robinson on points in fifteen rounds in London, England, but in September of 1951 Ray Robinson was rematched with Randy Turpin in New York City and regained his world title by a ko in the tenth round. On 18 December 1952, Ray Robinson retired undefeated as world's middleweight champion and an elimination tournament followed between Randy Turpin, Charlie Fusari, Carl Olson, and Patty Young with Olson finally winning international recognition in 1953. But in December 1955, Ray Robinson again returned to work and knocked out Olson in the second round in Chicago but, in turn, was deprived of his title by a fifteen-round decision to Gene Fulmer who, in turn, succumbed to Ray Robinson who won the title for a fourth time by knocking out Gene Fulmer in five rounds in Chicago. In 1957, Carmen Basilio won the title on a split decision from Robinson in New York, but Robinson won the title back for the fifth time on a fifteen-round split decision from Carmen Basilio in Chicago. When the N.B.A. vacated Robinson's title in 1959, Gene Fulmer and Carmen Basilio met in San Francisco with Fulmer stopping Basilio in fourteen rounds to gain N.B.A. recognition. However, in January 1960, Paul Pender won the world's title by a split decision over Ray Robinson in fifteen rounds in Boston, Massachussetts and was recognized by a number of organizations as the world's titleholder. Terry Downes won a piece of the title by stopping Paul Pender in nine rounds in London, but Paul Pender regained that title by winning a fifteen-round decision over Downes in Boston. But in 1962, Dick Tiger won the W.B.A. title by winning a unanimous fifteen-round decision over Gene Fulmer in San Francisco. Then for less than a year there was no completely internationally recognized world titleholder. Pender retired on 7 May 1963 and when Tiger ko'd Fulmer in seven rounds at Ibadan, Nigeria, he became the official title holder. He, however, lost the title in December of 1963 by being outpointed by Jose Giardello in Atlantic City, New Jersey, but again regained the title by unanimous decision over Giardello in Madison Square Garden at the end of fifteen rounds. As will be noted, this was a most active division with many closely matched boxers. In April of 1966, Emile Griffith of Weehauken, New Jersey, defeated Dick Tiger in a split decision, but lost the title in 1967 to Nino Benvenuti of Trieste, Italy, in fifteen rounds in Madison Square Garden. Benvenuti was an Italian and former Olympic titleholder. In 1967 Emile Griffith regained the world title by outpointing Nino Benvenuti at Shea Stadium in Flushing, New York by a split vote. Then in March of 1968, Nino Benvenuti of Italy regained the world's title by a unanimous decision at the end of fifteen rounds and the title remained in Italy until 7 November 1970 when Carlos Monzon of Argentina ko'd Benvenuti in the twelfth round in Rome, Italy. Carlos Monzon, who is still the world's middleweight champion and as this book goes to press a formidable and outstanding competitor with a record, since he won the world title, of twelve ko's, three decisions in fifteen defenses in a period of over five years. Monzon koed the WBA champion Tony Licata of New Orleans and will fight Rodrigo Valdez of Columbia the W.B.C. claimant next.

WELTERWEIGHT CLASS

The welterweight class came into being about 1880 and records indicate the first champions were Paddy Duffy, Mysterious Billy Smith, Tommy Ryan, and Rube Ferns. Then came two all-time greats, Joe Walcott and Dixie Kid. Joe Walcott, a Barbados black born in 1872, though only 5 feet 1 inch tall and a welterweight, beat many good heavyweights including Joe Choynski and Peter Jackson, as well as lightheavies and middleweights such as Philadelphia Jack O'Brien and Mike Donovan. He fought the best men in every weight from 1890 to 1911.

Walcott won the welterweight title in 1901 by a knockout over Rube Ferns at Fort Erie, Canada. Although he lost on a disputed foul to Dixie Kid in 1904, the Kid outgrew the division and Walcott was champion until outpointed by Honey Melody in the latter part of 1906.

The Dixie Kid (Aaron L. Brown) was an American black who also fought middles, lightheavies, and heavies, and outgrew the welterweight class. Like other old-timers, he followed the ring a long time. He knocked out his first opponent, Tony Rivers, in one round in 1899, and his last opponent Bill Bristowe, in two rounds in 1914.

Ted Lewis and Jack Britton then toured the United States and Canada as the leading contenders for the welterweight title from 1915 to 1919, barnstorming and fighting each other. They fought each other sixteen times. Their many fights, all close and entertaining, revived interest in a division which had failed to attract the public after 1906. Britton finally emerged the winner and champion of the series and of the weight classification by a knockout at Dayton, Ohio, on St. Patrick's Day, 17 March 1918. Britton eventually lost his title to the "Rumson Bulldog," Mickey Walker in 1922 before the latter grew into a middleweight.

Then followed a succession of champions featured by the comeback of Jackie Fields, an Olympic world's amateur champion. He won the professional title in 1929 from Joe Dundee, lost it to young Jack Thompson in 1930, but regained it in 1932 from Lou Brouillard. Jimmy McLarnin and Barney Ross (later to become a World War II hero) were great modern 145-pound champions but were overshadowed by Henry Armstrong, a black marvel from California. Armstrong made ring history by being the first and only man ever to hold officially three world's professional championships in three weight classifications at the same time. (Terry McGovern unofficially won the bantam, feather, and lightweight titles.) When Armstrong whipped Barney Ross in 1938, he was already both feather and lightweight champion. Fritzie Zivic, Red Cochrane, and Marty Servo followed Armstrong as champions in the welterweight division. The next champion considered by many as a candidate for all time honors was Sugar Robinson, a wily black boxer.

After successfully defending his welterweight title against Kid Gavilan, the "Cuban Hawk," Robinson invaded the middleweight division, announced that he was ready to give up the welterweight class, but only after he was assured of a "shot" at the middleweight crown. However, by a rather arbitrary ruling, the New York State Boxing Commission no longer recognizes the possibility of a man holding more than one championship. It discourages a cham-

pion from becoming a contender in a heavier class without resigning his first title. From a business standpoint, however, it can easily be seen that no boxer should be forced to resign his championship merely because he is good enough to be a definite contender in the next higher class. However, there was no dearth of topnotch material in the welterweight class. Three of the most colorful, if not the best, contenders in 1947 were Cuba's Kid Gavilan; Hawaii's Frankie Fernandez; and Filipino Bernard Docusen from New Orleans.

After a lot of maneuvering by the New York State Boxing Commission and the N.B.A., it was finally agreed to recognize the winner of a Ray Robinson-Tommy Bell fight as the world's welterweight titleholder. The fight was held on 20 December 1946. Robinson gained the title via a fifteen-round decision, but vacated the title after winning the middleweight championship on 14 February 1951. In an N.B.A. elimination, Johnny Bratton won the title by decisioning Charlie Fusari in fifteen rounds in Chicago in 1951. In May 1951, Kid Gavilan defeated Johnny Bratton in fifteen rounds in New York in a bout recognized as a world's championship contest by both the N.B.A. and New York State, although this decision was not accepted universally. But on the retirement of Charles Humez of France, Kid Gavilan gained international recognition by defeating Billy Graham. On 20 October 1954, Johnny Saxton won the title over Kid Gavilan in fifteen rounds in Philadelphia, and in April 1955 Tony DeMarco knocked out Johnny Saxton in fourteen rounds at Boston winning the crown, but was himself knocked out by Carmen Basilio in twelve rounds in Syracuse. Then Johnny Saxton rewon the title by outpointing Carmen Basilio in Chicago only to be knocked out by Basilio later in 1956 in Syracuse. Basilio then relinquished the welterweight title after winning the middleweight crown, and Virgil Akins won the vacant title by knocking out Vince Martinez in four rounds in St. Louis, Missouri but was himself deprived of the title by Don Jordan in fifteen rounds in Los Angeles. Benny Kid Paret then won the welterweight title by a unanimous decision in fifteen rounds in Las Vegas, but in April 1961, Emil Griffith won the title by knocking out Benny Paret in the thirteenth round at Miami Beach, Florida. Paret, however, regained the title by outpointing Griffith in a fifteen-round split decision in Madison Square Garden. Then Emile Griffith regained the title by knocking out Benny Paret in the twelfth round in Madison Square Garden. Paret died as a result of injuries received in this bout, one of the very few ring fatalities to world champions or former world champions. In March 1963, Louis Rodriguez won the title by outpointing Emile Griffith over fifteen

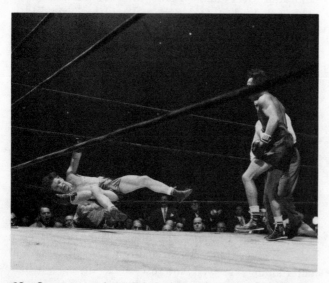

68. Suspension! Al Davis knocked down by Henry Armstrong, 15 June 1944. (Press Association Inc.)

rounds in Los Angeles only to be beaten on points in Madison Square Garden in fifteen rounds by Griffith in June 1963. Emile Griffith then retained the title in four championship fights from 1964 to 1966, but in 1966, the title was taken away from him by the New York State Commission because he had gained the middleweight championship title. No champion, by the way, by international ruling can hold two titles simultaneously although there is no real sound, sane reason why this cannot be done if the boxer can handle his weight limitations. A comparatively unknown named Curtis Cokes, in winning a decision over Manuel Gonzales in the Dallas Municipal Auditorium in 1965, was accepted as the world's titleholder. Curtis Cokes, with a euphonious sounding name, was a bit of a mystery as he was practically unknown to boxing fans, yet he won the world's welterweight title according to the W.B.A. on 24 August 1966 by a decision over Manuel Gonzales, and a universally recognized world's welterweight title by defeating Jean Josselin in Dallas in November of 1966. He seems to have successfully retained the title in many fights in 1967, 1968, and part of 1969 only to be ko'd by Jose Napoles of Cuba twice in 1969, both title fights. Jose Napoles lost the world title when he was ko'd in turn by Billy Backus of Syracuse, New York in the fourth round of a title fight. But Jose Napoles came back and regained the title by koing Billy Backus in the fourth round in 1971 in Syracuse.

In the summer of 1975, Napoles was caught in not the best of condition by Armando Muniz of Los Angeles and was further handicapped by a bad cut over his left eye but was given an unusual winning decision when the bout at Acapulco was stopped in the twelfth round. Muniz had been warned for butting in the third and fifth rounds. Napoles, at age thirty-five or more, was saved by the unanimous decision of the doctor, referee, and judges. Napoles was paid $150,000 while Muniz received $15,000. However, Napoles showed his great class by a rematch with Muniz in Mexico City. It was a fierce and bloody battle and although handicapped without any question by age and by too many fights, Napoles still proved the champion and discouraged Muniz with an eighth-round knockdown. Napoles has been a professional boxer for seventeen years, has fought eighty-one times and has held his world title for seven years with only a short break.

LIGHTWEIGHT CLASS

The lightweight class, second oldest division in boxing, began in the United States as far back as 1868. Arthur Chambers was the first nationally

known and accepted champion until he retired in 1879, although records seem to indicate that Abe Hicken was the titleholder from 1868 to 1872. Jack Dempsey, the Nonpareil, began his unmatched career as a lightweight. However, the name of Jack McAuliffe, the Napoleon of the prize ring, dominates the early lightweight class history. McAuliffe, one of the greatest fighters to step into a ring, strangely enough was contemporary with two other all-time greats, Nonpareil Jack Dempsey and John L. Sullivan. However, of the three men, only McAuliffe retired without a single defeat in his entire career. This record was unmatched by any of the earlier fighters except Jimmy Barry of Chicago, bantam champion of the nineties. From 1885 to 1896, McAuliffe was considered champion, although his claim to the world's championship was never fully justified, for his battle for the world crown with Jim Carney of England resulted in a seventy-four-round draw. When the fight was stopped, Carney actually had much the better of it. McAuliffe later went on the stage and became a great monologist. He never lost his extraordinary intelligence and sense of humor, and died happy, in 1937, at the age of seventy-two.

Kid Lavigne of Saginaw, Michigan, who succeeded the great McAuliffe, was able to do what his predecessor had failed to do—bring the world's title to America. In 1896, Lavigne went to London and knocked out Dick Burge, the British and European champion, in seventeen rounds.

The all-time greats of the lightweight class, besides McAuliffe, are Joe Gans, Benny Leonard, and Henry Armstrong. Joe Gans, the old master, is generally considered the greatest boxer of the game. He was an American black, born in Baltimore in 1874. He started boxing in 1891 and was managed by Al Hereford, one of the cleverest managers of all time. He fought almost up to the time of his death from tuberculosis in 1910. To show the wizardry of Joe Gans, the record shows that prior to the onset of ill-health, or from 1891 to 1908, over a seventeen-year span, in approximately 200 fights with lightweights to heavyweights, he lost only five fights and these to such opponents as heavyweight Sam Langford, Terry McGovern, and George McFadden, and later reversed most of these. He was world's champion from 1902 to 1908.

Benny Leonard (Benjamin Lerner) was born in New York City. He is often compared to Gans and enjoyed the longest reign—eight years—of any lightweight champion of the world in the gloved fist era. He won the title in 1917 by a ko over Freddy Welsh and retired undefeated in 1925. He emerged from retirement in 1931, because he had lost all his money in bad investments, and won about twenty-one fights as a welterweight but was knocked out in

1932 by Jimmy McLarnin. After war service as a lieutenant in the United States Maritime Service, Leonard died of heart failure while refereeing a fight for the New York State Boxing Commission in 1948.

While there have been many great lightweight champions in more recent years, they are all topped by Henry Armstrong, a human dynamo who captured the feather, light, and welterweight world's championships. In 1947, a black fighter named Ike Williams became the undisputed world's lightweight champion and improved with each fight in defense of his title. Billy McCarney, Dumb Dan Morgan, Jimmy Wilson, and all the old-timers among boxing experts expressed the belief that before Williams hung up his gloves, he would earn a place among the all-time greats of his class. The constant and rapid improvement of Ike Williams even led to much discussion of a Robinson-Williams fight where a great lightweight champion, who had run out of opponents in his own weight, would meet one of the greatest welterweights of all time.

From 1947 to 1951 Ike Williams held tight sway over all lightweights, but his story is no different than that of all boxers—namely, as he got older (he fought 171 times in seventeen years) he ran out of gas—namely, on 25 May 1951, James Carter of New York KO'd Williams in the fourteenth round. James Carter then lost his title to Lauro Salas on points in 1952, but rewon it by decisioning Lauro Salas in a fifteen-round fight in Chicago. After several success-

ful defenses of his title in 1952 and 1953, Carter finally succumbed to Paddy DeMarco in a fifteen-round decision only to come back that same year, 1954, to win back his title from Paddy DeMarco, stopping him in the fifteenth round in San Francisco. However, in 1955 he was beaten by Wallace Bud Smith in a Boston decision and again lost to Smith some months later. Smith, a great amateur and AAU titleholder who won sixty-five out of seventy amateur bouts, lost his title in 1956 to Joe Brown in New Orleans, Louisiana by decision. When Smith tried again in 1957, he was KO'd by Brown in the eleventh round. Joe Brown of New Orleans, "old bones" as he was called, was managed by the well-known manager, Lou Viscusi, and was all service lightweight champion during World War II and had an unusually long boxing career, namely, on a professional basis alone—from 1946 to 1970—twenty-four years. He won the title from Bud Smith in August 1956 and successfully defended it many times all over the world including the Americas, England, the Philippines, and Europe. Finally he lost, partly due to old age, in a decision to Carlos Ortiz in Las Vegas in April 1962, but continued to box all over the world. "Old Bones" last bout was in 1970 at age forty-four. Carlos Ortiz defended his title which he won from Joe Brown in 1962 in the United States, Philippines, and Japan, but lost his crown to Ismael Laguna in Panama City by a decision. He, however, regained the title from Ismael Laguna in San Juan, Puerto Rico by

69. Benny Leonard getting up in his fight against McLarnin as Arthur Donovan counts.

a fifteen-round decision and retained his title until 1968 when he lost a decision to Carlos Cruz in Santo Domingo. Carlos Cruz of the Dominican Republic retained the title for one year, but then lost it to Mando Ramos of Los Angeles by a KO in the eleventh round. Cruz and his family died in an airplane crash off the coast of the Dominican Republic in 1970. Mando Ramos, who won the world title from Cruz in 1969, lost it by being knocked out by Ismael Laguna of Panama in March 1970. The latter then lost his title in September 1970, to Ken Buchanan of Scotland by a fifteen-round decision. Buchanan, after successfully defending his title on a number of occasions from 1970 to 1972, finally lost it in June 1972 to Roberto Duran of Panama by a KO in the thirteenth round and retired in 1973. Duran is still the world's lightweight champion.

It was Duran who fought in the live companion piece to the Ali-Frazier TV showing at the Nassau Coliseum on 30 September 1975. The attendance was a surprising 14,396 persons, or, in money, $241,106. It was a nontitle fight and a comedy feature between Duran and Edwin Viruet who made faces and stuck his tongue out at Duran all through the bout as he kept circling and running around in circles, intent on two objectives—making Duran look bad and avoiding any possibility of being knocked down. Duran cannot be blamed for his failure to make a good fight nor for his failure to catch up with his opponent and is still considered a great champion on a pound for pound basis.

FEATHERWEIGHT CLASS

The featherweight all-time list should include young Griffo, Jem Driscoll, and Johnny Dundee. Young Griffo, the Australian "shadow" who came to this country around 1894, was unbeatable, whether trained or untrained. This was the man who would stand on a handkerchief and dare anyone to hit him or make him move off. He was so quick he could pick flies out of the air with his hands. His defense was so perfect few boxers could hit him. Jem Driscoll was England's greatest featherweight who boxed at catch weights—or the weights he chose—whether or not he belonged in that category. He invaded the United States in 1901 and boxed a ten-round no-decision exhibition with Abe Attell, one of our best champions, who held the title here from 1908 until 1912. The Englishman clearly showed his superiority over the best here, and certainly was entitled to be recognized as the world's champion, even though he never officially won the title. Attell will be remembered for his participation in the "fix" of the infamous World

Series of 1919. Johnny Dundee, the Scotch Wop, born Joseppe Carrora, who liked a Scotch name, Scotch kilts, but not Scotch Whiskey fought over 300 battles. He won the title in 1923 from Eugene Criqui, a Frenchman who finally ended Johnny Kilbane's twelve-year reign of "no decision" bouts. Though Criqui was able to catch up with Kilbane, he was himself knocked out by Dundee. Dundee resigned his title in 1925 because he could no longer make the weight.   Willie Pep (William Papaleo) who became world's featherweight champion in 1942 by defeating Chalky Wright, was credited up to 1948 with one of the greatest records ever compiled by a boxer in the last fifty years. During that time, he had lost only one fight in 125 starts—to Lou Angott. His two strings of sixty-two consecutive victories are unusual in competition. His father turned him over as a successful amateur boxer (Connecticut State champion in 1938 and 1939) to veteran manager Lou Viscusi who handled him thereafter. Not even a serious airplane accident, which hospitalized Pep for some time, interfered with his record.

In 1948, Willie Pep lost his second fight—out of almost 150 starts—and the world's championship to Sandy Saddler, but in one of the greatest boxing exhibitions ever seen, defeated Saddler convincingly in a rematch and won back his title. However, Pep could hardly defeat both age and good opponents. Four colorful contenders in the persons of Sandy Saddler, Ray Famechon of France, Henry Davis, and Elis Ask of Finland awaited the opportunity to win his title.

70. Willie Pep, world's featherweight champion (1946–48, 1949–50). (Courtesy of Willie Pep and the Ring Magazine)

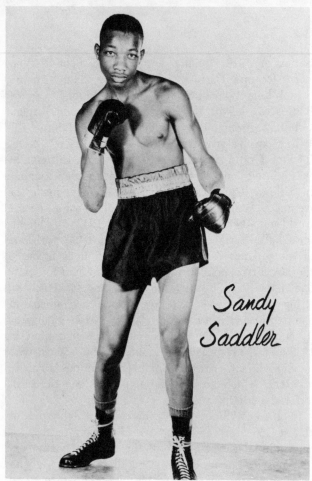

71. Sandy Saddler, world's featherweight champion (1948–49, 1950–57), (Ring Magazine)

Finally on 8 September 1950 Sandy Saddler finally rewon the title by halting Willy Pep at Yankee Stadium when Pep was unable to answer the bell for the eighth round due to an injury. Saddler was, incidentally, inducted into the Army in 1952 after defending his title successfully a number of times, and the N.B.A. recognized Percy "Kid" Bassey as an interim champion. In 1956, Saddler suffered an automobile accident in which he was seriously injured, after which he relinquished his title in 1957. After an elimination tournament Hogan "Kid" Bassey won the title by stopping Cherif Hamia in the tenth round in Paris and held it from 1957 to March 1959 when Davey Moore knocked him out at the end of the thirteenth round at Los Angeles, California. Davey Moore was more successful than his predecessors and kept the crown until March of 1963, namely, for four years but was ko'd in the eleventh round in Los Angeles, California, by Sugar Ramos who, in turn, was knocked out in the twelfth round in Mexico City by Vincente Saldivar whom we must signal as an outstanding champion and generally considered as a great perofrmer. He defended his title many times in many places. He ko'd Mexican Sugar Ramos in 1964, Floyd Robinson of Ghana in

1966, defeated on points Mitsunari Seki of Japan, in fifteen rounds, knocked out Seki in the seventh round in their next fight in Mexico City, in 1967, defeated Howard Winstone of Wales, in Cardiff, Wales and ko'd him the next time out in twelve rounds in Mexico City, and then announced his retirement. During an interim period of 1969, Johnny Famechon of the famous French boxing family of Famechons, but of Australia, won the title by decisioning Jose Legra of Spain in London. But Vincente Saldivar of Mexico returned to the ring and defeated Famechon in a fifteen-round bout in May 1970. Then out of the Far East in Japan came one Kuniaki Shibata who knocked out Saldivar in the thirteenth round of a championship fight in Tijuana, Mexico in December 1972, only to be knocked out in May 1972 by another Mexican, Clemente Sanchez, who vacated his title as he could no longer make the 126 pound limit. The championship was then split according to the various control bodies between Ernesto Marcel of Panama and Jose Legra of Spain. Then for a time the claimants recognized by various bodies were Billy Chacon of Los Angeles, California; Ruben Olivares of Mexico; and Alexis Arguello of Nicaragua. As of the prepublication deadline of this book, the generally accepted champion is Alexis Arguello of Nicaragua.

BANTAMWEIGHT CLASS

The names of the men who lead the bantamweight class in the history of boxing are George Dixon, who held the title from 1888 to 1891 and the featherweight crown from 1892 to 1900, Jimmy Barry, Terry McGovern, and Pete Herman.

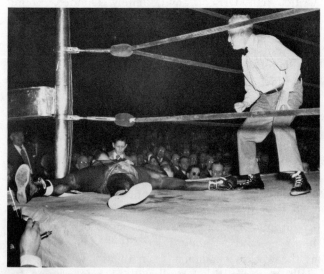

72. Downbeat of a knockout count—Jimmy McAllister knocked out by Willie Pep, 30 April 1946.

"Little Chocolate," as George Dixon was called, was a Halifax black who was king of the little men in the Gay Nineties. He even went to England to seek out worthwhile opponents and became undisputed bantam and featherweight champion of the world. He was a clever boxer and a devastating hitter for his size. George Dixon is important in the story of boxing, for it was his terrific punch for his size that led to our present padded ring floors. Until 1882, fights were held either on stages or on floors of pine-board or on turf. In a fight that year at Coney Island, New York, Dixon knocked out a fighter named Fred Johnson who hit the floor with the back of his head with such force that he almost died from concussion of the brain. As a result, the ring floor at the very next fight was crudely padded, and a new practice started, leading to our present padded but fast ring, which is constructed of tightly stretched canvas over felt, woolen or blanket padding.

McGovern won the bantam title in 1899 after Jimmy Barry had retired undefeated. Barry had held the American title since 1894 and in 1897 in London, England, obtained the world's title for America by knocking out Walter Croot in twenty rounds. Croot died after the knockout but Barry was exonerated by a coroner's jury. McGovern then relinquished the bantam title and defeated George Dixon in 1900 for the featherweight championship but lost it to Young Corbett in 1901.

Terrible Terry McGovern was therefore double champion at the turn of the century and sought opponents in the United States, Canada, Australia, and England. He was a principal in one of the few early, but widely publicized, international matches among the lighter men when he fought Pedlar Palmer, the British champion, at Tuckahoe, New York, in 1899. This international match did not last long, as the customary fury of McGovern's initial attack ended the fight in the first round. No opponent lasted more than a few rounds with McGovern in his prime.

Another great bantam, and one who remained a bantam, was Pete Herman, an Italian-American from New Orleans. Pete's followers traveled all over the country to see him fight and win. He never let them down and was one of the most popular champions of any weight in modern times. Herman became champion on 9 January 1917, when he outpointed the heavy-hitting Kid Williams. Although defeated by Joe Lynch in 1920, Herman came back to win his title again in 1921 but lost it a few months later when he was outpointed by Johnny Buff. Herman later became totally blind.

Joe Lynch who had held the title for a short time before, knocked out Johnny Buff in the New York

City Velodrome on 10 July 1922, and then the very popular New York boxer Abe Goldstein outpointed Joe Lynch in Madison Square Garden in fifteen rounds in March of 1924 only to be outpointed in turn by Eddie "Cannonball" Martin in the Garden in December of 1924. Charlie Rosenberg in 1925 outpointed Martin, but was deprived of his title when he was unable to make the weight for a scheduled championship bout with Bushy Graham, and the title was in controversy until 1927 when Bud Taylor beat Tony Canzoneri to win world recognition. But Taylor vacated the crown and from 1928 to 1929 Bushy Graham obtained some recognition, but also outgrew the class and, finally, in June 1929, Al Brown outpointed Vidal Gregario as a result of an elimination tournament and was recognized as the champion. In 1935, Baltazar Sangchili outpointed Al Brown at Valencia, Spain in fifteen rounds. He in turn was knocked out by Tony Marino in fourteen rounds in New York City and, in 1936, Sixto Escobar knocked out Tony Marino in thirteen rounds. Thirteen months later, Harry Jeffra beat Escobar on points in fifteen rounds in the New York City Polo Grounds. Then Escobar reversed the decision in 1933 in Puerto Rico and retired as champion in 1940. The title was in doubt for a while until Lou Salica gained official support of all until 7 August 1942 when Manuel Ortiz decisioned him in twelve rounds in Hollywood, California. Then came an almost unprecedented reign when Ortiz successfully defended his title eight times in 1943 and four times in 1944. He went into the U.S. Army in World War II in 1945 and, after his discharge, defended his title three times in 1946, winning all by KOs. In 1947 he was surprised by Harold Dade who defeated him by decision, but Ortiz promptly regained his title from Dade on points in 1947. After almost eight years in command of the division in a fifteen-round bout in faraway Johannesburg, South Africa, he was defeated by Vic Toweel by decision in 1950. But in 1952, again in Johannesburg, the title changed hands when Jimmy Carruthers KO'd Vic Toweel in one round and remained champion until 1954 when he retired undefeated after successfully defending his title against Chamran Songkitrat in Bangkok, Thailand. In September 1954, Robert Cohen of France defeated Songkitra in fifteen rounds for the title, which he held until KO'd by Italian Mario D'Agata in the sixth round in Rome. A North African, Alphonse Halimi, who learned his boxing in France, then decisioned D'Agata in Paris in 1957, but was then stopped by Joe Becerra, another Mexican, in the third round in Los Angeles. Joe Becerra retired in 1960 and there was a period of some confusion with respect to the titleholder, but the title finally was clearly earned by Elder Joffre, a Brazilian, who was the accepted champion for several years. This was until, in 1945, Fighting Harada of Japan outscored Joffre in Tokyo. The title remained in Japan until Lionel Rose, an Australian, beat Harada on points in Tokyo in 1968. The next year Ruben Olivares, of Mexico, defeated Rose by a fifth-round ко in Los Angeles, but Olivares was in turn ко'd by his fellow Mexican Chucho Castillo in the fourteenth round in Los Angeles. Then Ruben Olivares regained his title in 1971 on points at Los Angeles, California, with four rapid changes in less than three years— Rafael Herrera, Mexico; Enrique Pinder, Panama; and Romero Anaya, Mexico. The next champion, Arnold Taylor of South Africa, had a record of twelve kos, seventeen wins on decisions and four losses in a short six-year career. He retired because of weight problems but later returned as a featherweight.

After several claimants in an unclear situation on the championship, Soo Hwan Hong of South Korea became the accepted bantamweight titleholder. However, in June 1975, Alfonso Zamora, Olympic silver medal winner at Munich in 1972, ко'd Hong in the fourth round before some 14,000 spectators in Los Angeles, Calif. Zamora, at age twenty, becomes the youngest bantamweight champion in ring history. It was his twenty-first ко out of twenty-one pro fights. As the manuscript of this book is turned in, Zamora of Mexico is still the titleholder.

FLYWEIGHT CLASS

The flyweight class always brings up four names in two almost contemporary groups. The first group includes Jimmy Wilde and Pancho Villa. The other group includes Kid Chocolate and Fidel LaBarba. Jimmy Wilde was one of England's and the world's first and best flyweight champions. He was so small-boned and light, that even as a flyweight he gave away considerable weight, and often fought under considerable weight handicap. He was the fistic idol of England for years. He finally lost his title to a Filipino, Pancho Villa, who knocked him out in 1923. Villa died in 1925. Fidel LaBarba, a California schoolboy, won the title by defeating Frankie Genaro in 1925. He then retired to enter Stanford University, but later returned to the ring as a bantam and feather. LaBarba had previously won the World's Olympic Flyweight Championship in 1924. LaBarba, together with Jackie Fields and Petey Sarron, all later professional champions, were teammates of the late Eddie Eagan and the author on the 1924 United States world champion United States Olympic Team.

By a coincidence, LaBarba's predecessor, Genaro, was the 1920 World's Olympic Champion. Kid Chocolate was a Cuban sensation who came to New York and proceeded to lick everybody in sight. Chocolate and LaBarba fought three interesting bouts, with Chocolate winning two out of three.

No class or division suffered so much confusion as well as being the last to be recognized, namely, in 1910, and then only in England. The United States only recognized this division in 1920. No real world champion internationally recognized can be listed before Benny Lynch in 1935 or after Lynch's retirement from this class in 1938. However, in January 1943, Jackie Patterson ко'd Peter Kane in one round in Scotland and was internationally recognized as the flyweight champion, but in 1947 Rinty Monaghan defeated Little Dado Marino in London in fifteen rounds for N.B.A. recognition, although the British still recognized Patterson. In 1948 Monaghan ко'd Patterson in seven rounds to receive all world recognition. Rinty Monaghan not only became world flyweight champion, but was also an accomplished singer. Monaghan, like Charles Kid Thomas, sang from ringside at all his fights. Monaghan retired in 1950 and Terry Allen was considered the champion, but Allen was outpointed by Dado Marino in fifteen rounds in Honolulu. In 1952 Yoshio Shirai won a fifteen-round decision over Dado in Tokyo. Then, in November 1954, Pascual Perez, Olympic flyweight champion from Argentina, won the title in a fifteen-

73. Elis Ask, great featherweight prospect from Finland, his manager, Jack Dempsey, and Willie Pep, world's featherweight champion. (Einar Thulin)

TERRY McGOVERN

YOUNG CORBETT

74. Terrible Terry McGovern finally meets his match in young Corbett. (N.Y. Athletic Club)

round bout in Tokyo. Perez was an outstanding champion, a pet of the Argentine Dictator, Juan Peron, and retained his title for about six years, until April 1960, when he was defeated by a decision at the end of fifteen rounds with Pone Kingpetch in the latter's native Bangkok. But Pone lost it in 1962 by being ко'd in the eleventh round in Tokyo by Fighting Harada, the Japanese champion. In January 1963, however, Pone Kingpetch became the first man to ever regain the flyweight title by defeating Fighting Harada in fifteen rounds in Bangkok, but was ко'd in September 1963 by Hiroyuke Ebihara in the first round in Tokyo. But again Pone Kingpetch came back to win a decision over Ebihara and once more regained his title, but was beaten in 1965 by Salvatore Burruni, an Italian, in a fifteen-round decision in Rome. Then it seemed that the championship changed hands so rapidly that it was hard to keep track of. The champions were Walter McGowan of Scotland, Chartchai Chionoi of Thailand, Efran Torres of Mexico, Erbito Salvarria of the Philippines, and Venice Burkorsor of Thailand, who resigned his

75. Rinty Monaghan, Irish world flyweight champion from 1947–50 who was also a great singer and could have made the opera but chose to sing before his fights. Retired as champion for a singing career. (Ring Magazine)

flyweight title to fight as a bantamweight in 1973. Two Mexicans, Miguel Canto and Vincente Pool, were the leading contenders in 1974, with Canto being accepted generally as the champion in early 1975 and still the current titleholder.

There has been less and less interest taken in this class in the last few years, especially in the United States, due to the fact that Americans are evidently eating more and growing bigger, and there are fewer and fewer flyweights, namely, men who weigh less than 112 pounds. Also, opportunities as jockeys represent far less punishment—riding as opposed to boxing—for flyweights in the world of sports.

NEW JUNIOR TITLES

No treatment of weight classifications in modern times can avoid the much later addition of the so-called "junior" titles. They are all of very recent vintage and, in some cases, have been abandoned. Their creation, recognition, and legal or official approval is far too controversial to bear telling. Suffice it to say that over a period of years, from the 1920s on, generally speaking, only in the United States has there been any concerted movement for new weight categories. However, only two have earned any official recognition—although there have been efforts for junior flyweight, junior bantamweight, junior featherweight, and junior middleweight classes.—Junior lightweight and junior welterweight are the only survivors.

On 29 April 1946, Tippy Larkin, of Garfield, New Jersey, defeated Willie Joyce of Gary, Indiana in a twelve-round bout, which the Massachusetts State Athletic Commission recognized as the junior welterweight championship of the world. On 18 November 1921 Johnny Dundee and George "KO" Chaney fought for the championship of the 130 pound or junior lightweight class. Dundee won on a foul in the fifth round.

No official records exist in recognition of junior titleholders except those of junior lightweight and junior welterweight, although there were some claims of the maintenance and even recognition of junior titleholders in the junior middleweight class. In 1971 this title was won by Koiche Wajima of Japan from Carmela Bossi of Italy in Tokyo. Both men weighed in the 152–153 pound range.

However, junior welterweight and junior lightweight classifications have now become generally recognized with 140 pounds and 130 pounds as the maximum weight limits, as opposed to the 147 pounds and the 135 pound weight limits of the regular or usual weight limits of the welterweight and lightweight classes.

Many experts believe the junior titles are definitely synthetic because the weight differences of the regular classifications were arrived at by definite analysis and experience in the evaluation of weight, size, hitting power, and physical capacity to withstand punishment with proper increments of weight differences, namely, from flyweight to heavyweight, thusly: 6–8–9–12–13–15-pound differences to the unlimited difference over the light heavyweight 175 pound class limit.

The recognition of three added, although synthetic titles, has, of course, been of some promotional and financial value, but the three new classes have no great following and the titleholders rarely fight only within their class. The latest convert to acceptance of the new categories, *Ring Magazine,* has, of course, helped.

75A. Victor Galindez, current Light Heavyweight Champion of the World (**Courtesy,** Ring Magazine)

75B. Carlos Monzon, current Middleweight Champion of the World (**Courtesy,** Ring Magazine)

75C. John Stacey, current Welterweight Champion of the World (**Courtesy,** Ring Magazine)

75D. Roberto Duran, current Lightweight Champion of the World (**Courtesy,** Ring Maagazine)

75F. Alex Arguello, current Featherweight Champion of the World (**Courtesy,** Ring Magazine)

75E. Ben Villaflor, current Junior Lightweight Champion of the World (**Courtesy,** Ring Magazine)

75G. Miguel Canto, current Flyweight Champion of the World (**Courtesy,** Ring Mazagine)

FEMALE BOXING

As in all sports and fields of human endeavor, women want and are getting equal rights. Women in fencing, bowling, riding, shooting, basketball, and even in wrestling, have been emancipated. Women will now be in attendance and graduate from West Point, Annapolis, and the Air Force Academy. Perhaps future generals and admirals will be women. Women have won Olympic medals in competition not only among themselves but against men. Women have now invaded boxing. Believe it or not, professional women boxers and boxing matches have been licensed in several states. A query to the New York State Athletic Commission resulted in the answer that women applicants and women bouts in any weight classification would be turned down but if taken to the courts, based on the latest precedents, the New York State Athletic Commission would have to follow any legal ruling with respect to boxing competition for women. However, at least one other state is regularly licensing women boxers and women boxing matches, and therefore women's boxing must be included in this book as the latest development in the story of the fist.

75H. Caroline Svendsen, "First Lady" of prize-fighting (Courtesy, Ted Walker)

76. Dr. Eddie Flynn of New Orleans, Louisiana. United States Intercollegiate National Amateur, and World Olympic welterweight titleholder in 1932, but refused to turn pro. (New Orleans Item)

In Nevada, women prizefighters have been duly licensed, and in Virginia City, in an impromptu boxing site next to the Bucket of Blood Saloon in the former silvermining town near Reno, a preliminary bout was run off with Caroline Svendsen the winner by a ко in fifty seconds of the first round in a women's welterweight bout. The loser was Jean Lange of Phoenix. Both obtained their licenses with the help of the antisex discrimination ban. Miss Svendsen is half French and half Danish, has blue eyes, blonde hair stacked on top of her head, and is twice a grandmother, having first married at thirteen. She is twice divorced and currently single. Her unusual breakthrough, her knockout, and her glamour broke another record. Her story and picture were featured on the front page of the *Wall Street Journal* of 4 November 1975.

Whether women's boxing in all weights, in all or in some countries, will follow, remains to be seen, but a start has certainly been made and duly noted. In Southeast Asia, reports of professional boxing and savate matches (a form of boxing using both feet and fists, first developed in France) were customary and seen by many between the two World Wars.

77. Fidel La Barba, amateur, Olympic, and, later, world's professional flyweight champ.

8 • Mirrors of Boxing—the Fist in Literature, Art, Theatre, Movies, Radio, and T. V.

The saga of the fist is mirrored in art and literature. In every age and in every country, boxing has inspired lasting poetry and prose, while artists working in many mediums have depicted it in enduring masterpieces. Boxing has also appealed to dramatists from time immemorial. The theatre, motion pictures, radio, and more recently, television have projected the drama of boxing. Ancient Socrates opined centuries ago, "Do you not suppose that a single boxer who is perfect in his art would easily be a match for two or more well-to-do gentlemen who are not boxers?" This same theme has been used effectively for centuries in all forms of entertainment.

Except for a few hieroglyphics and paintings in tombs of the pharaohs, there are no records of boxing in the Ethiopian or Egyptian period, but it was a favorite subject for decorated vases and primitive friezes during the Minoan period in Crete. These have been discovered within the last seventy years and can be seen in many museums. One of the most famous is a Minoan vase found in Cyprus, dating around 1100 B.C. The antiquity of the sport is most evident in this piece of ancient artistry, for it shows that boxing had attained a prominence in Crete great enough to cause its spread to colonial Cyprus, and implies the development of the sport by many previous generations.

The first Golden Age of boxing in ancient Greece was also the first Golden Age of boxing in art and literature. In fact, it can be safely said that our present era, while surpassing the ancient one in the sport itself, has not surpassed it in its art and literature.

The first writer of ancient times to come to our mind is Homer, who gives us our clearest picture of the sport over three thousand years ago. A bout between Euryalous and Epeios is described in the *Iliad*, and in the *Odyssey* he chronicles the life and fistic record of our first world's heavyweight champion, Odysseus (Ulysses).

Plato, Socrates, and Aristotle all showed great interest in boxing and reveal to us a general concept of its purpose and practice in ancient times. Plato makes the following surprisingly modern statement:

Surely, if we were boxers, we should have been learning to fight many days before, and exercising ourselves in imitating all those blows and wards which we were intending to use in the hour of conflict; and in order that we might come as near to reality as possible, we should put on soft cestus that the blows and the wards might be practiced by us to the utmost of our power, and, if there were a lack of sparring partners, the ridicule of fools would not deter us from hanging up a lifeless image and practicing at that.

Plato knew that boxers had to train and that it was better for them to wear heavy training gloves or work on a heavy bag than to pull punches in training. Who can doubt therefore that boxing was well developed in those ancient days? Theocritus, in his *Dioscuri*, describes for us the great boxer Pollux. Literature has confused us with respect to this character, for he is sometimes called Polydeuces and there are at least four entirely different versions of his fight with Amycus.

Lucilius, who came much later, when boxing had

78. Early Italian school of painting Ulysses and His Men—**showing use of rocks in hand as early fistic weapon. (Courtesy of Vassar College Art Gallery)**

78A. Famous painting Thumbs Down, **depicting Roman gladiator in combat. (Courtesy of Frick Art Reference Library)**

deteriorated, might well be compared with the late Damon Runyon. In his *Epigrams* he used the boxing jargon of the day and poked fun at poor characters dented by fists, such as, "Augustus who once had a nose, a chin, a forehead, ears and eyelids, but lost them all in the ring." He acquaints us with the fact that boxers who assimilated too much punishment walked on their heels in ancient Greece just as they did along "Jacobs Beach" yesterday. He tells us of one old punch-drunk fighter who married a "dame" who beat him and sent him out to beg every day. Another he describes as being devoid of memory and having a head "like a sieve or the lower edge of a worm-eaten book."

The Roman poet Virgil writes about Greek boxing, particularly the fight between Dares and Entellus. Pausanias, however, is our greatest source of ancient information on boxing. He was the "columnist" of his day, although his greatest living work is a detailed description of Olympia and its magnificent statues and the works of the great Greek sculptors. These statues of the gods, the goddesses, and the Olympic victors have been, with few exceptions, destroyed. Unfortunately, earthquakes, a river changing its course, wars, and the jealous sabotage of the Romans have left very few of them, and we must rely mainly on the record of Pausanias to recreate Olympia and the Golden Age for us.

As if to prove the high esteem in which athletics were held by the ancients, while many of the vases, friezes, and statues that have come down to us depict scenes from, or heroes of, other games and sports, boxing is clearly the favorite. It would appear that the Romans were jealous of Greek superiority in athletic contests, for they are responsible for the destruction of almost all the statues of the greatest Olympic boxers and most of their records. Extensive search has resulted in finding only the base of a statue of Theagenes, a statue of a seated boxer believed by all experts to be Cleitomachus, and pieces of the statues of Caprus, Agias, and a few other less known boxers and wrestlers. A number of statues of Milo of Croton, more famous as a wrestler than a boxer, have been found. However, none of these is an athletic pose, but all depict him as he died, with his hand caught in a tree and being eaten by wolves. Probably this appealed to the Romans' sense of humor, who did not destory any of these, believing that they ridiculed a great Greek athletic hero.

It is unfortunate indeed that the mirror of boxing has come down to us so badly cracked, but even in that condition it casts a bright light on the first Golden Age of boxing. The statues that are left are among the greatest works of sculpture in the world.

The Roman era resulted in the decline of boxing and this is reflected in the paucity of art or literature on the subject. Artists of Roman times dipped into the past for their inspiration, for the true spirit of athletics had waned with the advance of Rome, and the glories of Greece were fading. It must be remembered that Rome brought dictatorship and the end of Greek democracies and boxing has always died with tyranny—as proven by history.

One thing that makes a study of the development of boxing somewhat confusing is the fact that the ancients were flagrantly guilty of anachronisms. A modern writer or dramatist describing a boxing scene of a previous age would portray it as it existed in that period. Movies and the radio today spend much time on research just to prevent anachronisms. However, the Romans deliberately and consistently misinterpreted the details of the past. Virgil, the Roman writer, describes a bout that took place a thousand years before his time, in Homer's day, yet he puts on the hands of the boxers the cruel Roman cestus and runs off the match according to Roman rules. Homer tells us definitely that boxing in his time was carried on either with the bare fist or with soft leather thong wrappings.

For twelve hundred years, between the fall of Rome and the beginning of modern boxing in England about 1700, the sport was hibernating. During this time it was no longer a subject for writers or artists, and in the absence of any record we rightly conclude it was nonexistent. But with its awakening in England, we find Richard Steele, Samuel Johnson, Paul Whitehead, the French writer Diderot, George Coleman, William Hazlett, and great artists such as Hogarth, all reflecting its rebirth in their works.

Samuel Johnson in his dictionary of the English language, tells us that "box" came from "bock," meaning "the cheek" in Welsh, and signifies a blow on the head given with the hand. He further claims that "to box" is "to fight with the fist" and that a "boxer" is "a man who fought with his fists." Diderot, in his Encyclopedia, offers the best description ever given of the various forms of Greek and Roman cesti, showing that he must have made an exhaustive research into the development of the use of the fist both as a weapon and in sport. According to him the primitive glove derived its name "cestus" from the Greek word meaning "ants." The connection was based on the fact that the sensation resulting from a punch with the cestus was similar to that caused by the sting of ants. Another version of the origin claims that it means "girdle or wrapping," hence leather wrappings for the hands.

Generally speaking, literature and art reflect the ups and downs of the sport. Figg, Broughton, and later Gentleman Jackson, all attracted artists and

79. Dempsey and Firpo, painting by George Bellows. (Whitney Museum of American Art)

writers to the prize ring, and its followers included Thomas Moore and Lord Byron who were close friends of Gentleman Jackson. Lord Byron for many years took boxing lessons from Jackson, and in spite of his club foot was considered an adept boxer. In this connection it is interesting to note that a number of men with physical deformities have been successful boxers and usually terrific punchers. Tami Mauriello, who once fought Joe Louis, limps; William Perry, called the "Tipton Slasher," English bare-knuckle champion in 1856, had a game leg; an intercollegiate boxer from the Massachusetts Institute of Technology in the early 1920s, named O'Malley, was a successful competitor and terrific puncher in spite of a definite limp.

Lord Byron, in addition to being a good boxer, was interested in all phases of the game. It is said that his interest in boxing led him to investigate personally the home of its first golden era and that this trip to Greece, while urged on by the same reasons which have sent many a modern pugilist to foreign shores—creditors and women—was undertaken to search for the statues and records of Theagenes.

When Byron sparred with Jackson he wore "mufflers" or "Broughtons," as boxing gloves were called in those days, and in spite of his size, 5 feet 8½ inches tall, he was rated by his contemporary boxing friends as a "hard hitter." He voiced the attitude of the fashionable young men of his day when he wrote in his *Hints from Horace*:

> And men unpracticed in exchanging knocks
> Must go to Jackson ere they dare to box.

The prints, engravings, mezzotints, and paintings of boxing in the past two centuries are outstanding. One of the most interesting private collections in America was once owned by Mr. Paul Magriel.

Like the Romans and the Greeks and our writers today, some writers of the English bare-fist period were ironic in their description of pugilism, notably Victor Hugo in *The Man Who Laughed*. A great admirer of boxing in this time was Sir Walter Scott. In fact, he thought so well of the sport that he undertook to act as an adviser to young men interested in becoming prizefighters. In writing to one of these, he stressed the difficulties of professional boxing: "I do not find fault with your ambition to try to stand in the London P. R., but mind you are not made foolish in the experiment. The accepted men of every class in the great metropolis of England have

all been put to the test of severe trials before they were enabled to obtain anything like popularity or eminence. So beware of the ridiculous."

No account of boxing in literature can omit reference to George Borrow's *Lavengro,* William M. Thackeray's poem inspired by the Heenan-Sayers fight, and Thomas Hughes's *School Days at Rugby.* Sir Arthur Conan Doyle's *Rodney Stone* was inspired by the Quinn-Naylor Glasgow fight between two rival gang leaders. The influence of boxing on Doyle is evident in his fabulous detective creation, *Sherlock Holmes.* Holmes, it will be remembered, was a handy man with his fists, a prominent amateur often approached by managers and promoters to turn professional. However, unfortunately for boxing and fortunately for detective story addicts, he remained faithful to the profession chosen for him by Doyle.

At the beginning of the twentieth century we find the start of a long and celebrated line of reportorial writers on boxing.

O. Henry and Arnold Bennett contributed important writings on the sport and Richard Harding Davis in his newspaper story, *Gallegher,* projected the trials and tribulations, the color and dramatic suspense, of prizefights in the days when they were illegal and when spectators not only had to stand for hours exposed to all kinds of weather, but were liable to the intervention of the police, with the subsequent night in jail and trial in court.

No coverage of boxing literature could omit Nellie Bly, the first newspaperwoman assigned to boxing. She even went to Muldoon's White Plains training camp, chaperoned by her mother, to give the world an account of the Muldoon-Sullivan training routine. While forbidden to witness the Sullivan-Kilrain fight, she was the first person to interview Sullivan after the fight.

Many well-known contemporary writers began as sports reporters and were particularly interested in boxing. Among these, to name just a few, are Joe Williams, Sinclair Lewis, Paul Gallico, and Westbrook Pegler. The first great reporter of fights in the United States was Robert H. Davis, whose *Ruby Robert* and the descriptions of the Fitzsimmons-Corbett fight will probably live forever. Jack London, Irvin S. Cobb, Ernest Hemingway, Donn Byrne, Ring Lardner, and Damon Runyon also contributed boxing literature that will never die. Joe Williams, the dean of sports editors with a special interest in boxing, labelled the original 1949 edition of this book "the world's heavyweight champion of all books on boxing."

The articles and poems of Grantland Rice, the dean of modern sports writers, cannot be overlooked. No era of boxing will have a more accurate or a more colorful contemporary recorder than "Granny." The columns of Arthur Daley and Red Smith often highlight the fist and its followers. Many excellent writers today are specialized writers on boxing. Among these are Al Buck, former boxing editor of the *New York Post Home News* and president of the Boxing Writers Association; Elmer Ferguson, sports editor of *The Herald*, Montreal, Canada; Harry B. Smith, sports editor emeritus of the *San Francisco Chronicle*; Jesse Abramson, boxing editor of *The New York Herald Tribune*; Lester Bromberg of the *New York World-Telegram*; and—the giant among boxing writers in foreign fields—Horacio Estol of Buenos Aires, Argentina. Dan Parker takes the prize for being the most vitriolic writer to take more than an occasional interest in boxing.

Dan Parker accused me on 17 February 1961 of a connection with Frank Carbo, which cost him and his publisher an apology and a cash settlement when I sued for libel. My only connection with Carbo was that a French fighter I comanaged, Laurent Dauthuille, fought Jake LaMotta for the world's middleweight title. LaMotta was alleged to have been a Carbo controlled boxer. I am absolutely certain that the title fight, which was won by LaMotta, was on the level. I was fortunately able to prove not only the fact that I had no connection with Carbo, but that the publisher had previous relations with me in connection with an FBI and Army Intelligence matter and knew I had the highest security clearance.

New York Mirror

GREAT AMONG THE WORLD'S GREAT NEWSPAPERS

235 East 45th St., New York City   MUrray Hill 2-1000

Office of the Editor

February 17, 1961

Dear Sir:

In connection with the settlement of a recent lawsuit brought by you on the basis of certain statements of Dan Parker, susceptible to the interpretation that you were associated with one Frank Carbo, I wish to make the following statement:

Investigation has not revealed that you had any such association, or even acquaintance, with Frank Carbo except that he sought to acquire an interest in a contract you had as manager of a boxer and that you rejected these advances.

In my opinion, Mr. Parker misinterpreted your article on the political supervision of boxing and that his conception of your meaning was unjustified. You will no doubt agree that Parker is a sincere enemy of the skulduggery incident to boxing, and was perhaps overzealous in grasping every opportunity to belabor Carbo for his machinations. We were advised by counsel that an impartial tribunal would not interpret your article as Parker did, and that counsel was devoid of any material which would impair your standing.

Please be advised that there was never any malice in connection with the item and that the management of the New York Mirror continues to hold you in the same esteem as before and regrets this inept publication.

Yours truly,

GLENN NEVILLE
Editor-in-Chief

General John V. Grombach
113 West 57th Street
New York 19, New York

81. Letter of apology from the New York Mirror **to the author in connection with the cash settlement of a libel suit in which an incorrect and libelous claim was made against the author by the Hearst newspaper.**

MIGHTY MIRROR—SECOND LARGEST DAILY AND SUNDAY CIRCULATION

133

. Boxing experts consider this oil by McClelland
rclay one of the finest contemporary action
intings. (N.Y. Athletic Club)

Jeffrey Farnol, of course, is in a class by himself. His articles and romantic novels revolving around boxing are among the most interesting in literature. *The Amateur Gentleman*, a favorite of several generations, has been published and republished, dramatized and redramatized, adapted for stage, screen and radio, so often and in so many languages, that a count is difficult. Unfortunately, through improper handling, a dramatization of this delightful novel was not successful in a radio presentation starring Leslie Howard.

No story about radio would be complete without an account of the history of boxing on the airwaves. The first World Championship fight to be broadcast was the Dempsey-Carpentier contest on 2 July 1921 (N.B.C.). Then came the Leonard-Tendler, 27 July 1922; Leonard-Tendler, 23 July 1923; Johnny Wilson-Harry Greb, 31 August 1923; and. Dempsey-Firpo, 14 September 1923. Many people believe the first network broadcast on many stations of a world championship fight was the first Tunney-Dempsey fight. Actually, the first world championship fight to be broadcast to the entire world on a commercial basis with every kind of promotion and merchandising tie-up was the Baer-Carnera fight (N.B.C.) sponsored by The B. F. Goodrich Co. The first of the now famous Gillette Cavalcade of Sport broadcasts, which still brings boxing and sports events to the world via commercially sponsored broadcasts, was the radio reporting of the next heavyweight title bout, the Baer-Braddock fight. Both these commercially sponsored world broadcasts, and the next major fight—the Baer-Louis fight broadcast by General Motors—were arranged in connection with Baer's original fight contracts. Thereafter, world championship fight broadcasts were no longer sold or bid for individually but the broadcasting rights became a part of overall contracts or arrangements made by Jacobs at the time the fighters were signed. Thus broadcast and television rights were then sold by the promoter for his own best interests, which were not necessarily for the best interests of the fighters.

The first major fight to be televised in the United States was the Baer-Nova fight, 1 June 1939 (N.B.C.). The first television broadcast of a major fight in Europe (England) was that of Tommy Farr vs. Max Baer, 15 April 1937. Amateur fights and exhibitions had been broadcast in the United States previously by the Columbia Broadcasting System. Commercial television licenses were not granted until just before the war, and the war then interfered. But N.B.C.-R.C.A., unable to do any commercial television and needing actual experience in this medium, installed sets in various veterans' hospitals and broadcast fights as a special service to the wounded veterans. Then N.B.C. for some time handled the telecasts to the fights from Madison Square Garden through an overall agreement with that organization which gave the fighters and their managers no negotiating rights whatever. John Royal, himself an ardent fight fan and ex-boxer, as N.B.C. Vice-President in charge of television, was responsible for the veteran broadcasts. It is doubtful if he had personally missed any championship fights.

With the amalgamation of many of the biggest interests in professional boxing into the International Boxing Club (IBC), alias Octopus Inc., the radio and television rights had become highly involved in promises, agreements, and doubts. In 1949, IBC had committed the television rights to their Madison Square Garden fights to Gillette and N.B.C., the television rights to their St. Nicholas Arena fights to Gillette and C.B.S., and had until then decided to stop televising their big outdoor fights in fear that television might compete with the boxoffice. If the big fights were to be televised later, the rights were to be divided between N.B.C. and C.B.S. but were to be sold on a catch-as-catch-can basis to sponsors —although it was rumored Gillette had an option on N.B.C. fights and a beer manufacturer on C.B.S. fights. The radio rights to Madison Square Garden fights were to go to Gillette as first initiated by the author in 1935 and Gillette would also have the radio rights to IBC outdoor fights. These fights would be carried by American Broadcasting System although major world's championship fights could be put on a number of networks and short-waved to the world as well. N.B.C. and C.B.S. were not too interested in weekly fights as 10:00 P.M. Eastern Daylight Saving Time interfered with major commercial program schedules.

Of course the problem which eventually broke down this entire system was that top stars in boxing, like top stars in any entertainment medium, and their managers soon discovered that they could get far more money on a purely competitive basis for each appearance. The author, as radio manager of Max Baer, after obtaining the radio rights to a single fight and because of the entertainment appeal of Baer fights, once had five sponsors bidding for the radio rights and (notwithstanding an agreement between the major networks not to bid against each other) an approach from one network to "purchase an option."

Later, a LaMotta-Robinson match placed on the open market in both radio and television would bring far more money to the fighters than their share in the single broadcast of the year-around IBC contract with Gillette who were forced to take the IBC's John Doe versus Charlie Klotz fight on the following week.

Television, according to well-informed sources in

1949, had increased and not decreased interest and attendances in wrestling and baseball. Radio, although scheduled to be the death knell of home records, resulted in the largest sale and upsurge the phonograph recording business ever experienced. Boxing, on the other hand, was the greatest factor in the start of the motion picture industry and the greatest attraction in television. Major fights on the radio have not only outpulled the greatest entertainment programs studded with picture stars, but have attracted more listeners than even the fireside talks and speeches of President Roosevelt in World War II. A survey made by the author showed that a 1949 fight in New York City was seen via television in 16,500 bars and restaurants in New York City alone.

Today and tomorrow, 1975, and thereafter, literally hundreds of television stations are and will be located all over—not only in the United States, but over the entire world. The genius and inventiveness of man that has harnessed the atom has also made possible not only television but the relay of television waves of light and sound via satellites. Today, a fight at Cape Town, South Africa, New York City, United States, London, England, Moscow, Russia, Buenos Aires, Argentina, Kinshasa, Zaire, or on a temporary coral reef or a newly formed rock island belonging to no one and without taxes or controls, can be televised to thousands of arenas, stadiums, and theaters all over the world. As extraordinary as this may be, it is the present mirror of boxing that these same fights can later be televised into the homes of millions to advertise razor blades or beer. More writers and artists will be inspired to produce masterpieces of art and literature on the fist and world champions of boxing.

In the field of modern art, Thomas Eakins, Dame Laura Knight, and George Bellows have given their talents to the portrayal of boxing. To many boxers and followers of the sport, one of the greatest artists to portray boxing scenes and characters was a man identified primarily with pictures of feminine glamor. McClelland Barclay, an outstanding athlete himself, and an excellent boxer, was able to bring to his pictures an accuracy in technical detail which the fighter

and fight fan appreciated. When Commander Barclay was reported missing in action and later declared killed in action in the South Pacific, the sport lost one of its most articulate patrons. One of his finest fight paintings was exhibited for a long time in the lobby of The New York Athletic Club.

James Chapin, a leading modern artist, has been interested in the sport since boyhood, both as spectator and amateur. This is apparent in his accurate and sensitive fight pictures, *Fighter and His Manager*, *Negro Boxer*, and *Beaten Boxer*.

82. Famous boxing painting by George Bellows: Introducing John L. Sullivan—1923, with permission from private collector.

James Montgomery Flagg also has done some colorful paintings and murals of world championship fights and world champions. He did the mural of the Dempsey-Willard fight that hung for many years in Jack Dempsey's restaurant in New York City. When the Dempsey restaurant closed, Dempsey gave the painting to the Smithsonian Institute in Washington.

Today boxing is also brilliantly mirrored by the statues and sketches of Mahonri Young, the lithographs and oils of Robert Riggs, the paintings of John Groth, and the lithographs and water colors of Joseph W. Golimkin.

The artists of each period in which boxing flourished were attracted by the drama of the sport, the color and physical qualities of the fighters. Paul Landowsky, J. Ellys, John Berridge, Ben Marshal, T. Gericault, and Currier and Ives portrayed fighters and fight scenes, and even Staffordshire pottery reproduced Tom Molyneux, the first of the great Negro fighters in modern times.

An exhibition of art in boxing entitled *The Ring and the Glove* was presented at the Museum of the City of New York between 19 November and 4 April 1948. It drew great attention and later toured the United States.

In the opinion of many experts, both in and out of the ring, the best contribution in verse which mirrors the sport today both from the standpoint of sympathy and technical exactness is the narrative poem *The Set-Up* by Joseph Moncure March. March, later a writer in Hollywood, was born and brought up in New York City on the upper West Side. As he himself states, "I lived in a district where the citizens had an intense and scientific preoccupation in the art of bouncing their knuckles off somebody's jaw and from an early age I took for granted that being expert with my fist was important." He boxed in amateur contests while in college and was coached by a black ex-prizefighter, Doc Newport. Although always a fight fan, it was years later before he wrote *The Set-Up*. He was inspired to do so by a painting by his friend James Chapin, an artist already mentioned in this chapter. Chapin's large canvas of a black prizefighter sitting in his corner with his handlers above him made March decide to write a narrative about a black prizefighter, and *The Set-Up* resulted. The poem was the basis for a 1949 R.K.O. picture bearing the same name.

One man in our time has done more for the establishment of permanent and complete boxing records than any other individual alive or dead. This man, the late Nat Fleischer, had devoted an active lifetime to the collection, evaluation, writing, and publication of boxing facts. His *Ring Record Books* and other reference works present, in orderly fashion, data culled from thousands of sources. His stories of pugilism and pugilists, his boxing manuals, and *The Ring* magazine which he published were and still are a definite part of the sport today. They are worthy continuations of the first boxing manual by Captain Godfrey, published in 1747; the first record book by Pierce Egan, published in 1812; and the first boxing magazine by Thomas Fewtrell in 1790—all of which dealt with the bare-fist era in old England. Today, Fleischer's son-in-law Nat Loubet carries on the magazine and the Boxing Encyclopedia and Record Book.

The theatre, motion pictures, and radio have turned to boxing for plot and characterizations, with varied success. On the stage, *Is Zat So* and *Golden Boy* were authentic and entertaining plays. Radio, due to the fact that it is controlled by commercial and not by artistic interests, has been less successful. Radio has attempted to present in its leading boxing roles either fighters themselves, or actors who do not properly fulfill the visual picture. The sad

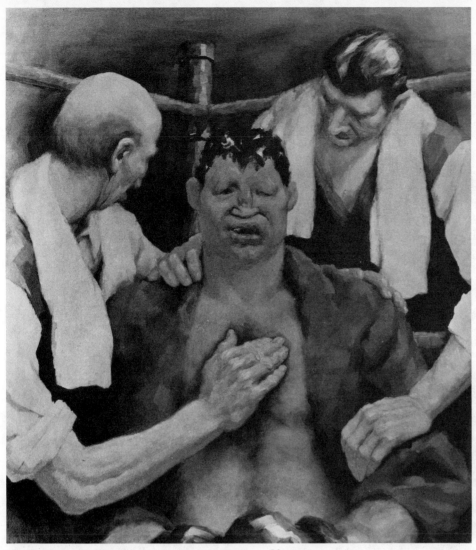

83. Boxer and handlers, painting by James Chapin.

fate of *The Amateur Gentleman*, already mentioned, is illustrative of the latter. Most boxers are not actors, and even those who have some ability must be carefully directed and coached. Above all else, their vehicles and the character they project must be carefully studied and planned. Failure results if this is not done. James J. Braddock in a comedy skit series and the earlier dramatic ventures of Jack Dempsey, bear this out.

However, there have been some notable fistic radio successes such as the sports program of Jack Dempsey which dramatized his important fights, and the radio program serials of the voluble Mr. Baer. The success of these was due to several factors— type casting, individual coaching, and sympathetic direction—but especially to a vehicle conceived for and a script written to suit the personality of the star.

In Max Baer's first coast-to-coast serial, *Taxi*, sponsored by an automobile tire manufacturer, he was "a taxi driver with a penchant for blondes." The blondes kept hiring his cab and then lured him into any number of heroic or comedy situations. This series was tied up with the commercial broadcast of the Baer-Carnera fight. At that fight Baer wore silk bathrobes —the one for his entrance having his motion picture name "Steve Morgan," from M.G.M.'s *The Prize-Fighter and the Lady*, and the robe for his exit showing his radio name, Al Harper, across the back. In his second coast-to-coast series the following year, Baer was *Lucky Smith*, a private detective "with a punch," who preferred "action to theory." The prominent playwright and director, Garson Kanin, then an actor, played Baer's sidekick in both these serials. The program was tied up with Baer's first defense of his title against Braddock. This may be an important turning point in the saga of the fist because it marked the first time that other considerations, beyond a share in wagers or in profits from the paid attendance of spectators, impelled a champion to put his title "on the line."

Without a coast-to-coast weekly commercial radio program and a possible motion picture based on it, and the sale of the fight broadcast along with the serial, Baer would not have been interested in fighting Braddock. It is further questionable if he would

137

Broadcasting of the Max Baer Radio Program
Berkeley Carteret Hotel   Asbury Park N.J.

Policastro Studio
Asbury Park N.J.

84 Max Baer broadcasts his weekly serial, "Taxi," from a portable studio at his 1934 training camp. Among the cast shown with him are Garson Kanin, Graham McNamee, and Jerry Macy.

have fought at all under the aegis of the Madison Square Garden, and this might have broken up a long monopoly of the control of the world's heavyweight championship—a control first held exclusively by Tex Rickard and the Madison Square Garden Corporation, later acquired by Mike Jacobs and the Twentieth Century Sporting Club and previously covered in detail in this book. Baer signed for the Braddock fight only because a radio series and a movie were tied up with the world broadcast rights promised him by the Garden if he signed for a world's championship fight, and Braddock was the only contender available. Baer and his manager, Ancil Hoffman, took the match because their share of proceeds of the sale of the radio series and the world fight broadcast rights was far in excess of the forty percent share of the gate the champion would receive for defending his title, and they furthermore knew that if Baer retained the championship (which was

expected) the picture rights and renewed radio contracts would be worth a great deal more. The renewal options on Baers' radio serial, plus a movie option to "picturize" the serial if he had defeated Braddock, totaled a half million dollars.

Radio, therefore, a mirror of boxing, was, on this occasion, responsible for the first time for bringing about a world's championship fight and an unexpected transfer of the title.

From a publicity angle, there is also an interesting anecdote to tell for the first time relative to this program. At the height of the serial, and just prior to the Braddock-Baer fight, the sponsor wanted worldwide, front-page publicity for his broadcasts and for the worldwide fight broadcast which he had contracted to sponsor. Max Baer was "accidentally" shot in a tense moment as he was making a "pinch" in one of the weekly *Lucky Smith* mysteries. The burned clothes, the blood, ambulance, and nurses, were all part of the plan and resulted in first-page stories everywhere. For a few days there was even some talk of a postponement of the fight.

There is an interesting slant about radio and boxing. Before any fighter or boxer broadcasts on the air, he must belong to the radio actors' union and pay his annual dues. Fortunately, boxing has not yet become that complicated, so if a radio actor wants to be put to sleep by the lethal punch of some pug, he does not have to join any boxers' union; but he has to be licensed for a fee by the New York State Athletic Commission, if the fight is an official one.

Boxing has been a popular subject in motion pictures from its very beginning. In the early days of the industry, the British did some outstanding pictures based on Pierce Egan's stories of life in old London, which were so much admired by Thackeray. The lives of some of the bare-knuckle champions were dramatized for the films, and in the picture *The Call of the Road*, probably the greatest of the British fight pictures, the producer filmed the fights in Epping Forest outside London on the very sites of the original contests.

In 1924 an American motion picture on the fight game called *The Gay White Way* was filmed by Cosmopolitan Pictures in the old Madison Square Garden. Anita Stewart was the star and the longest boxing sequence in this picture was a match between a professional heavyweight from England and an American amateur. Jack Dempsey was featured in another Cosmopolitan Picture, *The Idol of Millions*,

86. The Baer brothers, Bud and Max.

the same title as his last and most successful coast-to-coast radio series. In 1931 R.K.O. made a prize-fight picture called *Slow Poison*, starring James Gleason. In 1932 Paramount produced a picture entitled *Madison Square Garden*, starring Jack Oakie, Thomas Meighan, Marion Nixon, Warren Hymer, William Collier, William Boyd, and Zasu Pitts, and brought to the screen many old-time boxers such as Tommy Ryan, middleweight champion from 1897 to 1907, Billy Papke, and others. A boxing picture, *The Milky Way*, was one of Harold Lloyd's best pictures and the same story was later readapted as a starring vehicle for Danny Kaye, called *A Kid from Brooklyn*.

Max Baer established a new record in the motion picture business when he was starred with Myrna Loy, Otto Kreuger, Walter Huston, and others in a picture entitled *The Prize-Fighter and the Lady*. In addition to starring Baer, it featured Jack Dempsey as referee and Primo Carnera, then world's heavyweight champion. For the second time in boxing history, two contestants met in the prizering prior to their championship fight when Baer and Carnera fought for the world's championship in the motion picture story. Its counterpart was the sparring match in full-dress clothes between champion Sullivan and challenger Corbett on the stage of the San Francisco Opera House prior to their championship tilt.

It is interesting to know that in the motion picture in question, Carnera and his managers insisted that the champion had to "win." After many nights of argument on the movie set a compromise was reached and it was agreed the "picture" fight should end in a draw.

The problems surrounding the handling of Baer and Carnera on the movie lot, particularly in their fight scenes, were difficult. The picture was held up for many days by the artistic temperament, not of the actors, but of the fighters, and was finally finished only because M.G.M. called upon its trouble shooter,

85. "Tell your mother the hell with the dishes, Max Baer is playing at the movies." (Esquire Inc.)

William Van Dyke, to handle the situation. Van Dyke, a tough character who later became a Colonel in the Marine Corps, sized up the situation as follows: He could browbeat Carnera but would have to think up something more spectacular to get Baer under his thumb, which he proceeded to do. At the psychological moment when Baer started an argument, Van Dyke pretended to lose his temper, drew a revolver from his pocket and fired it at Baer. At the same time, a movie prop man dropped a heavy sandbag from a scaffold so as to miss Baer by inches, and another helper swung a portable crane arm against the back of Baer's legs, clipping him neatly and flopping him on his back with a sharp thud. Baer turned deathly pale. Mr. Van Dyke apologized but added rather firmly, "Will you behave?" Baer behaved from then on.

Baer, after boxing Carnera for the cameras, was certain he could defeat him in the ring. Corbett, it will be remembered, after he boxed the champion on a stage, believed he could beat Sullivan because of his own superior boxing ability and style. Baer believed he could beat Carnera because he had successfully intimidated the champion in the movie ring and also because he had discovered that Carnera was a tremendous and slow-moving target for a right hand.

Although a disappointment as a boxing champion, notwithstanding a great physique, a literally killing right hand, punch and plenty of stamina and good speed, there is no question that Baer was the greatest showman in boxing history. He could pass as a professional actor, singer, and dancer, and was very good looking. He made more money from motion pictures, radio, and television outside of actual boxing than any other pugilist. Besides being a competent showman, he could play an excellent game of bridge and was better than average on a golf course.

While on the subject of arts, the connection of boxing with astrology, numerology, palmistry, graphology, or crystal-gazing should be discussed. There is one thing certain. The letter "J" is the north star, the right number, the life line, or the crux of boxing insofar as heavyweight championships are concerned up to 1952.

First, let us list the generally accepted World Heavyweight Boxing Champions from 1880 to 1952 who have held their titles for approximately seven years or more. They are: JOHN L. SULLIVAN 1882–1892; JAMES J. JEFFRIES 1899–1906; JACK JOHNSON 1908–15; JACK DEMPSEY 1919–26; JOE LOUIS 1937–49.

Next, the English bare-knuckle heavyweight champions who held their titles for approximately seven years or more. They are: JAMES FIGG, 1719–30; JACK BROUGHTON, 1734–50; JACK SLACK, 1750–60; TOM JOHNSON, 1783–1791; JOHN JACKSON, 1792–1800; TOM CRIBB, 1809–22.

Ten out of the eleven greatest boxing champions had a "J" as one of their initials, two of these had J in their initials twice, and one, three times. In addition, in modern times there were champions, JAMES J. CORBETT, JAMES J. BRADDOCK, JAMES J. TUNNEY and JERSEY JOE WALCOTT, four more double J's. To make our J hang higher, let us not forget JAMES J. WALKER, JOHN (Tex) RICKARD, JAMES J. JOHNSON and MIKE JACOBS. According to one graphologist, Rocky Marciano put a curse on the initial "J" by annihilating Joe Louis and Jersey Joe Walcott, while an astrologist claims that Joe Frazier will regain his title!

Here is another fact which might be wrapped up in the stars. No world's heavyweight champion had ever regained his title. Many had tried, but none has succeeded. Corbett led champion Jeffries on points for twenty-two rounds in a twenty-five round fight, but was knocked out in the twenty-third. Jack Dempsey "knocked out" champion Gene Tunney for the now famous "long count," but lost on points. However, thirty-three years later, Floyd Patterson won back his title from Ingemar Johansson with the magic "J" and Cassius Clay-Muhammad Ali, without "J" in either name won the title back.

Boxers themselves have made some contributions to the artistic side of living. Obviously, because of the nature of the sport, the professional boxer seldom has the required education or opportunity to attain artistic stardom. Notwithstanding this handicap, many boxers and most champions have tried to write, just as almost everyone else has tried at one time or another; others have been musicians, successful actors, or have painted. Jim Tully, a veteran of forty-three professional ring battles, turned to writing and became an accepted and world-known literary figure. He dedicated his most famous book on the prize ring, *The Bruiser*, to "my fellow road-kid, Jack Dempsey."

Victor McLaglen, a professional heavyweight who once fought Jack Johnson, (and one of the few to not be put to sleep by a KO) probably leads the list of actors who were former fighters. There are other old-time fighters turned actors who did not attain either his prominence in the ring or on the screen. The present generation of boxers has, with more opportunities, fared better. Among comedians we had Max Baer and Maxie Rosenbloom, a former world's light heavyweight champion, and in motion pictures there was former middleweight champion Fred Steele, who became as much in demand in Hollywood as he once was in rings all over the country.

87. Victor McLaglen in the Quiet Man. **(Academy of Motion Picture Arts and Sciences)**

Fidel La Barba, former world's flyweight Olympic champion and later professional champion took his ring earnings, finished college and became a successful writer for 20th Century-Fox. Mickey Walker, former middleweight champion, turned to the palette and oils and became recognized as an artist of promise.

James J. Corbett was an excellent actor and toured the country in a production called *Gentleman Jim,* in which he played the part of a college hero. William J. Brady, prominent theatrical producer, was his friend and manager and the producer of this play which enjoyed great popularity. After retiring, Corbett became an actor in vaudeville and was one of the first boxing champions to break into the movies as an actor.

Prior to Corbett, John L. Sullivan had been as much a trail-blazer in the theatre as he was in the ring. Those who saw him say he was positively the worst actor of all time, but it made no difference. He was a matinee idol with the ladies. His artless play,

88. Photo from the Eagle Lion Studios showing Dempsey and Robert Preston squeezing Susan Hayward between them on the set of Walter Wanger's technicolor Tulsa. **(Courtesy of Walter Wanger and the Eagle Lion Studios)**

Honest Hearts and Willing Hands, played to crowds everywhere for many years. The plot called for the hero son of an honest blacksmith to thrash the villain at an Irish fair. Fortunately for a long line of villains, the fight was with gloves. *Honest Hearts and Willing Hands* toured America, Canada, and Australia, and is reported to have netted Sullivan two hundred thousand dollars.

Both Dempsey and Tunney tried acting on stage and screen with no great success. Tunney's picture, *The Fighting Marine*, if seen today would be good for many laughs even though it is not a comedy. Gene Delmont, an exfighter, became a movie character actor of some prominence during this period.

No account of the theatre would be complete if it omitted Canada Lee, the most accomplished actor developed from the modern prize ring. His colorful career is discussed elsewhere in this book.

As boxing became an acceptable sport, many famous writers were retained to report championship fights, and their enthusiastic and colorful accounts helped immeasurably to further interest in pugilism. Prominent among these are Jeffrey Farnol who covered the Dempsey-Carpentier fight for the *London Daily Mail*, and Arnold Bennett who reported the bouts Cochrane promoted in London.

George Bernard Shaw once showed more than a passing interest in boxing; in fact, he wrote a most entertaining book on the English bare-knuckle P.R. called *Cashel Byron's Profession*. In this story he shows a wonderfully keen feeling for boxers and their peculiar psychology. Certainly Cashel Byron in some ways is a literary and earlier Gene Tunney. Shaw regretted the level to which boxing had fallen in the last of the bare-knuckle days and declared that the sport was dying of its own intolerable tediousness.

Shaw also threw some light—or confusion—on another great literary figure's interest in boxing. He said Thackeray "loved a prize fight as he loved a fool." Thackeray was known to be a follower of the game and was seen by many of his friends and several journalists at the Heenan-Sayers fight. Naturally, being a Britisher, he thought Sayers had won but denied he himself had been present at the fight and wrote for *Punch* an anonymous verse of protest against the claim that he was a spectator.

Speaking of anonymous poems, no consideration of

90. Boxing scene from Gentleman Jim. (Warner Bros. First National)

verse and boxing can overlook the most popular and the most famous poem of the sport, *The Nonpareil's Grave* (see appendix). The first Jack Dempsey, known as "The Nonpareil," whose name was Kelly, was born in Ireland, and arrived in New York as a boy in 1880. Three years later, when watching a boxing show, Kelly volunteered to substitute for one of the contestants who did not show up, gave his name as Jack Dempsey, and won the contest. This encouraged him to become a professional fighter. In five years, although never weighing more than 150 pounds, he won sixty out of sixty fights from boxers of all weights from welters to heavies, and the world's middleweight championship. His style, skill and abilities earned him the "Nonpareil" title. In 1889 he was knocked out for the first time by George Le Blanche in San Francisco in the twenty-second round by a pivot punch thereafter barred as illegal. He never recovered from this knockout and an illness contracted about this time, and in 1891 Bob Fitzsimmons stopped him in thirteen rounds to become world's middleweight champion. In 1895, Dempsey made his last appearance in the ring and

later, in an attempt to regain his broken health, left for the West but died in Oregon. M. J. McMahon of Portland, Dempsey's lawyer, was so incensed by the neglect of his many admirers of other years during Dempsey's last illness, that he wrote a poem anonymously, had a thousand copies printed and sent to Dempsey's friends. It was printed and reprinted around the world and Dempsey's friends, out of remorse, finally raised funds and erected a proper memorial to one of the most phenomenal boxers of all time.

Sir Arthur Conan Doyle's *Rodney Stone* and C.E. Pearce's *Corinthian Jack* were carefully filmed by the English, as only they are able to do, with a minimum of Hollywood ornateness and expense and a maximum of authenticity of feeling and fact. After many versions of *The Amateur Gentleman* and gangster pictures with fights as background, Hollywood finally produced an exceptional picture involving boxing and fantasy. In *Here Comes Mr. Jordan*, a boxing champion (Robert Montgomery) dies by error and not in accordance with heavenly schedule. His manager (James Gleason) has the body cremated, so when the spirit is forced to return to earth, it cannot find its body, and a really new problem in the saga of the fist is presented. The picture was a tremendous artistic and financial success and is the favorite of a host of professional boxing champions.

The Great John L., released by United Artists Corporation and produced by Bing Crosby, was a fictionalization of the life and career of John L. Sullivan. *Body and Soul*, starring John Garfield, another picture of United Artists, featured many professional fighters of championship fame.

In late 1947 and early 1948, Hollywood suddenly became very interested in fight pictures. The *Champion* with Kirk Douglas, the *Set-Up* with Robert Ryan, and the *Duke of Chicago* followed *Body and Soul*.

Unfortunately, all of these projected the worst side of boxing and made many people believe that boxing was almost exclusively a racket for criminals, gamblers, and gangsters.

It is hoped that Hollywood will present the other side of boxing in the future, for, like every sport and activity of man, and man himself, boxing contains both good and evil.

One of the finest and most enjoyable movies on boxing and almost a factual one is Walt Disney's *The Happiest Millionaire* starring Fred McMurray and covering the beginning of the Rickard and Dempsey period and featuring millionaire Biddle, the original financial supporter of Rickard and also Madison Square Garden.

92. Still from Walt Disney's boxing picture The Happiest Millionaire, **based on the life of Anthony J. Drexel Biddle, original backer of Tex Rickard and the Madison Square Garden and the judge of the Dempsey-Willard fight. Shown here is Lesley Ann Warren. (Courtesy of Walt Disney Productions)**

Boxing is often introduced into plays or pictures for dramatic contrast or for humor. In *The Bells of St. Mary*, Ingrid Bergman, as a nun, successfully teaches one of her parochial school pupils the manly art from what she had been able to pick up from a boxing manual. Jimmy Cagney has portrayed many a cocky little fist-thrower. The school boys learned boxing to defend themselves from the bully in *How Green Was My Valley*.

The late Errol Flynn, the actor, was once an amateur boxer but denied that he competed for a place on the Irish Olympic team. He kept in fair shape by fencing and playing tennis and had his eyes sharpened by occasional scraps in the movies and in the better night clubs. As Hollywood's keenest boxing student, he had refereed many amateur bouts and was the hero of probably the most convincing picture about boxing history ever made, Warner Brothers' *Gentleman Jim*. In this picture Flynn played the part of James J. Corbett and re-enacted some of the high spots in the career of the first universally accepted world's champion. There is no doubt that Flynn wanted to play the part of Dempsey in a picture based on the life of the Manassa Mauler. Several years before he passed away he specifically requested that it be stressed in this book that his boxing days were over and that he had now become only an actor, for he felt that in *Gentleman Jim* and in another fight picture, the *Perfect Specimen*, the boxers assigned to spar with him in the pictures had all tried to "go to work on him." A talk with some of these, however, brought forth the admission that Errol could still take care of himself and that he was a "bad actor" in the ring.

The Crowd Roars, a 1939 M.G.M. picture, is based on the story of Jackie Fields and Joe Salas. Joe Salas

91. Boxer-actor Flynn as actor-boxer Corbett. (Warner Bros. First National)

93. The Happiest Millionaire. Shown here is the set of Mayor Biddle's private gym with rare boxing memorabilia. (Courtesy of Walt Disney Productions)

won the national amateur featherweight boxing championship in Boston in 1924 and became a member of the Olympic Boxing Team. Featherweight Jackie Fields had an off day, and was eliminated by a decision in the same tournament. Both boys came from Los Angeles, went to school together, took up boxing together, boxed for the same club, and had come across country together. Both had the same ambition—an Olympic championship and then a professional championship. Jackie Fields, because of his record, was added to the Olympic team as an extra but official member, as were several others, since in 1924 each Olympic team could enter two men in each weight class. Fields worked and persevered and at his request Spike Webb, the Olympic coach, gave him special instructions. When the final entries were made by Coach Webb, Salas and Fields were chosen as the two United States contestants in their weight. They both fought and won five fights to meet in the final. For three rounds they fought toe to toe. The fact that they were close friends made no difference. At the end both were punched out. After a tense moment the officials awarded the bout and the

World's Olympic Championship to Fields. The two friends ran across the ring and fell into each other's arms as the band played "The Star Spangled Banner." As two American flags were hoisted to the first and second place flagpoles, two California boys in tears stood locked in each other's arms. Jackie Fields later turned "pro" and became the World's Welter-

94. The Happiest Millionaire. Shown here is Fred MacMurray landing a blow on the chin of "A marine boxing champion"—William Weldman, Jr. (Courtesy of Walt Disney Prod.)

weight Champion and, believe it or not, worked for a time with Joe Salas for M.G.M. studios.

Not to be outdone by the past or former heavy-weight champions, Joe Frazier is musically inclined and in his spare time he leads a band "The Knock-outs." It is even reported that on one of his hot sessions at Ceasar's Palace in Las Vegas he broke an ankle.

Cassius Clay, aka Muhammad Ali, tried acting in December 1969. He made his active debut on Broadway in the black power musical "Buck White." However, the show closed barely before it opened so Ali could hardly get a rating as a showman outside of the ring!

The dramatic power of boxing was again demonstrated in late 1976 by the film *Rocky*. Written by and starring an unknown actor, Sylvestor Stallone, it dealt with a club fighter's accidental chance at the heavy-weight championship. Audiences by the millons responded to the underdog-hero, and the film garnered ten Academy Award nominations.

Naturally, in talking about the literature of boxing, one cannot duck the sharp punches of fistic jargon which can be divided into two periods and classes. The slang of the English bare-knuckle days, given us by boxing's earliest historian, Pierce Egan, was the same as that of our earlier boxing days. The second phase is the jargon of our present-day cauli-flower-ear industry.

In the days of the "P.R." (prize ring) and the "noble art," "Old Q," the "dandies," the "fancy," the "gentry," and the "bucks" all enjoyed "mills" as we do "shows" and "bouts" today. Many a man would get lost trying to find "Mile End Road" or, even more likely, after leaving it he could not find the site of the "square" or "mill" in "Epping Forest" or "Epping Glades" where the clandestine fights were held. "Giving the office" did not signify getting arrested or avoiding arrest, but was information given the boxing fans by forest sentinels posted in the woods by the promoters to direct the spectators to the particular place chosen for the fight, to keep away the police or to give the alarm when the police arrived in force.

In an open space amid hornbeams and giant oaks stood the ring. Gentlemen in colorful attire sur-rounded it and within its confines fought tough shaggy-eyebrowed men, swinging lustily with bare fists. They, like their Greek and Roman predecessors, first maneuvered for position so that the sun was in the opponent's eyes, although the most important fights started at twelve, noon, so as to put the sun directly overhead, where the almost blinding but neutral ring-lights are today.

Then, as today, and as in the days of the Greeks, boxers acquired an unusual number of wrinkles in their foreheads from holding their head down well over their Adam's apple and looking with some strain at their opponents from under their eyebrows and into a glaring light. These English "pugs," like the Greeks or our boxers today, puffed and snorted while boxing to clear their noses for breathing through the twisted septums and broken bones of flattened probosces.

Today's slang of Fistiana is no less colorful than that of the bare-knuckle days. "Jacobs Beach," instead of "Epping Forest" was its center after World War Two. The late "Uncle Mike" Jacobs and his deaf "mouthpiece" Sol Strauss, "Dumb Dan" Morgan and others talked about their "boys" who were either "cuties," "canvas backs," "southpaws," or "suckers for blondes," and discussed "bouts," "cards," "take," "cuts," "ice," and the like. Don King and John Daly use the same language today. Slang or no slang, past or present, writers and artists have proved that the spectacle of a fight has always appealed to man's primitige instincts, and boxing's cruel beauty to his aesthetic appreciation.

In the future, boxing will continue to inspire thrilling narration, poetry, and drama. Artists in many mediums will continue to depict the sport's beauty, symmetry, rhythm, and savage quality in oils, water-color, charcoal, bronze and marble. In addition to books, the theatre, radio, and pictures, the drama of future fights will be broadcast to the world by television in a fraction of a second. By this comparatively new medium, art, education, and democratic civilization will continue to spread throughout the world and with these fleeting carrier waves distributing understanding and tolerance will also proceed the sport of boxing. The stirring punches of the great fighters of tomorrow will come alive on the television screens of the future.

9 • Boxing and the World— Civilization, Politics, New York State Athletic Commission, National Boxing Association, Oddities, and War

Historians and persons familiar with the story of boxing know that civilization and the sport are closely related. Since this is not a textbook of history or a book on sociology, all the causes, reasons or results of this relationship will not be described, but certain facts will be given.

The first inescapable fact is that boxing and civilization have been together consistently and constantly. In the periods during which civilization was at a low ebb, boxing was absent, and at other times it has advanced or retreated in line with mankind's progress or decline.

Let us examine the record. The first record of boxing was found in Egypt, and certainly we know that the Egyptian civilization was centuries in advance of that in other contemporary countries. Based on minimal evidence of the end of the Paleolithic Period and the earliest Egyptian civilization, boxing may well have started nine thousand years ago. We then find the sport in Crete, where the Minoan civilization led the then known world. Each of these countries enjoyed comparative political freedom and practiced an early form of democracy. Each also maintained a great navy and depended on its maritime trade for power and leadership. This overseas trade extended to the Aegean and Mediterranean seas. In both these cases, boxing went hand in hand with democracy and thalassocracy, a term which designates an essentially maritime nation.

Thalassocracy has an even closer connection with boxing than democracy, and all three are intimately woven with man's progress and civilization, no matter how highbrow this statement may sound. Egypt and Crete were both early centers of boxing and they were both freedom-loving sea powers.

Civilization, democracy, thalassocracy, and boxing continued their connection in Egypt and Crete. The area or country that became the hub of civilization for centuries after Crete was Greece. Greece and her democratic city states enjoyed political freedom and considerable tolerance. The Greeks were dependent for their leadership on naval power and overseas trade. And there in ancient Greece, boxing thrived, developed and enjoyed its first golden age.

The Greeks, threatened in our day, were among the first to espouse political freedom and democracy. The very word democracy is a Greek word. This same Greece was the scene of international (intercity) boxing competitions that did not stop even for wars.

After centuries of the highest type of civilization, the beginnings of democracy and a highly developed interest in boxing, Greek naval power and maritime trade waned. Eventually the Romans took over. They controlled the seas, and the Roman Empire, originally a relative democracy, became the acknowledged focal point of civilization. The outposts of the naval power and maritime trade of Rome rivaled those of England before World War II. Boxing went with this shift of dominance, but as the Roman Empire tumbled, boxing as an athletic contest deteriorated into a spectacle of cruelty and was finally outlawed. When the Roman Empire crumbled, civilization went into the period known as the Dark Ages. There may have been naval powers during this period, but certainly civilization and democracy were not on the march.

The relationship between civilization, democracy, and boxing continued, however, for the Dark Ages of history tolled curfew for the fist also.

After the Dark Ages and the renaissance of civilization, boxing reappeared. With the Renaissance, we find a decided shift in the center of civilization. Now certainly, if the relationship which we traced before boxing died was merely a coincidence, we should expect to see it reappear in Greece or in Rome where it had been before it was snuffed out. But in neither country was political freedom or democracy to be found, so boxing did not reappear in its former homes.

Instead, it reappeared in England, the hub of world power, around 1680. It prospered there for two hundred years. In this era, England had greater political freedom and tolerance than any other country coupled with a dominant position in sea power and maritime trade. Then, although boxing still continued there, the control and development of the sport moved to America.

Even this last move is consistent. The United States became the stronghold of democracy against all forms of dictatorships, and its power was and is based to a great degree on its naval strength and world commerce.

So no matter what the cause or result, the association or relationship of boxing with civilization, democracy, and naval power has been direct and consistent for over 9,000 years. The only thing left to explain is its 1,200 year sleep. That can be attributed to the fact that nowhere during this period was there political freedom, tolerance or absence of dictators, and wars of conquest. For in reverse, boxing has always been stifled whenever and wherever there have been dictators and plans of world conquest.

Today, professional boxing conducted on any major scale is to be found in the United States and its possessions and in the British Empire, but was, until very recently, practically nonexistent in Russia and the areas under Russian control. In addition, even to one ignorant of political ideology, it is apparent that when and if a country departs from certain democratic concepts, boxing goes out the window. This was particularly evident in both Fascist Spain and Communistic Hungary and Poland. Cuba had a great Olympic 1972 heavyweight champion but dictator Castro would not let him turn professional. Communism would certainly not allow two men fighting for a world title to divide ten million dollars. That would certainly make them extreme capitalists! It is all a bit startling and surprising, but until refuted by better or more thorough research, the facts must be accepted.

Let us hope that boxing will soon flourish throughout the world, or at least continue thriving in our own country.

Even Russia, about two years ago, indicated that perhaps at that time its government might be developing a change of policy toward a more democratic ideal, and that perhaps it was not adopting any plan for world conquest, by becoming interested in boxing. One of the leading United States boxing experts was approached confidentially by a high ranking official representative of the Russian government for the express purpose of trying to arrange boxing relations between the United States and Russia. It is understood that the discussion explored the possibility of Russia sending over boxers to compete here with our leading amateurs and even with our professional fighters. Also the possibility of sending an outstanding boxing coach or trainer to Russia was discussed, and finally a Russian tour for Joe Louis was suggested. In November 1975, ten amateur heavyweight boxers from the USSR fought against ten U.S. heavyweights in the Madison Square Garden. The score was 6 U.S. wins against 4 USSR wins. The Russian team then toured the United States, meeting other U.S. teams to acquire more experience and U.S. boxing know-how.

According to the statements made, it appeared that boxing was then beginning to be popular in Russia. Boxing, along with other sports, is conducted there along the same lines that produced Germany's splendid Olympic team in 1936. Sports in Russia are conducted by the govenrment and, to a great degree, are part of its physical training program, and connected with the industrial recreation program. According to one source, top athletes are more or less subsidized and their standard of living is based on the importance of their athletic activities. This, of course, departs completely from our own concepts as to what differentiates professionals from amateurs. Actually sports in Russia are part of their ideological propaganda program.

It would be interesting to conjecture what status Russian athletes would have if they came over here to establish friendly relations through the medium of boxing. Would they be professionals or would they be amateurs? Based on communist doctrine there can be no true professional sports, yet their amateurs are subsidized to prove that their amateurs are superior to ours. The fact that this does not make sense is not our fault! None of our professional boxers would be satisfied with civil service pay or government subsidy in lieu of large guarantees.

Here again we have but to go into the past to find an answer. The ancient Greek athletes did not compete for cash prizes, but in most cases made their living through government subsidies. The winner of an Olympic, in addition to getting his palm and his crown of olive leaves, received financial help. Most democratic city-states rewarded top athletes with subsidies, for instance, if any Athenian won an Olympic crown, he was given the right to eat at government expense for the rest of his life. Prominent citizens vied with each other to bed and board Olympic champions. Yet, the Greek athlete was considered an amateur. It is believed that as long as a Russian boxer did not compete in professional fights here for money, he would be considered an amateur.

In connection with Communist ideology in boxing, a Shanghai Soviet newspaper once published a comment about "Young George," a boxer. It revealed the thoroughness of Soviet indoctrination of its converts. It explained how young George had won all his fights on points or by decisions because knockouts were not consistent with his ideals. "The Soviet sportsman cannot comply with the demands of the bourgeois public for a bloody boxing match in which the boxer is crippled and for which he receives only a few dollars . . . ," the boxer volunteered. The paper went on to say that "his correct behavior in the ring will assure him success in the Soviet Union." Fortunately in America even the underprivileged and unknown can win fame and more than a few dollars in boxing without pulling their punches or waiting for decisions from commissars, no matter what their race, religion, or nationality. Argentine Louis Firpo, Jewish Max Baer, German Max Schmeling, Irish James J. Braddock, French Marcel Cerdan, Filipino Pancho Villa, Black Sugar Robinson, Black Joe Louis, all got their chance, and many others, such as Canada Lee, were able, because of our democratic system, to make other careers for themselves. More recently, the deployment of top boxers and world champions has included many countries in all continents of every race, creed, nationality, and social position. Even persons with criminal records have not been prevented from top objectives in the sport. There is no discrimination against minorities. Eight out of the last ten world heavyweight champions in the last thirty-eight years have been black. As against one out of fourteen in the previous fifty-five years.

In addition to the unusual historical relationship between civilization and boxing, facts and figures show that the sport of boxing has also gone hand-in-hand with the most intelligent political thinking throughout the ages. It has played an important part in the political lives of famous men, kings, rulers, administrators, and presidents. Theseus, the cunning politician who united many communities into the city-state of Athens, was the man who introduced boxing to Greece; Cato, the Roman philosopher, taught it to his son; George IV of England was a friend and pupil of Gentleman Jackson and absorbed many a punch; Teddy Roosevelt was a boxer and boxing enthusiast; and in our cabinet there was James Forrestal, our first Secretary of National Defense, with a nose

and two ears slightly altered by fists. Louis Johnson, the second Secretary of National Defense selected by President Truman, was also a former boxer. Johnson was heavyweight champion at the University of Virginia, and the top caliber of boxers at this college was later established beyond any doubt in intercollegiate competition. Last but not least, King George VI appointed a former boxer to succeed his own brother as Governor General of Australia (another maritime democracy where boxing is popular). William John McKell was born in New South Wales in 1892, the son of a butcher. After various experiences and occupations, he was for a time a professional boxer and fought in the prize ring while studying to be a lawyer and even continued after he had hung out his shingle. After retiring from the ring, he practiced law, became Minister of Justice, then Prime Minister of New South Wales until his appointment in 1947 as Governor General of the newest continent. President Ford has a background as a prominent college football player and a coach of football and boxing, and his nose looks like it has been disturbed by a fist.

The fist as well as the handshake has played an important part in politics. It has secured votes. In Rome, politicians, consuls, emperors, and would-be emperors obtained popularity and political support by promoting spectacles and bloody prizefights featuring both men and beasts. In old England, many an aristocratic sponsor of boxing was more interested in the mass appeal and publicity based on his connection with some amphitheatre or champion fighter, than in the sport itself. Many loved the sport, but also used the ring to political advantage.

In the United States the very start and development of boxing were tied up with politics. That is why the story of the formal beginnings of the sport of the fist in America belongs in this chapter. A semi-political grudge fight led to the naming of the first boxing champion of America when in 1816 a Jacob Hyer challenged Tom Beasley. Hyer won. Beasley's friends refused to be enthusiastic about Hyer's prowess, so Hyer in anger replied publicly that he could lick any man in the United States, and that he was champion. No one accepted the challenge, so Hyer became champion.

On 13 September 1842, Chris Lilly, an Englishman, and Tom McCoy, Irish-American, fought in a vacant lot somewhere between Yonkers and Hastings, New York. The men were 140 pounders and the battle, which was a grudge affair, lasted 120 rounds, or two hours and forty minutes. The end came when McCoy was ko'd and died. The result of this fatality made it impossible for boxing to continue. Yankee Sullivan, one of the first claimants for the

American championship, who had merely been a spectator but had offered advice to Lilly, and was an ex-convict from Australia, was arrested, tried, and sentenced to two years in the state prison. From that day on, boxing was strictly illegal. It was, therefore, only with the help of politicians and politics that the fight game was able to survive and develop in the United States.

In the '80s and '90s, there were no great fistic activities because of state laws barring fighting. California and Louisiana because of politics and profits first tolerated, then legally sanctioned, "gloved duels." New York then followed with the Horton Law in 1896 and Nevada approved boxing in 1897, specifically to permit the Corbett-Fitzsimmons fight in Carson City.

Newspapers of those dasy show clearly that boxing and politics were definitely connected, and many an election was determined at the polls by a candidate's support of the fist as a medium of entertainment, as a means to support gambling, and as a source of jobs to build up political patronage. When corruption crept into boxing in 1900, the New York Legislature repealed the Horton Law. Ten years later it was revived under the Frawley Law, but died again in a few years. Boxing laws, boxing politics, and boxing were strictly on a catch-as-catch-can basis in various cities and states from 1895 to 1920.

In 1919 the boxing situation and politics surrounding boxing in America were put on a more tolerable

96. Left foot to the jaw—1945. Two world wars spread savate to Bangkok, Siam. (Andre Barraut)

basis through the efforts of an Englishman—William Gavin. Gavin came to America in 1918 and started an organization patterned after the National Sports Club in London. He drafted a set of rules that were his adaptation of the Marquis of Queensberry code. These rules were to be used in the club located at Forty-first Street and Sixth Avenue which was sup-

150

ported by Major Anthony Biddle and other individuals in New York's financial community, and for which Tex Rickard had agreed to become matchmaker.

However, when everything looked all set, it was discovered that politics had to be considered. A law had to be passed to permit the club to conduct boxing on its premises. Gavin turned his set of rules over to James J. Walker, then New York State Senator, and they were introduced and passed as the "Walker Boxing Bill." When it seemed certain that the bill would pass by the proper alignment of politics and politicians, Rickard walked out on Gavin and his International Sporting Club and obtained a lease on Madison Square Garden through Al Smith. As a result of this, when boxing became legal in New York in 1920, Rickard was the main beneficiary and not poor old Gavin who had started it all. So it was Gavin to Walker to Rickard that put boxing over in New York, but the essential link was the right politics and politicians to pass the necessary legislation at the right time.

Anthony Drexel Biddle, the major and original financial supporter of Rickard, and as a result definitely responsible for boxing in New York State and for the Madison Square Garden, is often referred to as "the forgotten man of boxing." He was also known as "the happiest millionaire." He was a great boxing devotee who would challenge anyone to a duel with gloves, a friend and second of Philadelphia's Jack O'Brien. He was commissioned as a Major in the United States Marine Corps Reserve in World War I and was a bayonet expert. He was a judge of the Dempsey-Willard fight at Toledo, Ohio. On 4 June 1919, at 3:30 P.M., with a ringside temperature of 114 degrees, before a sweltering and suffering crowd, Biddle put on a not too well-received exhibition drill with a squad of Marines he had brought to the fight at his own expense. Needless to say, Major Biddle's enthusiasm for boxing and his happy good nature led to his daughter's book *The Happiest Millionaire*

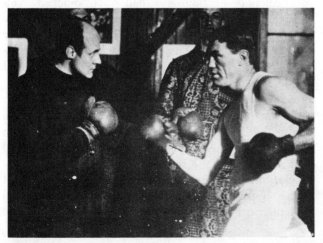

97. Marine Corps picture of Mayor Biddle and Philadelphia's Jack O'Brien. (Courtesy of Walt Disney Productions)

dramatized for stage and screen with Fred McMurray.

"Jimmy" Walker, aided by Gavin who started the ball rolling, and Rickard who picked it up and ran with it, were the major factors in putting boxing where it is today. Walker, like many other characters connected with boxing, was versatile. He was an outstanding public speaker, an athlete, and an accomplished musician, as well as a famous wit. When elected to the State Senate from Greenwich Village in 1910, he began a lifelong association with boxing fans, Al Smith, James A. Farley, Caleb Baumes, and Battling Marty McCue, the ex-prizefighter characterized by Walker as one who carried the Marquis of Queensberry rules into the Legislature.

In the State Legislature, Walker not only legalized boxing, but also adopted the Gavin rules and initiated the state licensing and control of all persons officially connected with boxing bouts—referees, judges, boxers, managers, trainers, seconds, physicians, and others, under an executive body of three commissioners.

He left Albany to become Mayor of New York City. As Mayor he never forgot his first love—a love that was a major factor in obtaining political support, patronage, and votes—boxing. He never missed an important fight and even put the gloves on from time to time in friendly bouts. He claimed that "boxing was the only sport in which you meet one opponent at a time, and he is always in front of you."

Walker once told me a boxing story about himself explaining that it was the only case on record where a man had knocked himself out. The scene was Leone's Restaurant near the Madison Square Garden where impromptu bouts among the customers were often held after closing hours. According to Walker, on this particular night he asked Jimmy Johnston, fight manager and former boxer, to go a few rounds with him, but to take it easy. Walker sparred until he was so winded he decided to end it all by throwing a haymaker at Johnston. Johnston saw the punch coming, ducked, and Walker hit the floor full length, chin first.

Notwithstanding this story on himself, Jimmy was a good boxer, knew the game and enjoyed a good fight in or out of the irng. His performances at his yearly appearances at the Boxing Writers' Dinners were so outstanding that in 1947, the first dinner the late Mayor missed, everyone agreed that "there should have been a chair left because if anybody dominated the dinner it was " 'the little man that wasn't there.' " When contributions were made to the Damon Runyon Cancer Fund by this organization, they were "in memory of Jimmy Walker."

The great success of boxing under the Walker Law

98. James J. Walker decorating Joe Louis. (Press Association Inc.)

99. Number 1 coach vs. Number 1 commissioner; Spike Webb and Eddie Eagan square off.

and Gavin's rules in New York State killed off prejudice against it elsewhere. Politicians in various states, seeing the great opportunities provided in taxes, visitors, profits, and especially in jobs and political patronage, all spelling votes, followed suit and legalized boxing in most states.

Later, some states, to prevent abuses and to strengthen boxing, attempted to form an organization that would have national control over the sport. However, this association did not succeed, principally because New York, Pennsylvania, California, and Massachusetts refused to join. As these states enjoyed the largest interest in boxing, the National Boxing Association never got national control. It has been said that the reason the four states refused to join was that politics and boxing were too strongly merged in these states; that the Boxing Commissions of these states and the licensing of referees, judges, managers, fighters, and others having been set up in conjunction with political patronage those in control did not want to give up their position of power. Another reason, advanced by just as large a group, was that these states, after longer experience with fights and fighters, saw no reason for relinquishing any of the powers or controls which they had developed effectively and efficiently, to a new and untried group.

The New York Athletic Commission, who control boxing in New York State, consists of three appointees or commissioners selected by the Governor of New York State. These appointments are considered lush political jobs. The senior commissioner or chairman received $10,000 per year in 1949 and was permitted by law to engage in another occupation while serving as commissioner. Today the present senior commissioner is James A. Farley, Jr., the son of James J. Farley, who held down the same job from February 1924 to February 1933. The present Chairman was appointed in August 1975, and his compensation is $35,250 per year. The other commissioners earn $110 per day when serving at commission meetings. Deputy commissioner Marvin Kohn who is also the public information officer was invaluable in the preparation of this book.

The fist had even dented the national political picture before World War II. Henry Wallace frequently boxed in the Senate gym and released photographs of himself boxing with various Washington political figures. According to a reliable source, Senator Ellender of Louisiana had once knocked Wallace out cold with a right to the chin in a friendly bout in the Senate gym in 1941. Senator Ellender was once known in Tulane University boxing circles as "Houma Kid." More recently, President Gerald Ford, a long time member of Congress, was once boxing coach at Yale University.

In the proceedings and debates of the 77th Congress, the Hon. C. Wayland Brooks, Senator from Illinois, with the consent of the Senate, read and had printed into the record a talk by James G. Conzelman on the importance and value of body-contact games, especially boxing, to the young man's mental and physical approach to war.

Boxing, in addition to being involved in politics, was engaged in talks with the Federal Government during World War II. Mike Jacobs negotiated with the War Department and almost put over an unusual deal. He sold to the Secretary of War and the Army's Bureau of Public Relations the idea of a Joe Louis vs. Billy Conn world championship fight for charity. However, the Secretary of War and General Surles were not informed on the big business of beakbusting. They did not realize that in addition to the normal proceeds of a fight of this type, there are many subsidiary and complicated additional revenues, among the most substantial of which is the *Ice*. The *Ice* is the amount of money made on ticket manipulation. You will find, for instance, that while a so-called ringside seat may enable you to see the fight fairly well with a good pair of field glasses providing your line of vision is clear, another ringside seat may be only fifteen feet from the ring.

Ringside rows usually follow a crazy pattern of lettering, such as row A, row AA, row AAA, row A-1, A-2, or AA-1, AA-2, and so on. In the final analysis there are ringside seats that are immediately behind the press seats, and ringside seats that are so far away that field glasses are necessary to get a good look at the ring from them. Ticket speculators ask for much more *Ice* or additional bonus for a really good ticket than for a mediocre one, and more for a mediocre one than for a bad one. When you consider the number of tickets of all types, particularly ringside tickets, that are available in an outdoor world's heavyweight championship fight, you can readily see that the *Ice* is no mean figure. Of course, television and closed circuit theater presentations that can be seen equally well from all seats have practically eliminated this promotion gambit . . . except for the "home" ringside spectators.

Nothing, of course, was said about the *Ice* in the negotiations between Mike Jacobs and the then Secretary of War or his representative. The only compensation which the fighters were going to have as originally discussed was their training expenses. However, because of the fact that they were both in service and both owed a considerable amount of income tax, Jacobs and his lawyer Strauss later appealed to the military authorities to the effect that it would be a nice gesture at least to help the poor boys pay their income tax. Furthermore, because of the fact that the boxers were fighting for nothing and bridging over their absence from the ring in service, strange rumors persisted on Jacobs Beach from usually reliable sources that the fight was a "fix" and would be a draw. In other words, the fight sponsored by the War Department was allegedly to be used as a sort of trailer or advertisement for a later

fight after the boys were released from service. However, some of the tough newspapermen who had been brought into the Army Public Relations and put into uniform and who knew all the angles in professional fight promotion, finally convinced the War Department that no matter how honest and sincere Mike Jacobs and the other principals might be, the fight should not come off. Perhaps rumors of Carbo's interest discouraged the colonels and generals.

The story is a classic example to show that boxing was so important that it led to negotiations between its leading promoter and the government of one of the Big Three during the greatest World War in history. Army brass in Washington wasted hours and days sweating and stewing over Mike Jacobs's plan while a full-sized war was going on. Jacobs, on the other hand, was probably sincere in wanting to do his bit in raising money for a worthy cause.

Just to show that there is nothing new under the sun, we can go back thousands of years and find that when Xerxes, Emperor of Persia, had given up trying to invade Russia and decided instead to throw his powerful army into Greece, and was trying to force the pass of Thermopylae, the Greeks insisted on holding their championships just the same, and Theagenes of Thasos was given a leave of absence from the Army in order to defend his title. This was in 480 B.C. or 2456 years ago!

In the United States in the last half of the twentieth century boxing and politics have a connection. It is a healthy one. The reader on a subway train or bus opens his tabloid to the sports section, and turns only later to politics. The popularity of the spectator and professional sport has been proved a sign of political peace. When a man does not get the excitements provided by war or politics, he has to get it by projecting himself into football, baseball, or boxing. The relative political peace of the English-speaking people explains both their interest and their superiority in sports. Let us hope that Madison Square Garden and Yankee Stadium may resound with the cheers of the public for the victors of the ring for years to come, rather than thunder with the ominous uproar of mass meetings leading to hatreds, political war, or worse.

At the helm of the fistic ship in New York State in 1949 was Governor Dewey's appointee, Senior Commissioner Eddie Eagan. Outside of New York State, Eagan was not always looked up to. The *Washington News* once characterized Eagan as "the biggest sports flop of the year." It went on to "award him a piece of limp lettuce with the banner lines: 'Never did one man do so little with so much.'" It wound up by alleging that "it is still plainly self-evident that no matter what the official documents may say, Mike Jacobs is the New York authority." Of course it must be remembered, in evaluating the above, that the District of Columbia was a member of the N.B.A. and was outside the New York boxing orbit, and by the same token outside of the vast realms of Jacobs promotions.

Eddie Eagan was an interesting character. As an amateur boxer in 1920, he was one of the world's best. In the 1924 Olympics he had passed his peak. Eddie Eagan was absolutely and supremely honest, but congenitally naive and trusting. As a result of this factor, he must have been handicapped as a boxing commissioner at first, facing some of the toughest and most agile minds in any business. A few years in the job wised him up considerably. Many people believe he was wrong when he said he should not have a staff of investigators, but perhaps Eddie was an optimist or perhaps he was right and others are the optimists.

The following story about Eddie Eagan, to illustrate the point, is one that few people are acquainted with except officials of the 1920 and 1924 Olympic Teams. In 1920 Eddie Eagan left what little ready cash he had with him at the Olympics in his clothes or in his baggage, and it promptly disappeared. This was not too unusual, as there were no guards, and the Olympics are a magnet, and the quarters of athletes are fairly accessible to contestants and spectators. This experience, however, should have taught Eddie a lesson, and put him on his guard. But in 1924 at the Olympic encampment where the boxing team was quartered, at the Chateau of Prince Murat, adjoining Versailles, again Eagan left all his money around, and again it disappeared, never to return. In both cases Eagan complained bitterly to the Olympic officials and United States Olympic team managers, and it is believed he was reimbursed for his loss in both cases.

As great a job as Eagan did, it is too bad that Eddie was not sufficiently independent of politics to govern boxing with absolutely no reference to it. There is no criticism of Eagan or of boxing. To show the very definite connection between boxing and politics, and that the Greek tribunes, the Roman senators, the Lords of Parliament, the members of the Commons, and our present-day politicians are all worshippers of votes and as such wield an influence on boxing based on politics in addition to the best interests of boxing, we have a story from personal experience. This story also shows that Tammany or Reform, Democrat or Republican, the basic principle is the same.

In 1928, I asked my old friend General Phelan, at that time the senior New York State Boxing Commissioner, for a license as a boxing referee or judge, and for occasional assignments. I had refereed hundreds of fights, and had considerable background in the sport. After several talks and a formal request in writing, a letter from General Phelan, on New York State Athletic Commission stationary, was finally received. It said generally that to be appointed, licensed, or assigned as a referee or judge of boxing in the State of New York, one had to be recommended, passed on, and supported by the Democratic leader of his district or through Democratic party channels, irrespective of qualifications.

Seventeen years later the Republicans had taken over the political control of the State of New York. A commission of an allegedly nonpolitical nature had been appointed to improve and control boxing for the good of the game only. The senior Commissioner, appointed by Governor Dewey, was Eddie Eagan, a former fellow officer in World War II and a former teammate on the Olympic Boxing Team of 1924, who knew that the author was interested only in the sport, was unreachable by gamblers or outside influences, and knew the game.

So again the author applied. This time, however, he explained that he was interested only in helping the sport and would be glad to serve as a judge gratis, or turn his fees over to some boxing charity. He further explained that he had refereed and judged professional fights in other states where he had been duly licensed as a competent boxing official. The author wrote that he hoped Eagan could use him in some way, particularly as a judge.

Back came the answer. It was practically a carbon copy of the letter received from a Democratic appointee seventeen years before. It was surprising, first to see that in seventeen years, just as in seventeen hundred years, the connection between boxing and politics could not be changed; second, to see that experience in the field and even the licenses from other states were secondary to consideration of political patronage; and third, to see that Eddie Eagan would send such a letter and officially admit that he did not have the power to license, appoint or employ whom he wanted, based only on their being experienced, competent and above influence. It is felt that in publishing this letter from Eagan, as almost a carbon copy of General Phelan's, we indicate a field for improvement. There are many sportsmen who are available, who have the education as well as experience as competitor, referee and judge, and who have licenses establishing their competency in other states. Politics in New York State should not make anyone's eyesight better or worse.

Today as we move out of the Republican administration of Governor Nelson Rockefeller and Mal-

STATE OF NEW YORK

DEPARTMENT OF STATE
THOMAS J. CURRAN, SECRETARY OF STATE

DIVISION OF STATE ATHLETIC COMMISSION
155 WORTH STREET, NEW YORK CITY 13
PHONE CORTLANDT 7-9800

January 22, 1945

Colonel John V. Grombach, G.S.C.
New York Athletic Club
180 Central Park South
New York 19, New York

Dear John:

    Thank you for your letter of congratulations.

    I expect to have a lot of fun although a lot of hard work at the same time.

    Regarding Judges, it is necessary to clear such applications in regular channels usually with the political leaders or assemblymen.

    Good Luck to you in 1945.

        Sincerely,

        Eddie

        Edward P. F. Eagan

100. Letter from Eddie Eagan.

EDWIN B. DOOLEY
CHAIRMAN

STATE OF NEW YORK
DIVISION OF STATE ATHLETIC COMMISSION
DEPARTMENT OF STATE
NEW YORK, N.Y.
10007

December 9, 1974

General John V. Grombach
111 West 57th Street
New York, N. Y. 10019

Dear General Grombach:

    Thanks for your letter of December 4th.

    In the light of your long experience in boxing, both in amateur and professional circles and the fact you were a member of the U.S. Olympic 1924 Boxing Team, it appears to me you would make an ideal prospect for a sound and safe Judge.

    If you wish to pursue it, the procedure is to have a physical examination and fingerprinting and fill out certain forms which I will send you on request.

    As I see it, there is nothing to stand in the way of your becoming a Judge except your age. Even that is not an insurmountable barrier.

        Sincerely yours,

        Edwin B. Dooley

        Edwin B. Dooley
        Chairman

EBD:RL

101. Letter to author from the Hon. Ed Dooley, Chairman of the New York Athletic Commission indicating politics or political sponsorship no longer dictate appointments or selection of boxing officials in New York State as in previous administrations.

---

colm Wilson and their Chairman of the Athletic Commission Edwin Dooley, we find a very unusual and encouraging lack of political influence in this commission and evidently complete freedom from political interference and control or influence. More as a standard operating procedure and because of my past books and past articles on boxing, I decided to write the same kind of letter to the Chairman of the 1974–75 Commission as I had sent to Eagan in 1945 and to Phelan in 1933 or before. (According to my records, the letter to Phelan was written in 1928 evidently as a commission member and before he became Chairman.) This latest letter, dated in late 1974, offered my services as a boxing official (i.e. as a judge), for the thirty-year difference and the forty-two-year span would disqualify me as a referee. Back came the answer, which is reproduced in this book and can be compared with Eagan's letter showing that political influence or support is now no longer needed to become a boxing official—only competence, honesty and, of course, a physical examination . . . in other words, the only issue is what will be good for boxing.

We cannot leave a mention of the late Eddie Eagan however, without discussing the Eddie Eagan Point System, which is an adaptation of many various point systems in boxing. Eddie conveniently sent his friends a sample scorecard for Christmas, giving them a KO decision for the sake of Santa Claus. This system, plan, and card, should alone justify Governor Dewey's appointment. It is by far the best and most practicable system used anywhere to judge a boxing bout. If honestly and correctly followed, the system should result in properly determining a winner of any bout no matter how close.

We believed the system and the card too complicated, especially for the busy referee in the ring watching the fighters during rounds and the fighters in their corners between rounds. However, after studying the California system and card and others, and after a half an hour spent with Eagan in which he explained the system as if he were instructing one of his judges, we are convinced of the superiority of the Eagan system and card. The text of the Eagan or New York Point System is as follows:

The point system to show the margin by which a contestant wins the round is solely to aid the judges in making a final determination. The officials base their judgment on four items: 1. Clean hitting; 2. Effective aggressiveness; 3. Defense; 4. Ring generalship. Evaluation by points exists in the minds of the officials and they put down the margin by which a contestant wins a round. The points take into account all the elements that go into winning a round.

(1) One point is scored for the boxer winning the round by a bare shade, zero for the loser. If the official must actually reflect and consider which boxer won the round, he will give one point to the winner. It is desirable that no round shall be looked upon as even. A winner should be determined.

(2) When the round is a clear win, two points will be credited to the winner and zero for the loser.

(3) If it is a one-sided round, the winner will receive three points and the loser none.

(4) If it is a one-sided round plus one or more knockdowns, the winner of the round will receive four points.

Knockdown can count one or two points, depending on the judgment of the officials. The official must determine the value to be placed on the knockdown. In marking a contest, the official shall judge the round as though no knockdown has occurred and, after arriving at this decision, he can add or deduct points. Hence, if a man has clearly won a one-sided round by a 3–0 margin and during the round happens to get knocked down, he still might win the round or at least tie it; that is, he might have one or two points deducted from his score. The result of the round might be a 1–0 in his favor.

The "no foul" rule exists and will continue to exist in the State of New York. The referee will tell the officials when he is taking the round away from one of the contestants because of a foul; the referee being the sole judge when a foul occurs. In such a round the man who is fouled will be awarded the round. However, the points will vary according to what happens in the round. If a man winning a one-sided round by a 3–0 margin commits a foul, he will lose that round and the possible points. His opponent will be given the round and one point. *However, he must lose the round.* On the other hand, if a man is losing the round by a big margin and he commits the foul, he will lose the round by four points, the maximum. If the round is about even and a foul is committed, the one fouled is awarded the round and given one point.

The New York rules permit referees to give a warning to a boxer before penalizing him with the loss of a round. Taking away a round should be exercised with appropriate caution.

Although the text may sound complicated, when explained by Eagan it is not too difficult. If, for instance, in any given round, two boxers are very evenly matched except that one has a slight margin because he is the aggressor, the referee or judge can merely put a check mark in that box under that round and give the round to the aggressor by 1–0. The card and boxes are not necessarily to be used except as an aid to the official in determining (a) the winner of the round, and (b) the margin by which the round was won. However, it is discretionary with ring officials to award the contest to a boxer who has won a lesser number of rounds than his opponent has, if he has inflicted more damage, proved his superiority, finished in better shape, and has more points. This is provided for in the New York State Boxing Commission rules. In the last case it is clear that a boxer could lead in the early rounds by a bare margin in each such round and then be badly beaten in the last rounds and all but out on his feet at the final bell. By the Eagan system the winner at the beginning might have more rounds won but the point score might be even because of the greater margin of the late starter's rally in the late rounds. In such a case, the officials could and should give it to the man who had his opponent all but knocked out at the finish, notwithstanding a tie-point score.

The present-day system or method of judging boxing bouts in New York State and in many other places in the world follow the same general pattern and principles. Today's New York State Boxing or Athletic Commission has printed up a general treatise on judging boxing bouts. It is written by William Recht entitled "At the Ringside With a Boxing Judge." William Recht is a top New York State boxing official and judge, highly regarded by the present Commission and by the boxing profession. Although it may have a few differences or a transposition of order of elements, it is basically very similar to the Eagan system.

So we can see that the entry of politics, commissioners, lawyers, some with boxing experience such as Eagan, have helped the sport by improving its rules and giving it proper and efficient control, even though it may have kept out a few helpers who dislike asking for political favors or who erroneously believe that "the job should seek the man."

In this connection, no discussion of modern boxing, especially in New York State, should omit one of its most peculiar characters who not only sought a job and a place in boxing but also drove plenty of people crazy doing it. He finally, however, made a real contribution to the sport. Prior to both Colonel Eddie Eagan and General John J. Phelan, the Senior Boxing Commissioner was James A. Farley, later

Club: MERRY CHRISTMAS & HAPPY NEW YEAR

Col. John V. Grombach, G.S.C.

Name: _____ Name: K. O. Tough Luck

WINNER OF ROUND	CLEAN EFFECTIVE PUNCHES	RING GENERALSHIP	AGGRESSIVENESS	DEFENSE	POINTS	1946 1947	POINTS	DEFENSE	AGGRESSIVENESS	RING GENERALSHIP	CLEAN EFFECTIVE PUNCHES	WINNER OF ROUND
W						Dec.						L
W						Jan.						L
W						Feb.						L
W						Mar.						L
W						Apr.						L
W	HEALTH	HAPPINESS	PROSPERITY	FRIENDSHIP		May						L
W						June						L
W						July						L
W						Aug.						L
W						Sept.						L
W						Oct.						L
W						Nov.						L

Col. John V. Grombach, G.S.C.

is Winner of All Points

in all Rounds

Edward P. F. Eagen
SIGNATURE

102. New York State Athletic Commissioner Eddie Eagan's scorecard.

Postmaster General, who followed George Brower and William Muldoon, the first publicized commissioner. In Farley's regime there was an epidemic of fouls. Boxers accidentally or on purpose hit their opponents below the belt and were declared losers, while the winners usually lay writhing in pain on the ring floor. This led to betting abuses, for gamblers usually declared all bets off in case of a foul. Also, many boxers on the losing end of a fight began to acquire the habit of falling to the floor, alleging they had been fouled.

A disgruntled witness to many of these real or illusory fouls was a newspaper telegraph operator whose job required him to sit in the press row, with his fist on a telegraph key, and describe the fights he saw. A foul always annoyed him, as it did the writing fraternity whose prepared accounts he relayed along the wires. One day he informed his associates he had discovered a foul-proof cup to end all fouls. His reporter friends immediately named him "Foulproof" Taylor. Undaunted, he perfected his discovery in his cellar in Brooklyn and soon started going to fights wearing his invention which he guaranteed would immunize a man against any low blow. He would walk up to his newspaper friends at the fights or in places where they retired for libations.

"Hit me," exclaimed Foulproof Taylor, as he stood before some sports writer.

"Kick me if you want," he would triumphantly add.

The protector was a sponge rubber and aluminum arrangement quite small, but strong and able almost to withstand the kick of a mule. Attired in a white sweater on which was written "Foulproof Taylor," the proud inventor picketed the offices of the boxing commission, sports stores, boxers' training camps, and the offices of sports editors.

"Go ahead, hit me here," Foulproof used to say as he stood with legs apart and stomach out, hands by his sides.

Soon he proved to all that with his protector there was no longer a low blow that could hurt or incapacitate the wearer.

As a result of this invention and its bizarre but imaginative creator, Farley decreed that a man who went down would be counted out no matter where he had been hit. So, there were no more fouls or at least no more fights won, lost, and ended by them. This was a great departure from the old rules and another advance in the progress of boxing, attributable to politics in the form of a boxing commission with absolute authority, and last but not least to Mr. Taylor.

Although Mr. Eagan and the New York State Boxing Commission instituted many excellent reforms, it must be admitted that, like everything else in the world, there was plenty of room for improvement.

In September 1951, Eagan was replaced by Robert K. Christenberry, who served through December 1954. Although Mr. Christenberry's background did not include any boxing experience, as an experienced executive in the hotel business he did not harm boxing, although he made some questionable decisions such as trying to reverse fight decisions by his own appointed officials, which, of course, were reversed in court. From January 1955 to December 1958 Julius Helfand, a gangster-chasing lawyer, was the boxing commissioner, followed by Melvin Krulewitch from January 1959 to June 1966. Then in July 1966 (to July 1975) came Edwin Dooley, famous all-American football player with a blarney stone ability to express himself and the Irish love of flying fists. His nine years in office matched the record of another Irish-American, James Farley, who held sway over boxing in New York State from February 1924 to February 1933. Dooley evidently had the full backing of Governors Rockefeller and Malcolm Wilson to run things for the good of boxing only, as he proceeded to do. Evidence of this is that an application to Dooley by the author resulted in a letter welcoming the possibilities of using an experienced and competent official irrespective of political support, connections, or endorsements. Dooley's letter, compared with Eagan's (both photographed and in this book), indicates a great improvement in the approach of obtaining proper officials, irrespective of politics. Before leaving the subject of the New York State Athletic Commission, most books on boxing refer to the famous William Muldoon as the first chairman or commissioner. However, research in the New York State files indicate that a Joseph Johnson was the earliest incumbent, serving from August 1920 to April 1921.

The first Jersey Joe Walcott-Joe Louis fight demonstrated many weaknesses of the New York State system. First it was arranged as a mere exhibition since the bout was originally scheduled for a nonchampionship ten rounds. In the words of the commission—

It will also be permitted for a heavyweight champion to engage in a bout of a lesser number of rounds than fifteen when his championship will not be at stake, provided he agrees that he will box the outstanding contender for the championship within six months from the date of his last championship bout, at the time he contracts to participate in a bout of a lesser number of rounds.

According to this rather punchy sentence, the Commission was able to approve the exhibition bout and at a $30 top, even though the Garden, the promoters, and the Commission should have known better. The day of a high-priced exhibition is past. The press and the public then went to work and the Commission backtracked. This automatically should make the rule ready for Nat Fleisher's Boxing Museum. It is definitely obsolete.

The Eagan System, while a step in the right direction, may be, according to many, a hop, skip, and jump landing too far into space. As the situation stands, New York fights are generally decided on the basis of rounds won. That does not necessarily work out. The first Louis-Walcott fight, for example, demonstrated that very point. In addition, it demonstrated that professional officials, especially those super-saturated with boxing lore, can believe in one of the fighters so overwhelmingly on his past performances as to become blinded to what goes on before their eyes if it is totally unexpected. More amateur officials or a greater distribution of refereeing and judging assignments among prominent business or professional men intimately conversant with boxing, or among other less professional types of officials drawn from the ranks of ex-fighters not dependent on the sport for a livelihood, would introduce new arbiters with broader perspectives and more flexibility because they would not be so close

to the subject. In any case, such officials could follow the Eagan System or the language of the rule book better, or help simplify that system and language.

There is no doubt in the minds of many experts that the Louis-Walcott, 5 December 1947 decision was the result of some of the officials' memories of Joe Louis over the previous ten years rather than the exact measure of what he did on 5 December. In other words, men who live mostly in the fight game and officiate continually may not always have an open mind, and may be confused by rules which systematize and complicate the simple question of who whacked hell out of whom. A famous boxing coach once said there was only one rule by which to judge the winner of a bout. He said he selected the contestant he would prefer to be at the end of the bout—the one who got whacked around or knocked down less. "To hell with points or rounds," he added.

The last word in judging and scoring boxing bouts, as far as the New York State Athletic Commission, is projected by an official booklet by William Recht already referred to. Basically it is pretty close to the Eddie Eagan system, but the text and explanations are more clearly and simply written.

Professional boxing is a contributor to both the national and state budgets through taxes, but because of its nature, has become partly or entirely controlled by the states. The National Boxing Association, a purely voluntary body, previously mentioned, had done a great deal for the sport and had been able to accomplish many reforms and some coordination, but was neither recognized by, nor had any standing in some states. In 1949, it enjoyed considerable prestige with A. J. Green and Heinie Miller as its top executives. Miller, former president of the N.B.A., was a well-known former boxer, boxing official, and Colonel in the United States Marine Corps and Secretary of the District of Columbia Boxing Commission.

However the N.B.A. in the opinion of many unfortunately dropped its usefulness and prestige in trying to overreach itself. It became the self-styled World Boxing Association (W.B.A.), and tried to have every state in the United States have a vote, but gave only one vote to other countries so that, for instance, France, Germany, Sweden, and England had only four votes against the United States' boxing interests, which had forty-eight votes (at that time). Needless to say, this made little sense. Pretty soon another group came into being, the World Boxing Council (W.B.C.). If these two had combined, many troubles in the sport could have been solved and many improvements in world boxing could have been attained. As it is, recognition of different champions leads only to confusion. The recognition of the European boxing body or of the New York State Athletic Commission or of *The Ring* magazine is as likely to be correct and accepted as those of the two allegedly controlling boxing bodies. The W.B.A. has become famous for its inclination to want to strip champions of their titles on the slightest pretext and have even questioned such "greats" as Monzon and Napoles while they were still in their prime. Why have several versions of a championship? As far as the author is concerned, based on some fifty years of contact with the late Nat Fleischer and *The Ring* magazine, he would take *The Ring*'s choice and now that of Nat Loubet in preference to that of either of the new (alleged) world boxing bodies.

Without going into any criticism of the legitimacy of the various authorities, the sport suffers. In contrast, one can point to the central control of professional football in the United States. One thing is certain—that boxing should have but one overall controlling body or single coordination, certainly insofar as the United States is concerned and one single coordination of all national bodies for control and standardization, and one source of recognition of world champions. However, there is no agreement between the principals and the experts in boxing on whether the control should be governmental or private. Most experts believe that boxing control should not be political and not based on any bureaucratic organization supported by taxes. The success of baseball in governing itself is often referred to, but baseball is not worldwide. With the advance of the worldwide TV era in boxing and with the little experience in faraway countries as against the experience of the controls in well-established boxing countries, there is as a result greatly reduced controls. In other words, major fights and world championship contests may not be controlled properly with every possible test against doping or any illegal or unethical interference or influence. After all, the controlling authority on a boxing match in Zaire, Indonesia, Macao, or Madagascar cannot compare with that afforded by some controlling organization such as in New York State with over three-quarters of a century's experience.

As a specific example of possible safeguards (or lack of safeguards) by a controlling body, the New York State Athletic Commission was asked this question in recognizing the 1975 change in the world's heavyweight championship: "Did they have one of their personnel present at the Zaire fight?" The answer was: "No." When the press reported that Foreman had claimed being poisoned before the fight, the New York State Athletic Commission was asked if urine and blood tests had been made on both fighters before and after the Zaire fight and, if so, were the results available? The answer was that they doubted if any had been made, although even Olympic athletes are tested against drugs as are racehorses. Which brings up the case of Carlos Monzon, currently middleweight champion of the world, who is barred by the European Boxing Union from boxing in Europe because of his refusal to pay the ten thousand British pounds fine for refusing to take a dope test in Paris at his fight with José Napoles in February 1974.

A strange story that this book cannot omit is that of a retired boxing referee who, after lots of punishment, scored a final KO, or at least a technical KO, over the Madison Square Garden. He not only had the Garden on the ropes but managed, at the same time, to stagger the New York State Athletic Commission by making it look like it might have been subservient to the Garden boxing management.

The story, one of the most unusual in boxing, started in Madison Square Garden on 15 September 1970 when Davey Feld, age fifty, a former Brooklyn boxer—promoter—night club operator, who now runs a liquor business in Miami Beach, was forceably ejected from ringside, not too gently, by Madison Square Garden security police under the orders of Garden matchmaker Teddy Brenner and the then Garden boxing president, Harry Markson. A platoon of Garden bouncers grabbed Feld when he either refused to leave his seat (assigned to officials at ringside) or when he attempted to climb into the ring to referee a bout he had been officially assigned to referee by the Chairman of the New York State Athletic Commission, Edwin B. Dooley, that very morning. The scheduled heavyweight fight, the main event, was between Floyd Patterson and Charlie Green. According to the testimony, it would appear that Patterson objected to Feld's refereeing, which caused Dooley to threaten Patterson with a lifetime suspension from fighting in New York State and a $5,000 fine if he refused to accept the Commission's choice of a referee, or ran out on the fight. Yet, at the last minute, Dooley evidently changed his mind due to claims by the Garden's boxing management with respect to the possibility of a riot and a general refund of all tickets. In any case, when Feld either tried to make good on the commission's original appointment or, after being notified by Dooley to take himself out, merely wanted to keep his ringside seat to see the fight (this was never fully determined at the trial), he was thrown out bodily and, according to some testimony, was physically injured. It was established, however, that he was knocked to the ground several times, punched any number of times, headlocked, and, finally, lifted and bodily carried out of the Garden by six special Garden guards. This was contended as not doing any good to his arthritic bones or to his teeth, under treatment, not to mention the public humiliation and shame. Of course Feld came back swinging from his battle against heavy odds. He sued the Garden for one million dollars!

The story behind the story involved the fact that Feld had quite properly stopped a fight between Pedro Agosto and Forrest Ward in 1969 when Agosto, dazed and unable to defend himself, stumbled about the ring. Teddy Brenner, the Garden matchmaker, who either was trying to build up Agosto or felt that the stopping of a fight arranged by him was critical of his matchmaking abilities, jumped up and shouted "Feld will never work in the Garden again and if I can't help it, I'll get him!" Feld's next major assignment at the Garden after this was on 15 September 1970 when he was objected to at the last minute—although appointed by the Commissioner the very morning of the fight.

Another story behind the story is that the Garden was anxious to buildup Patterson all over again for a second Clay fight, although he had been knocked out twice in one round each by Sonny Liston seven or eight years before. Patterson had even, a year before, lost a decision to Jimmy Ellis in Stockholm; nevertheless, the boxing management of the Garden and Patterson and his manager, under the circumstances, wanted to be sure that the referee could be counted on as neither handicapping Patterson's style or confidence. So Patterson seemed to have some edge on the Garden boxing promoters and the Garden, with its threats of a riot and returning of ticket money (including state tax), seemed to have caused the Commission to overrule itself even though one story claims Commissioner Dooley seemed to be adamant with respect to his appointment of Feld as referee. The evidence seemed to indicate that the fault, if any, was that of the Garden and its management.

The last round of this unusual boxing bout was in the Manhattan Civil Court in October 1975. As announced by most of the press, the result was "Feld by a TKO." The Garden led with frequent references to Feld's real name being Samuel Kelman, but received some staggering counter-punches when Kelman explained he had adopted the name Feld to prevent his mother from knowing he was boxing from age thirteen. He had some one hundred amateur and professional bouts, before becoming a $150 per bout referee. It was also brought out that the Garden may have caused the commission to check Feld out with the FBI, without any result. The Garden, seeing that Feld's punching was too much for them and that they could not score on Feld, reached an out-of-court settlement, although the settlement was definitely less than a million dollars. The amount of the settlement was declared confidential and not to be disclosed by anyone according to the orders of the judge. It therefore cannot be disclosed but was believed to have been in the very low six figures. In any case, Feld had this to say, "I'm extremely happy as I feel like I beat the Garden and repaid them for what they did to me. . . . It was not merely a monetary matter." So ended one of the most unusual bouts in recent boxing history.

No sport as old as boxing is without its unusual angles. Just as oddities in the news are inescapable, strange happenings in boxing frequently occur.

For instance, a one-armed boxer would be assumed to be even less useful than a one-armed paperhanger, but the courage, perseverance and abilities of man have proved such a statement incorrect. Tommy Rodgers, twenty-year-old one-armed Harvard junior from Pittsburgh, on 27 March 1947, won the 155-pound championship of Harvard University with a knockout in the finals. In the first round, he and his opponent, Somerby Dowst of Exeter, New Hampshire, sparred cautiously; in the second round, they started slugging. Rodgers, a chunky lad who lost his left arm in a train wreck a few years ago, took a couple on the head but landed a fast hard one on Dowst's chin. It sent Dowst down for a count of nine. When Dowst regained his feet, Rodgers nailed him again. The bout was over and a one-armed boxer had won a championship.

While on the subject of unusual happenings in boxing, it would be interesting to explore the point of whether a world's champion could ever lose his title in a nontitle bout. This issue has been discussed and written about by newspaper writers and dramatists for years. Every time a world's champion, particularly the world's heavyweight champion, goes on a barnstorming tour either challenging all comers or fighting local stumblebums, the point is raised and many articles written about the possibility that an unknown might, by accident, defeat or knock out the champion.

The strange part of it is that it really happened. A champion was beaten, although not knocked out, by an unknown. Early in the present century, on account of the laws of various states, many fights were conducted on a no decision basis, although there was always the newspaper decision which was the opinion of the majority of the sports writers who witnessed the contest. This decision was usually more or less accepted.

On 19 December 1902, James J. Jeffries, world heavyweight boxing champion, fought an exhibition or nontitle fight with an unknown named Jack Munroe, in Butte, Montana. According to all accounts, Munroe gave Jeffries what was then called in the *Police Gazette* a thorough "lathering," and won the unanimous newspaper decision from the world's title-holder. There was much controversy as to whether Munroe was not the champion because of his unquestionably having given the champion a beating. Munroe proceeded to prove his surprise defeat of Jeffries was no fluke by beating such outstanding heavyweight fighters of his day as Peter Maher, Tom Sharkey, and Jack Johnson. On 26 April 1904, as a result of popular demand, Munroe fought Jeffries again in an official world's heavyweight championship bout. This time Jeffries knocked out Munroe, retaining his official title and ending the controversy.

Munroe later enlisted in the famous Princess Pat Regiment of Canada and lost an arm at the battle of Vimy Ridge in France in World War I. Munroe died 13 February 1942, in Toronto, Canada, where he was always known as the "Champ."

One of the many interesting prospects in store for the ring and one that some day may come to pass, is for a world's champion in an exhibition, nontitle, or unofficial bout, to be knocked cold. If all the conditions were according to rules and such a knockout were legitimate in every way, the question as to who would then be champion might be difficult to determine, especially in the heavyweight division where no weight, official weighing-in or weight limit is involved.

The easiest and most popular way in which champions in other weight divisions can ply their trade without risking their crowns, is in the "overweight" contest. By the expedient of having their opponent or both weigh over the limit allowed for their class, the bout automatically cannot involve the title for that class. But, naturally, since the heavyweight class has no limits, this fool-proof means of protecting titles is not possible in the senior division.

No book on boxing would be complete without the story of the Duke of Albemarle. In 1681 he forced his servants to take up boxing and entertained himself and his family by arranging matches between his various servants, just as years later the Southerners did with their slaves in America. Thirteen years before James Figg's birth, a London newspaper carried the following comment: "Yesterday a match of boxing was performed before his Grace, the right honorable Duke of Albemarle, between his butler and his butcher, the latter won the prize as he hath done many times before, being accounted, though but a little man, the best at this exercise in all England."

Nero, in A.D. 67, wanted to bribe the Olympic judges to let him win a boxing championship. The latter were afraid that someone would cross Nero up and injure his royal person, so they sold him on the idea of participating in the chariot race instead, where, with better equipment and finer horses, he could win going away. Nero should have "stood in bed," for even in the chariot race he came to grief, although it is not known if some pre-race libations were responsible. He fell from his chariot in the race and came very near being crushed to death, but as a deal had been made with the Hellanodikai (chief judge) for one million sesterces, originally offered for the boxing championship, Nero was crowned victor of the chariot race. However, Nero's championship in the chariot race was the same as it would have been in boxing, namely, he won on the floor by a foul.

Probably the most interesting story ever told about William A. Brady, and incidentally about William Muldoon, is the one concerning the motion picture of the Corbett-Fitzsimmons fight.

Corbett knocked down Fitzsimmons in the early rounds, although succumbing to Fitzsimmons's solar plexus punch later, losing the championship. William Muldoon, the famous solid man, was timekeeper at the fight. One night some time after the fight, motion pictures of the contest were being shown in New York at the Academy of Music, and Muldoon dropped in to see them. The film unreeled without more than normal remarks from the audience, until the part that showed Fitz being knocked down by Corbett. Then a voice from audience shouted, "Stop the film." It stopped, showing a beautiful still of Ruby Robert Fitzsimmons on the canvas.

The person who had interrupted the picture then sprang on the stage and to Muldoon's surprise there stood William A. Brady, the manager of the ex-champion.

"Excuse me, ladies and gentlemen," he said, "if you will please follow the rest of this film you will see that James J. Corbett was really done out of his championship by foul means."

He then gave the order for the picture to proceed, inviting everyone to take out his watch and follow the count. As the picture proceeded, he counted aloud while Muldoon was doing the same silently on the screen. The count went to thirteen, or well over the knockout time, and was followed by shouts from the audience that Fitzsimmons was not really the champion.

Brady continued, "You see, Corbett knocked out Fitzsimmons."

Muldoon arose and boomed out, "You're a liar."

Brady could not answer this accusation, since he had bribed the operator who turned the hand crank, to slow down the picture. James J. Corbett, himself, convinced Brady to quit making any repeat performances of this little travesty and with excellent sportsmanship admitted that he had been fairly beaten by Fitzsimmons.

An interesting incident with respect to timekeeping brought on by the modern era is one that occurred in a major fight in New York, a state which prides itself on running fights perfectly.

One of the rounds of a major heavyweight fight, commercially broadcast to the world, appeared to us to be short. The author immediately repaired to his radio studio in the Steinway Building where the fight broadcast had been recorded. The engineers were asked to identify the turntables the broadcast had been recorded on. We then tested them with a stroboscope to be certain there was no speed variation or error that would make any time consideration incorrect. They were perfect. We then played the records on the same turntables and timed the round from bell to bell, which could be heard in the broadcast behind the fight commentator's talk, and, sure enough, the round was definitely short by some twenty seconds.

Brigadier General John J. Phelan, then Senior Commissioner of the New York Boxing Commission, was immediately informed and told he could come up to our studio to hear it for himself, and that he could bring any engineers or watch experts he desired. However, he not only refused, but also told the author he was crazy. "You can forget your stroboscope and your probosis" cried the General! The General claimed that it was impossible for the timing of any New York State Boxing Commission fight to be wrong, and that it was the equipment and recording that were wrong. As a result we conducted further tests which further proved the records and recordings were correct and the round was short.

We recommend, (although it has probably already been accomplished) since we are in the "Age of Science," that only electric clocks that will automatically ring a bell alternately three minutes and one minute apart after the first bell and will also buzz the "seconds out" warning, thirty seconds before the start of each round be employed. By being occasionally checked, such a piece of equipment would eliminate the human element or any influences affecting the time, timing, or time-keeping of rounds in championship fights in the Atomic Age. A knockdown, the action of the crowd, the excitement of the action in the ring, human error or accident, any or all might contribute to incorrect timing.

The knockdown count is another item based on a human rather than a mechanical or mathematical equation. In a 1948 fight at Madison Square Garden with Eddie Eagan at ringside, Arthur Donovan, stellar referee of the New York State Boxing Commission, and Jack Watson, official timekeeper, the following incident occurred: Marcel Cerdan, middleweight champion of Europe, knocked down Lavern Roach of Texas, but toppled over him, and then jumped up again. The referee started a count, but the timekeeper did not. Then the timekeeper did, while the referee was still begging a count. The result was that Roach got up at nine, although Nat Fleischer claimed to have clocked Roach's rest at thirty-two seconds. The author timed it as nineteen seconds. According to Ring Lardner's son John, a sports writer who knows his boxing, Frenchy Cerdan said, "I admire your tall women and beautiful buildings, but not your long timekeepers."

Croquet and boxing are rarely connected, but they once were, in the reign of Gentleman Jim Corbett. Corbett went in for croquet in a big way and played a "wicked" game. However, in Jacksonville, Florida, while training for his fight with Mitchell, Corbett met his match. Jack Dempsey, the Nonpareil, who had been horribly beaten by Fitzsimmons after the former had passed his prime, was sick but still good enough at croquet to beat Corbett.

Speaking of croquet at the turn of the century naturally brings up the ladies. Women rarely, if ever, went to prizefights in those days, much less ever entered the ring. The first woman to enter the ring was Mrs. Fitzsimmons at the Corbett-Fitzsimmons fight in Carson City. When Corbett was leading, she dashed into Bob's corner between rounds, sponged his face and gave him advice in a lusty fashion. Mrs. Tex Rickard saw an early fight, concealed in a booth, but later went to a Jeffries fight with Mrs. Jeffries. A woman dressed like a man got into the Sullivan-Corbett fight in New Orleans.

Some boxers have been musicians. One Jack Doyle, the Irish Thrush, sang from the ringside before and after his fights. The Voice, Frank Sinatra, is said to have been a boxer and occasionally throws punches on and off the screen. However, except for the Romans, no one has forced musicians to box. A Roman Emperor once forced some Greek flute players, who were performing badly at a festival, to put on cestus. They were not pleasing the audience, so they were ordered to fight. Their boxing afforded great entertainment to the Roman crowd. This happened in 167 B.C., but there is no record of musicians ever performing in the ring again, either with their flutes or their fists.

Boxing still makes its impression in the field of music. James Petrillo, former head of the musicians' union in the United States, was a former boxer. Ferruccio Tagliavini, the Italian tenor of the Metropolitan Opera, was such an ardent fight fan that he

103. Number 1 boxing fan in American Golden Era, Arturo Toscanini, world-famous conductor.

104. Most famous double-knockout in boxing history; referee, after picking up Ad Wolgast, counts Rivers out, 4 July 1912. (N.Y. Athletic Club)

risked spoiling his voice by yelling his favorites on at the Garden. He once said, "I like very much the box—it is very dangerous for me when I sing on Saturday because on Friday my voice is for Madison Square Garden." Arturo Toscanini, world famous conductor, was an ardent boxing fan. He would frequently phone the author from all over the world for an opinion before or after some fights and desired to be introduced to Jack Dempsey, Primo Carnera and Max Baer.

One of the most unusual angles found in digging around for material for this book was the fact that for hundreds of years English medical authorities have been performing autopsies, particularly on their famous men. Up until some time ago, the famous man who had the largest heart ever found was Lord Nelson, of Trafalgar fame. On the other hand, the smallest human heart ever found by the British medical authorities was that of Hooper the Tinman, who was English or World's Heavyweight (bare-fist) Champion in 1795.

Doctors tell us that the strain of athletics has a tendency to enlarge the heart, but evidently it didn't work out in this case of the Tinman, who fought a 180 round fight in 1790 that lasted over three and one-half hours. Perhaps the explanation was that Hooper, like many champions, had a killer instinct and therefore little heart!

Double knockouts are the most frequent of ring oddities. However, the most famous, the oddest and the only championship double knockout occurred during the Rivers-Wolgast event at Vernon, California. Rivers, with the exception of Aurelia Herrera, was the greatest Mexican fighter of all time. He and Ad Wolgast, lightweight champion, hit each other at the same time in a ferocious match on a hot summer day in 1912. Both men went down, Rivers claiming a foul. Jack Welsh, the referee, deliberately picked up Wolgast and counted Rivers out.

With the advent of television we not only have to worry about time and sound or music for a program, but also color. At the Cerdan-Abrams fight at Madison Square Garden on 29 March 1947, Eagan and the New York State Athletic Commission changed their color scheme for fighters' tights. Cerdan was assigned black trunks with white waistband and white stripes down the sides and front; Abrams was given contrasting trunks of white with black waistband and black stripes down the sides and front. The purpose was to better identify the principals for the television clients. Previous to this fight, the standard color combination in New York State was black and purple and fight managers requested information as to who was going to pay for the new trunks. The television people said they did not request the change. A television expert states that off-white is preferable to white. This opens up all sorts of possibilities, including the painting of colored bands around fighters' arms, legs, and bodies. A decorator even suggested that for television one fighter might be painted like a zebra, while the other should be spotted like a leopard, which should make identification easier.

A well-known Englishman once said that "boxing is the image of war with none of its guilt and only twenty-five per cent of its dangers." All of the ancient boxers, and most of the bare-knuckle fighters in England, partook of both, however. Corporal Shaw, an English prizefighter, killed ten Frenchmen at the Battle of Waterloo with his own hand, according to contemporary accounts and Sir Walter Scott. Shaw was finally killed by a musket shot and was immortalized in a popular poem of the time:

Oh! Shade of the cheesemonger! You who, alas,
Doubled up by dozens, those monsieurs in brass.
Oh! That great day of milling, when blood lay in lakes!
When Kings held the battle, and Europe the stakes.

Barney Ross, the ex-world's welterweight champion, was credited with having killed twenty-two Japanese on Guadalcanal in the Southwest Pacific in World War II. In 1948 he enlisted in a volunteer fighting force to defend the State of Israel in Palestine.

The soldiers in World War I were especially

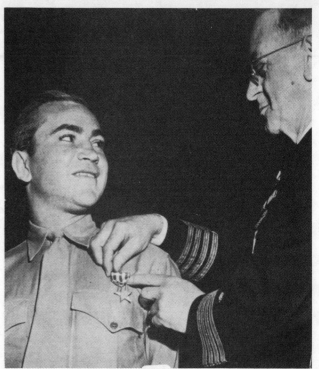

104A. Barney Ross being decorated for bravery in action as a Marine at Guadalcanal by USN Capt. Pratt. (United States Navy photo)

trained in both boxing and bayonet fighting. Particularly outstanding in each of these was Captain Bob Roper, who later became a first-rate professional heavyweight. His younger brother, Tom Roper, followed him into the prize ring only to be knocked out by Joe Louis.

It is impossible to give here the number of boxers who entered or were killed in World War I. It is just as difficult to mention those who were in World War II, but it is known that the courage, aggressiveness, and self-reliance, which boxing teaches, enabled many of them to accomplish much for their country. An idea of what boxers as a group did in this war can be had by mentioning a few from but one place, the United States Naval Academy:

Slade Cutter, according to Spike Webb, the greatest heavyweight boxer ever to attend the Naval Academy, undefeated in four years, was a submarine commander in the Pacific and sank eighteen Jap ships, totaling over 100,000 tons, in three cruises. Decorated and honored, he stated that "the best training for war is boxing."

Another ex-Navy boxer was Commander Bruce McCandless, '32, who was awarded the highest honor, the Congressional Medal of Honor.

John J. Powers, a member of the Navy Boxing Team in 1934–35, and nephew of the famous fight manager, Jimmy Johnston, was killed in action and awarded the Congressional Medal of Honor posthumously.

Gus Lentz, Navy intercollegiate heavyweight champion in 1926, was killed in action.

John Fitzgerald, an intercollegiate lightweight champion in 1929, commanded a submarine and was a prisoner of the Japs for two years.

Colonel Paul Moret, Marine Corps, killed in the Southwest Pacific and posthumously awarded the Legion of Merit, was captain of the Navy Boxing Team in 1930.

Admiral "Bull" Halsey was a boxing representative of the United States Naval Academy to the N.C.A.A. (the intercollegiate control body) from 1928 to 1930. He was a great fight fan and supporter of boxing and the boxing program of the Navy. He was a boxer himself when he was a midshipman in 1904.

William L. Peterson, killed in action over Tokyo two days before the end of the war, was captain of the 1942 Navy Boxing Team the last year of intercollegiate boxing. George S. Lambert, killed in action, was captain of the 1935 Navy Boxing Team.

Boxers were scattered over the seven seas by World War II and, it is believed, spread the sport farther than ever before. Boxing gloves became well known in the farthest islands in the South Pacific, in the teak forests of Burma, in the temples of Siam, and even in the mountain fastnesses of the Himalayas. Boxing became popular in Scandinavia and in Africa. Colonel Bill Maglin, light heavyweight champion of West Point from 1919 to 1924, Provost Marshal of Korea, taught his Korean police force how to fight with their fists. Colonel Mike Buckley, one of the hardest hitting middleweights ever to box for West Point, worked out with the boxers in the Anzac outfit he was attached to as an observer in the fighting in North Africa before we entered the war. When that outfit was all but annihilated by Rommel's armored cavalry, Mike was captured by the Germans, but, because they were not interested in boxing or holding an American observer, he was turned over to the Italians who sent him to Rome and let him work out in an old Roman gym there. Colonel Demas Craw, killed in the North African invasion and posthumously awarded a Congressional Medal of Honor, was never on a boxing team at West Point but learned to box there from Billy Cavanagh. While Military Attache to Greece during the Axis occupation and before we entered the war, Craw was almost pushed off the street by an official Italian Staff car. He successfully blocked the Fascist car, however, but became engaged in an argument and later a fight with its officer occupant and his chauffeur. He knocked out the Italian officer with a right to the chin and routed the chauffeur with flying left hooks, to the great delight of the Greek crowd.

Another boxer who distinguished himself in World War II was Lou Barba, born Louis Barbagelata of Greenwich Village. He fought Braddock and other leading heavyweights in the late twenties and was once sparring partner to Max Schmeling. Barba was in the Merchant Marine where he served as a physical director. Twice a member of ship crews that were torpedoed, he was shot in the back by machine gun fire from a German submarine intent on destroying the survivors of a torpedoed ship. Although he miraculously escaped, he eventually died of his wounds and exposure.

During World War II in Nazi-controlled France, the national and local boxing associations and groups became the cells of a very active underground organization. Many of the outstanding managers, promoters, and fighters in this way became clandestine allies to the British and American troops in uniform. Discovery and capture by the Germans meant death before a firing squad to these men. Andre Barraut, manager of Laurent Dauthuille, top French middleweight, was a prominent member of the French boxing underground and had many narrow escapes. Very often meetings at the neighborhood gymnasium, boxing workouts, and training were the screens or cover for planning sabotage of key industry, communication, or transportation; plotting escapes for allied airmen from Nazi imprisonment; or relaying military information destined for the headquarters of General Eisenhower. There is even a case on record where these secret channels were used clandestinely to distribute rare and dangerous equipment from the United States—sets of boxing gloves. So here we find boxing gloves as the cover for the punches of the forces of democracy.

David "Mickey" Marcus, one of the stars of "Mickey" Cavanagh's (Kid Glover) all-time best West Point teams in the early Twenties, taught the United States 27th Division boxing and hand-to-hand combat in Hawaii for use in the South Pacific in World War II. Later, on the personal staff of President Roosevelt at Teheran and Yalta, he talked boxing to the Allied leaders. After World War II, Colonel Marcus offered his services to Israel, and was killed before the city of Jerusalem by a stray Arab bullet several days before the final truce. Later, the accepted and official report was that Marcus had been killed by a trigger happy sentry who had challenged him on his way to his quarters. Marcus, not knowing Hebrew and answering in English, had further confused the sentry. Then, much later, secret intelligence sources reported two different versions of an assassination plot. While acting as Commander-in-Chief of the Jewish Army defending Jerusalem, Marcus introduced boxing as a compulsory part of the training of the Israeli Army he organized. Marcus, between his West Point days and his reentry into military service, was a lawyer and once Commissioner of Correction of the City of New York. Boxing played more than a recreational part in the career of David Marcus.

165

104B. Great American boxing coach Spike Webb, United States Naval Academy, United States Olympic Boxing teams, 1920–24–28; via United States Navy, he coached boxing all over the world. (Courtesy of U.S. Naval Academy)

While stationed at Governor's Island as a Lieutenant of Infantry after his graduation from West Point, Marcus studied law at night school and helped his schooling and his family financially by fighting professionally as *Danny Mars* in Metropolitan Brooklyn, and Long Island rings. His professional boxing career was abruptly stopped when his Colonel, on a party, wound up as a guest at a prizefight. The Colonel was astounded to recognize one of the participants as one of his shave-tails.

From approximately 1920 to 1930 the United States Navy sent its great United States Naval Academy boxing coach "Spike" Webb around the world with the annual midshipmen cruises. He coached many United States Olympic and United States international boxing teams, gave boxing lessons at many ports of call of United States fleets, and contributed to the spread and advance of boxing toward the present worldwide era.

Finally, during World War II, Tunney and Dempsey toured the world on inspection trips to check up on the Navy and Coast Guard physical training programs respectively. Joe Louis and a troupe of champions and sparring partners and other boxing groups gave exhibitions everywhere, primarily for our GIs but invariably seen by many of the local inhabitants.

There can be no question but that boxing came to many strange places for the first time, and, judging by its reception, came to stay.

10 • Great Actors of Boxing— In and Out of the Ring

There has always been hero worship of the strong man and the manly qualities of courage, brawn and vigor. Combine these qualities with the thrill of boxing as a sport, and there emerges a fit subject for the public to venerate—the king of the ancient arena and of the modern ring. If, as Shakespeare says,

All the world's a stage
And all the men and women merely players;
They have their exits and their entrances;
And one man in his time plays many parts,

Then surely the ring is that stage also, and the spotlight of centuries has played upon boxing. The actors of boxing have been many and have shone brightly in the annals of time. Certain characters stand out in the cavalcade of boxing through the ages. Many of these have been dealt with in their proper niches as champions in the history of the sport, in the development of the sport's technique or in other parts of this book. Consequently they will not be dealt with again in this chapter, even though they did command the spotlight and are actors worthy of the applause of their audience.

Milo of Croton, over two thousand years ago, is probably one of our first great actors; also Eurydamas of Greece who certainly got his teeth into his boxing role. He swallowed all his teeth which had been battered out, rather than show his opponent he had been hurt, forcing the latter finally to give up in despair, thinking that his most telling blows had had no effect.

In the days of Rome, when boxing became part of the bloody spectacles of the Colosseum, the actors came and went rather rapidly. However, this period gave us one of our greatest players in the earlier era of boxing. This amateur rose from a mere spearholder to not only the star role, but also to manager, director, writer, producer, and emperor as well. But we are getting ahead of our story.

Primo Carnera was a piker in size, appetite, boxing, and wrestling ability when compared to this champion who lived approximately 200 years after Christ. It was not a promoter like Mr. Leon See who first saw this giant, but an emperor. Emperor Severus of Rome, while returning from an expedition to the East, halted in Thrace to celebrate the birthday of Geta, his youngest son. Athletic games were the order of the day, and thousands of people came from miles around. Among these was a young barbarian of such gigantic stature and great muscular development as to attract the attention of all. In rude dialect he asked to take part in the boxing and wrestling exercises to contend for prizes. The Roman soldiers refused, at first, for frankly they were afraid both of his size, and of what would result in loss of prestige if a Thracian peasant beat a Roman soldier. However, subsequently the refusal was reversed, and the strongest and toughest camp followers were chosen to compete with him. The young barbarian defeated sixteen of these in succession. After being given many gifts by the Roman soldiers, he was told by them that he might enlist in their army. This he did, and the next day was seen among a crowd of recruits by the Emperor, who took an immediate liking to him. The Thracian giant followed the mounted emperor at a dead run for a long and fast journey without the slightest appearance of fatigue. The remarkable endurance of the young barbarian astonished the emperor.

"Thracian," he said, "are you prepared to fight after your run?"

"Ready and willing, Sire," answered the youth, with alacrity.

The strongest and toughest soldiers of the army were selected and pitted against him. He knocked out seven in rapid succession. As a result of this, the emperor made him a member of his personal guard. This young barbarian, whose name was Maximin, had judgment and shrewdness as well as valor and strength, and soon advanced in the favor of the emperor. To make a long story short: this giant, called by his soldiers Hercules, gradually rose in rank and importance until in a later reign he finally led the army in revolt and assassinated the emperor who had succeeded Severus.

Maximin then became Emperor of Rome. His rule was not too successful, however, as he became violently suspicious of everyone, accusing them of conspiring against his life. On one such occasion he had over 4,000 persons put to death without trial. As a result of this, there was civil war, and he was finally assassinated by the Praetorian Guard. However, let us examine Maximin only in comparison with other giants of the fight game. It is said he was never defeated in wrestling or boxing. Contemporary reports tell us he was eight feet in height, weighed over 400 pounds, and had the strength and appetite to match. It was stated that he could drink seven gallons of wine at one sitting and could eat forty pounds of meat in a day. He could move a loaded wagon with his arms, break a horse's leg with his fist, crumble stones in his hands, and tear up small trees by the roots. This king of the arena and Emperor of Rome overshadows all other actors in the sport in accomplishment and in size during the period preceding the Dark Ages.

It is a tradition of the stage that the show must go on. So we find, during the 1200 years when boxing disappeared, that certain personalities with a flair for drama were trying without success to keep boxing alive.

Richard Coeur de Lion, a king with a punch, who should have been an actor, did some boxing as well as crusading. Robin Hood, not a bad actor either, and his green rangers, especially Little John, occasionally resorted to fisticuffs to vary their performances.

The legend of Richard Coeur de Lion's boxing is fairly cloudy. One story is that while disguised as a mendicant he boxed with a French prince, and by accident killed him with a blow of his fist. Original sources fail to give us much confirmation or detail of Richard's fistic activities. However, history does tell us how Richard tried to intimidate a Saracen king by an exhibition reminiscent of our old Greek boxing friend Polydamas. Richard ordered out a bull, and with his two-handed sword chopped off its head with one cleaverlike blow. But the stunt boomeranged, for the Saracen king was not impressed. He too gave a demonstration of his swordsmanship for his followers and those of Richard, by throwing a feather cushion into the air and cutting it in many pieces with a sharp bladed scimitar while it fell.

After the Dark Ages, the rebirth of the science of the fist found boxing literally on the stage, and its exponents, although fencing masters, were forced to put on stage shows in order to attract trade and pupils. The famous boxers of early modern boxing, James Figg and John Broughton, were consummate showmen, not only in their own performances, but also in producing "shows." They operated their own theatres—amphitheatres, if you please—and developed these and their boxers and incidentally boxing, until they were all in public demand.

It is interesting to note that actors today have sometimes to grow beards like James Mason, or shave their heads like the late Dick Powell. The actors of the eighteenth century stage shows or prizefights shaved their heads. If you will study the pictures of James Figg and John Broughton with the shaved heads of their profession you can readily see why they were often called "twins." Actually, they were no relation, any more than Jack Dempsey and Max Schmeling, who also looked alike.

It was Figg and Broughton who first discovered the box-office success recipe used today by every wrestling promoter in the business, and used by Tex Rickard in his promotion of the Dempsey-Carpentier fight, namely, the recipe of pitting the villain against the hero, the mug versus the unsophisticated youth, the battered and bludgeoned veteran against the rising unmarked fighter, the foul fighter against the clean one. James Figg always had as villain of his shows one Buckhorse, a great backsword fencer, fighter, and boxer, who had been so badly chewed up that he was quite a horrible sight. James Figg also extended his "acting" to opening up boxing booths at fairs.

The next great actors of boxing were Daniel Mendoza and Richard Humphries, called the "Gentleman Boxer." In fact, they were such good actors and such great personalities that their repeat performances of really punishing fights helped boxing through one of its darkest eras.

Then we come to Gentleman Jackson, the aristocrat who opened the boxing school on Bond Street and hobnobbed with the upper crust. He has been discussed in his regular niche as one of the great champions of the sport. So has John Gully, probably one of the greatest actors of all time on the boxing scene. In addition to his parts in the ring, Gully had a gift for figures and the power to do rapid calculations. This talent, coupled with a knowledge of horses, made him turn to horseracing. At the outset of his career in this field, he was a backer and not a bookmaker. Later he became the leading bookmaker in England, and served the royal family. With his savings and winnings he began to buy horses. His purchases were all good, and soon his stable was the best in England. Like all actors, Gully had certain superstitions and prejudices—on names, for instance. The name in this case was Mameluke. It belonged to a horse, the first famous one that Gully owned, and one that almost ruined him. It was in 1827 when Gully, generally considered to be the betting agent of George IV, purchased Mameluke, Derby winner of the year before, from Lord Jersey for approximately $21,000. Dirty work in the famous St. Leger race made Mameluke lose, and Gully dropped $200,000. However, Gully recouped and finally sold the horse at a profit; in fact, like many a successful actor whose vehicle always makes money, Gully could not touch anything without being successful.

After he was graduated from butcher into a debtors' prison, his entry into boxing led him to the English or world's championship; his entrance into racing finally made him the greatest bookmaker, the owner of the greatest stable in the world, and winner of the Derby; his entry into politics elected him to Parliament; and later, when he went into the coal business, he wound up by owning most of the mines in one region of England. With respect to the Derby, what few people know is that Gully was not satisfied to win one Derby, which was among his great ambitions. His horse, Pyrrhus I, won in 1846, and in 1854 one of his horses, Andover, won the Derby, and another of his horses, Hermit, finished third. Gully at the age of seventy was described as "an old gentleman, strong and venerable, with snow white hair and lilac coat, and a not unkindly face."

On shifting the main scene of boxing from Enland to America, we automatically meet with a galaxy of showmen, not the least of whom were Morrissey and John L. Sullivan. John Morrissey was born in Ireland, but came over to America with his parents who settled in Troy. Morrissey began his career as a deckhand on the Hudson River boats. The story of his start in the fight game is an interesting and dramatic one. In the early days of New York City, boarding houses for immigrants flourished and the owners vied with each other for customers by having so-called runners meet the immigrants at the docks. The runner's assignment finally reduced itself to the business of licking the runners of other establishments.

Our young "player" was projected into this situation. He soon found that one Tom McCann was king of the runners, and so he proceeded in true Morrissey fashion to hunt down the said Tom McCann in the bar-room of the old St. Charles Hotel on lower Broadway to settle the immigrant situation with him right then and there. In the course of the scrimmage that followed, everything in the place was smashed, including a barrel stove which spilled its glowing coals over the floor. This was an important factor, for in an interchange it happened that Mr. Morrissey hit the floor first, and the glowing coals spurred him up and at Mr. McCann with such terrific heat that he knocked his opponent cold even though he himself was smoking, and his clothes were burned. As a result of this episode, he was known from then on as "The Old Smoke." In 1850 Morrissey caught the gold fever and went to California. It was there that he first made his entry into the prize ring. Formerly he had only been champion on a catch-as-catch-can or rough-and-tumble basis. Because of his tremendous appetite for punishment, which never could be satisfied, and his prodigious strength, he defeated everyone. Morrissey was recognized later as champion perhaps of the world, but certainly of America, especially after he defeated John Heenan. After this battle, Morrissey announced his retirement in accordance with a promise made to his wife.

Morrissey, attracted the attention of Commodore Vanderbilt, made a great deal of money in Wall Street, became interested in gambling houses, was very successful with them, took up horse racing and was a winner at that, and was responsible for the entire racing plant at Saratoga, New York, which eventually became famous. Later, like Gully, Morrissey entered politics, was elected to Congress from the Fifth New York District, and served with success for several terms.

Another great character actor of boxing, Ben Hogan, played many parts. Born a German, he became Irish by substituting "o" for one of the two "a's" in his original name. He was a gambler, inventor of America's first gambling ship, business man, professional acrobat, boxer, wrestler, competitive marksman, pirate, Civil War spy, oil magnate, and finally evangelist.

Hogan began his career as a peddler in Syracuse, and was later a cabin boy on an Erie Canal barge. It was in the latter job that he had his first informal bout against the barge fleet bully. He fought forty-three bouts under the *Police Gazette* rules. He then went to New Orleans and later became a pirate actually participating in attacks on, and sharing in the spoils of several merchant vessels. By good luck both as a pirate and gambler, Hogan returned to New York with $50,000 but lost almost all of it in a tavern on Cortlandt Street near the Hudson River. However, he did enter show business, and soon owned a successful traveling show or circus. He was the star of his own show, changing makeup and costumes and "doubling" as acrobat, tumbler, master of ceremonies, and strongman. The last included boxing exhibitions and a challenge to fight anyone in the audience.

The show finally failed, and Hogan returned to New Orleans where he killed an infamous bully in self-defense. The Civil War was then raging. The judge gave him the choice of jail or enlistment as a spy for the Confederacy. He chose the lesser of two evils. As soon as he got into Union territory he made for home, and shortly thereafter enlisted in the Union Army and left on a transport for southern combat duty. His ship was wrecked off Atlantic City and on rejoining his regiment he was made a Union spy because of his experiences, and was infiltrated back to New Orleans with some of his former pirate friends. They obtained work on a famous blockade runner that brought the Confederacy medical supplies, and biding their time finally captured her with a valuable cargo and sailed her to a northern port, winning commendation and prize money.

After the war, Hogan teamed up with a well-known gambling house hostess, Katherine Grant, known as "French Kate." They soon owned a chain of gambling houses and even opened one in Saratoga, New York, opposite the best-known gambling center in America, that of John Morrissey, the prizefighter Congressman.

After many years of prosperity, Hogan and Kate suffered tremendous losses. Hogan determined he would go after what Americans considered the world's heavyweight championship, then held by Tom Allen. Hogan had never once been licked in either his formal or many free-for-all bouts interspersed throughout his career.

The battle took place in 1873 at Council Bluffs near St. Louis, and Hogan wagered over $10,000 on himself. The fight was held in a rather desolate spot. Allen had an early advantage but in the third round in one of the wrestling sequences common to earlier boxing, Allen's knee caught Hogan low and dropped him beyond recovery. Hogan and his seconds claimed a foul, the referee declared Allen still champion, but called off all bets and returned the stakes to both principals. A free-for-all ensued among the spectators, with one killed and fourteen seriously injured before it subsided.

The fight was a turning point for Hogan and French Kate, for they prospered again as if to compensate for Hogan's bad luck in losing his opportunity at the heavyweight title. But when French Kate died of pneumonia, Hogan was so desolate that he could find solace only in religion and became an evangelist. Like the British heavyweight champion, Ben-

105. Flaming Ben Hogan, pugilist, pirate, gambler, Civil War spy for both sides, oil magnate, evangelist, millionaire . . . the greatest romantic figure in the history of boxing, 1844–1906.

106. French Kate—beautiful, gambling world queen who became a heart and business partner of Ben Hogan on his floating gambling palace, gambling dens, and expensive flamboyant sport houses. It was her death that led to Hogan's turning to religion.

digo, Hogan turned from a life of fighting and gambling to one in the service of God. When Ben Hogan died, he was mourned by many people in all walks of life, who remarked that here was another case where boxing had developed a useful citizen who in his last years had helped mankind and shown admirable character.

107. John L. Sullivan—1888

Naturally, we cannot discuss great actors of the ring without having to bring in the Great John L. His accomplishments, whether good, bad, or indifferent, outside of the ring were as famous as those within. There has never been an actor with his fists that has captured the imagination of his time quite to the same extent as the Boston Strong Boy who held the heavyweight title for ten tempestuous years.

John L. Sullivan as an actor in the ring was in a class by himself. Sullivan's huge bulk, tremendous strength, powerful hitting, ring ferocity, innumerable conquests, eccentric conduct, nasty but at the same time lovable personality, all combined to capture, hold and multiply the public interest. Sullivan was considered invincible.

He began his career as a baseball player and wrestler. The Cincinnati Reds of his day were about to hire him. In 1878 Sullivan began to show his fistic wares on the stages of Boston theatres. The number of fights which Sullivan had and his record are really

108. John Morissey, who went from the ring to the United States Congress.

unknown, for he barnstormed, challenged all comers and, in fact, fought many nonactors in the audience for years. John L. Sullivan like another great actor, John Barrymore, turned to firewater to satiate his unquenchable thirst for excitement. At one time his favorite dish was "a stein of bourbon and be quick about it." Sullivan could put away more liquid refreshment than any other two men.

John Barrymore as a youth was an excellent amateur boxer, just as Sullivan, the boxer, was an excellent actor. John's father, Maurice Barrymore, who was contemporary with John L, was an even tougher fistic competitor than his son. He sparred with Corbett, won several amateur tournaments, and also fought a grudge fight in Boston in front of the old Park Theatre with Robert Hilliard. Barrymore won by a knockout after more than an hour of battling.

The modern American golden era of boxing from John L. Sullivan to Joe Louis is replete with great actors, both in and out of the ring. Time and space make it impossible to cover all these. Many were prominent actors in the ring, many were great outside of the ring, and many played star parts. Some of our outstanding actors of boxing in this period may be known only to the close followers of the sports, but others may have been so unimportant as boxers that they may not be known at all, but they nevertheless made their mark beyond any question. They are entitled to consideration in our survey of the so-called greats.

No chapter on the great actors of boxing can over-

171

109. John Gully—from a debtor's prison to millions and Parliament via boxing.

look a counterpart of a triumvirate found in all old books or plays or movies. In one reference or another one always hears of "The Three Musketeers" —three great characters who were contemporary and friendly and equally famous. So it is in boxing. Nowhere in the annals of boxing did three supergreat boxers come along at the same time, yet so different in size and weight they could hardly be matched against each other.

There was Jack Dempsey, the Nonpareil; Jack McAuliffe, the Napoleon of the ring; and John L. Sullivan, the Boston Strong Boy. Who can ever match such a combination? The color, appeal, drawing power, supreme skill, and all the attributes of boxers were wrapped up in all three of these great characters in the same period in ring history.

Jack McAuliffe, the Napoleon of the ring, was a lightweight, 5'6" tall, 133 pounds, and was the world's lightweight champion from 1885 to 1896. Unlike the other two Musketeers, neither time nor age, nor disease nor odds ever beat the Napoleon of the ring, Jack McAuliffe. He had fifty-six fights in eleven years without a defeat in bouts of from one round to seventy-four rounds. It took him that long in one bout to take out his opponent.

Jack Dempsey, the Nonpareil, also Irish, was middleweight champion from 1884 to 1891. He was 5'8" tall and weighed 150 pounds. He had sixty-eight fights and lost three. One by a κo delivered illegally and by a man who had not made the proper weight; later he was κo'd and lost his title to Bob Fitzsimmons by being knocked out in the thirteenth round

and lost a decision in 1895. However, he had become a victim of tuberculosis before losing any one of his fights and was very sick for the last two. Also, although a middleweight, he fought anybody and everybody at any weight.

John L. Sullivan, Irish-American, was 5'10½" tall and weighed 190 pounds. He boxed from 1878 to 1905. He was heavyweight champion from 1889 to 1892. He had thirty-five fights and lost only one.

Besides the top actors from the standpoint of boxing alone, which are dealt with elsewhere, we are forced to name Joe Grimm and Leach Cross. Joe Grimm, born Saverio Giannone, was an amazing personality in the early twentieth century, whose claim to fame, strangely enough, was based only on his astonishing ability to take punishment. He had no boxing ability, no punching power, no great strength, no ring cunning, but it was his boast that no one had ever knocked him out. Actually he competed in about 250 contests from four to twenty rounds, against lightweights to heavyweights. He performed in the United States, Canada, Australia, New Zealand, West Indies, and Europe, and even in the San Carlos Opera House in Naples.

His "act" was to lean over the rope and shout to the crowd, "I am Joe Grimm—I fear no man on earth." After taking the most horrible beatings, at the end of every fight he would again lean over the ropes and mumble, "I am Joe Grimm—I fear no man on earth." On the basis of this unusual act and on the superior abilities of Joe Grimm as an actor in his character, he was matched with the world's heavyweight champion Fitzsimmons—one of the most terrific punchers of all time—on 14 October 1903, in Philadelphia. At the end of six gory rounds a badly chopped-up, unrecognizable figure of a man staggered to the ropes and, spitting out teeth through smashed lips, triumphantly announced, "I am Joe Grimm—I fear no man on earth."

He fought the great of almost all weights, including Philadelphia Jack O'Brien, Peter Maher, Joe Walcott, Dixie Kid, Joe Gans, Gus Gardner, Jack Blackburn, Jack Johnson, and Sailor Burke who after three tries knocked him out. Even by 1910, it took Sam McVey twelve rounds to knock him out in Paris, France. In 1913, Grimm retired after being saved by the final bell from a knockout from the fists of a comparative unknown.

Although Grimm's claim to fame may be dubious, there is no question of his place in the parade of boxing, especially when it comes to acting out a part to the finish. The finish in this case was death in an insane asylum in 1939.

Leach Cross was a lightweight, but not mentally. He fought around 1910, and developed the most "canny" defense of the modern era of boxing. He was no Joe Grimm. He boxed from a shell, "all elbows and arms," and while he was not powerful or a great puncher or an unusual boxer, his defense was almost impervious. In fact, so exasperating was Leach Cross' defense that he attained a success rarely matched by any other actor or boxer. He built up a tremendous following who always went to see him fight, hoping that someone would solve his exasperating defensive style and that they would have the pleasure of seeing him knocked cold by some opponent. Seldom, if ever, was anyone recompensed for his trouble, for Leach Cross in his prime could not be caught up with, although he was knocked out once by Dick Hyland from California in forty-one rounds.

Even outside of the ring and after retiring, Leach Cross followed his tradition of successfully exasperating his customers, for he became a prosperous dentist, and no doubt worried many a patient by pulling out his teeth or drilling into them with his dental buzz saw.

Yesterday, but in our contemporary era, in addition to such characters as Max Baer, Max Rosenbloom, Fred Steele, and others already dealt with in our chapter on stage, screen, and radio, there is one fighter although passed away to join "the invisible caravan," who was a most excellent one to complete our account of life's players from within the ropes. This actor, in true Shakespeare tradition, had played many parts. Canada Lee, prizefighter, musician, jockey, and actor, declared that, were he to relive his life, he would choose the ring all over again. There is no doubt about the merits of Mr. Lee's record in any of his careers. As a prizefighter he fought over two hundred contests; as a musician, he played at Aeolian Hall in the students' concerts; as a jockey, he came in first at some of the best tracks, including Saratoga; and as an actor, we quote Mr. Richard Watts of *The New York Times* after the opening of *Native Son*: "As for Mr. Lee's performance in the leading role, it is honest, moving and generally impressive and gives the play not only force, but dignity and a wry sort of pity."

Born Lee Canegata, the name by which he has been known since his first amateur bout was given him by Joe Humphries. Getting his last name first and then mispronouncing it, "Canada Lee" was announced to the waiting audience, and Canada Lee it remained thereafter. His fourteen-year-old son, however, is a Canegata. His grandfather was a West Indian importer and ship owner. His father ran away to the United States where he brought up his family.

After returning from eventful but unprofitable years as a jockey when weight forced him to look for other interests, Canada Lee wandered into the Salem, Massachusetts, Crescent Athletic Club in the basement of the Methodist Church. Willie Powell was trainer there. He took over the smooth-looking young black and in two years made him into an amateur lightweight champion. The story of his first professional fight is dramatic and amusing. In 1925 he turned professional, and who should be his first opponent but the same Willie Powell. Lee was scared, but his former trainer consoled him. "Don't worry. It won't take a minute. I'll just break your neck." Lee, however, knocked him out. In eight years he had piled up two hundred fights, and moved from lightweight to welterweight, and then to middleweight. He never won a championship, though he fought three champions either before or after they had held the crown. He made and spent about $100,000 during these years. Finally, a blow from Andy Di Vodi detached the retina of his eye, and he had to leave the ring. No matter what success he had met on the stage, his greatest satisfaction was found in the ring. He gave his reasons for loving a good fight, and his reasoning seems to contain the very essence of the sport's appeal. He said that he enjoyed the rhythm of the sport, the feints and the science that make one's opponent do what you wanted him to do. Being a boxer taught him to think quickly and clearly. It taught him how to handle himself and how to meet any situation.

The transition from the ring to the stage came about naturally but unexpectedly. After a several months' engagement in a night club, he dropped into a W.P.A. theatre project where Frank Wilson, one of the greatest black actors and a fight fan, was trying out actors for a play *Brother Mose*. Lee didn't ask for it, but he got a part. After that came the role of Blacksnake in *Stevedore*; Banquo, in *Macbeth*, and then the lead in *Native Son*, which plummeted him to fame and the higher income tax bracket. Two plays by Saroyan next gave him the opportunity to extend his acting ability, then Hollywood and the Hitchcock picture, *Lifeboat*, with Tallulah Bankhead, brought him international recognition. In 1944 he played in *Anna Lucasta*, the next year Margaret Webster cast him in the role of Caliban in Shakespeare's *Tempest*, featuring Vera Zorina. This actor, now rated "distinguished" by the leading critics, turned co-producer and actor-manager, and appeared in his own plays, *On Whitman Avenue* and *South Pacific*. When a rush call went out for him to fill the part of De Bosola in the *Duchess of Malfi*, starring Elizabeth Bergner, he became the first black ever to take a white man's part. The Boston audiences were engrossed by his performance. He was made up like a white man. One reviewer said, "His ears are cauliflowered, nose broken, one eye off center, and yet when one watches him, one never notices these things." In spite of his theatrical success, Canada Lee never lost his love for the ring, and for a time trained and financed the young black heavyweight Buddy Moore. The sparring was a little tough on the mentor, but it served as a very positive link with a happy past.

The arena of yesterday and the ring of today resemble the stage of yesterday and the stage of today in many ways. The stage has its plays and its actors who are seen and heard by the audience and the public. However, the stage also has its nonetheless important backstage participants, and so it is in boxing. In addition to the fighters who enjoy the spotlight of public attention, the roar of crowds and the acclaim of the multitudes, there are the out-of-the-ring characters, sponsors, promoters, managers, referees, seconds, and trainers. They also have contributed to the fight game through the ages.

In the old days when civilization, business, and life were far less complicated, there was probably less need for these characters. In addition, the lack of detailed records has made it impossible for us to recreate sufficient detail to tell you about them if they existed. The first character that did a great deal for boxing and enjoys a position unmatched in boxing history is, strangely enough, a Saint Bernardine monk. He was an ecclesiastic who lived at the beginning of the thirteenth century. As a priest in Siena, Italy, he became alarmed by the number of deaths and serious injuries caused by the practice of dueling among his parishioners during this period. Fights, for no matter what cause, with the sword or the poniard always resulted in fatal or hardly less grave consequences. Business competitions, arguments, courtships, drunken brawls, or even fancied insults, each led to the spilling of blood and the loss of life.

This priest had evidently been a Greek student and decided that if he could prevail upon the hot-headed citizens of his parish to clench their fists in anger rather than to draw their swords or poniards, he would accomplish a great deal. So he went around the countryside, as no one ever had before, or since, teaching boxing to the youths in order that they might beat each other up with their fists rather than kill each other off with their swords. This new form of competition quickly caught the fancy of the neighborhood, so much so that soon the citizens wanted to mix it with each other for fun. The result was that the good priest not only became a teacher of boxing, but a promoter and matchmaker and even a referee. He arranged many amateur contests under rules that made boxing a healthy exercise. He supervised all boxing in his area and saw that no real damage was done. This good priest was born ahead of his time, therefore he alone with his small community could not conquer the cruelty and viciousness of his time, nor overcome the inertia of the period.

Although some claim that boxing comes from "box," which was a word borrowed from the Danes by the Welsh, meaning a blow on the cheek, there are also many who believe that our term "boxing" comes from the good father who first described the sport as "the art of boxing up an opponent." In any case, this Saint Bernardine monk is a major character behind the scenes of boxing and might well in many ways be considered the first since classical times.

The next behind-the-scenes character in boxing is a dual personality. He might be called the Dr. Jekyll and Mr. Hyde of boxing. He gave much, and then took away much from boxing. He was responsible for helping the rise of boxing, and he was also almost solely responsible for deliberately throwing boxing into one of its darkest periods. He sponsored and helped boxing and then turned against it to become one of its greatest enemies. This man was the Duke of Cumberland. His entire career was one of conflict. The son of King George II and Queen Caroline of England, he was a great athlete and boxer as a boy. He was forced into a naval career, but became so dissatisfied that he joined the army where his abilities and his name and connections soon resulted in his becoming a general. He commanded armies in active combat in Europe and was able, courageous, and loved by his men, although he was the severest of disciplinarians. He displayed such energy, ability and tact that the British people selected him to stop the rebellion of Prince Charles in 1745. He was recalled from Flanders where he had been fighting the French. Although only twenty-four, in 1746 he was the most experienced general in the British "loyalist" forces. He and his army defeated the Pretender at the Battle of Culloden in Scotland. On account of the merciless severity with which Cumberland treated fugitives and rebels, he became known as "The Butcher."

He became the greatest sponsor of boxing from about 1740 to 1750 and backed Jack Broughton and his amphitheatre during these years. Then, because forty-six-year-old Broughton lost to Jack Slack and the Duke lost over $50,000 in bets, he accused Broughton of a "fix" and turned against him and against boxing. He even took action to make boxing illegal and practically ran the sport out of England. This may well have changed his luck, for shortly after, in 1757, he was forced to surrender to the French and disband his army. His disgrace was completed by the King's refusal to be bound by any agreements with him and he was forced to retire. In his retirement, he applied the same discipline to himself he had enforced on others, and not a whimper was ever heard from him. However, before he died in 1765, he had regained much of his popularity and again sponsored boxing. If ever there was a dual character, part good and part bad, both in and out of boxing, it was the Duke of Cumberland. His influence on world history and on boxing alike as viewed today were, however, far more good than bad. He definitely deserves a niche in the boxing hall of fame.

Next in our behind-the-scene parade is probably the best-known sponsor, follower and good samaritan of boxing, whose name is synonymous with the sport: The Marquis of Queensberry. Actually, the Marquis of Queensberry hardly deserves the prominence he enjoys. While there is no question of his great interest and love for the sport, and while there is no critiicsm of what he did for boxing, it must be admitted that he is the beneficiary of a series of peculiar errors. After all, the Marquis of Queensberry's greatest contribution to boxing is allegedly his rules. However, the truth of the matter is that he did not write the rules that bear his name.

He is also credited with having almost single-handedly brought boxing back to light. However, a study of boxing history and the Marquis reveals the fact that boxing saw far darker days and lived to tell the tale, than those days prior to the intervention of the Marquis; and that even had the Marquis not lived, no one can doubt that boxing would have survived and also have come into its own without him. Consequently, in removing much of the credit from the Marquis of Queensberry on these two points, we have little left to support—what is an undeniable fact—that the Marquis' name is almost synonymous with the sport of boxing.

The Marquis did not help boxing out of its darkest period because the darkest period of the modern rebirth of boxing was from 1750 until approximately 1784. It was definitely on the upgrade by the time the Marquis came along. It also was ripe for sounder rules. In addition, the period marked a time of geographical transition, and whether the British will agree or not, the control of boxing was moving to America. All these facts must be taken into consideration with respect to many beneficial factors along with the timing of the Marquis' interest and sponsorship.

It had taken almost a century to prove to everyone that the London Prize Ring rules were outmoded by the development of the sport and were definitely no longer of much value. The boxing glove, as such, had been developed by Broughton around 1750, and one hundred years had convinced both competitors and spectators that gloves should be used. So here again we find destiny in favor of the Marquis.

Arthur Chambers, an English lightweight who later came to America, was the real author of the famous rules which are generally credited to and bear the Marquis' name. They were first presented in 1865. Incidentally, it was not until 1872 at a tournament in London, sponsored by the Marquis, that the rules were followed, and that all contestants wore gloves, fought three-minute rounds, with wrestling barred. However, even the idea of gloved competition was not the Marquis' at all. If anyone doubts that, we refer them to a Paris newspaper of 8 October 1818. They will read there the following item:

> Yesterday at Aix-la-Chapelle a great exhibition was made by English boxers. The two champions were built like Hercules, and were naked to the waist. They entered the place with their hands guarded with huge padded gloves. After a severe contest, one of them, more adroit than his rival, struck him so violent a blow on the breast that he fell, and victory was thus decided.

In fact, it is doubtful if the Marquis of Queensberry and his rules would have gained much momentum had it not been for the hundred years preceding him, and for the quick adoption of his rules in America by John L. Sullivan, not in 1892 as most books state, but in 1888. However, John Sholto Douglas, eighth Marquis of Queensberry (1844–1900), was an important and beneficial character in the backstage parade of boxing. He is not to be confused with "Old Q.," William Douglas, the fourth Duke of Queensberry (1724–1810), who was also a patron of sports, especially horseracing, and whose escapades and extravagances were notorious. According to many, even the confusion between these two Queensberrys accrued to the benefit of John Sholto.

Although writers are not actors, no book on boxing can avoid the dramatic impact of Pierce Egan and his *Art of Self Defense*. As we look through this book published in 1845, over one hundred years after the return of boxing in England and Ireland, we see that the book was dedicated to no less than the Duke of Wellington. We cannot but marvel at the same terms, expressions, descriptions, and instructions on how to box. Among the everyday instructions to the boxer is the caution that he should never get mad or lose his cool. This was a must in 1845 and is still a must in 1976. The sketches all show a normal boxer's stance, almost the same as that prescribed today with perhaps the hands or guard kept a little too low, a little less bending of the body, and less weight forward—but with most southpaws still with their right hand and right foot forward. That is all except southpaws with a right-hand stance, which results in a definite curl of the left shoulder for that surprise haymaker. One of the most interesting but little noticed part of Egan's book is his determination to visit "the grave of the great late champion of Ireland in Dublin, Dan Donnelly . . ." whom George IV, when regent, had knighted for his "great pugilistic striking power." Donnelly was buried with great pomp and circumstance in Bully's Acre near Kilmainham.

When we get into our modern era with the complications of everyday life surrounding boxing, we find that boxing progressed only in proportion to the imagination and efforts of certain individuals behind-the-scenes. Sam Harris, William A. Brady, James W. Coffroth, Tex Rickard, Hugh D. McIntosh, and Charles B. Cochrane were, with many others, responsible for the forward surge of the game to its current golden era.

Jeff Dixon of Biloxi, Mississippi, United States Army aviation officer and camera technician in World War II, is the "might-have-been actor" of the present and future boxing period. After World War I, Dixon, who had been a member of the AEF, settled in Paris and became the Tex Rickard of Europe. He acquired control of the "Palais des Sports" in Paris, and promoted all kinds of boxing and athletic attractions. He has been credited with originally discovering many European entertainment and athletic stars, from Sonja Henie to Primo Carnera. Dixon dropped everything to join the United States Army Air Force in World War II, and was later killed in action. By a strange coincidence, he died not so far from the Palais des Sports and the Seine River he loved so well. A plane on a photographic mission which he had volunteered to help, was shot down by the Germans near Orly Field, Paris. Had he lived, many believe he would have become the greatest boxing promoter of the future and might have exercised a more beneficial and more gentlemanly influence on the sport than Mike Jacobs.

While William A. Brady was getting his first theatrical experience in the fight game, another youngster, destined to become a great figure in the theatrical world, was entering it via the fist. Sam Harris, world-known theatrical producer, in an interview with the *New York Herald Tribune* in 1925, when asked to describe his life in a few sentences, stated: "I started selling towels in a downtown office building, then I managed Terrible Terry McGovern, a champion prizefighter. During this time I became associated with the theatrical world which later led to the firm of Cohan and Harris, out of which grew Sam H. Harris, and that is all there is to it." So, the well-known producer of dozens of successful shows, owner of many theatres, and comedian in his own right, began as a prizefight manager when he handled Terry McGovern, the world's featherweight champion.

To quote a writer of twenty-five years ago: "When Terry McGovern flashed out of Brooklyn, Harris managed him, and when he became famous, Harris presented him in the red-blooded epic of the great theatre in-doors entitled *The Bowery after Dark*." As an actor, according to Harris, Terry was the world's greatest in-fighter. Terry McGovern and boxing helped Harris get a start, and shortly thereafter Harris controlled three theatres in New York, two in Chicago, and two in Boston. Harris produced all of the famous Irving Berlin Music Box Reviews in his own theatre, and produced dozens of others including: *They Knew What They Wanted, Six-Cylinder Love*, and *Little Old New York*. He always said that he had to work hard in order to feed his fighters and his stable of race horses. However, he was partly kidding, for according to reports, he never managed a fighter after McGovern. Here is, indeed, a colorful character behind the scenes of boxing who moved on to a position behind the scenes of the stage. To show that boxing left its bulldog imprint on Sam Harris, one has but to mention the fact that in 1916 when he was worth millions he sued someone for $47.54 and collected.

Charles B. Cochran was another theatrically minded man with a dramatic flair, and a love for boxing. While primarily a theatrical producer of many successful plays in England and America, in partnership with William Brady he promoted fights and managed fighters in England. His most successful sponsorship was in connection with Georges Carpentier, the orchid man of France. Therein, however, was his greatest disappointment. It had been his dream to bring the great French light heavyweight to America for a fight with Jack Dempsey; in fact, at one time Mr. Brady and Mr. Cochran were in on the Dempsey-Carpentier preliminary negotiations, with Mr. Cochran putting up some money. Cochran and Brady had a binder on Carpentier. However, when Kearns and Dempsey refused fifty percent of the gate from Rickard and demanded $300,000 guarantee instead, Carpentier and Deschamps countered by raising their guarantee to $200,000. Brady was called in with respect to raising his ante and that of Cochran, but could not confer with Cochran about what was considered an unprecedented guarantee, for Cochran was ill in the hospital. Rather than risk his friend's money, he withdrew. It was not until after the fight that Cochran learned he was not in on it. Brady, remorseful over his partner's disappointment and the fact that the Dempsey-Carpentier fight, carried through by Tex Rickard alone, had been a tremendous success, cut Cochran in on a show which was successful, and thereby netted him some profit, although it is extremely doubtful if he made as much as he would have on the fight. Rickard had told

Kearns when he refused fifty percent of the gate receipts and asked instead for a $300,000 guarantee, that he had thrown away $200,000, and strangely enough that was exactly what Kearns and Dempsey lost by demanding the guarantee.

Cochran also managed famous wrestlers such as Hackenschmidt, Zbyszko, and Madrali. He saw every wrestling and boxing match he possibly could. Cochran believed in charging very high prices for his fights and, to assure his getting them, he at one time had options on both the Olympia and the Holborn stadiums. Cochran once made the statement that "no matter how good two fighters of a lighter class may be, they cannot pull like a bum in the heavy-weight class." He promoted the Freddy Welsh-Willie Richie fight in London and the Mickey Walker-Tommy Milligan fight.

The latter was the most spectacular fight Cochran ever planned. He had made a large guarantee, $110,000 to Mickey Walker, and $15,000 to Milligan. He put Mickey Walker up at Taggs Island where his training costs amounted to about $3,000 a week, so that the press could be near for interviews and pre-fight publicity. Walker was, of course, a very colorful character, especially for England, and his manager, Jack Kearns, created great consternation by refusing to choose a referee from a list of the best submitted, but demanded that the Prince of Wales referee the fight. Cochran and even the public became annoyed with the demands of Kearns and Walker, and finally submitted three more names, among which was that of Eugene Corri, demanding an immediate decision. Kearns, driven into a corner, choose Corri. The fight had been planned for a huge outdoor stadium at Blackpool, England, seating 100,000, where a profit was a certainty, but difficulties arose, and at the last minute it had to be arranged for the Olympia where the seating was so limited that Cochran lost over $75,000.

William H. Brady, the theatrical producer, was another behind-the-scenes giant in boxing. At the age of fifteen he began his career as a messenger between the old press club and the old Madison Square Garden. His connection with the game and his handling of his first world's champion was, as he afterwards remarked, the most backward arrangement on record. Brady produced a play, *After Dark,* but it was not doing so well. He signed James J. Corbett, a handsome young clerk from San Francisco who was an outstanding amateur boxer, to come east and give sparring exhibitions as an added attraction at the performance.

Brady, who had become quite a judge of fistic ability, had heard enough to convince him that James J. Corbett might well be the next world's heavyweight boxing champion. He had heard how this young amateur had gone thirty rounds wearing riding gloves with the famous professional Joe Choynski. In addition, Brady knew that Corbett had sparred with the Great John L three rounds in full evening dress, with gloves, and that Corbett had discovered that Sullivan had no knowledge of the science of boxing and could be easily opened up by feints. Another indication of his early promise was the fact that this young man had gone sixty rounds with the great Peter Jackson. So Brady's invitation was perfectly timed. The young man came from the West to delight the people who saw the play, *After Dark.* Brady paid Corbett $150 a week for his nightly sparring exhibitions. According to Brady, Corbett was like Baer. He could sing a song or read a line like a professional and had he not become a boxing champion, he could well have been famous as an actor.

He had another play written called *Gentleman Jim,* especially for Corbett, and to help his theatrical plans and Corbett's theatrical career, Brady began to cook up a world's championship fight between Corbett and John L. Sullivan in order to publicize his new play.

Brady also proved his flair for publicity and showmanship. He maneuvered things so that Sullivan wound up on the day of the fight sore as a boil and full of hate. Again like Baer, Corbett and Brady chose Asbury Park as a training site. Brady stopped at nothing to undermine Sullivan's morale. He had lithographs printed stating that "James J. Corbett, Champion of the World, will appear in Madison Square Garden in New York two weeks after the fight." These were posted on every billboard and shanty between New York and New Orleans. Furthermore, there was a superstition that a particular corner of the ring was the lucky one. Brady won that on the toss. Sullivan was known to have his own superstition which he had carefully guarded during his ten years as champion. He believed that the boxer who entered the ring first, went out last— feet first. Brady, by some trickery, forced Sullivan to enter the ring first in New Orleans, sarcastically exclaiming, "Champions first, Mr. Sullivan."

Although the odds favored the champion four to one, Brady bet $3,000 on his man through Steve Brodie of Brooklyn Bridge fame. The fighting tactics of Corbett were new to the fans, since he was the first of a new school of fighters that endeavored to avoid being hit. These tactics were first met by jeers from the audience, but Brady prompted Corbett to stop the bout and talk to the crowd. Corbett coolly turned away from the champion and told the audience not to worry, that they would get their money's worth. After Corbett won the championship, naturally Brady made money for Corbett and himself in every direction. Here are a few of Brady's ideas which made money and helped promote boxing:

One of the most amusing was the use of Corbett's hand as a model for a paperweight. An impression was made in plaster of Paris and $60,000 was the champion's share of the profits of the sale of his paperweight fist.

Another amusing and profitable incident was the unusual fight staged by Brady between Corbett's trainer, a fighter named Jim Daley, and—a Kangaroo. Daley won, but not before he had gotten a wallop from the kangaroo's hind leg right in the stomach, knocking him clear across the ring and out of it. It happened at the Chicago World's Fair in 1893 and was talked about and written about for years. Needless to say, it added to the public's interest in boxing and in the heavyweight champion.

William A. Brady's strongest love, however, was the theatre, and he toured Corbett very successfully throughout the United States and in addition took his plays and his champion abroad to London and Paris. Corbett appeared in the *Folies Bergères* and was matched in a French boxing contest with the savate champion. This type of boxing legalized the use of the feet as well as the hands. Corbett received a hard right foot to the jaw which hurt, and then proceeded to knock out his French opponent.

Back in America, Brady and Tom Edison cooked up the first motion picture fight. Corbett was matched against Peter Cortney for the express purpose of making a motion picture for the Kineograph Company, and this picture later was sent all over the world. Many claim that the first big money ever made by motion pictures was with the help of the fight-ring and boxing. If so, the motion pictures as well as the stage, vaudeville, radio and television owe a debt to the game.

William A. Brady next turned to baseball and started the Paterson, New Jersey club of the Atlantic League, with Corbett playing first base. Corbett was a good first baseman, but strangely enough, not a good hitter. However, since there was no Judge Landis or even Happy Chandler in those days, a little money to the opposing pitcher and the right pitch was thrown when Corbett was at bat. The result was hits for Corbett and $1,000 a day at the boxoffice, which was mighty good money in those days. However, the story is that, before Corbett quit baseball, the pitchers were pitching their best, Corbett's hitting had not fallen off, and Brady's high batting average continued.

The team of Corbett and Brady finally broke up, but there was no ill will. When Brady was looking for new fields to conquer and was becoming more and more interested in the theatre, Corbett decided to open a saloon on Broadway at thirty-fourth Street. Brady did not go along with this idea, as he did not think Corbett was the type to make a success in this field, and he did not care to become involved with the responsibilities of such an operation, so Corbett and Brady in a very gentlemanly way agreed to disagree and parted, even though it is said Brady offered Corbett a partnership in his theatrical business. If this is true, Corbett undoubtedly rued the day he split, for shortly thereafter Brady's next play, *Way Down East,* brought him a fortune.

However, William A. Brady was not through with his first love. Although now a successful theatrical producer and manager, Brady was to manage another world's heavyweight champion and another "James J." The giant Jeffries, once hired by Brady as a sparring partner for Corbett, pursued Brady and persuaded him to take over his management. The story of how Brady hired Tommy Ryan to coach Jeffries, and how he and Jeffries developed the famous Jeffries crouch is well known. What is not so well known is that Brady was disappointed in Jeffries as a champion because the latter could neither act, nor was he enthusiastic about touring the country and the world in plays conceived or dug up by Brady. While boxing was Brady's first love and his path to success, he devoted his entire energies to the theatre after Jeffries. He was, nevertheless, one of boxing's most colorful, creative, and imaginative impresarios.

Other managers worthy of mention in the cavalcade of the fist begin with Billy Madden, a sparring partner of John L. Sullivan who later became his theatrical booker and perhaps the first official fight manager in modern boxing. Charles H. Davies, known as the "Parson," was a well-known fight manager at the turn of the century. Martin Julian, brother of Fitzsimmons' acrobatic wife, and Sam Fitzpatrick, manager of Fitz, were colorful managerial characters of their time.

In more recent years the following managers enjoyed considerable prominence: (though many of these have passed on)

Billy Gibson, manager of Gene Tunney, Benny Leonard, and others.

Leo P. Flynn, "the Carpet Bagger of Fistiana," the mass manager who piloted as many as sixty-two fighters at one and the same time, and who also was one of the greatest matchmakers ever employed by the Madison Square Garden.

Charles Harvey, importer and exporter of boxing champions to and from Europe.

Frank A. Churchill, who sought and found Filipino fighters, including Pancho Villa.

Francois Deschamps, the first "Svengali" manager, who handled Georges Carpentier.

Leon See, who first saw Primo Carnera in a circus.

Harry Pollok, who managed Freddie Welsh and many other prominent fighters.

Max Waxman, the man who had directed more world's champions in his lifetime than any other manager and was the business manager for Jack Dempsey. Waxman, according to many, was one of the shrewdest managers between the two World Wars. He was the son of a highly erudite rabbi of Jerusalem. Max's hobby was criminology and criminal law. Managing fighters became an avocation as he was engaged in fifteen different businesses, all successful.

Nate Lewis, known as "the old bald eagle of the Boul. Mich'," was a fight promoter and manager from Chicago for fifty years. He managed Charlie White.

George Engle, manager of Harry Greb.

"Dumb Dan" Morgan, who is not dumb and had managed close to a thousand fighters.

Phil Glassman, developer of Lew Tendler.

Paddy Mullens, manager of Harry Wills, the "Black Panther."

Frank "Doc" Bagley, who became interested in Gene Tunney after his discovery by Billy Roach and who sold Gene Tunney to Billy Gibson for $5,000.

Jimmy Bronson, who handled one of the most famous boxing families of modern times, the Zivics.

Scotty Monteith, pilot of Johnny Dundee, the "Scotch Wop."

Dan McKettrick who specialized in Irish Americans and managed Billy Glover (Billy Cavanagh).

"Pa" Stribling, who handled his son "W. L."

James Dougherty, "the Baron of Leiperville, Pa.," who managed big George Godfrey, specialized in black fighters and became a Leiperville City Commissioner. Dougherty refereed the fight between Dempsey and Gibbons in Shelby, Montana.

The Dundee brothers of Miami who have performed as promoters, managers, and trainers. Angelo is the trainer and the strategic and tactical corner advisor for Muhammad Ali.

Ancil Hoffman, the "Small Dane," who made a fortune in restaurants and real estate before becoming a promoter and later manager of Max and Buddy Baer. Perhaps Ancil was the most honest and selfless fight manager in modern boxing, who battled Max Baer to retain for Baer a retirement income from his rapid fortune, as the author well knows.

Jack Curley, "the Mahout of the Pachyderms," manager of heavyweight wrestlers and boxers. He believed in handling only weighty clients and numbered Jess Willard among his herd.

Al Weill, "the Vest," matchmaker, promoter, philosopher, and wearer of fancy waistcoats, who managed many champions and who rated higher than

diplomats with head waiters in Washington. His most famous fighter who terminated their relationship was Rocky Marciano.

Fred Digby, editor of the *New Orleans Item*, who specialized in trying to keep the war between the states going by bringing up Dixie talent to the big Eastern cities.

English-born James J. Johnston, "the Boy Bandit," a former boxer who became one of the characters of Broadway. Johnston was known as "the greatest rejuvenator of washed-up bums." On the other hand, he helped elect Jimmy Walker mayor of New York, by staging a "3.2 We Want Beer" parade. After his death the Smithsonian is said to have asked for his desk as a relic of fistiana in the roaring twenties.

Eddie Mead, who piloted Henry Armstrong to three titles.

"Pop" Foster who fathered Jimmy McLarnin.

Joe "we wuz robbed" Jacobs, Jewish manager of Nazi Max Schmeling.

Fight managers notwithstanding motion picture concepts are not all "mugs," nor do they habitually wear sweaters and caps but they are masters of promotional devices. Jack Kearns was the King of the Ballyhoo, and his publicity "angles" would have done credit to a Herbert Bayard Swope or the greatest public relations men in the world. He must be held at least partially responsible for the "Manassa Mauler," the "Rumson Bulldog," and the "Battle of the Century" tags which spelled dollars to two of his charges, Jack Dempsey, and Mickey Walker.

Jack Curley who was once a bell boy in the Planters Hotel in St. Louis and a dishwasher in a cheap restaurant, later became a captain of waiters and a maitre d'hotel at a "swanky joint." He had what it took to manage not only wrestlers and boxers, but to handle the dance tours of Rudolph Valentino and the lecture tours of William Jennings Bryan. Curley was also the manager of Emmeline Pankhurst and, as such, was partly responsible for women voting today. Curley managed Annette Kellerman and the Vatican choir on their American tour.

Angelo Pucci, a younger manager, earned a great reputation by earning more than $400,000 for himself and Tippy Larkin in ten years of fighting. Larkin, a "glass-chinned" boxer, who never was a real champion, was flattened on many occasions, but always came back because of Pucci.

Tom Jones who managed three world titleholders was a successful business man while Phil Schlossberg spent twenty-five years in the U.S. Navy before turning fight manager.

Billy McCarney's death in 1949 was mourned by followers of boxing all over the world. McCarney was a college graduate who aimed for the priesthood, switched to law, thence to sports writing, and then into boxing promotion and management. The "old professor," as he was affectionately known, probably was a friend of more people in boxing than any other two men in the world. It was sad but significant that his death resulted from a cold caught at the Cerdan-Zale world's middleweight championship fight.

The list of great managers is almost endless. Among the best are Joe Woodman, who managed Sam Langford; George Lawrence; Sammy Goldman, Sammy Aaronson, a great amateur champion; Tom O'Rourke; Dan Carroll; Johnny Buckley; Eddie Mack; Eddie Kane; Eddie Long; Tom McArdle, manager of Soldier Bartfield and Joe Jeanette; F. Bachman; Joe Gould, manager of "the Cinderella man," James J. Braddock; Miller Gilzenberg; Lew Brix; Harry Lenny; Sam Pian; Art Rose; Gig Rooney; Wad Wadhams; Charlie Rose; Lew Burston; Billy Duffy; Andy Niederreiter, "the Boy Promoter"; Hymie Caplin; Sol Gold; Charlie Cook; Jack Hurley; and Tommy Walsh, not to forget the late Yank Durham.

The most picturesque fight manager, and the one who left the most money when he died, was Al Hereford of Baltimore. He managed Joe Gans, the original young Peter Jackson, and Harry Lyon. He is unique in the fact that he left an estate worth well over a million dollars.

Promoters as such were unknown until Roman days, when the most famous promoters of course were the consuls, emperors, and politicians, and their promotions were not for cash, but for votes and popularity. The bloody spectacles of Rome were free to the crowds, even though they cost the State plenty. When boxing was reborn in England, there were sponsors and gamblers but no promoters, and even when boxing first moved to America, fight promoters were still practically nonexistent. Pugilists and their backers put up side bets, winner take all, and it was the custom to pass the hat among the spectators. The funds so collected went to the winner or were split 50–50 depending on how the contestants had previously decided.

The test of a promoter or of promotion in boxing is not in the planning or presentation of a fight, but is purely financial. When a group or an individual guarantees money and arranges a fight for paid attendance, gambling that the proceeds will exceed the guarantee, this is promotion. Up until the Fitzsimmons-Dempsey "the Nonpareil" middleweight championship, the arrangement of bouts was on a haphazard basis. This was the first time that an individual or a group had put up cash, in this case $11,000, gambling on getting it back plus a profit out of the box-office receipts.

This original promoter in the history of boxing was the Olympic Club of New Orleans, which staged the Bob Fitzsimmons-Jack Dempsey "the Nonpareil" fight for the middleweight championship of the world on 14 January 1891. In 1892 the same Olympic Club promoted the Fitzsimmons-Maher fight. The California Athletic Club of San Francisco, which staged the Corbett-Jackson fight 21 May 1901, also was an early promoter. Because all the foregoing clubs actually had other interests in attracting visitors to their towns and were not entirely promoting the fights for box-office profits alone, many old-timers feel that the first true fight promoter was the Bohemian Sporting Club of Amsterdam Avenue and 81st Street, New York City. This club staged the Myers-McAuliff, Dixon-Shelly, Sullivan-Corbett fights on 5, 6, and 7 September 1892, at the Olympic Club in New Orleans. The Bohemian Club had working arrangements with the Olympic Club of New Orleans, Broadway Athletic Club of New York, and National Sporting Club of London. It had its own boxing rules.

It was not until the advent of James W. Coffroth of San Francisco that any one individual became a promoter. About 1900 Coffroth decided that what clubs, syndicates, and groups could do, one man could do better alone; for one man would be untrammeled by a lot of opinions and fears and could make as much progress as his imagination dictated and the public accepted.

Coffroth was only twenty-two years old when he started in the fight game. He had just been graduated from law school and was attracted to boxing after seeing some fights in New York and San Francisco. Coffroth's boxing business concept was very simple. He paid the fighters sixty percent and sometimes seventy-five percent of the gross receipts. The total share for the fighter was usually split up sixty percent to the winner, forty percent to the loser, or seventy-five percent to the winner and twenty-five percent to the loser, or in a few cases ninety percent to the winner and ten percent to the loser. The remaining twenty-five percent to forty percent of the gross receipts went for expenses plus Coffroth's profit. Coffroth successfully promoted fights for about twelve years, then abandoned boxing and promoted racing in Mexico and amassed a fortune before he died in 1943. His was the first individual promoting based on financial considerations in the history of boxing.

Tex Rickard was next. He first came to public notice when, as a former gambler from the Alaskan gold rush, he showed up in a mining gulch in Nevada called Goldfield and offered $30,000 to Joe Gans and Battling Nelson to fight there for the lightweight championship of the world. His next large venture was in 1910 when he offered $101,000 for the July Fourth fight between Jim Jeffries and Jack Johnson. Tex Rickard probably played the largest single part in ushering in the second golden era of boxing which, from a financial standpoint, was the forerunner of our inflation of receipts in the Television Era.

The third and last great trail-blazing promoter in the history of boxing was Hugh D. McIntosh of Australia, who died in England in 1941. His promotions were mainly in Australia. McIntosh, in addition to being the promoter, refereed his own fights and also handled his own motion picture and subsidiary rights. He is most famous for having promoted the Jack Johnson-Tommy Burns world heavyweight fight in Sydney, Australia, originally scheduled on Christmas Day, 1908. To show the canniness of this Australian, he made his own motion pictures of that fight and personally toured Australia, New Zealand, England, and the United States with them, making close to $300,000 net profit on this operation alone. Later in the twenties and early thirties McIntosh became prominent in Australian politics as a newspaper publisher and as Australian theatrical czar. However, during this period he never forgot his first love, and he lured dozens of American fighters to Australia, the last famous one being Young Stribling of Georgia.

Tex Rickard, alone of the three, taught and trained his own successor. During his phenomenal rise to fame and fortune, Rickard more and more depended on Mike Jacobs for the handling of his tickets. The association of the two men became quite close and Jacobs learned much about boxing from Rickard who knew the game, having participated in many impromptu fights and having done considerable refereeing of his own championship fights.

Jacobs learned all there was to know about promotion from Rickard and, because of his strong hold on the ticket situation and an intimate knowledge even greater than Rickard's of the means for the disposal and sale of tickets, became the logical successor of the No. 1 promoter of boxing. The basic financial arrangements and methods of promotion used by Mike Jacobs during his control and by Tex Rickard and others, follow closely the pattern set by Coffroth. Where Mike Jacobs differs from the others is in his effort to obtain a monopoly by tying up by contract on an exclusive basis all champions and championships, and thus extending his control over fighters and managers. This, as we have seen, led to IBC and an even worse monopoly.

Besides being a great promoter, Tex Rickard was the No. 1 figure behind-the-scenes in the annals of boxing. He did more for boxing than any other in-

110. The greatest boxing promoter of all time— Tex Rickard

dividual in the modern era. Therefore we should devote more space to this star actor in the fistic cavalcade. He was born, as his name implies, in Texas, and he was born with a gambler's instinct. His first gambling and promotional venture was undertaken at the age of twelve. He had saved money earned by doing chores at local ranches. This he ventured on a local gambling table and returned home with $150. He told his mother she could have $50 but that he wanted the remaining $100 to buy a merry-go-round advertised for sale in a nearby town. He explained that he figured there would be money in running it for local entertainment. He lost money on this deal but the promoting fever never left him from that day until his death. He became town marshal, wandered to the Yukon, then to Africa, but it was not until he went to the mining town of Goldfield, Nevada, that he hit upon the combination that was more or less to decide his future.

In Goldfield he acquired a gambling house, "The Northern," and got his share of the mining boom that during the first year brought the little town $20,000,000 in gold and silver ore. Water in Goldfield cost more than beer. The citizens wanted to publicize the town and a committee was called to decide on a means of doing so. Several ideas were proposed. One man suggested sending up a balloon with $5,000 in a basket, finders to take all. Another proposed that a lake be dug in the middle of the town and filled with beer for the thirsty. A third idea was to import camels and have the first and only camel racing and gambling track in the world. Rickard suggested that he promote the Nelson-Gans fight there to draw the attention of the world to Goldfield.

He wired a proposal to Battling Nelson's manager, Billy Nolan, who answered, "Raise the bid to $30,000 and we will accept." Nobody took Rickard seriously, because it was believed Goldfield was too far away from civilization for the venture to succeed.

However, newspapermen descended on Goldfield to see if Rickard had any real money. Rickard pulled out a bag of gold pieces and displayed it in the window of "The Northern." He finally signed up Gans and Nelson, the former through Benny Selig, his manager, and the fight came off on schedule, Gans winning on a foul and Rickard winning a $30,000 net profit. The town won, too, as it was jammed with visitors and was featured in news stories throughout the world. After the fight, Rickard felt that the town had done its best for him, that its mines would soon run out, so he sold his gambling house and bought another at Rawhide, Nevada. Once again, general opinion held that he was making a mistake. However, the mines did run out at Goldfield, while rich ore was struck at Rawhide and Rickard was in on the cleanup there. When his gambling house burned down, Rickard had already withdrawn his money and had bought a million dollars worth of gold mines.

He then decided to take his family to New York and study the fight game in the big city. He also decided he had to impress New York's "city slickers," so he lived in the most expensive suite in the old Waldorf and spent money like a drunken sailor. He plunged heavily in the stock market and lost most of his fortune.

He turned to fight promotion to recoup and became the most sensational promoter in boxing history.

The press at this time was clamoring for a match that would bring Jim Jeffries out of retirement. Everyone wanted to see Jack Johnson licked and everyone believed that Jeffries, who had run out of competition and retired years before, could do it. As it was against the law even to promote or bid for a fight in New York, the bidding was done in Hoboken. After winning the bid, Rickard was faced with the little matter of convincing Jeffries to train and fight again. Rickard had won the bid with a guarantee of $101,000 in cash, defeating even Coffroth. Rickard also persuaded Jeffries to return to the ring. The greatest fight of that time was set.

The fight was first scheduled for California. Governor Gillette had given his permission to hold it there and Rickard started building the stadium. The protest in the state was so great, however, once the news had gotten out, that the governor was forced to withdraw his permission, although Rickard had already sunk $35,000 in construction work. Then Tex managed to get permission from Reno, Nevada, to stage it there. The stadium in California was pulled down, the lumber loaded and taken to the new proposed site and reassembled. The fight, on July Fourth, was won by Johnson with Rickard as referee. After the fight, Rickard was $20,000 richer.

He now went to Buenos Aires, bought cattle and settled there to make a new fortune. It was while out on the range with his cattle that he met Theodore Roosevelt. A close friendship began that continued until the President's death.

When Tex returned from South America, the general opinion was that he intended to stage a Jess Willard fight. The rumor gave birth to the idea and Rickard promoted the Willard-Moran fight in the old Garden, which was a flop as a fight but netted Rickard $30,000.

Rickard's next profit was $60,000, won betting on Wilson, not the fighter, but the college professor who won an election for the presidency of the United States.

From then on Rickard promoted practically every important fight that took place until his death. Rickard also turned his attention to acquiring the old Madison Square Garden. There was a heavy mortgage on the old Garden; boxing had been outlawed in New York State, but when it began to look as if fights would be sanctioned in the state, everybody wanted the building. Rickard got it on a ten-year lease for $400,000-a-year rent, against such political opposition as Tammany Hall represented in the person of Joe Humphries.

Governor Smith gave Rickard the lease because, after listening to his plans for attracting the public, he said Tex was the only man with enough ideas and promotional technique to be successful. Rickard planned bike races, political rallies, swimming meets, and other events, and elicited support from Wall Street. At the last minute his backers failed to come through with the money and Rickard turned to John Ringling with a proposal for him to back the Garden in return for using it for his circus. Ringling fell in with the idea and thus the lease was acquired by Rickard, and circuses became inevitably associated with both the old and the new Garden.

The Dempsey-Carpentier, Benny Leonard-Tendler, Dempsey-Firpo, and the Dempsey-Tunney fights were all Rickard promotions and all highly successful because of adept publicity and ballyhoo angles. Even the old Garden, which had previously been a "white elephant," prospered under Rickard. In the first six months it took in over half a million dollars. For outdoor fights Rickard built a huge wooden bowl at Boyle's Thirty Acres in Jersey City for 90,000 people to witness the Dempsey-Carpentier fight.

After the Tunney-Heeney fight on which Rickard lost $155,000, he embarked on a series of new ventures including the new Madison Square Garden, and a sports center and dog racing track at Miami. However, he died before any of those schemes were really minting money as all Rickard enterprises usually did. He died, according to many, because, although he was a man of proven physical and moral courage, this gambler who staked his all so often was afraid of an operation, and waited too long before having it performed. In any case, there is no doubt that when he died, boxing lost one of its greatest characters and the off-stage actor who contributed the most to its current high estate.

The referee is the invisible man of boxing. While actually in the ring during all fights as the so-called third man, he is hardly noticed by the audience and rarely mentioned in any accounts of fights. In fact, it is his duty to conduct himself in the ring and move about so as never to be in the way of the fighters or the line of vision of the audience. When you stop to realize what this means, you will realize that a boxing referee has no cinch.

In the old days a referee also ran innumerable dangers from defeated gamblers, because a referee was the sole arbiter of the fight and combined the duties presently performed by the referee and two judges.

Notwithstanding their complete anonymity while in the ring, there have been well-known referees in the history of the game.

George Siler from Chicago was perhaps the most famous of all early referees. He started officiating in the bare-knuckle days in the late nineteenth century when fights were for side bets and when the followers of each contestant backed their men to the limit. When the decision went against their man, the losers usually blamed the referee, who consequently led an exciting life. Siler refereed for about twenty-five years and was the hero of many escapes from injury or worse. He refereed thousands of bouts and was so honest and so expert that he was almost always the first choice of fighters themselves, especially when there was a title at stake. His bravery and resourcefulness became traditional.

Professor John Duffy was another pet of the fighters. He is famous for having refereed the Sullivan-Corbett fight in New Orleans in 1892 and most of the fights of Bob Fitzsimmons. The last of the great bare-knuckle heavyweight fights were refereed by John Fitzpatrick of New Orleans. Wyatt Earp set a style for referees by insisting on always wearing a holster complete with loaded gun in the ring. James W. Coffroth, leading promoter in the early boxing days in America, preferred Billy Roche of New York City and Eddie Graney of San Francisco, who refereed most of his fights.

Referees in more recent days generally come from three sources: first, managers and promoters; second, sportswriters and newspapermen; and third, ex-fighters. All of the important fights in Europe before World War I were refereed by Gene Corri of London, who was considered by many, especially in Europe, the greatest referee of modern times. Al Smith of New York, Captain Bill Daley of Boston, and Jimmy Bronson were all referees drawn from the promoter-manager ranks. Gene Buckley, later the first state boxing commissioner of Massachusetts, was the leading referee in New England for many years. Snowey Baker refereed all the important fights in Australia in the early part of the twentieth century until he moved to California about 1925. Honest John Kelly was the third man in the ring for the Corbett-Fitzsimmons fight.

Sometimes champions have shown great partiality in the selection of referees for all their fights. However, this did not mean that the referee of their choice favored them. An example of this was Hector McGinnis, who refereed practically all of Johnny Wilson's fights when he was middleweight champion. One of the toughest places in the world for referees used to be Boston. Captain Cook was the first man to get away with refereeing in fine style there, being followed by Captain Daley, Jack Sheehan, Maffitt Flaherty, Hector McGinnis, eagle-eyed Charlie White, and Johnny White.

Sportswriters who have gained their share of fame as boxing referees are Jack Sheehan of Boston, Ed Smith of Chicago, Bat Masterson of New York, Otto Floto of Denver, E. W. Dickerson of Grand Rapids, Fred Digby of New Orleans, Joseph Murphy of St. Louis, Tom Andrews of Milwaukee, George Barton

111. Jack Dempsey, the Manassa Mauler, the greatest actor of modern boxing based on the box office . . . without closed-circuit TV.

of Minneapolis, Ed. W. Cochrane of Chicago, Matt Hinkle of Cleveland, Dan Donnelley of Boston, Harry Stout of Milwaukee, Ed Purdy of Chicago, Charles Eyton of Los Angeles, Howie Hodgkins of Boston. All of these newspapermen were outstanding referees, as were Jack Welsh and Willard Bean of Salt Lake City.

Among the boxers who became famous as referees are: Corbett, Fitzsimmons, Jeffries, Tom Sharkey, Jack McAuliffe, Jess Willard, Gunboat Smith, Benny Leonard, Bill Stribling, Jack Dempsey, Gene Tunney, Billy "Kid" Glover Cavanagh, Arthur Donovan, Frank Fulham, and many others. Bill Forbes of the *Brooklyn Eagle* made a great name for himself as a referee in professional, amateur, and intercollegiate competition.

No list of referees should omit the names of Harry Ertle, E. W. Smith of Chicago, Johnny Gallagher, Colonel Charles Short, U.S.A., Harry Stout, and Malache Hogan of Chicago. More recently more top referees have been developed such as Art Mercente, Zach Clayton, Henry Gibbs, Jay Edson, and others.

George Blake, one of the most famous boxing coaches in the United States and once coach at the famous Los Angeles Athletic Club, was one of the greatest referees in the United States before World War II. Probably his most famous action as a referee was to stop the Schmeling-Stribling fight in the last round, rightfully to save Stribling from serious injury, but it took considerable courage because it gave Schmeling credit for a knockout victory over a man whose record was particularly clear of knockouts. Blake's accomplishments as coach, however, overshadow even his refereeing. He developed many amateur and professional champions on the west coast, later went on to Hawaii and is considered by many to be responsible for the beginning of Hawaiian excellence in the sport. In recent years Hawaii has sent very successful teams to this country to compete in our national amateur championships.

In this connection it is interesting to see how one man with technical knowledge and personality can start an interest in a sport, and produce such excellence in it among people who have never participated in it before, as to carry them to world prominence. We have an example of this in Australia, where Romany Jem Mace first introduced boxing, which resulted in great interest in the sport there and the invasion of the United States by many champions and near-champions from the Antipodes, including Bob Fitzsimmons. In one other sport, which, by the way, is close to boxing, we have an even greater example. A noted Italian fencing master named Santelli moved to Hungary at the turn of the century and interested the Hungarians in sabre fencing. It be-

came their national sport, and Hungary and the Hungarians have cleaned up most Olympic and world championships in this sport and weapon until recently, and are still among the best. Santelli's son, by the way, emigrated to America and was the coach of several United States Olympic fencing teams and the New York Athletic Club until retired for age.

Perhaps the greatest amateur boxer in the history of the modern game, John Gaddi, became an outstanding referee. Wounds suffered in World War I prevented him from following the professional boxing career in which he was expected to become a champion. He won the National Heavyweight Amateur Boxing Championship in 1917 and then went to war. The war and his wounds turned his hair prematurely snow-white, which further accentuated the lines of his strong, handsome face. Gaddi as a referee exerted an almost hypnotic quality over fighters in the ring after World War I.

Yesterday when almost half of the important boxing bouts in the world were held in Greater New York or in New York State, the favorite referees and judges of the New York State Athletic Commission were naturally the ones who came in for the most public attention. For many years the work horse of the New York State Boxing Commission was Arthur Donovan, and for that reason he became the best known of modern-day referees. As boxing rules have attained greater perfection over the last twenty years, they have also ended the single-official system. Therefore, today, because there are two judges who rule on a fight as well as the referee, the importance of the latter has become minimized. In other days, the referee was the final arbiter and only judge. Today he is the most important member of a court of three.

Arthur Donovan was, as we already know, the son of the famous Mike Donovan, once world's middleweight champion. He was a quick-thinking, quick-moving man who had been known in an important fight even to catch a punch with his hands, thereby avoiding the possibility of a boxer's committing an unintentional foul—always unsatisfactory to the public and to the game.

If the referee is the invisible man of boxing, the trainer is the unheard-of man of the sport. I feel certain that even boxing experts cannot recite any list of famous trainers and their clients or wards. However, no discussion of personalities or players on or behind the fistic stage can overlook a few of the best-known trainers.

The best-known old-timer, and in fact the father of prizefight training, is Captain Barclay Allardyce of Ury, Scotland. He was born in 1779 and fell heir to the family estates at Ury at the age of eighteen.

His vocation was improving the art of agriculture. His avocations were riding to the hounds and other sports, especially walking and the training of athletes. He was a thoroughgoing sportsman and a scientific trainer. While he was in Cambridge he built himself up by self-imposed exercise.

At the age of twenty-seven he could lift a half ton and at seventeen he could walk six miles in an hour. For the latter, he won $500 on a bet. At twenty-one, he walked sixty-five miles in twelve hours, including time out for refreshments. He later did one hundred miles in nineteen hours.

He accepted a wager to walk 1,000 miles in as many successive hours at the rate of one mile in each and every hour. His plan was carefully thought out and he was trained by Mr. Smith of Owston in Yorkshire. He varied his clothing to suit the weather, a greatcoat in rain, a flannel jacket on other days, strong shoes, two pairs of coarse stockings. He started at midnight, 1 June 1809. He performed best in rainy weather and on dry days had a water-cart go over the road to keep it cool. Toward the end of the ordeal, he suffered so much from a muscle spasm in his legs that he could not walk a mile in less than twenty minutes, but about 8 days before he finished, the sinews of his right leg became much better, and odds became ten to one in his favor, having been two to one and five to two during his leg trouble.

On 12 July at 3:15, forty-five minutes before the necessary end of the race, he came in with perfect ease through a crowd that had been lining the course for days. The crowds awaiting his victory were unprecedented in size and included all the gentry and many members of the court. Bets aggregated $500,000, and Barclay's prize was $5,250. According to one account, he won close to $100,000 in bets on himself.

When Barclay trained Tom Cribb, the heavyweight champion, he became the first trainer of a professional boxer in modern ring history. His methods included the initiation of "road work," still used by present-day fighters in training. Suffice it to say that Barclay was a tough taskmaster and a martinet, but he believed that anyone he trained could lick anyone else. He wagered and won $60,000 on Cribb in the second Cribb-Moylneux fight after he had trained Cribb for three months. Barclay was a colorful character and was unequaled until the appearance of William Muldoon in America.

William Muldoon, America's Barclay, called by some the "Czar of Boxing," by others the "Father of American Boxing," was a wrestling champion, a boxer, the second Commissioner of the New York State Athletic Commission (January 1921–April 1923), and above all else was a physical trainer and conditioner

—one of the greatest in the game. His contribution to boxing is a great one, and there is no doubt of his place among the behind-the-scenes actors of fistiana.

In 1870 he helped organize the first athletic association in the New York Police Department, of which he was physical instructor. After wrestling, boxing, and instructing, Muldoon settled down to his main love and interest. He became the leading trainer and conditioner in America, first in an establishment on East 22nd Street in New York, then in nearby White Plains. Even President Grover Cleveland once planned to have Muldoon help him take off some weight.

An interesting fact unearthed about Muldoon is a public statement by him that had he been able to train John L for the Corbett fight, the Boston Strong Boy never would have lost. Many of the boxing experts of the time believe this statement.

Today the trainer is an essential part of a boxer's life. In fact, in many cases he has developed into

112. William Muldoon in his prime.

not only a conditioner but a second, technical adviser and member of the board of strategy as well. When fight time comes, a fighter usually has his trainer and manager in his corner to advise him in what to do and what not to do. Even during the progress of a fight, particularly in clinches, a fighter glances occasionally toward his corner for instructions. These he gets by means of a system of signals just like those a batter or catcher in baseball gets from the bench.

Among the most famous trainers of modern times are: Joe Palmer, crack trackman, boxer, referee, and author, who dedicated a book to the Duke of Windsor; Jimmy De Forest, who usually was successful except when his own fighter, Firpo, fired him; Dia Doblings, the English trainer who handled Mike McTigue, McLarnin, and many world's champions; Heinie Blaustein, who trained five world's champions out of Baltimore, Maryland; Hymie Cantor, who trained and managed Ruby Goldstein; "Doc" Robb, the first trainer of Benny Leonard and who handled many old champions; Mannie Seamon, trainer of Joe Louis after the death of Blackburn and who also trained Leonard; Charlie Goldman, who trained Lou Ambers, Al McCoy, Marty Servo, and Rocky Marciano; Gus Wilson, trainer of Jack Dempsey; Gene Lutz, who conditioned Freddie Welch and Young Stribling; Nick and Dan Florio, who put Genaro and many little fellows in shape and handled Jersey Joe Walcott; Izzy Kline, conditioner of Barney Ross, also of Max and Buddy Baer; and Bill Gore who kept Willie Pep in great shape. More recently, the Dundee brothers, Sandy Sadler, and Archie Moore have become great trainers.

The most famous training team of modern pugilism was the team of Whitey Bimstein and Ray Arcel. They grossed between a quarter and a half million dollars in fifteen years, then agreed to disagree and broke up. They still operated for a long time but separately. They were each considered among the greatest brain-trusters of the padded ring. A fighter who had one of them in his corner had a whole general staff behind him, and a fighter with both of them in his corner could almost find out what his opponent was going to do in each round. However, both helped carry many an opponent of Joe Louis's out of the ring, feet first.

Boxing in the last hundred years has developed its own specialists in fistic promotion. The boxing press agent or publicity director has become another important behind-the-scene player. Walter St. Denis, one of the greatest of these, died while he was with Mike Jacobs and the Twentieth Century Sporting Club, although his connection with boxing goes back to Joe Gans and Jim Corbett. St. Denis wrote up

boxing as early as 1905 for the *New York Globe* and is the man who first sponsored Robert Ripley and who suggested the "Believe It or Not" series. In 1915 he was also a promoter and put on fights including the Packy McFarland-Mike Gibbons bout at Brighton Beach. He was boxing publicity director for the Madison Square Garden from 1926 to 1934 when he joined Mike Jacobs. Murray Goodman is probably the present dean of boxing publicity. He handled the Zaire and Manila championship fights. He received an award for helping the sport of boxing from the Boxing Writers Association. He is always on the alert to help any author write a book, play or motion picture that will help the sport.

The boxing stage includes even women actors, rarely in the ring, but nevertheless important factors behind the major ring characters. None of the feminine actors identified with boxing can surpass Algernon Swinburne's *Dolores*.

> Thou art fair in the fearless old fashion
> And thy limbs are as melodies yet,
> And move to the music of passion
> With lithe and lascivious regret;
> What ailed us, oh gods, to desert you
> For creeds that refuse and restrain?
> Come down and redeem us from virtue,
> Our Lady of Pain!

Adois Dolores McCord, the darling of the poet Swinburne, of the writers Charles Dickens and Alexander Dumas, American Venus, author, actress, journalist, was not only one of the great dramatic characters of boxing but was almost solely responsible for the first publicized International World's Championship on 17 April 1860. She made John Camel Heenan, bare-knuckle heavyweight champion of the United States, challenge Tom Sayers, the English champion. She then married Heenan in 1859, but divorced him because he did not win the fight and the world's title.

Miss McCord's career reads like a motion picture epic. Born in New Orleans, Louisiana, in 1835, she wrote her first published poems at the age of thirteen, and appeared as a dancer at the old French Opera House in Havana at the age of fourteen. At fifteen she was criminally assaulted by her mother's lover. Shortly thereafter she began an almost lifelong affair and friendship with a New Orleans ballet dancing teacher. She then traveled in his show throughout the United States and Mexico, dancing, riding horseback, and doing male impersonations. On a buffalo hunting trip she and a male companion were captured by Indians. Because her male companion was a coward, he defeated her attempt to escape, for which she horsewhipped him when they were finally rescued. Their rescuer, the chief of the Texas Rangers, became her lover. After returning to New Orleans, Dolores married her music teacher, a well-known artist, Alexander Isaacs Menken, and became known as Adah Isaacs Menken; but this marriage did not last. She toured as leading lady of a show and, it is reported, was the cause of at least one duel. Next she became an expert on horseracing and moved to Kentucky, where her beauty, intelligence, and acute race tips were commented on by Horace Greeley.

Her next stop was New York, where she met, fell in love with, and married the American heavyweight champion John Camel Heenan. With a clever eye to publicity she made a new theatrical tour as Mrs. John Camel Heenan. However, when Heenan failed to become world's champion in his match with Sayers in England, for which Mrs. Heenan was responsible, Dolores divorced her pugilist husband. Her next husband, acquired before her divorce from Heenan was legal, was Robert Newell, a well-known writer. On their honeymoon the couple visited Washington and the White House and lunched with President Abraham Lincoln, even though Dolores was an outspoken Southern sympathizer.

Because Dolores insisted on a Western tour of *Mazeppa* in which she appeared on horseback clad in what in those days was considered almost nothing, she became known as "the naked lady." When she showered too much attention on a millionaire gold miner known as Handsome Billy Thompson on the Pacific Coast, her husband Newell left her. Her agent Ed James was then smart enough to schedule a European tour. In 1864 they sailed for England by way of Cape Horn, a few months' voyage. Her success in England was immediate and complete.

James Barkley, a king-pin gambler who had followed Dolores to England from California, proposed to her repeatedly but she did not marry him until several years later. Her tour in England and France made her the toast of Europe. In England she became an intimate friend of Charles Dickens and Algernon Swinburne and exchanged poems with them. In Paris her constant admirers and companions were Alexander Dumas and Théophile Gautier. Her intelligence and beauty were admired everywhere.

On returning to New York she married Barkley, who died or committed suicide a few months later, leaving Dolores a large fortune. The world was at her feet. Offers of marriage came from the United States and all over the world. After a short eastern tour she sailed for England again. All London crowded *Mazeppa's* every performance for four months. She received over $1,500 weekly, which in those days was an unprecedented salary. Her friendship with Swinburne during this period turned into a well-known romance, which some claim was mainly conceived by Dolores as a publicity stunt. The British Government was even moved to order her expulsion, which merely increased her profits. But finally Dolores became tired of either her love or her publicity stunt and after a British provincial tour went to Paris, where she met Napoleon III and the King of Greece. A scandal broke here too, in connection with her goings-on with Alexander Dumas, but this again served only to increase the size of the Dolores audiences.

All during this period Dolores insisted on being known as Adah Isaacs Menken and on retaining the Jewish faith, which she had adopted on marrying Menken. Many believe, because of this, that the musician Menken was the only man she truly loved, although in many interviews she stated that she would never have divorced Heenan if he had won the world's heavyweight boxing championship. No one ever accused this strange woman of not being generous. She gave away millions. On her last visit to Paris, when she was herself in insecure financial circumstances, she helped Dumas with practically the last remnants of her once-great fortune.

Not only was her fortune gone by 1868, but she had developed cancer, and while she continued her mad pace, she knew she was doomed to a painful and almost immediate death. While performing in a theatre she collapsed and died at the age of thirty-three. Many people of her time, including the boxing and theatrical worlds, agreed that she had no equal in physical beauty, intellectual greatness, or human understanding and generosity.

When the news of the death of Dolores reached Heenan, the American heavyweight champion, he firmly assured the press that she alone had been his inspiration, had consoled him for his loss to John Morrissey, had spurred him on when he fought Sayers for the world title, and that she had warned him not to come back to her without winning the world's championship for America. No woman has ever played a more important role in boxing than Adah Isaacs Menken, born Dolores McCord.

Algernon Swinburne wrote a poem to remember Dolores and also to have her remembered:

> For the tale of our life as it closes
> Is darkness, the fruit there of dust,
> No thorns are as sharp as a rose's
> and Love is more cruel than lust;
> Time turns the old days to derision,
> Our loves into corpses or wives,
> And marriage and death and division
> Make barren our lives.

112A. Dolores, wife of Heenan, early U. S. heavy-weight champion, and four other men and the darling of poets and kings.

Before we pass over women actors on the boxing stage, we must refer to one whose role was almost equal to Dolores. This was Ann Livingston. She had been a childhood friend of John L. Sullivan at Roxbury, Massachusetts. Then suddenly they met again in the mid-1880s after Sullivan had left his first wife in 1882. Ann Livingston, born Naylor, was in the theater. She was tall and willowy, with bright blue eyes and blonde hair. Ann had married her booking agent but she left him. She was the most talked about actress in New York, Philadelphia, Boston, and Washington. After the childhood chums met again, they were practically inseparable. Ann travelled all over the world with Sullivan. Dressed as a man she was a witness to his title fights against Mitchell at Baron Rothschild's Chantilly Chateau and against Kilrain in Richburg, Mississippi in 1889. In this fight Kilrain's seconds threw in the sponge in the seventy-fifth round in a temperature of 105 degrees in the shade. Shortly thereafter, not affected by the sun, Sullivan gave his girlfriend, Ann, some $15,000 in cash and lots of valuable jewelry, but he had started to drink heavily. They quarreled and finally separated. Sometime after 1890, after failing to recover her acting popularity, Ann opened a theatrical boarding house on Third Avenue near Chatham Square in New York City, but it failed and shortly thereafter she died sick and penniless. When Sullivan heard about this he was very sad. He did not remember when he was drunk and had accused her of infidelity and then struck her across the face, nor did he remember how she had then knocked him out by hitting him over the head

113. Ann Livingstone, John L. Sullivan's girl friend —Police Gazette—1897.

with one of his Indian clubs. All he remembered was that he had loved her very much. All he could do was to pay for her burial but he could not bring her back!

There is one more actor in boxing to discuss—"the Shadow." The shadow is a challenger, usually for the heavyweight title, who never gets his chance until it is too late. The shadow is usually handicapped in some way, sometimes really for no good reason except that most shadows are good, so good that the champion or his managers want no part of him. Peter Jackson was the shadow of John L. Sullivan and Corbett. Sam Langford was the shadow of Jack Johnson. Harry Wills was the shadow of Jack Dempsey.

Shadows usually get their chance, but after they have seen their pugilistic prime. All of them, or perhaps none of them at his best, could have won the championship. This uncertainty is also what makes them shadows.

Modern radio broadcasting has introduced another actorlike character to boxing—the announcer. Major White was the first well-known radio fight announcer in the crystal-set days of Champion Jack Dempsey. Then Graham McNamee, with his "Ladies and gentlemen of the radio audience," took boxing lessons better to adapt his dramatic delivery to the description of some of Baer's fights. His "He's down," "He's up" left many a fight fan limp with excitement in his own home. Ted Husing, Bill Stern, and Bill Slater, leading sports announcers, have all had a try at boxing also. Don Dumphey and Red Barber have broadcast many fights for Gillette's Cavalcade of Sport, and as a result are identified by thousands of radio listeners with boxing.

However, the Greek chorus of boxing, who speak the prologue and epilogue and comment on the course of events in the sport, are the announcers actually in and of the ring. These gentlemen belong to no other sport and are truly characters of the stage of boxing —the ring. The golden era of American boxing is almost taken care of by just two of these loud-voiced gentlemen.

Joe Humphries was the first of these. In the latter part of his career, a fat old gent with a round face, a bulbous nose and a bald pate, he would clamber into the ring, remove his false teeth and place them in his pocket. He would then literally bellow his "Ladies and Gentlemen," and his introduction of the fighters. Humphries came from the old gas-house district of New York City around First Avenue from 16th to 23rd Streets. His hangout was the Anawonda (Tammany) Democratic Hall. He knew all the prominent politicians in his youth. Humphries's particular friends were old Judge Moss, James Foley, the "Aldy" (Willie Kennelley), Tammany leader of the district, and Charlie Murphy, the leader of Tammany Hall.

Joe became interested in boxing and boxers as a kid. A great friend of the great fighter Willie Lewis, he acted as his bodyguard and took him home almost every night. Whenever Willie was out after dark, Joe Humphries had to be with him, take him home, and wait until Willie's mother could come downstairs with a lamp or until she could light a gas-jet in the house. Although Willie was a mighty middleweight with his fists and feared no one in the ring, he was desperately afraid of the dark.

Humphries's first experience as announcer was gained in the ring of Kramer's Bowery Arena, where fights were held before they moved to the car barn which later became the first Madison Square Garden. When the old Garden opened, although Humphries had tried to get the franchise or management of the Garden or, at least, the conduct of boxing there, Rickard installed him as the master-of-ceremonies.

In the early days Humphries and his voice were able to fill the old Garden without the aid of microphones, and Humphries's motions, personality, and screaming tenor voice could stop any disturbance or vocal objections from the audience. He became a fixture of all world's championship fights and some of his expressions have become standard today, such as "winner and still champion." Other expressions, probably not necessarily connected with him, such as "in this corner," are identified with him by all old-timers. He was the Number One announcer and master-of-ceremonies of boxing almost to his death.

Only yesterday the role of Humphries was being capably played by Harry Balogh. Balogh served an apprenticeship as announcer in the New York State National Guard Armories, which used to conduct weekly fights after World War I. He then wound up in "big time" and became the No. 1 announcer and master-of-ceremonies for championship fights. In addition, Balogh had taken on two extra roles—one in radio and one in television. One might say, to paraphrase Dan Parker, that Balogh has rocketed to the pinnacle of the pugilistic world with a dictionary in his right hand, a thesaurus in his left, a potent pair of lungs, and a tuxedo. He punched with words faster than any boxing champion could throw punches, and he was just as paralyzing. Harry, the "new look" in fight announcers, had discarded a tradition of two centuries. The pugilistic master-of-ceremonies had, until Balogh, been satisfied to send bruisers into the ring with direct and very down-to-earth talk, winding up with a stereotyped line—"May the best man win!"

Balogh's improvisation and exploration in the English language immediately marked him for success. Mr. Balogh was a humorist, but most amusing when in dead earnest. One night at the St. Nicholas Arena he was making an impassioned appeal for a March of Dimes collection about to be taken up in coin boxes by a group of beautiful models. After orating at length with much emphasis on the worthiness of the cause, Balogh threw a right with this punch line: "Now," he roared, "the pretty volunteers will pass among you with their little cans." Some of his other bon mots are "the man who, like good wine, goes on forever," —"the fighter who, like Tennyson's brook, improves with age,"—"may the arm of the worthier participant be elevated in token of victory,"—"undefeated in his last 57 pugilistic forays."

Probably his most famous warning to any crowd was uttered at the Carnera-Louis fight: "So I appeal to you to look at and view this great fistic encounter and boxing match with your minds free from prejudism." Occasionally Balogh even lapsed into foreign languages—also dug up for the occasion—such as, at a Gavilan fight when Harry appealed to the Cuban welterweight's followers, "Amigos, por favor, silencio, escucharme. Gracias!"

Balogh was also as well known for his sartorial splendor as for his mixed metaphors, and dangling participles. He had a dressing scale depending on the rating of the club where he worked. A neighborhood club rated a plain business suit—the Madison Square Garden called for a tuxedo—open air ball parks called for a white tuxedo jacket with black tuxedo trousers, and he became one of the earlier leading characters in television.

Probably the funniest story about Balogh is that concerning a free lance writer who went to interview Harry with respect to a proposed article for a national magazine. After some hemming and hawing, Harry finally inquired, "And how much, may I ask, is the remuneration for yours sincerely Harold Balogh?"

Strangely enough, with the disappearance of Harry Balogh came another announcer character who, in many ways, resembled him. This announcer, Howard Cosell, however, became famous and first found work and fame not in boxing, but in other sports, particularly football, although his technical knowledge of that sport was often questioned. However, he is always teamed up with top football experts, usually former stars of the game, and they support him and prevent him from going too far in forays into the theory and tactics of the game. So far his handling of boxing contests has been fairly limited, although he is a professed admirer of Muhammad Ali. Many persons accuse Cosell of a lack of tact which led to a disturbance at a broadcast on 23 January 1974 on the ABC Wide World of Sports show.

Incidentally, boxing is hardly a sports announcer's dream for a contest in boxing is very fast and short-lived. A fifteen round fight has actually only forty-five minutes of action with a minute's rest between rounds for any sum-up or comment. Since television allows all viewers to see the action, some persons pay little attention to the announcer. As a result, even a Howard Cosell can add very little to a televised boxing contest, particularly to any expert viewer. In fact many persons claim Cosell spoils many sports competitions he tries to narrate. Because the actual spectators or gates at prizefights are now unimportant, the ringside announcer has also become unimportant. The last of the great ringside announcers was John Addie who passed away in 1971. To prove this today, we often may have receipts from television audiences totaling millions of dollars with an actual physical audience of several thousand persons. Also, television announcers now often add their narration second-hand and, of course, in many different languages. Therefore, both ringside announcers and the many different broadcasters are no longer among the great actors of boxing. So here also we see a tremendous change as boxing becomes worldwide and seen by millions via TV, but with different announcers or narrators.

11 • Development of Boxing Technique and Summary of Current Theory—Stance—Footwork—Offense and Defense

When a caveman picked up a stone as a weapon and, instead of throwing it, held it in his hand and swung with it, boxing was born. When this same man or another found that by clenching his fists he had two natural weapons, the technique (i.e., the art and science of pugilism) began.

From the discovery of the fist to that of gunpowder, the submarine, the airplane, the tank, guided missiles, and the atomic bomb, man has sought an offensive weapon to aid him in the survival of the fittest. A strong offense is the best defense. This belief instinctively appealed to man in his battle for existence. So the first subject in the technique of boxing based on the chronological development of the use of the fist, is "hitting," because it has to do with the offensive urge.

The art of hitting is the art of obtaining maximum power in a blow with the fist. From records, pictures, and statues, we know that originally blows were struck by swinging and, later, by hooking. Such a method developed from swinging a club and hitting with a stone in the hand. Both the cat and the bear families instinctively hit in this manner. The ability to hit straight from the shoulder is not a natural act. It cannot be learned by chance. Even experience does not teach it. Straight hitting with body follow-through is an art that has taken centuries to develop and perfect. Similarly, the shortening of blows was the result of the perfection of technique rather than of instinct.

114. Minoan boxers, Crete, 1100 B.C.

Man is not naturally ambidextrous. On the contrary, with the exception of an occasional "southpaw," the right hand is used normally with greater flexibility, strength, and power than the left hand. As a result, from the very beginning the right hand was the principal hitting or punching hand. The boxing scenes on Minoan and Greek vases, friezes, and statues prove this beyond any doubt, though there are evidences that the left hand also was used for hitting.

The position of the right arm and hand in Greek art shows that:

191

1. It was used for a round-house blow—hook, chop, or cross.
2. It was sometimes raised above shoulder height in readiness for a full swing, straight right or downward chopping or swinging blow.
3. It was sometimes "cocked" as in modern pugilism—evidence that a straight punch was to follow when an opening was made with the left hand.

Although T. K. Frost, Prof. Mahaffy and other experts and archaeologists claim that the Greeks did not know or use the straight punch, E. N. Gardiner and other authorities disagree with them. After considerable study of Greek art, we are convinced that the Greeks had developed the straight punch from the Homeric or pre-Olympic period through the first golden era of the sport and that it was very much in evidence in the boxing championships from the 60th through the 142nd Olympic.

T. K. Frost is on weak ground and "leads with his chin" when he tells us that the cauliflower ears of the Greek boxers indicate that the Greeks used only swinging blows. The cauliflower ear is with us today, yet our fighters use straight punches as well as hooks, crosses, and swings. In addition, most prominent Greek boxers, unlike ours today, competed in the field of wrestling and entered the pancratium or free-for-all competition of boxing and wrestling. In these, they were subjected to fierce and sometimes deadly headlocks which certainly were rough on the ears.

Wrestlers were often responsible for the earmarking of boxers and hitting sometimes was not sufficient to win in these combination boxing and wrestling matches. The fact that Kreugas, a great Olympic boxing champion, was killed by the wrestler Demoexnos in the finals of the pancratium championship at the Nemean games attests to this. In another pancratium contest, Archacian was posthumously awarded the championship because a toehold he finally put on his opponent made the latter give up. However, during the contest, Archacian had been under the pressure of such terrific headlocks and strangle holds that when his opponent quit, Archacian rolled over, was proclaimed champion and then died.

In our modern era, King Levinsky, fish-peddler and boxer, and Ray Steele, college graduate and heavyweight wrestler, met in St. Louis, Missouri, 20 November 1935, before a crowd of 15,000 in a modern pancratium. At the bell, both contestants rushed out of their corners. Levinsky swung a right hand hay-maker for Steele's chin and missed. Steele grabbed the King, picked him up, spun him above his head in an "airplane twirl" and threw him on the ring floor, falling on top of him. There was very little more wriggling before Steele pinned both Levinsky's shoulders down. Time thirty-five seconds. This shows that a boxer should never lead with his

115. Greek Boxers, fourth century B.C. (British Museum, London)

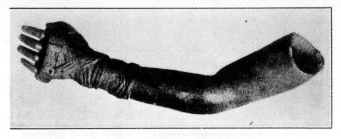

116. The soft glove (Library of Congress)

right, even against a wrestler. The Greeks knew this in 500 B.C.

Promoters tried to match Dempsey and Frank Gotch in a boxer-wrestler match—when the Manassa Mauler was champion, but it never came off. Generally speaking, both in Greek and modern times, wrestlers have beaten boxers in free-for-all contests. In the entire history of the Greek Olympics only two boxing champions (Theagenes and Cleitomachus) were able to win in both boxing and the pancratium, while seven Greek wrestling champions received both palms in the same Olympics.

Another and more certain proof of the straight punching habits and abilities and the highly developed technique of hitting among the Greeks is a study of the cestus or ancient boxing gloves. The development of these indicates to anyone acquainted with boxing that straight and efficient hitting was practiced in this entire period.

The first cestus originally used in Egypt, Crete, and at the outset in Greece consisted merely of leather strips or bands wrapped around the hand, fist, thumb, wrist, and arm to the elbow, with no special hitting surface. This was replaced in the Homeric period and the beginning of the Hellenic or Olympic period by what is called the "soft glove" cestus, which was very close to our present-day gauze and adhesive tape wrappings except that leather was used, and the wrapping was continued halfway up the forearm. The interesting feature of the wrappings was that they were particularly thick and contained many layers on the knuckle, back of the hand and over the four fingers between the second joint and knuckle proper, the latter being the only hitting surface used in straight punches. The wrappings on the back of the hand, thumb, and arm indicate that boxers of that era still used the swing, hook, and even rabbit punch or clublike swing from over the head. The special wrappings on the hitting surface however conclusively prove that the Greeks were learning to shorten their wild swings into hooks and crosses delivered with the hitting surface of the fist, and also were using the straight punch which only involved the surface presented by the wrappings over the fingers between the second joint and the knuckle proper.

Later, in the Hellenic or Olympic period when

117. The hard glove (Library of Congress)

boxing became more important and vast crowds saw men fight with their fists for "world" championships, the cestus or ancient boxing-glove underwent another change. It became what is referred to as the "hard glove." The wrappings around the thumb, hand, wrist, and forearm became simply protective and defensive bindings to prevent bruises and broken bones. A close-fitting glove covered the hand, leaving the upper joints of the fingers free and the palm open. The wrappings extended above the wrist half way to the elbow and terminated in a rim of fur. This fur was the actual forerunner of our current single or double (training) wrist padding. Without connection with the wrist and arm wrappings, the "hard glove" could be slipped off the hand.

However, the best and most modern feature of this "hard glove" was the hitting surface, three thick rings or bands of leather joined together, one alongside of the other, giving the appearance of a sort of a doughnut, the edge of which was the hitting surface over the four fingers and between the second joint and knuckle or edge of the hand. The fingers in closing (to make a fist) grasped the other side of this leather doughnut. This was the hard glove used in the Olympic and other Greek game championships. It can readily be seen that modern punching or a close facsimile of it must have been practiced, for otherwise this hard glove would not have been effective. We have two indications to prove that it was effective. A great number of boxers were killed during this period. This was the result of punching with the surface described above, the same hitting surface used today, and one which must have involved straight punching. The other clue to its effectiveness is that the boxers, when deprived of their hard glove as an offensive adjunct and as a protection for their hands, were generally defeated by wrestlers in the pancratium. With the hard glove

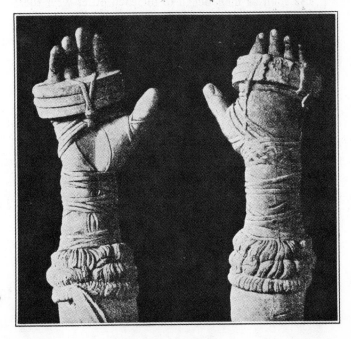

and its hitting edge the boxers would undoubtedly have knocked most of the wrestlers bowlegged. As it was, with unprotected hands, the boxers probably broke their fists on the wrestlers heads before being dumped on their backs.

Most evidence indicates that the Greeks hit only to the head in their boxing competitions, and any blows to the body were purely accidental. Punches to the stomach were considered fouls. However, when the fist was used as a weapon and not for sport or when used by the so-called barbarians or uncivilized tribesmen, body blows were probably employed. Statues of Greeks and "barbarians" in defensive poses, with bare knuckles indicating a fight and not a boxing competition, show them in position to guard against body punches. However, most Greek statues of boxers with cestus show an unusually high guard. While their bodies were left exposed, the ancient Greeks were very careful to guard their faces and heads, especially against rabbit punches or clublike swings from above by their opponents.

In the Roman period, however, there is evidence that body punching was practiced with the loaded cestus, which brought the guard down. While body punching was not unknown in early English boxing, it was not used as much as it is today, and even in America in the days of John L. Sullivan, James J. Corbett and Bob Fitzsimmons, the head and face were the major and almost exclusive targets for attack. For an interesting illustration of this point we have put an 1897 picture of Bob Fitzsimmons in fighting pose alongside of a photograph of an antique statue of Pollux in boxing position dating back to approximately 1500 B.C. The poses are 3,397 years apart. In both, the left hand is held in a position to guard the head against overhand righthand swings, while the right hand is held ready to be thrown at an opponent's head or chin.

As soon as men began to hit each other with their fists, they began to think about defending themselves. Instinctively, the very first defensive move was to push one's opponent away with an outstretched left hand to cause the opponent's right swing to fall short of its target or to upset the balance of the opponent in such a way that he could not even start his swing. The chances are that the next instinctive move was the parry with a sudden movement of one's hand from the inside or outside meeting an oncoming blow either to deflect the blow from its original path or to break the force of the blow or prevent the blow from landing at all. Strangely enough, these are still the two basic defensive moves of the modern boxer, although they have been greatly developed as well as supplemented by other defensive tactics.

To return to the defensive left hand, we find Egyp-tian and Minoan (Crete) friezes and vases and, of course, Greek vases and statues, with the left hand held almost straight out and with the left foot forward so that the attacker cannot possibly be missed and so that the opponent's righthand blow will be short. Most of the boxing scenes of the Greeks uniformly show a stance very similar to our present one, particularly with respect to defense and the use of the left hand. The left foot in the Greek stance was directly in front of the right. This also was to improve defense.

118. Early Greek boxers. Drawing from a contemporary vase.

With the left hand the Greeks held off their opponents or pushed their opponents "off set" or off balance, and thereby broke up their offense and their righthand punches. They also, with the straight left, measured their opponents for their own righthand follow-through or knockout swing. The ancient pugilist, by hitting or pushing his opponent with the left hand at the moment the latter was about to throw a punch, threw him off balance and thereby prevented him either from starting the blow, or, if the blow was already started, prevented it from landing with any great force. The left hand, by its position in the opponent's face, also served as a sort of range-finder or yardstick for a right-hand swing. However, according to the evidence unearthed, the defensive tactics of the ancients stopped here.

Just as war is a constant see-saw between offense and defense, so is boxing. As soon as the crude defense described above began to make itself felt, men developed offensive tactics in addition to the left-hand push-punch, the half swing, the righthand haymaker or full-swing, and combinations of these. Man next evolved the "rush" by which he rapidly closed with his opponent in order to throw one or both hands to the head. Man also developed more than one type of swing with either hand, shortened his swings to hooks, and finally, it can be seen from Greek art and the cestus, began to learn to hit straight from the shoulder with either hand and with body follow-through. As soon as these blows developed, someone discovered that in parrying a right hand, one could immediately follow the parry with a blow or, better yet, could meet a blow from an opponent with a blow of his own that would land first.

That was the beginning of "countering" in boxing. Countering is still a most important element in the fight game today. Joe Louis was the greatest counter puncher in boxing history. As soon as countering tended to favor the defense, the offense got busy and developed many different kinds and types of blows as well as blocks, and then fighters began to discover that all their hitting and offense and all their parrys, blocks and defense needed strategic mixing, and we were first introduced to ring craft or generalship.

118A. Joe Louis' stance, 1947 (Ring Magazine)

A tall man found that he could get along best with a "straight left" defense and that his best strategy lay in keeping a smaller opponent away. If he let the smaller opponent keep rushing, the shorter man would wear himself out and then the taller man could swing with his right hand at the target whose range had been measured by the left. On the other hand, a small, stocky, fast man discovered that he could do best by beating a tall man's left down, getting inside the tall man's guard and swinging with both hands. One morning some young boxer made a startling discovery—if he maneuvered in such a position that his opponent faced the sun, his opponent would be temporarily blinded by its rays during which time a KO punch could be landed. All these simple tricks and more were discovered when ring craft started.

While it is difficult to be sure when blocking began, most people believe it came after parrying, although it is today the first line of defense. Blocking means taking a blow on some part of the body which is not too susceptible to injury. Unlike the parry, it is purely defensive, for blocking does result in absorbing some punishment, and usually disturbs balance, thus preventing countering and even creating openings for other blows from the opponent. As the art of blocking developed, blows were blocked with the hand, elbow, forearm and shoulder. Then someone found that blocking could also be combined with countering and could be almost a spring-board for the counterattack; the see-saw between offense and defense continued.

About this time it must have become obvious to man that the effectiveness of his hitting and his defense, of his offense and his countering, of his blows and his blocks were dependent on the correctness of his basic position. This led to a careful study of the position of "on guard" or to what we refer to today as "stance." How to stand in such a way as to be able to move in any direction and yet to be able to hit, block or counter, to take the offense or defense, became all important. Every offensive and defensive consideration went into determining the proper stance, that is, the position of the feet, body, hands, and head, to fit best into both offense and defense. The present-day boxer's stance is the result of centuries of development.

Next, boxers began to realize that no matter how good they were, some tired more quickly than others, some could take punishment better than others, and some could hit better than others. Those who were inferior and had perseverance refused to accept their inferiority and went out into the jungle to try to acquire what they lacked. This was the beginning of training. Training involved diet in order to improve stamina and capacity to absorb punishment. Training also involved lung endurance (wind) and the development of the muscles, particularly those in the arms, shoulders, and legs. Training also meant constant practice so that the proper actions and reactions would become automatic and spontaneous.

As soon as training and the art of training began, together with all the other developments already pointed out, it became clear that a successful boxer had to have a fairly large repertoire of blows, punches, parries, counters, and combinations of all these which he could practice so often and so thoroughly that they would become almost instinctive and would be used without thought whenever the proper occasion arose in a fight.

Then some cunning beginner or wily veteran came along and discovered, perhaps by accident, that at the last moment, in fact just a fraction of a second before the impact of a blow from an opponent, a punch could be avoided by suddenly lowering, pulling back or turning the head, or by pulling back, turning or twisting the body. This led to the art of ducking and slipping. From this evolved the fact that even a second later, a person could also avoid serious punishment by simply moving his head or body away from a punch in the same direction as the punch. In other words, just as one catches a baseball today, one can avoid the full impact of a punch by "riding" with it. This is now known as the art of "rolling."

So far, it will be noted that boxing involved no great mobility, but as all these complications came into it, man realized that he could attack or defend himself, apply ring craft, generalship, and all the other adjuncts to better advantage if he used his feet as well as his head, and thus footwork came into being.

Probably last in the chronological evolution of boxing technique came the feint. After all of the other points had been developed to some considerable degree and after feinting had developed in the allied art of fencing, it invaded the fistic sport. While there is some minor evidence that feinting was practiced in Greek boxing and in early English boxing, we find feinting, generally speaking, is a late development of modern boxing, and is one of the last technical advancements due at least partly to the influence of fencing in the renaissance of boxing. Feinting was first used as a major factor in a championship fight by one of its greatest and earliest exponents, James J. Corbett.

Of course, much of the technique of boxing began to take definite shape only when formal fistic competition began. We can only go back positively, though hazily, to the Egyptians and clearly to Crete for any indications as to the rules of the first formal competitions. These in turn led to the fairly well-known rules in early Greece and the better-known Olympic rules in the first golden age of boxing.

There were no weight classes, and consequently superior strength, size, and weight were the deciding factors. Next, there were no rounds. All fights were fought to a finish. In cases where both men fought to exhaustion, they drew lots for the order in which they would proceed to get free "shots" or knockout punches at each other. The absence of rounds and regular rest periods led to stalling, during which both contestants took it easy. Defensive tactics and stalling occurred in both the ancient Greek and the more modern English Era.

119. Bob Fitzsimmons' stance, 1898. (Nat Fleischer). Compare with illus. 120 (p. 197).

In Greece, even in the Olympics and other great games, contestants could, by mutual consent, take a rest during the progress of a fight. The statue attributed to be that of Cleitomachus is believed to show him during a rest period in his fight in the finals of an Olympic boxing championship against the handsome Egyptian Aristonikos. Although Cleitomachus was the local defending champion, at first the crowd was for his opponent. One story tells us that the foreigner led at the beginning of the fight, with the crowd in his favor; just as the Frenchman, Carpentier, was the favorite of an American crowd in the first part of his fight with Dempsey. Then the tide began to change and a rest period was agreed to by mutual consent. During this rest period Cleitomachus audibly upbraided the crowd for backing the foreigner. The famous statue shows him resting and also shows the results of the beating he obviously took in the early stages of the fight. After the rest period, the crowd began to cheer for their own local Greek champion and Cleitomachus won by a knockout.

An interesting rule in all early boxing, which showed that the ancients were neither as stupid nor as cruel as we are led to believe, was the one which permitted any boxing competitor to indicate his desire to give up by merely holding up his right or left hand with a forefinger pointed upward. We fortunately have pictorial proof of this on a Cretan vase of the sixth century B.C., showing a defeated boxer in a position similar to that of many a beaten boxer to-

121. Greek-Roman fighting stance as against boxing stance. (Atkins Museum, Kansas City)

day, but holding up his hand with forefinger extended to admit defeat and end the bout. In early Greece there were no neutral corners or rules against hitting a man partially down but who still showed fight.

The Greeks, it is believed, did no wrestling, cross-buttocking, or throwing of their opponents as in early English boxing. We also know that, notwithstanding much to the contrary, the Greeks used their feet as well as their heads and fists. There was frequent maneuvering for position, and for sunlight. In addition, there is evidence to prove that Greek boxing, like today's, developed the human figure to the typical boxer's proportions. Greek boxers had thin legs, large shoulders, and long muscles indicating speed afoot, and hitting power.

Hundreds of pictures, statues, and friezes show beyond doubt that the Greeks used a stance approximating our own today and requiring the same basic footwork. It is clear that forcing tactics were considered amateurish or barbarian, and caution was a prime factor. As a result, many fights in the early Olympics were slow and long. That is probably the reason for the rule permitting a "breather" by mutual consent. Defensive tactics were favored. Because, there was no limit of space or restriction of area and because of the old rules, close fighting was discouraged and all boxing was at long range.

We have proof of the early beginning of footwork in boxing. The Roman, Statius, wrote that a certain

120. Pollux's stance, 1500 B.C. (Library of Congress)

boxer "avoided a thousand deaths which flitted around his temples by quick movement and by the help of his feet." Philostratus, in an effort to revive ancient Greek boxing, wrote: "I do not approve of men with big calves in any branch of athletics and especially boxing. They are slow in advancing and easily caught by an opponent." Other mentions in Greek contemporary sources refer to boxers "ducking," "slipping," and especially of their being "light of foot".

Even the modern practice of putting grease or vaseline on the face or body to help assimilate a beating with the fist comes from the Greeks, the Minoans of Crete, and the Egyptians, all of whom put oil on their bodies before competition and removed it and bathed after their bouts.

Naturally, since the Greeks only hit to the head, there was some difference between the theory of attack and defense of that day and the modern theory. As has been already said, even in English bare-knuckle days, the head was preferred as the main target for punches. The English bare-fist fights, which left the hand open for grasping or grappling, definitely brought on considerable in-fighting as well as actual wrestling. The ancient boxers in Greece, however, kept wrestling completely out of boxing. They got their wrestling, by entering the pancratium, in which, from a study of Greek records, we find the boxer often being subdued by flying mares, leg holds, toe holds, strangle holds, headlocks, kicking, and above all else, by the bending back of his fingers. This latter trick not only made many a boxer quit, but ruined many a Greek fist for all time. The most famous exponent, if not the originator, of this technique of bending a man's fingers backward until he yelled "uncle" or until his fingers and hand were broken, is believed to be Sostratos, who won the 104th, 105th and 106th Olympic wrestling championships (364–356 B.C.) and also took on all the boxers at one of these Olympics, winning both the wrestling and pancratium titles.

Under the rules in force for boxing in the old Olympics, it was forbidden to hit with open hands or to poke anyone in the eye with fingers or thumb.

122. Boxer giving up, sixth century B.C. (Library of Congress)

One more technical point between boxing in the Greek Golden Age and boxing today is in the distribution of weight or balance. The advantages of leaning slightly forward in order to duck, slip, or roll while retaining complete balance and the ability to hit, was unknown to the ancients. Greek and Olympic champions fought standing fairly straight like the old English boxers. However, the early English boxer had learned enough never to lean back or bend his rear knee when attacked, but to use his left hand and move away with both feet. The ancient Greek, shown on statues and art work, made the terrible mistake of leaning way back out of reach of an opponent's swings and sometimes even bent the right knee. This position further proves that the Greeks did not use their feet or move around as much as the modern boxer. Being hit in this position over a couple of hundred years, however, must have taught man that he was too far off balance and could be easily bowled over if hit. Also, man must have learned he could not hit or make any other offensive gesture from this position.

On page 194 is a tracing of a sixth century B.C. vase showing early Greek boxers sparring. It will be noted that both figures have a stance similar to the modern conventional one, left foot in front, right back, toes forward, left hand straight. The right hand is very much higher than would be expected, supporting the belief that the ancient sport's target was only the head. The position, however, leaves no doubt that straight punches were forthcoming.

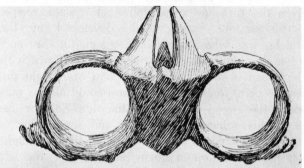

124. Drawing of bronze myrmex found in Greek and Roman ruins. (N.Y. Public Library)

When the Romans adapted boxing for their gladiatorial spectacles by adding the loaded cestus, the loser was usually the first man to be hit. All skill was abandoned. If a champion, no matter how clever, received one chance blow from the lead or loaded fist of an opponent, his brains were literally batted out. This naturally killed the game as well as the contestants. To make matters worse, the Etruscans, who learned boxing from Trojan emigrees from Greece under Aeneas (778 B.C.), used a myrmex or limb-piercer. This was a pointed instrument attached to the cestus in such a way as to pierce or dent into the head, body, or arm of anyone hit. The Romans learned about this little fistic pick from the Etruscans and used it on their boxers in the gladiatorial spectacles. The spectators at the Roman Circus Maximus shouted for blood, and the myrmex gave it to them, but as a result the fist disappeared for 1200 years.

When boxing did come back in England, it was introduced by fencing-masters. As a result, the boxing stance was made to approximate the fencing stance and to good effect. By that time, fencing had advanced to the point where the small sword or thrusting weapon was preferred to the broadsword or sabre. The use of the straight thrust or lunge against any side sweep or slash had been developed. The principles of advancing, retreating, much of our modern boxing footwork, and our straight punching came from fencing.

The prizefighter like the fencing master found that in advancing or retreating, if the approximate po-

123. Roman boxing (N.Y. Athletic Club)

sition of "on guard" was maintained, any attack or defense was possible at any instant. The first principle in boxing or fencing is always to make the first step or half or quarter step in any direction with the forward foot and then to bring up the other foot to the same relative position as before. In retreating, a boxer or a fencer first takes a small step back with the rear foot, then follows with his forward foot to the same relative position. In this way, a boxer or a fencer maintains his most effective pose. Even the turn in boxing follows the same recipe.

The straight punch, while developed by the Greeks, was reborn again in England, for the fencing masters knew that a straight lunge or thrust with the sword in attack, or a stop point or straight defensive point to an opponent's arm could always outspeed the sweep or cut from the side. So they applied this principle to boxing and found that a straight right could stop a swing and that a straight left jab could stop most anything. In fact, the left jab is a close imitation of the basic fencing lunge.

The fencing masters who developed the "gentle" art knew that, since in fencing only the right hand, which held the sword, was used it should be forward with the right foot forward and the left hand should be used as a counter-weight to help the balance and especially to help recover from extended lunges. They found, however, like the Greeks, that in boxing two hands could be used and the left was the best for defense and preparation, while the right was best for the final attack and the more telling blows. This led to a stance similar to fencing but on an opposite diagonal. In boxing, the left hand and left foot were forward and the right hand was placed where it could serve not only as an aid to balance but also where it could parry or block an opponent's punches and where it could be thrown to the opponent's head. The original boxing stance of the early English prizefighters was adapted from their fencing position of "on guard."

For those who do not believe that boxing should credit fencing for most of its technical development in modern history, we will quote from one of the earliest manuals on boxing ever written in our modern era. As far as we know, there is only one copy of this book in the western hemisphere. It was written by a fencer and fencing scholar, Captain John Godfrey, printed by T. Gardner, 1747, London, and entitled: *A Treatise Upon the Useful Science of Defense Connecting the Small and Back Sword with Some Observations Upon Boxing, and the Characters of the Most Able Boxers Within the Author's Time.*

From the title itself, it is easy to see that much of the technique discussed by the author is common to

125. Boxing stance in 1810 (Molyneaux, left, influenced by fencing stance of early "prizefighters" who fenced and boxed in 1743. Right, Broughton)

both fencing and boxing. The basic principles common to both enabled the art and science of boxing to develop with far greater speed in the last two centuries than its earlier advance in Greece in a dozen centuries. Fencing was truly responsible for this. Captain Godfrey says:

Boxing is a combat depending more on strength than the sword: But art will make up for strength in it also.

The strength of man is chiefly in the power of his muscles and that Power is greatly to be increased by Art. The muscles are as springs and levers which execute the different motions of our body, but by Art a man can give an additional Force to them.

The nearer a man brings his body to the center of gravity, the truer Line of Direction will his muscles act in, and consequently with more resulting force. If a man desires to strike a hard blow, let him put his feet as firm as possible; the power of his arm will then be considerably greater than if but lightly closed and the velocity of his blow vastly augmented by it.

The position of the Body is of the greatest consequence in fighting. The center of Gravity ought to be well considered, for by that the weight of the body being justly suspended, and the true equilibrium thereby preserved, the body stands much the firmer against opposing force.

This depends upon the proper distance between the legs, which is the first regard a boxer ought to have or all his manly attempts will prove abortive.

In order to find the true position, the left leg must be presented some reasonable distance before the right, which brings the left side towards the adversary; this the right-handed man ought to do that, after stopping the blow with his left arm, which is a kind of buckler to him, he may have the more readiness and greater power of stepping in with his right hand's returning blow.

In this posture he ought to reserve an easy flexion in the left knee, that his advances and retreats may be quicker. By this proper flexion his body is brought forward so as to have a just inclination over the left thigh, insomuch that his face makes a perpendicular or straight line with the left knee whilst the right leg and thigh in a slanting line, strongly prop up the whole body, as does a large beam an old wall.

So, strange as it may seem, modern boxing or at least the technique of modern boxing stemmed from fencing. Many other interesting and unusual facts about boxing are available to anyone with a knowledge of boxing who can find the time to study the original source material now available.

For instance, the Greeks in the old Olympics used their left fists, hit straight with both hands, had a stance quite similar to ours, and used their feet as well as their heads and their fists. This is a revolutionary statement to make, but records unearthed by modern excavations prove it.

Next, modern boxing, particularly its technique, was given a fast pick-up when reborn because it based most of its theory on centuries of fencing technique.

These facts knock a lot of preconceived ideas aside. For instance, John Jackson, the "Gentleman boxer," is credited with being the first exponent of the straight left lead. James J. Corbett was said to be the first boxer to use the left jab and the first man to use feinting in boxing. Ben Brain was alleged to be the father of the straight right in 1786. We are told that the school of Belcher, Bendigo, and Sayer started footwork in the ring. Several sources tell us that Jack Dempsey discovered the way to throw a left hook with knockout power and invented the triple punch or 1–2–3. Others tell us that Broughton discovered the left to the stomach in London, that Fitzsimmons created the "solar plexus" punch at Carson City, that Jack Johnson invented the right uppercut, Firpo discovered the rabbit punch or clublike swing and that Louis developed counter punching to its present perfection. None of these statements is entirely correct. All these men became great experts or exponents of the specialties attributed to them in the theory of boxing. However, in boxing as in many other fields, there is very little new under the sun, and millions of fists over thousands of years have developed the art and science of boxing to what it is today.

Just as the introduction of the mask and the foil or practice weapon helped develop the theory of fencing, the modern boxing glove gave boxing its greatest modern impetus and in addition helped quicken the pace of its technical development. John

Broughton, known as "the Father of Modern Boxing," therefore earned his title, although it must be remembered that the hard glove, soft glove and cestus were used in Greece, Crete, and Egypt for thousands of years. The padded glove in modern times enabled boxing to spread to clubs, colleges, and schools. As expressed in an advertisement for Broughton's school:

Persons of quality and distinction should not be deterred from entering into a course of these lectures, because they will be given with the Utmost Tenderness and Regard to the Delicacies of the Frame and Constitution of the Pupils, for which Reason Mufflers (gloves) are provided that will effectively secure them from the Incovenience of Black Eyes, Broken Jaws and Bloody Noses.

Just like the ancients, the early English boxers were influenced to a great degree by rules. Boxing outgrew both Figg's and Broughton's rules. In 1838 an interesting change was adopted. Under the rules laid down by Broughton, when "time" was called and either of the men was not able to walk to the scratch (center of the ring), their seconds carried them to it. Two fighters, Brighton Bill and Owen Swift, were so badly beaten and exhausted by this sort of "help" that finally both had to be carried by their seconds, not to the scratch but out of the ring. Subsequently one of them, Brighton Bill, died. This caused a wave of reform and new rules—The London Prize Ring Rules. According to the new rules "at the expiration of thirty seconds, unless otherwise agreed, each man shall rise from the knee of his bottle-holder (substitute for a stool in those days) and walk to his own side of the scratch unaided—and that either man failing to be at the scratch within eight seconds shall be deemed to have lost the battle."

Butting, blows below the belt, use of fingers, kicking, and kneeing were all not only defined as foul, but declared sufficient to forfeit the fight. The new

126. Between rounds, early nineteenth century, drawing from a contemporary print.

rules also gave an unusual responsibility to the referee and umpires. In case of police interference they were to determine quickly the time and place for the continuation of the fight, that is, if the fighters were not arrested.

English bare-fist prizefights featured much close "in-fighting" and not a little wrestling. Attack and straight-up defense and much use of the left jab were common. Most punches were aimed for the head, although there were many exponents of body punching. Tom Cribb employed a body attack frequently, particularly in his second fight with Molyneaux.

Incidentally, it was at this fight and in this period that an interesting technical point was broached which has led to controversial discussions all over the world. Someone advanced the theory that since a Negro's skull was thicker than a Caucasian's, he could stand more punishment than a white man. Another theory advanced was that, conversely, a black could not stand as much punishment about the body. The result was that, for the last century and a half, white boxers have repeatedly applied this belief in the ring. However, no one knows for sure if there is any basis for it. As a matter of fact there have been many championship fights in which blacks have successfully withstood all kinds of body punishment, and examples where blacks like whites have been knocked out by a single punch to the chin and its resulting shock to the base of the skull.

Training has been important in both the history and the technical development of the fist. Up until the fifth century B.C., boxers were developed along Homeric principles. It was merely a natural and healthy part of living, and the contests were natural and spontaneous. Then with the Olympics, formal contests became professionalized and with specialization came trainers and gymnasiums. In fact, early statues and vases show that up until about 600 B.C. boxers had the normal classical Greek figures with standard proportions (calf, biceps, and neck measurements the same.) Then, beginning with about the 30th Olympics and increasingly thereafter, boxers showed the definite effect of special training for boxing, just as most boxers do today—thin, long-sinewed legs, heavy, well-muscled shoulders and arms, large neck to withstand punishment around the head and jaws, broken noses, cauliflower ears, and rather heavily muscled bodies. In this connection, Jess Willard is the only heavyweight champion of modern times who had the classic Greek proportion: calf, bicep, and neck all measuring 17½ inches. By present standards his build was not considered ideal for boxing nor was he one of our greatest champions.

Training and trainers go way back in history. A Menandar of Athens trained Olympic winners around

127. James J. Tunney's stance—1925. (N.Y. Athletic Club)

481 B.C. Pythagoras of Samos, after winning the Olympic boxing championship about 500 B.C., became the greatest trainer of boxers in antiquity. He is credited with introducing meat into the boxer's diet. Prior to that, people including boxers were mostly vegetarians. Even doctors and early physicians entered the lists of training. They were especially interested in boxers.

Only one training schedule of old Greece has come down to us. It is called the *Tetrad*. According to this scheme, certain training duties were assigned to specific days, with no exceptions in the routine. This plan covered the routine for four days, then was repeated with occasional days of rest. The first day involved "light and quick movements to prepare the boxer." The second day "tested his powers of endurance or extended them." The third day "relaxed him in gentle exercises." The fourth was "to develop defensive practices."

Strangely enough, when boxing started again in England, training was almost neglected, if not ignored, for nearly a century. I attribute this fault, along with the credit for technical advancement, to fencing. Fencing, especially to A.D. 1700 and up to its connection with boxing, was more of a necessity than a sport and was never concerned with training or special physical conditioning. That is probably because fencing did not call for any great physical stamina or involve any physical punishment other than cold steel through one's entrails. Naturally men figured that, regardless of good or bad physical condition, a sword wound would kill or incapacitate them.

Therefore the early English boxers, who were also fencers, had little or no training regimen. However, when Tom Cribb, the British champion, was almost beaten by Molyneaux, people began to sit up and take notice. It was quite evident that Cribb had been in no physical shape to fight any first-rate opponent.

So the right time and the right place had come

for an epoch-making milestone in the saga of the fist. All that remained to appear was the right man. He did, in the person of Captain Barclay Allardyce of Ury.

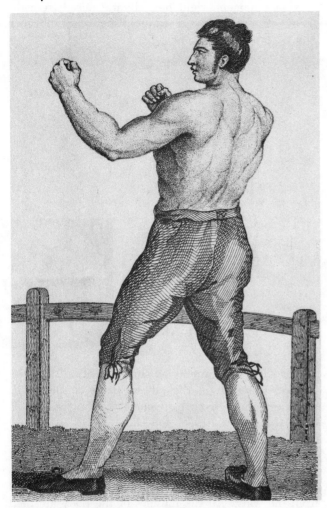

128. Tom Cribb's stance—1810.

Jess Willard

129. Jess Willard's stance—1918.

Captain Barclay, as he was called, was the famous pedestrian who was to become the first scientific trainer of prizefighters in modern history. He brought champion Tom Cribb up to Ury, Scotland, before Cribb's second fight with Molyneaux in 1810, and put him through a course of rigorous training. Cribb was deprived of thirty or forty pounds of his weight and given the wind of an antelope. For the first time in modern history, a fighter had to do "road work," walking and running out-of-doors. On first arriving, Cribb could walk only a few miles. The day after his arrival in Ury, he was heavily dosed with medicine and for two weeks was permitted to stroll about as he pleased. At the beginning of the third week, he was induced to do some real walking: first, ten miles, then twenty, then thirty. In addition, Cribb, who did not take kindly to his regime, was compelled to run a quarter of a mile every morning and every evening. In five weeks, he lost twenty-eight pounds. This kind of training would be considered absurd today, but Cribb took it and got rid of the fat he had picked up as the keeper of a tavern in London.

Barclay was a martinet and was the English counterpart of William Muldoon who successfully trained John L. Sullivan, another great but softened and intemperate champion. Barclay once explained how he made Cribb walk sixty miles on his second day of training in order to get something to eat. Between walks and running, Barclay kept Cribb sparring and giving boxing lessons. He allowed him a minimum of food.

So changed was Cribb's appearance after three months of Barclay's training that when he appeared in the ring to meet Molyneaux for their second fight, the black fighter exclaimed, "This is not Master Cribb. This is a strange man whom I do not know." Cribb was a strange man, for he knocked out Molyneaux in the eleventh round and danced a Scot's reel in the ring to celebrate his triumph, something like Jimmy McLarnin's somersaults after a win in the roaring twenties.

From then on, trainers and training became more important in boxing. The next great trainer who again called the public's attention to this important department was William Muldoon.

The story of Muldoon is well known. A professional strong man, world's champion wrestler and a fanatic on physical culture, he was hired for $10,000 to take over John L. Sullivan, the "Boston Strong Boy," and put him in shape to fight Kilrain. Sullivan had been on a several years' binge. Wine, women, and song had been his only occupation. In fact, it is doubtful if Sullivan had tasted water in a long time, according to many old-timers. Unlike Cribb,

203

Sullivan was difficult to handle because he was a bully and often boasted that he was afraid of no one. However, he was afraid of one person—William Muldoon. That was the real reason why Sullivan's friends had hired the wrestler to put the boxing champion in shape.

The greatest advance in ring technique, style, and generalship was made after the shift of boxing supremacy to the United States and immediately following Sullivan. However, that development, since 1892, has been so rapid and so involved that it is difficult to trace or describe. Also, the picture of the last fifty years is so close to us that we cannot properly evaluate or analyze it, or pick out any high spots as we have done after looking back over the vast panorama of the fist from the beginnings of recorded time.

Since we have covered the probable chronology in the development of the technique of boxing and commented on additional facts relative to its theory, we will now present the art and science of the fistic sport today in the manner normally used in teaching.

We will attempt to make our reader at least a mental champion in the theory of the ring. How shall we do it?

A thumbnail summary of boxing techniques was worked out and written many years ago by the author of this book with his coach, Billy Cavanaugh, aka Billy Glover, boxing coach of the U.S. Army, a veteran of ninety-six professional fights as a lightweight to middleweight and years of coaching, seconding, and refereeing. Thereafter, and with further help from Jack Dempsey while Dempsey was under contract to the author for a radio series and "a giveaway proof of purchase boxing booklet," the thumbnail manual was completed.

It is basic and fundamental, but if the reader can digest it completely, he will be thoroughly indoctrinated in today's theory of boxing or at least be thoroughly conversant with the latest principles.

ON GUARD POSITION

The first and most important thing to learn is the "on guard" position. Since the primary purpose of boxing is hitting, it is the position affording the best opportunities for hitting. However, since modern boxing also is based on the theory that "you can't be beat if you can't be hit," the "on guard" position is also the one affording the best protection.

The proper "stance" is therefore designed for both offense and defense—hitting, blocking, parrying, ducking, countering, slipping, rolling, and the ability to advance, retreat, side-step, and other maneuvers.

In the correct "on guard" position you can do all of these things. To get "on guard," stand naturally with your heels together, then advance the left foot about fifteen or eighteen inches directly forward, feet flat on the ground with the toe pointed directly at your opponent, right heel slightly raised from the floor, weight evenly distributed between the feet, knees very slightly bent.

130. On Guard

131. The Fist

The left upper arm is advanced a little, with the forearm raised from the elbow, hand clasped with knuckles turned toward opponent. The right hand is carried at the center of the chest, knuckles up and out. Both elbows are tucked in, covering the ribs. The left shoulder is slightly advanced, with the head and especially the chin gathered behind it. The upper part of the body is inclined slightly forward from the waist. All the muscles of the body are held collected but without any tenseness or tautness. The left hand should be carried high and on a level with the chin.

In addition to the "on guard" position, another thing to be learned before one starts to box is how to clench the fist properly. Close the fingers into the palm of the hand, then close the thumb down over the outside of the fingers, as in the illustration. Never close the fist with the thumb inside or sticking up over the clenched forefinger.

Now, practice clenching your fists and your "on guard" position.

Then from the "on guard" position, it is possible to advance, to retreat, or to circle one's opponent to the left or to the right.

The first principle of any movement or foot work in boxing is always to make the first step in any direction with the first foot in that direction and follow with the other foot the same distance.

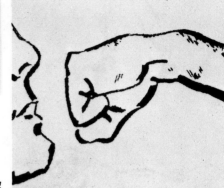

32. Shifting forward   **133. Shifting backward**

135. Hand in jabbing

To advance, from the "on guard" position, raise the left foot slightly and advance six or seven inches. Then draw or glide the right foot up after it, ending in the original "on guard" position.

To retreat, from "on guard" position, raise the right foot slightly and step backward about six or seven inches, drawing by a gliding motion the left foot after it, ending in the original "on guard" position.

To circle opponent—to the LEFT. Remember that a boxer who keeps moving is much more difficult to hit than one who does not. In order to circle to the left, from "on guard" position, first a step is taken to the left front, with the left foot, then pivot or turn upon the ball of the foot, swinging or gliding the right foot to the rear and facing right.

To circle opponent—to the RIGHT. In order to circle to the right, being "on guard," first a step is taken by the right foot to the right rear and then the body is pivoted on the ball of the right foot, swinging or gliding the left foot to the rear and facing left.

In boxing, as explained, whether you move forward, or backward, or sideways, *always* retain the "on guard" position. You should never bring one foot past the other. You glide along, letting one foot follow the other.

You should practice the "on guard" position and practice moving forward and backward across the room, and also circle an imaginary opponent both clockwise and counterclockwise until you have perfected your footwork.

THE LEFT JAB

This is the first punch to be learned in boxing. The left jab is delivered from the "on guard" position by shooting out the left fist as far as you can reach, at the same time stepping straight forward with the left foot. The palm of the hand should be turned down. The arm should be extended to its full length and the body should lean well forward. The blow should be delivered with a snap, as the force of the blow depends not only on the full weight of your body behind it, but also on the snap or speed you put into it.

Your head should be bent slightly to the right to guard against a right counterpunch from your opponent. When jabbing, your right hand should come up alongside of your chin, elbow down with padding of glove toward your face and palm down. This is to prevent your being hit as you jab, by a left hook from your opponent. The jab is followed by an immediate and quick recovery to the position of "on guard."

Practice jabbing at either a punching bag or an imaginary opponent's head, or better yet, in front of a mirror to see if you are covered and can't be hit.

THE LEFT HOOK

A left hook is delivered by stepping in with the left foot and with the left arm rigid though slightly bent at the elbow. Hook it from the shoulder down onto the opponent's jaw, with elbow held down as far as practicable. The entire force of the advancing step should go into the blow, which, when delivered properly, is very effective.

In a similar manner, a left hook is delivered to the body. The elbow is held low, and the blow is delivered under the right guard. In delivering the hook to the head, the palm of the hand is turned down. Delivering a hook to the body lays a man leading or hooking open to a hard right counter. To avoid this counter or punch from one's opponent, one should strike quickly and bend to the right. The guard for the left hook to the head is to receive and break the blow against the palm of your right hand, or the right

136. The left hook and the position of the knuckles

137. Feinting

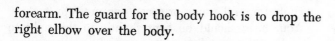

138. Ducking the left hook

139. Slipping the left jab

forearm. The guard for the body hook is to drop the right elbow over the body.

FEINTING

Feinting is the art of misleading your opponent with regard to your intentions. This may be accompanied by movement of eye, hand or feet, shift in body balance, or a combination of all these. The ordinary standard feint consists of pretending to strike with one hand and then hitting with the other when the opponent's guard has moved. Similarly, the eye may be cast at one point and the blow delivered at another, against which the opponent may be slow to guard.

A movement of the hand may indicate a lead to the chin and bring your opponent's guard up, while with the same hand you jab or hook to the body.

Feinting can be practiced, especially in front of a full-length mirror.

DUCKING

Ducking is quickly bending or weaving the body at the waist, thus allowing an opponent's blow to swing past overhead. It is often possible to duck under a left swing and then counter to the head or body with a right or left hook.

SLIPPING

Slipping is making a quick short movement, just removing the head or body from the path of an op-

ponent's punch. It is usually a quick inclining or turning of the head to one side or another to avoid a straight punch, although it may also apply to the movement of turning the stomach or hips or pulling them back to avoid blows to the abdomen.

THE STRAIGHT RIGHT

This is one of the most important punches and is the power punch; that is, the one that has the most force behind it if delivered correctly. When someone is knocked out, it is usually from a righthand blow to the jaw.

To deliver this punch, you must throw your right fist straight forward to your opponent's jaw, letting the right shoulder follow through with the punch, which causes the body to twist at the waist and brings the right heel up off the floor. Do not, however, take all the weight off the right foot.

This blow is usually preceded by a feint with the left hand and left foot during which the right foot can be advanced so as to be within good striking distance with the right hand.

The secret of imparting power to this punch is in the twist at the waist, throwing the right arm and shoulder forward, which is the "follow-through" that puts power behind the punch. This also brings the left side and arm back a bit, but the left hand should

141A. Left uppercut to the jaw

140. Slipping inside straight left

141B. Blocking left uppercut

141. The straight right

not, under any circumstances, be dropped when you deliver the blow.

THE UPPERCUTS

After practicing the various positions, footwork and blows, and becoming well versed in all the techniques given so far, you are now ready for another fundamental punch—the uppercut.

The left uppercut to the body is really an upward left hook to the solar plexus. The only difference is that it is delivered with a forward and upward movement of the fist, which is turned palm or fist upward when the blow lands. It is an in-fighting punch and must be delivered at close quarters inside your opponent's guard. It is never used as a lead punch.

To deliver this punch from position of "on guard," bring the left elbow close to the left side with fist palm upward. Lower the left shoulder slightly, bending the body somewhat to the left and bending both knees slightly. Then shoot the left outward and upward to the corresponding level of an opponent's solar plexus, at the same time throwing the weight forward and swinging the body toward the right with the blow, straightening the knees at the same

time. This slight turn of the body gives added strength to the blow.

The left uppercut to the jaw is delivered in the same way, except that the body is not bent so far to the left, nor the left shoulder so far back. The fist is shot more upward than in the case of the uppercut to the body.

The right uppercut to either the body or the jaw is executed in the same way as the left uppercut. However, the opponent must be coming *toward you* and into the blow to make effective use of this blow.

In the uppercuts, the arms are always bent, even when the punch is actually landing.

DEFENSE

If you have studied the instructions and practiced them, you should be able to master the fundamental blows in boxing. Now we will show how to guard against or defend against those same blows.

First, the LEFT JAB. The best and easiest defense is to parry it by slapping it aside with the right hand. The word "parry" in boxing or fencing means to ward off. Another method is actually to catch it with the open hand, palm out, and with the padding of your glove toward your face or jaw. Whether you parry or catch it, you should immediately counter or punch at your opponent, because he will be thrown slightly off balance and forward. The best counter is to throw a left hook to the jaw. Still another method of evading a left jab is by slipping. Only straight punches can be "slipped." As your opponent's left jab starts, quickly bob your head to the right, bending the body also slightly to the right. You will evade the blow and will be in a position to counter to his body with your own left.

142. **Parrying left jab**

143. **Ducking left hook**

A LEFT HOOK should be ducked. You duck by bending under the blow, by bending at the knees, waist, and neck. Never try to duck straight punches; only swings and hooks can be ducked. And remember to keep your eyes open and watch your opponent as you duck.

THE RIGHT CROSS

When a left lead to your jaw is attempted, slip inside the blow, then as your opponent's left hand passes harmlessly over your right shoulder, you step in about a foot and at the same time shoot your right fist over and across your opponent's left arm and shoulder to his jaw. The action causes your left hand and shoulder to be "cocked" or drawn back, leaving you in excellent position to follow up with a left hook to the head or body. The Cross is delivered with the elbow slightly bent, as in a Hook.

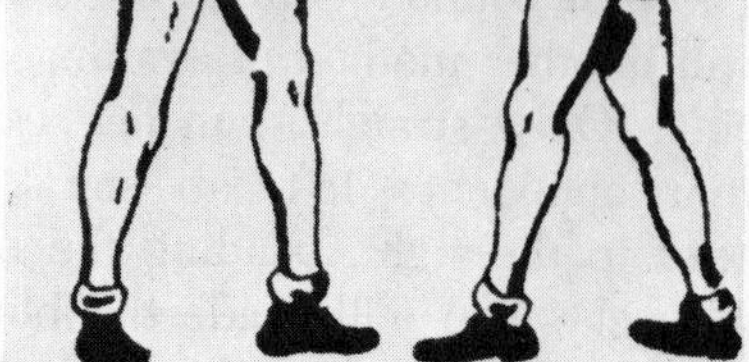

144. **The right cross**

145. **Blocking left uppercut**

BLOCKING

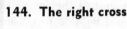

Blocking means preventing being hit at a vital spot by stopping punches with some less susceptible part of your body such as your glove, forearm, shoulder, or elbow.

This completes a thumb-nail summary in lesson form of some of the fundamentals in modern boxing technique developed over thousands of years, and quite properly ends our chapter on the art and science of the sport.

146. **Blocking right to the jaw**

12 • Homes, Finances, Results, Fatalities, and Future of Boxing

The story of boxing would not be complete without some discussion of the homes or houses of boxing—the headquarters of the fist throughout the ages.

Comparatively few buildings have been continuously headquarters or centers of boxing. The athletic amphitheatre of Crete, where rodeos also took place, is the first boxing center recorded.

Next, and identified with the first ancient golden age of boxing, is Olympia. If we could have seen Olympia as it was in the days of Theagenes or Cleitomachus, we would be amazed at how men centuries ago could possibly have outdone Hollywood. Scientific research and the most reliable and authentic sources have permitted us to reconstruct an exact model of what Olympia looked like in the Golden Age of boxing. In this book you will see a picture of Olympia, the home or center of boxing for many centuries.

The modern revival of boxing in England brought Figg's amphitheatre and then Broughton's, which was closed by the Duke of Cumberland when he removed his sponsorship from boxing. Then boxing went outdoors and underground for many years, because prizefights were illegal and had to be conducted clandestinely.

The first outdoor stands, it will be remembered, were erected for the Spring-Langan fight at Worcester. Then boxing more or less moved across the sea to the United States where it was held outdoors and underground for some time. Much boxing was also done in theatres until the sport began to be legalized and the fighters' fists encased in gloves. Athletic clubs arose in many cities and towns, while men from every walk of life—politicians, gamblers, and theatrical producers—turned fight promoters.

In this chaos Tex Rickard arose and became the world's leading promoter and took over the old Madison Square Garden in New York City.

On the northeast corner of Madison Square in the days of our great grandfathers stood the New York & Harlem Railroad station. Its days as a railroad terminal even then were numbered and, as the social life of old New York pushed uptown, Barnum of circus fame took the old building over and in 1873 converted it into Barnum's Hippodrome. Shortly after that it changed hands again and was called Gilmore's Garden, and during this period a youngster named William Brady ran messages between it and the old Press Club. In 1879 it was named once again, this time "Madison Square Garden." Evidently Barnum

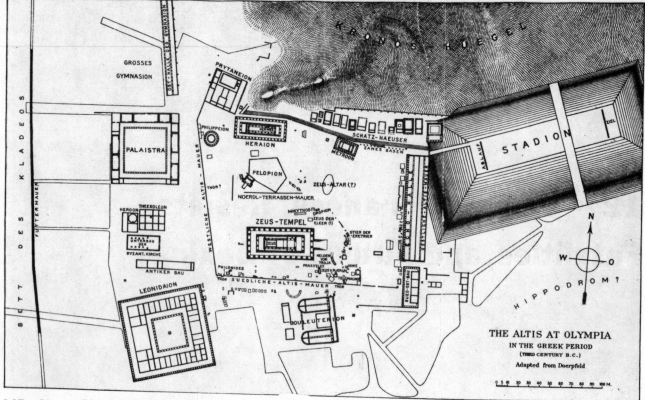

147. Chart, Olympia (Library of Congress)

kept his finger in the affairs of the old building during these changes, because when it was razed and the one designed by Stanford White put up on the same site, his name went on the list of directors along with those of J. P. Morgan and Darius Mills. The handsome new building—the safest, largest, and most convenient of its time—was a full square block in area. At its top, the statue of Diana, the work of Augustus St. Gaudens, stood 346 feet above the street, a spectacular height at that time. The winds that raged around her soon tore off her metal veil with which the sculptor had draped her. When the Old Garden was torn down to make way for the New York Life Insurance Company building, and Diana went to a museum in Pennsylvania, a surprising fact was revealed. The rivets that had failed to save her veil were nevertheless large enough to hold a battleship together.

The old, but actually the second Madison Square Garden was the house of boxing from 1890 to 1925. It had cost about three million dollars to build and occupied the block bounded by Madison Avenue, Fourth Avenue, Twenty-sixth and Twenty-seventh Streets. It was built by a syndicate headed by horse-show people. It was opened 16 June 1890, with an orchestra under the direction of Edouard Strauss, composer of dance music and conductor from Vienna, and a ballet under the direction of Leon Espinosa. The last attraction in this old landmark, sentimentally enough since it had become the house if not the home of boxing, was the Terris-Dundee fight 4 May 1925.

The day after, the Bartley ring was taken down for the last time, and crews of wreckers arrived to raze the old landmark amid the dust of years and the din of the day. Even the old Garden's ring had a history. Frank Bartley, to whom boxing owes much, developed the modern ring and most of its safest and most efficient features, and cannot be overlooked in the story of boxing.

The Old Garden, as it has been referred to since 1925, was the scene of varied events. It was there that William Jennings Bryan accepted the Democratic nomination for president; Adelina Patti sang; Jack Dempsey knocked out Bill Brennan; six-day go-as-you-please (walk, run, or crawl) races were held; and Wild West shows, aquatic exhibitions in the huge pool and the first automobile show took place. The circus was presented there annually. Just after World War I started the Garden was not doing so well, but Tex Rickard could see a boom coming up and grabbed it on a ten-year option. The first world championship fight in Manhattan was the Willard-Moran fight promoted by Rickard and held at the old Garden, 25 March 1916. It grossed over $250,000, and good times were back again. Sports fans had grown in number when the twenties rolled around and a new Garden was definitely needed.

In addition to containing the main amphitheatre or arena, the old Garden had many marks to show that it was essentially the home of the fist. Upstairs on the Twenty-seventh Street side was the leading training gymnasium for the local and itinerant prize-

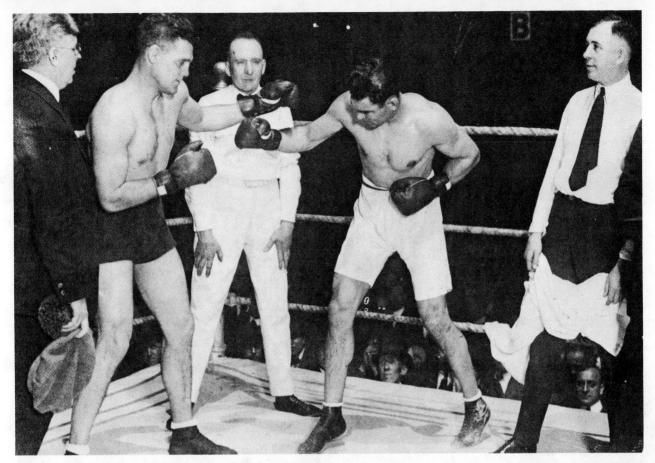

147A. 1920 Madison Square Garden hosting the Dempsey-Brennan world's championship fight. (Courtesy of the Madison Square Garden Corporation)

fighters. Here were rings, punching bags, handball courts, baths, dressing rooms, rows of seats for paid spectators who watched the pugs play and train, and who occasionally saw punches thrown with more abandon and force than dictated by training considerations alone. Here also foreign heavyweights were tried out, sometimes by some stumble-bum, sometimes by a brilliant amateur training among his betters to learn the ropes in order to fulfill an ambition to become a professional or to make a United States Olympic team.

This gym, owned and run by a jovial and shrewd physical culture enthusiast named MacLevy, was bigger, cleaner, and better equipped than many a gym today. It can be compared to Stillman's Gym, in the 1930s to 1950s. Bobby Gleason's on West 30th Street is now the mecca of fighters training in Manhattan. But MacLevy, who had an eye for business, ran his establishment twenty-four hours a day. He hired some of the more personable fighters to conduct gym classes and reducing courses for business men at night, working girls in the evening, and matrons and housewives in the morning. Between midnight and morning "happy" or "tired" gentlemen could always get Turkish baths. The professional boxers' training hours were from noon to five.

In the summer this gym expanded to the roof where there was an outdoor track, rings, and punching bag stands. Fighters as well as other customers could get fresh—though slightly soiled—air in their lungs and a healthy sunburn on their skins on the roof of the old Garden. Overlooking this beehive was Diana. Most of the MacLevy customers believed that Evelyn Nesbit Thaw had posed for the statue, just as she had for the figure on West Point's Victory Monument. The old Garden, incidentally, was inspired by the Alhambra in Spain and designed by the well-known architect, Stanford White, who was shot and killed by the late Harry K. Thaw over the same Miss Nesbit. A checkup, however, revealed the fact that because the figure was the work of St. Gaudens and in place when the old Garden opened in 1890, Miss

147B. 1924 Madison Square Garden hosting Democratic Convention to select presidential candidate. (Courtesy of the Madison Square Garden Corporation)

148. 1890 outside view of the old Madison Square Garden at Madison Square designed by Stanford White and built by the horseshow people; the home of boxing until 1925. (Courtesy of the Madison Square Garden Corporation)

Nesbit could not have posed for it so far back.

In this tremendous edifice, devoted primarily to boxing, were the private offices of Tex Rickard, the czar and patron saint of the industry.

The thought of the old Garden brings back nostalgic memories to all who ever visited it. While possibly not as large or imposing as the newer Gardens, all the old-timers believe it was far more colorful and romantic. If one ever boxed in its ring, one experienced a thrill never again equalled, even if the performance were only an amateur contest or one staged for a movie.

The next or number three Madison Square Garden was certainly the contemporary house of boxing from 1925 to 1968. It was between Eighth and Ninth Avenues and between 49th and 50th Streets in New York City. The arena seated 18,903 for boxing,

149. 1879 outside view of the original Madison Square Garden—the improved and converted Gilmore's Garden. (Courtesy of the Madison Square Garden Corporation)

15,500 for hockey, 14,500 for the bicycle races. It was constructed so that the audience's view was not obstructed by pillars, and it was equipped with devices that could change its character completely within hours. For instance, four hours after a hockey game, the ice could be cleared, 4,200 seats added, a ring set up and a boxing match begun. The arena could be frozen for the ice carnival in eight hours. Five hundred tons of ice were converted into snow by ice pulverizers for the winter carnival and 690 tons of earth were "rented" by the circus for its animal housing in the basement. The first boxing match, Jack Delaney-Paul Berlenbach, was on 11 December 1925.

Madison Square Garden was operated by a corporation headed by Stanton Griffis and Colonel J.R. Kilpatrick, a former all-American football player from Yale. This corporation owned the Rangers, while Mike Jacobs (Twentieth Century Sporting Club) controlled the boxing under a contract. The businessmen who controlled the Garden let or rented out boxing to Jacobs because they were afraid of it and believed it could be handled only by possible compromise with certain elements and by possibly overlooking certain principles. By the equivalent of a rental agreement, they were in a position to collect

150. 1935 outside view of Eighth Avenue and 49th Street, Madison Square Garden completed in 1925. (Courtesy of the Madison Square Garden Corporation)

some profit from boxing without any qualms or worries. In any case, the "boxoffice" was consistently good; Barnum and Bailey's circus had paid as much as $100,000 for its old twenty-seven day season; hockey ran over $700,000 a year; public meetings averaged $3,500 a week night and $5,000 on Saturday and Sunday nights. The new Garden cost $5,500,000 including land and building, and its informal opening was on 28 November 1925. While this structure was originally conceived by Rickard as the house of boxing, the fistic sport had no real home forever, for the Garden directors did not always want boxing in the intimate family, and boxing had outgrown the seating capacity of any covered building. When over 100,000 people would pay to see a fight, an outdoor stadium was the only home big enough for the sport.

This Garden has naturally fewer memories for old-timers but fresher memories for a more recent crop of boxers. Like the old Garden and the Olympia and the Cnossus amphitheatre, it featured rodeos, circuses, track meets, horse shows, and spectacles, besides boxing. It had not yet presented any gladiators nor any duels, although an exhibition of fencing involving several national champions was put on between the halves of the Olympic Basketball Tournament in March, 1948.

The Old or second Garden did present on one occasion an unusual combat with swords, refereed by John L. Sullivan. Sometime in 1890 or thereabouts, an Italian swordsman came over from Italy with a great reputation not only as a fencer, but as a *beau sabreur* and horseman. In order to obtain more fencing pupils for himself, he gave exhibitions in Central Park mounted on horseback and issued challenges to all comers to fence with sabres on horseback, claiming he could lick anyone. About this time there lived in New York a tough, husky Scot named MacTavish, who not only gave fencing lessons and instructed in the "manly art" of boxing, but could ride a bit. On hearing of the Italian's claims and challenges, MacTavish went into action. The result was a duel or mounted fencing match at the old Madison Square Garden, refereed by John L, put on as an extra feature at another event.

The Italian, on a beautiful but nervous horse, attired in velvet fencing suit, velvet gloves and light mask, appeared, armed with a light fencing sabre. The Scot, on a big horse of phlegmatic disposition, appeared in baggy clothes, a large mask, big gloves and a heavy wooden claymore (Scottish sabre). The contestants were announced and the referee introduced.

A roar went up from the crowd. The Scot took his place slowly at one end of the tanbarked circus arena of the old Garden. The Italian galloped his charger to the opposite end where his horse pranced and arched its neck. When John L gave the signal, both men put spurs to their horses—the Scot with little effect, while the Italian's horse sprang out of his corner and galloped furiously toward the bigger and slower steed.

213

151. Third Madison Square Garden, 1925–1968 home of boxing—winter version.

152. Yankee Stadium, 20 June 1946—home of boxing, summer version. Louis and Conn fight, gate, $1,925,564.

As the Italian came within range, the Scot stood in his stirrups and aimed a full sweeping slash from over his head at the Latin's head.

"Ping ping" went the Italian fencing master's light sabre, landing twice across the Scot's sword forearm as it descended. This of course should have given him the bout on points without any question, since if his sabre had been a real one, he would have severed the Scot's arm in two places. However, the Scot would not be denied, could not stop, or knew John L. Sullivan, for he simply finished his slashing stroke, hit the Italian on the head and mask with the heavy claymore with a full sweep of his arm and the weight of his body as he dropped from his standing position in the stirrups.

"Plump" went the claymore on the smaller man's mask and helmet. The Italian, knocked cold, slowly but gracefully slid off his horse to the tanbark amid the cheers of the Garden crowd.

"MacTavish the winner by a knockout!" shouted John L, thereby bringing to a close the nearest thing to a gladiatorial contest outside of boxing and wrestling in any one of the four Gardens. Unfortunately, there was no one to challenge the legality of the "knockout," the correctness of the decision, or the judgment of the great John L.

However, the third Garden suffered a depression. From over $1,000,000 profit in 1927 the Garden gain dwindled to $130,000 in 1931–32. However, Colonel Hammond and John Reed Kirkpatrick, were responsible for an upturn due mainly to basketball and ice hockey, although boxing proved a problem until Mike Jacobs took over the Garden's boxing management. Like Rickard who had Dempsey as his ace card, Jacobs held Joe Louis. Then the Garden fell under the control of IBC and a close monopoly broken up by the courts insofar as boxing was concerned. Based on a court order, IBC sold forty percent of Madison Square Garden stock to the Graham-Paige Corporation who increased its holdings to eighty percent in a new merged alignment and changed its name to Madison Square Garden Corporation. Irving Mitchel Felt became chairman and chief executive officer. He had formerly been president and was a super business executive. On 3 November 1960 he disclosed plans to the press to build a fourth Madison Square Garden—bigger and better than all the rest put together at some undisclosed site in New York City.

Already in 1949, capitalists, artists, architects, and city authorities began talking about a new and gigantic amphitheatre or "Garden" for athletic events and "spectacles," which, if the project was ever carried out, would probably have been the future home of boxing in New York City. The probably site was to be at 59th Street between Columbus Circle and Ninth Avenue. The building itself was even said to have reached the blueprint stage and was expected to cost over $60,000,000. While Rickard, the promoter, said to have been responsible for the third Madison Square Garden, namely, "the house that Tex built," would no doubt have been pleased that boxing was still a big enough moneymaker, he would have been shocked and surprised to know that the Garden management insulated itself during the monopoly period in boxing, namely, subcontracted boxing and thereby cut others into their profits. For political and financial reasons, the site and plans for a fourth Madison Square Garden at Columbus Circle were abandoned. Instead a huge, new business edifice was built at Columbus Circle as a much needed "Coliseum" for all kinds of shows and exhibits.

Two days after Mr. Felt's announcement of 3 November 1960 that the new Madison Square Garden Corporation would raise the money and build a fourth Madison Square Garden in New York City, he received a letter from J. W. Ewalt, vice-president in charge of real estate for the Pennsylvania Railroad Company. It proposed the building of a new Madison Square Garden on top of the Penn Station, a two square block site between Eighth and Ninth Avenues and between 31st and 33rd Streets. The obvious advantages of this site were merely suggested.

153. April 1965—Mayor Robert Wagner, Irving Felt, President of the Madison Square Garden Corporation, and W. Gerstnecker, Penn RR executive with model of the new garden to be built atop Penn RR Station. (Courtesy of the Madison Square Garden Corp.)

By 24 July 1961, Felt had investigated, decided, and begun negotiations. The number four Madison Square Garden has everything for every possible use including a companion 24-story office building. The reported cost of this current Madison Square Garden was $116,000,000. Insofar as boxing is concerned, on 22 March 1967, under Harry Markson, at that time managing director of boxing, Cassius Clay ко'd Zora Folley in the seventh round of the Garden's twelfth all-time world's heavyweight championship fight in the third Garden while the fourth Garden was under construction. But in truth, while workers were busy with number four, number three was still busy. There was no end, only a beginning. On 4

154. The current Madison Square Garden in New York City, the nearest thing to the home of boxing —1975. (Courtesy of the Madison Square Garden Corporation)

March 1968, Joe Frazier won New York State recognition as the world's heavyweight champion by a ко over Buster Mathis in the eleventh round in a double feature at the fourth Garden. The other feature being an Emile Griffith-Nino Benvenuti world middleweight title bout. On 8 March 1971, Muhammed Ali, formerly Cassius Clay, was defeated by Joe Frazier and almost ко'd for the world's title before an audience of 20,455 in the fourth Madison Square Garden for gate receipts of $1,352,950 (with ancillary rights of over $4,000,000), but with a TV closed circuit audience of millions for total receipts of approximately $20,000,000 ($16,000,000 according to a more conservative source.) More positive and unusual but official statistics which indicate why world title fights go to Zaire, Indonesia and the Philippines are: Madison Square Garden (New York) taxes for one fight were over $300,000 and each fighter's tax was $348,000. Total taxes of well over one million dollars were hardly encouraging to boxing promotion in New York.

To prove dollars in eight figures was no accident, on 28 January 1974, an Ali-Frazier No. 2 was again promoted at the Madison Square Garden. A crowd of some 20,748 composed the gate paying $1,053,688. Another approximate 1.5 million persons attended the closed circuit TV showings for total reported receipts of $18,000,000. The fighters

earned approximately 3.5 million dollars each—not bad for less than an hour's work! The fight, as well known, was given to Ali by a whisper, although many experts believe Frazier won.

While it is difficult to place the headquarters or home of world boxing, especially today, as it is entirely different from yesterday because of television, satellite relay, and closed circuit broadcasting, it is not difficult to place the center of boxing interest especially in the last few eras of boxing up to the present. In 1946, for instance, the U.S. led the world in this respect with a total of $14,000,000 to $20,000,000 paid attendance. Today the paid attendance of a single fight with television may well surpass those annual figures. However, in 1946, of the amounts given here, almost $7,000,000 were paid out for admission for professional fights in Greater New York City alone. The greatest of these, as well as many world champion contests, were held at Yankee Stadium and other outdoor installations with crowds that paid $2,000,000 or more in 1947 and 1948. However today, the actual site of a fight and its gate are relatively unimportant. Let us follow this interesting development from the old time super "production" of the second Tunney-Dempsey fight at Soldier's Field, Chicago with receipts of $2,658,660 and an attendance of 104,943 persons on 27 September 1927. On 21 September 1955, almost twenty-eight years later, the Marciano-Moore receipts, including TV and radio, were $2,074,000 with a ringside attendance of only 61,600 persons. On 13 March 1961, for the second Patterson-Johansson fight, receipts were approximately $3,400,000 although the ringside attendance was only 14,000 persons.

But that was only the beginning. Today, in the all-out worldwide and television era, we find boxing attendance and finances exploding from television satellite relays closed circuit performances, namely:

Date	Fight
25 February 1964	Clay–Liston No. 1
25 May 1964	Clay–Liston No. 2
8 March 1971	Ali (Clay)–Frazier No. 1
28 January 1974	Ali–Frazier No. 2
30 October 1974	Ali–Foreman No. 1
30 September 1975	Ali–Frazier No. 3

Receipts	Gate
$ 3,088,000	8,927
1,779,000	2,434
20,000,000	20,455
18,000,000	20,748
19,000,000	48,000
18,000,000	24,000

(All of the above receipts are reported or estimated.)

As a result of the fact that Cassius Clay, aka Muhammad Ali, happened to be the best boxer and champion and a colorful if not controversial personality at the time of this extraordinary explosion in the worldwide or television era, Ali has broken all financial records above and beyond even the wildest dreams of the past. Ali's receipts for but three fights totalled eleven million dollars! This should prove the greatness and opportunity for all—both in boxing and in Muhammad Ali's country, the United States.

When two boxers fighting for the world's heavyweight championship can be guaranteed five million dollars each, there is no question of the financial explosion of the sport and the importance of taxes. Countries, states, and cities, or the politicians of these will have to determine if, in a way, they want to kill the goose that lays the golden egg or not . . . or eliminate democracies and the free enterprise system and liquidate professional sports as the Communists have done. A fight like the Foreman-Ali fight in Zaire would have brought millions of dollars of business and visitors, etc., to New York City and with a reasonable approach on taxes, tremendous added income to a city and a state that are almost bankrupt. Instead, the promoters had to eliminate New York City as a possible prospective site for the fight. Not even the Madison Square Garden can beat the odds set up by current New York City, New York State, and IRS

taxes—especially when the competitive life of a boxer is very short and a world's champion is sometimes cut up into many small pieces. In other words, he is owned by many managers, helpers, and financial supporters. The story of this special but important side of boxing goes hand in hand with the saga of the fist.

To return to the history of the fourth Madison Square Garden, until recently and perhaps still the closest thing to the home of boxing and certainly not a site like Manila or Jakarta or Kinshasa, bidding for a fight for promotion and publicity, it is not doing well financially in boxing. The combination of King and Ali might be too much for the Garden at this writing. Reliable reports state that King, supported by Arab oil money, offered thirty-five million dollars to purchase the Garden but was challenged by negotiations with the New York City Off-Track Betting Corporation. The amount of their bid was not known, but officially this deal was permanently terminated and the Garden management stated that it would not be sold or leased to any governmental agency. It is reported, however, that a price was set for the purchase of the Garden at fifty million dollars. The estimated cost of the part of the Garden complex now reportedly for sale was over sixty million dollars.

However, in any consideration of Madison Square Garden as the fourth home of boxing, we must remember that it is actually and currently owned by the following: Gulf and Western Industries, 37.1%; Philip Levin estate, 12.5%; Penn Central (bankrupt), 10.4%; many others, 40%. Notwithstanding the refusal of the Garden to any offers to purchase the physical plant, the Garden has certainly not been financially prosperous. The Garden has not paid a cash dividend since 1926 when the third Garden was built at 49th Street and 8th Avenue. The minority stockholders on 9 October 1975 battled with all kinds of questions put to Mr. Alan Cohen, president and chief executive officer of the Madison Square Garden Corporation. Yet in 1974, five million customers attended 656 performances at the Garden, although very heavy mortgage payments and high operating costs made the Garden a corporate liability.

Nevertheless the *Wall Street Journal* carried a most unusual sidelight on the Garden's problems. It stated that Gulf and Western Industries, Inc., who own 37.1% or more of the Garden, predicted record earnings for 1976 and announced a record net income in 1975 of $140.1 million on a total revenue of $2.6 billion as against $2.3 billion in 1974. The Garden, of all things, was awaiting New York City tax help based on its real estate taxes, alone totalling $2.4 million, and admitted it had a net loss in 1974 of $4.7 million. There is no question that the Garden's multiple demons—television, taxes, and Don King—are very difficult. Never has boxing and boxing promotion been so dominated by a single person, namely, Muhammad Ali or Cassius Clay, whatever his legal name may be. Without him there would be no Don King but, as it is, the team of Ali and King must be included in any major fight promotion and even in any boxing feature the world over, due, of course, to the unusual combination of TV and satellite relay.

The financial side of boxing is interesting, but was never so complicated in earlier times. In early Greece, notwithstanding the fact that the sport was on a purely amateur basis, winners of various competitions were given cash prizes. There is a record that the boxing victor at the Ismenian games in early Greece, after wading through five days of continuous competition and many bouts, received one hundred drachmas. Research indicates that the drachma then was worth five times what it was valued at centuries later, and we have found centuries later that it was the average daily wage of an unskilled workman. Therefore, assuming five dollars a day average unskilled wage, the heavyweight champion of a major competition of Greece won a prize or purse of approximately $2,500.

As the sports became more professional in ancient Greece, boxers probably were able to get more and more subsidies, favors and cash prizes for their work. As far back as the sixth century B.C., Xenophanes foretold a decline in the prestige of athletics if the reward became more important than the deed. In the fourth and fifth centuries B.C., sources tell us that rich patrons of boxing, desiring to increase the field of competition, subsidized many contestants and offered large rewards. Sparta for a time even withdrew from the Olympics because of what it considered too much professionalism.

Even in ancient Greece there appeared to have been betting and gambling on fights and fighters, and in all likelihood a fighter who helped his sponsor win a fortune was given a part of it. In the funeral speech of Pericles we find the statement: "We love free speculation."

In the later days of the Romans the subsidizing of boxers continued. In addition, boxing was part of the gladiatorial shows which were given to the public free. The greatest prize given to a contestant in this time was his freedom, for in most cases he was either a slave or a convicted criminal.

When boxing started again in England in the form of stage or prizefights by teachers of fencing and as the "gentle art," the only financial aspect for the winner was the possibility of enrolling students or pupils. Later, prizes were offered and with the advent of amphitheatres such as those of Figg and Broughton, prizes turned to purses and the real modern prizefight

from a financial standpoint began. Then the financial side of boxing entered a new era, where the winner received the proceeds of a cash wager made on the outcome. This was closely allied with the sponsor system, for the rich lords who sponsored famous fighters usually put up the side bet or stake for the fighter and, in addition, wagered huge sums on the side. A winner usually received a handsome slice of his sponsor's winnings. When Broughton lost to Slack, Broughton's sponsor, the Duke of Cumberland, lost over $50,000, turned against Broughton and boxing, although he became the sponsor of Slack from that day on. In fact, Slack fought Bill Stevens, the Nailer, in 1766 with the Duke of Cumberland as his sponsor. Stevens was sponsored by the Duke of York. The two dukes bet over $50,000 on the outcome, and Slack and Stevens fought for $1,000 a side—that is, the winner took all, which was $2,000 for the sides, but the stakes had been put up by their backers and not by them.

In 1771 when Peter Corcoran, the Irish Champion, stopped Darts for the championship, almost $200,000 was won by the Irishman's backer, and Corcoran received close to $25,000. In 1885, $150,600 changed hands when Humphries knocked out Martin, the Bath Butcher, with the Prince of Wales, Dukes of York and Orleans involved in the sponsorship and the betting.

In 1784 Tom Jackling, born Johnson, the greatest money-maker inside the ring for the entire period prior to John L. Sullivan, was accepted as Champion. Johnson did not make his money by winning prizes, purses, or receiving guarantees or even percentages of gate receipts, but merely by betting on himself continually like a parlay. It is estimated by some that from 1783 to 1789, when he retired, Johnson had won over $500,000 in gate donations—which began about this time—his own bets and the then established custom of being paid from ten to twenty-five percent of the winnings of sponsors and gamblers. Johnson's earnings for his greatest fight against Perrins were as follows:

Perrins's side bet	$ 2,500
Bets on himself	25,000
Share in $100,000 winnings of a Mr. Bullock	5,000
Gate Donation	5,000
Miscellaneous contributions from sponsors and gamblers for their winnings	60,000
Total	$96,500

It must be remembered that, based on the value of money and the cost of living, this amount can be conservatively estimated by today's standard as being equivalent to at least $500,000, and Johnson's total gains at close to five million dollars.

Johnson was cleaned out by gamblers after he retired in 1789 and was forced to return to the ring to fight Big Ben Brain. We can study the greatest money-maker of the bare fist era as the unfortunate prototype of a loser in the early days of boxing in this bout. The loser really lost then, for he rarely got anything for his trouble but a beating. For being knocked out by Brain in eighteen rounds or one hour and twenty-one minutes, Johnson got nothing. As a matter of fact, Brain, who lacked a reputation, received very little either. The great financial winner was the Duke of Hamilton, sponsor and backer of Brain, who won over $100,000 on their contest. The Duke of Hamilton became a sort of financial betting and sponsoring wizard of his time in boxing.

Practically every time Hamilton sponsored or backed a fighter, the fighter won. When Brain died the Duke picked an absolute unknown, Hooper the Tinman. No sooner was he sponsored by the Duke than Hooper won consistently and eventually became champion. In one fight against George Maddox in 1794, Hooper got $1,000 for winning, while the Duke won $50,000. The Duke of Hamilton is said never to have missed a fight, but perhaps the excitement was too much for him, or his luck finally ran out, and he died suddenly in 1799 at the age of forty-three.

While John Gulley died a millionaire, he had made his money not so much in boxing but on horses, taverns, and coal. The financial rewards of boxing took a drop after Johnson until 1823, when fighters began to share the gate receipts, percentage from monies made from a new contrivance—stands where people could sit to watch a fight—and chip-ins from standees. During this entire period boxers, that is to say winners, received $500, $1,000, or $2,500 at the most. To show what slim pickings fighters had in those days, we have but to point out that Molyneux's entire English campaign of ten fights, including two championship bouts with Cribb, brought in less than $1,500.

A new development in the finances of boxing occurred in England in 1824 when the first grandstands or raised seats were supplied. They were a separate promotion by the builders, who guaranteed the fighters half the receipts if they would fight in front of the stands. The cost of a seat for this first experiment at the Spring-Langan championship fight was $2.50. The stand had a capacity of 4,000. Twenty-two thousand standees also viewed the fight. Spring won, and his financial earnings, based on winner take all, were as follows:

Langan side bet	$ 2,000
Half of grandstand receipts	5,000
Contributions from standees	20,000
Total	$27,000

Again boxing went into a period of at least financial decline, when even a champion could not collect

more than $2,500 a fight and there were no contributions from rich and generous sponsors, backers or gamblers. The famous Sayers-Heenan fight was for $1,000 a side. In 1887, however, an all-time financial high was reached when Kilrain and Jim Smith fought bare-fist in France for approximately $10,000. This was supposed at the time to be absolute tops and was considered beyond reason.

Then our financial study shifts to America, where originally the side-bet winner-take-all system for rewarding the fighters was employed. In defeating Paddy Ryan for the championship, John L. Sullivan won a $5,000 side bet. From a financial standpoint John L. Sullivan marks the beginning of the modern financial set-up and John L himself became the greatest moneymaker boxing had ever known until then. However, while Sullivan earned a great deal of money elsewhere, his actual ring earnings were small. The largest amount he ever received for a fight was $14,000, although it must be remembered that this would be equivalent to over $70,000 in purchasing power today.

During the career of John L. Sullivan, the current system of promotion began, involving a purse or guarantee or percentages of the box office to be paid to the principals of a fight.

Here is a breakdown of what many consider among the first promotions of modern boxing. It is from a financial report of the Olympic Club of New Orleans, Louisiana, an affiliate of the Bohemian Sporting Club of New York.

REPORT OF CONTEST COMMITTEE
FOR GLOVE CONTESTS OF
SEPTEMBER 5, 6 AND 7, 1892,
HELD AT THE OLYMPIC CLUB, NEW ORLEANS

Myers and McAuliffe

171	Box Seats at $15	$ 2,565.00
651	Reserved Seats at $10	6,510.00
2071	General Admission at $7	14,497.00
7	Subscribers' Tickets at $4.90	
		34.30
790	Members' Tickets at $2	1,580.00
660	Complimentary Tickets	0,000.00
4350	Total Admission	$25,186.30

Dixon and Skelly

122	Box Seats at $10	$ 1,200.00
602	Reserved Seats at $7.50	4,515.00
1757	General Admission at $5	8,785.00
9	Subscribers' Tickets at $3.50	
		31.50
751	Members' Tickets at $2	1,502.00
821	Complimentary Tickets	0,000.00
	Total Admission	$16,053.50

Sullivan and Corbett

223	Box Seats at $25	$ 5,575.00
1031	Reserved Seats at $20	20,620.00
1986	General Admission at $15	29,790.00

16 Subscribers' Tickets at $10.50	168.50	
833 Members' Tickets at $5	4,165.00	
884 Complimentary Tickets	0,000.00	
4973 Total Admission		$ 60,318.50
Grand Total		$101,558.30

Amount Expenses as per statement on file		$16,407.88
" Purse Myers-McAuliffe	10,000.00	
" Purse Dixon-Skelly	7,500.00	
" Purse Sullivan-Corbett	25,000.00	
Total Expense		$58,907.88
Amount Net Profit		$42,650.42

New Orleans, Sept. 21, 1892   Jos. L. Sporl, Chairman

In tracing the history of promoters, we. have seen how boxing owes a great deal to them, for by risking cash guarantees, they really supplied the life-blood to professional boxing. A promoter can sometimes lose all he has gained in one fight. For instance, Tex Rickard lost $155,000 on the Tunney-Heeney world's heavyweight championship fight because it did not "draw," while Cochran lost $75,000 on the Walker-Milligan championship fight only because he was maneuvered out of the scheduled stadium at the last minute.

So here we see the risks to a fight promoter under the guarantee and percentage basis. Nevertheless, prior to our present Television Era, fortunately or unfortunately, practically every city has one or more promoters who controlled certain managers, fighters, and audiences, and as a result had removed not only much of the speculation but perhaps also some of the color from the fight business. Immediately after World War II, Mike Jacobs practically had every title under contract and therefore had a monopoly of the boxing game as complete as any much-discussed public utility or international cartel. Still, as Mark Twain said, "There are always three sides to any question: your side, the other man's, and the truth." So-called monopolies in boxing have had certain advantages as well as disadvantages. Some people claim it has injured boxing and delayed the progress of the sport. Others claim that it helped in certain periods and will again.

One thing certain, without a Rickard or a Jacobs, whether benevolent or tyrannical, and illegal, the smaller promoters and the small clubs have, in our

155. The picture that inspired James Montgomery Flagg's famous mural and brought in the million-dollar age in boxing—Jack Dempsey battering his way to the world's championship over Jess Willard. (Courtesy of Nat Fleischer)

day, evaporated, and boxing as a business has deteriorated in the United States. New York State, once the center of boxing with the exception perhaps of an occasional major heavyweight or world's heavyweight championship fight, aided by the controversial attraction of a Muhammad Ali, is no longer active in professional boxing. California and Florida promoters, fight clubs, and boxers not reaching for millions furnish excellent competition and entertainment and somewhere another Rickard or Jacobs may be developing. According to many, the most promising true boxing promoter, not a speculator or financier of millions, is Pete Ashlock of Orlando, Florida, who also works out of Houston, Texas. To indicate the lack of interest in New York State—notwithstanding a wonderful reaction to my approach from the N.Y. State Athletic Commission to help sell state politicians on a change in the tax laws that would bring in, in the long run, more tax money to the state and more business to the city—two letters and nine phone calls to the public relations director for boxing at the Madison Square Garden Corporation could not earn me an appointment or even the acceptance of an invitation to lunch to help in the preparation of this book. What a contrast to my many meetings with Tex Rickard and Mike Jacobs and their publicity people! However the promotion and public relations consultant to Don King and the last two worldwide TV championships in Zaire and in the Philippines, Murray Goodman, is easy to see and most helpful.

156. Sock in the puss—modern version. (Wide World)

Present-day fights present far more complicated financial reports and involve as expenses such items as advertising, promotion, taxes, ushers, special police, carpenters, mechanics, ballyhoo men, dinners,

and gifts to the press, guarantees or compensation to the participants of the semifinal and preliminary bouts, rentals of ball parks, lighting, construction, and repair. In accounts receivable, in addition to the gate receipts, there are radio, television, and movie rights, testimonials, and other advertising tie-ups. Last but not least, today there are worldwide complications with television satellite relay and closed-circuit theatre and stadium showings all over the world involving major receipts and expenses.

The development of boxing as a big business from the beginnings of the modern promotion system to its current status is also covered in other chapters and statistical data on this subject are available in the appendix.

Suffice it to say that Mike Jacobs's publicity department reported in 1947 that the Twentieth Century Sporting Club in its first thirteen years' existence had run 478 fights with seventy-three world's titles at stake, grossing $25,546,099. When it is remembered that this figure covers but one club or promotion organization only up to 1947, it can be seen that boxing even yesterday was really big business.

However, yesterday's gates, spectators, receipts, etc., were easily obtainable and verified by all sorts of agencies and tax collectors—all within the confines of one city, one state, or one country. In other words, a single organization definitely promoted so many fights from 1934 to 1947 and collected so many dollars over twenty-five million. Today, even for a single year or a single major worldwide closed-circuit televised fight, this is impossible. All of the figures anyone can give and that are given in this book are based on reports and estimation and perhaps investigative procedure, but could be far off. How can one obtain and check the receipts of dozens to hundreds of closed-circuit television satellite relays of a fight at installations all over the world covered by intricate agreements involving sometimes as many as six legal or financial entities?

As an example of present day problems, it has been impossible to obtain any authentic figure for the number of paid spectators at Kinshasa. Reliable sources at the scene state that thousands of spectators sifted into the large outdoor soccer stadium after the fight had actually begun. A breakdown or a total of receipts on a worldwide basis can only be accepted, but never verified, nor can profits or costs or litigations be known. As an example of the difficulty of statistical gathering, the Ali-Frazier fight No. 1, where the gross receipts are quoted at twenty million dollars and where a United States and Madison Square Garden base would help, no confirmation could be obtained. No news of any resulting litigations were reported. Yet, several reliable sources estimate that many million dollars worth of lawsuits, claims, and litigations followed.

In the beginning of the broadcasting and monopoly era, when fighters and their managers did not know much about broadcasting and the advantages that accrued from it, therefore Mike Jacobs was able to continue his full and uninterrupted control of the radio broadcasts of his fights. He also, it is claimed, dictated to the fighters with respect to their movie, television and other subsidiary rights.

According to an article in a March, 1948 New York newspaper, Sol Strauss, acting for Mike Jacobs and the Twentieth Century Sporting Club, stated that, "We will positively not yield to the demands of the combined managers and boxers for any cut in the television income. I have talked the matter over with the Madison Square Garden Corporation's president, General John Reed Kilpatrick. He says if we cannot find the necessary fistic attractions, the Garden dates will be otherwise filled." It is difficult to believe that a corporation of big businessmen and financial interests would have supported Jacobs to the point of threatening to exclude boxing from the Garden, if the boxers were allowed to participate in the television of fights in which they were the principals.

Like everything else in life, and especially in boxing, many influences, actions, and reactions are misinterpreted or exaggerated. While we do not believe the Jacobs monopoly was as sound or as good for boxing as the type of operation conducted by Rickard, Coffroth, Cochran, or Dixon, times change. Perhaps without Mike Jacobs and his tight control of the boxing game before and during World War II, the padded ring might have gone into an actual decline, whereas the combination of Mike Jacobs and Joe Louis, just as Rickard and Dempsey, kept fists flying, the turnstile clicking and the public interested.

At the beginning of 1949 the Jacobs monopoly showed every sign of breaking up. To begin with, ill health had forced Mike Jacobs to the sidelines. In his absence the Madison Square Garden fights leased out to his Twentieth Century Sporting Club often showed deficits. Gradually some of the championships and star performers and their managers became free agents. In a vain effort to get new faces and a new crop of white fighters to face the ever-increasing array of top black fighters, and to add the color of international matches, Jacobs sent Lew Burston as pugilistic ambassador to Europe. However, Burston immediately found himself handicapped in his efforts because of the shortage of dollar balances at the disposal of European countries. Foreign fighters were willing to come in droves to America for dollars, but dollar shortages abroad prevented a proper

return to the foreign promoters. Not even Jacobs or the Garden could deliver many worthwhile American fighters abroad to be paid by the foreign promoters in kroners, marks, or francs. A round trip for an American fighter and his manager in dollars converted in local exchange was sufficient to make any trade look bad for the foreign promoter right from the start. Foreign fighters and managers also recognized the fact that Jacobs and Burston were not really interested in helping them or protecting them, but were primarily using them to inject a new hypodermic into the box office with new faces, new blood, international flavor, and national anthems.

In 1948 a new type of fight promotion organization was started called the Tournament of Champions, and renamed around Broadway "The Millionaire Club," for it was alleged to have been started by a group of very wealthy men whose main purpose was to improve the boxing situation by breaking the alleged Jacobs monopoly. Their main offering was the Cerdan-Zale middleweight championship fight at Roosevelt Stadium, Jersey City, which grossed $224,840. They also held contracts on Cerdan, the new world's champion, and Zale for a rematch. However, by 1949, the so-called "millionaires" had agreed to disagree and the Tournament of Champions organization became a shadow of its former self and fell into the hands of a public relations man who ballyhooed it into a television property.

By the middle of 1949, the Tournament of Champions had become an organization for the promoting of fights primarily for television purposes. It had rented a totally inadequate place from the standpoint of seating capacity in which to hold the fights, but it hoped to collect sufficient money by selling the radio and television advertising rights to make up the difference. The new partners who controlled this interesting experiment were the Columbia Broadcasting System, representing radio and television interests, and the Music Corporation of America, managers of bands and orchestras and other talent. However, these new principals, who knew nothing about the fight game, were unable to do very much, principally because with limited revenues they could not offer sufficient money to first-class fighters so that they would perform for them. Another factor tending to restrict their success is that any broadcasting, radio, or television they handled had to be on Columbia Broadcasting System or Columbia stations. Sports writers, perhaps egged on by the Jacobs organization, usually referred to this organization in late 1948 and early 1949 as Tournament of Champions, Inc. (Red). However, perhaps the organization marked a new promotion era in ring history, and in a way foretold the future.

Before the end of 1949, the entire boxing situation in the United States became affected by a merger and as already covered in this book in tracing the various eras of boxing, this merger became the subject of scrutiny by the antitrust Division of the Department of Justice. The Twentieth Century Sporting Club and the Jacobs empire (sans Mike Jacobs, retired) merged with the Joe Louis combine of Louis, Jim Norris, and Arthur M. Wirtz; the Madison Square Garden Corporation or its boxing interests; and the Tournament of Champions, Inc., partly owned by C.B.S. and Music Corporation of America. The result was called the International Boxing Club, IBC for short; Octopus, Inc. to the newspapers. The big six in the IBC according to a statement in their Ray Robinson—Steve Belloise 24 August 1949 program were Jim Norris, Ned Irish, Harry Markson, Al Weill, Ted Brenner, and Joe Louis. Arthur M. Wirtz was also listed as "one of the millionaire backers on the board of directors." According to the program, this combine was the "ablest combination that has yet taken over the sport in many years—and this despite the high respect due to Tex Rickard and Mike Jacobs, each of whom was tops in his respective era as a promoter." The program goes on to indicate that this organization will stage fights in many cities in the U.S. and have under its exclusive control most of the champions and contenders, or those whose claims will be recognized. Of course, we already know about the IBC and the monopoly and the final result. Its breakup was the rebirth of boxing.

Independent promoters in Europe continued to operate. Probably the No. 1 promoter of Europe after the death of Jeff Dickson was Jack Solomons of London, known as the King of Sock. He had promoted most of the major fights in England and brought over many leading American fighters, particularly heavyweights. Another very successful promoter in Europe was Eddie Ahlquist who promoted fights both indoors and outdoors in Sweden.

In Canada, the Forum in Montreal was a brilliant center of boxing and many champions have shown their fistic abilities there. In the summer, major fights are held outdoors. The promoter most responsible for this important center of boxing was the late Eddie Quinn. In the future it is believed Montreal will become an even more important fistic halfway house where European champions and American champions will meet. Montreal has also produced with the help of the Forum some great local talent, including Louis Kid Roy, Frankie Fleming, Johnny Greco, Dave Castilloux, and Danny Webb.

In Baltimore, Max Waxman, Louis Fisher, and George Goldberg may have claim to a record. They had promoted fights almost continuously every week for twenty-eight years, and often drew outdoors over $100,000 gates. Their fights had been held in the Coliseum, 5th Regiment Armory and Municipal Stadium. Kid Williams, the Dundee brothers, Chalky Wright, Harry Jeffra, and Red Burman were developed in these fistic incubators.

Before making a quick study of the current and future boxing situation, let us answer the question as to what becomes of fighters after they have served their usefulness in the ring.

Some fighters wind up rich, but they are very few. Some escape injury and go on to serve useful lives to their community, themselves and their families. But the average life span of a fighter is generally considered to be shorter than the average man's. In 1928 it was believed to be less than forty years, while today, with all vital and health statistics improved, it stands between forty-one and forty-two years. John Kofoed, well-known sports writer, once claimed that less than twenty percent of ex-professional fighters were even moderately well off and that for every successful boxer or ex-boxer in later life, he could mark a thousand failures.

The wear and tear of the ring cannot help but take its toll. In the bare-knuckle era, when contests continued until one fighter was knocked out or exhausted, fighters did not live long. Molyneaux died at thirty-four: Tom Johnson, Big Ben Brain, Jem Belcher all died young. Fitzsimmons, who fought in the ring when he was forty-five, died at fifty-six. Boxers who specialize in taking punishment wind up where you would expect them to wind up—in the madhouse. Ad Wolgast and Jo Grimm ended their lives there.

However, all in all, boxing does more for the physical development and character building of man than many other sports. The world today accepts it as beneficial except where greed and neglect are introduced. The fatality rate of boxing is exceedingly low. There were only four boxing deaths in the United States in 1943, five in 1944, six in 1945, and eleven in 1946. However, in 1946 a study shows that the causes of many of these could actually be traced to inadequate ring regulations, inexperienced managers, or hoodlum promoters. In 1945 Boxing Commissioner Leon Rains of Pennsylvania stoutly defended customs of prefight medical examinations, stating that as a result of these, his state has had only three ring deaths in the last fourteen years. Unfortunately, his claims did not stand up too well, for there were three ring deaths in Pennsylvania in 1946, the year following Rains's statement.

Investigations of several deaths in the ring during 1946 revealed the fact that the dead men had previously been suspended from the ring in some other state because of a heart condition or dangerous ailment of some kind.

This raises the question of where responsibility should rest. Al Weill who piloted Lou Ambers and Marty Servo to world championships, believe managers should be responsible for the condition of their fighters. That Weill practices what he preaches is shown by the fact that he was responsible for Servo's giving up his title rather than fighting with a bad nose.

The main burden of responsibility to prevent ring fatalities must be with the State Boxing Commissions. If they fail to take proper action, they will be held responsible by the public.

There were ten deaths in boxing in 1947, twelve in 1948, eighteen in 1949 and eleven in 1950. As a result of these and the death of Sam Baroudi, Akron and New York fighter, following his knockout in Chicago by Ezzard Charles of Cincinnati, the following recommendations were made:

(1) Full investigation of all promoters, managers and fighters and their records;
(2) That all boxers be required to carry a record of their fights, opponents, dates, places, medical report on treatment or hospitalization for any injury or disease;
(3) That Commissioner's medical examiner be allowed to stop fights;
(4) That any injured fighter be taken immediately to nearest hospital for "cardiograph and cranial X-ray study";
(5) That boxers from outside the state be required to file statement of intention to fight in the state thirty days before their initial appearance.
(6) That the N.B.A. establish a clearing house of information on boxers' records.

Based on proper coordination between various boxing agencies and better controls, ring deaths in boxing were seven in 1970, five in 1971, eleven in 1972 and only three in 1973.

However, the New York State Boxing Commission should have its own staff of investigators and liaison with all state and federal investigating agencies is also evident. Even in the field of preventing serious injuries and deaths such an investigating agency would be valuable. Only then could the Commission be certain that a boxer barred in some other state is not licensed in New York State, and that every manager would make sure his boxer was in excellent helath as well as condition. If managers knew a death or serious injury would be thoroughly investigated not only by the police, to determine if it was an accidental death, but also by boxing investigators, to ascertain why the accident happened, few managers would risk their license and public censure. When one realizes that many individual cities in the United States have more deaths in one day from automobile accidents than the total annual deaths in boxing, and one compares the incidence of accidental deaths in other sports to that in boxing, it can be seen that boxing is relatively safe and sane. Better control and further precautions, however, will reduce accidents to a minimum.

In addition to interest shown in the United States and in the British Commonwealth, there is great interest and progress in boxing in Latin America and in Europe. France probably leads in both interest, experience, and development of the sport after the Americans and the British. The French government exercises control of the sport throughout France, its colonies and protectorates through the Fédération Française de Boxe. This organization retains a technical director and trainer. It directs the French Institute of Sport and the organization of regional units. It trains boxers, coaches, referees, judges, selects champions and challengers, and issues ratings. The Fédération in connection with other government boxing associations also designates the European champions. In the last twenty-five or thirty years Frenchmen have held most of the championships of Europe.

The great trouble with French boxers is that they love their France so much that, as long as they can make any money in Europe, they do not come to the United States to develop themselves with the toughest competition available. As a result, so far even the best French boxers come to the United States after they have fought themselves out of competition in Europe and long after they have passed their prime. Eugene Criqui, Andre Routis, Georges Carpentier, Georges Thil, Marcel Cerdan, and Laurent Dauthuille were all outstanding examples of this. When top French fighters begin to come to the United States in their prime and season themselves by the kind of competition they can find here, then we can expect the French to break frequently into the world championship class.

One thing which is peculiar to France is that in that country practically all fight managers are former boxers, because the French government insists that a manager must know by experience how to throw a punch and block one. Most of the promoters are also ex-fighters, which is interesting as compared with the United States, where many promoters, like Mike Jacobs, had never put up their hands except to sign contracts, receive money or sell tickets.

The center of pugilism and the most advanced country in boxing in Latin America is Argentina. Both professional and amateur competition is outstanding there and public interest in boxing is very high. The English and the Irish brought the boxing glove to Argentina long before the introduction of the polo mallet, and with almost as much success.

While the French, in Europe, appear strongest in the middleweight and featherweight classes, in the Argentine the best prospects are all in the middleweight and light heavyweight divisions. However, with the development of outstanding performers these will come to America to try to win what Luis Angel Firpo almost had in his grasp—a world's championship and what Pascual Perez won and held for a long time. Today, Oscar Bonavena, heavyweight, Victor Galindez, Jorge Ahumada and Avenamar Peralta, light heavyweights, Miguel Castellini, junior middleweight, Carlos Gimenez, junior welterweight, Victor Echegaray, junior lightweight, and Jose Casas, featherweight, are serious contenders, while Carlos Munzon, outstanding world's middleweight champion, are all from Argentina.

The future of boxing, in the author's opinion, will prove even more spectacular than its past. Boundaries and distances in boxing hardly exist today with television satellite relay and closed-circuit theater broadcasting.

One more unusual and new trend in boxing is the fact that due to the tremendous cost of promoting world title fights and the unbelievable guarantees to the principals and the promotion value of worldwide TV coverage, countries and cities are prospects to underwrite, support, or bid for fights. Governments now feel a worldwide attraction is worth an investment, which may also turn in a major profit. Taxes can always serve as a safety factor. Don King, the present kingpin of boxing, is now soliciting countries and cities to finance his fights.

King reportedly tried to sell the Bahamas for a million dollars pocket money but Nassau settled instead for a February 1976 warmup for Ali. Nassau is reportedly raising the million dollars for a breather for Ali against some second-class opponent. Then another super-duper worldwide TV championship will be held in some nation or some city ready to put up five to seven million dollars hoping for better luck than Zaire and the Philippines. Hong Kong, the busy British Crown colony; Cairo or Teheran, supported by the Shah of Iran, or the owners of some sixty oil wells; and even Rio de Janiero, with the largest stadium in the world; are King's present prospects. According to reports, Hong Kong may have the inside track based on a gambling syndicate in Hong Kong and Macao, known as an even safer

hideout for unrecorded capital than Switzerland. After all, the current super promotor of boxing wants minimum taxes, controls, and problems, and the most money. The promotion is rigged so that the principals, namely, the promoter and the two principal opponents, get theirs no matter what! If the financial backers make money, fine, but, according to many, these operations have been no more successful than the world heavyweight championship between Dempsey and Gibbons, which all but wiped out the town of Shelby, Montana on 4 July 1923. There, a small town in 1923 put up $300,000, the last $100,000 had to be paid from the actual gate receipts of the fight. History does repeat itself, even in boxing.

According to the latest information, as reported by several boxing and sports writers, Muhammad Ali-Frazier 3 did "great" in New York, Philadelphia, Washington, and also at Miami where the super abilities of Chris Dundee were evident to promote a boxing feature; but the South, the Midwest, and the West Coast proved very disappointing. The opponent for Ali at this writing, if King gets oil or hush money, will be either Foreman or Norton and allegedly will be Ali's curtain call. However, with Ali's conceit and love of being "the greatest," it is doubtful he will quit before he is certain he is washed up as a fighter. All efforts to get some reliable figure on the financial backers' returns have failed, although some official and certified reports might well, some day, be made known. Most experts believe the Filipino government received very little back on its four million dollars advance. On the other hand, perhaps indirect gains and publicity warrant any actual losses by the sponsor. Moscow was mentioned several times by Ali who is better on ring strategy than on Communist business. Moscow has been awarded the 1980 Olympic Games but there is repeated report that this will depend on some device to raise the money for the games outside the Soviet Union—perhaps a giant worldwide lottery. However, even little Helsinki, as well as Mexico City and Tokyo, paid all their bills and for all construction for the Games. With respect to boxing promotion, can anyone imagine the Russians paying or advancing five to ten million dollars for the promotion of an Ali fight and for such an outstanding free enterprise endeavor? However, King might well find some enthusiasm on the part of Castro in a match between Ali and the Olympic heavyweight boxing champion Tiofilo Stevenson of Cuba, if Castro could be sure Stevenson would win. This would be another type of promotion that Communist Castro might well go for. However, based on Stevenson's showing in the 1975 Pan Am Games, he would be "duck soup" for Ali.

On the other hand, suppose the governments or city backers of our present-day super TV spectacles lose too much money. Suppose Zaire did lose seven million dollars as claimed by many and Manila also lost a tidy sum (reportedly four million dollars). Suppoes that even the Arab oil interests and the Far East gambling syndicates are no longer interested. This could mean a complete change in the promotion approach. It is doubtful if King can ever tie up with the Garden, the New York State Athletic Commission, and New York City and State taxes. Therefore, let us conjure up a world title fight on a coral reef in the South Pacific, or a new rocky island in the North Atlantic belonging to no country, or a fight on a ship or a platform on the open sea, all with no taxes or obligations beyond normal expenses, televised by satellite relay to over ten thousand theaters, stadiums, and arenas throughout the world. In addition, there will be video tapes and/or motion pictures later to be featured under commercial sponsorship over hundreds of commercial television stations, and later to be featured as a special presentation or motion picture on a commercial airlines, and then, finally, resold for old-time sports reviews in picture houses and over commercial television! How reminiscent of the old bare-fist fights on barges or in hidden rings in some forest with an audience of only a few hundred or a few thousand persons as against perhaps a similar scene today, but now with television and satellite relay seen and heard by millions. The actual gate or physical audience would be of no importance.

Fight fans in Abyssinia or Australia, Greece or Georgia, Tibet or Trinidad, Manhattan or Moscow, Zanzibar or Zamboanga will be able to see the champion of the world of any weight defend his title by going to the nearest closed-circuit installation or, ultimately, by merely turning a knob on his television set at home.

In any case and no matter how financed, but as a result of the vast spread of boxing to the world and into many homes, it will become (it is hoped) a salesman for democracy, tolerance, racial equality, and world peace, and handicap dictatorships of every kind. Competition and interest may mount to new heights as rivalry expands and brings new champions from Suva, Tallinn, or Seoul Kejo . . . or will Communism progress and capitalistic boxing profits for world champions be replaced by the average remuneration due to a very top worker in a new world of collectivism . . . who can tell?

Appendices

1.

THE AUTHOR'S SELECTION OF ALL TIME GREATS OF MODERN BOXING 1700 TO 1975

In chronological order without regard to comparative abilities but the selection influenced by both superior performance and the impact and contribution to the advance and popularity of the sport.

Heavyweight

1. James Figg
2. Jack Broughton
3. Gentleman John Jackson
4. James J. Jeffries
5. Jack Dempsey
6. Joe Louis
7. Rocky Marciano
8. Muhammad Ali

Light Heavyweight

1. Bob Fitzsimmons
2. Philadelphia Jack O'Brien
3. Georges Carpentier
4. Billy Conn
5. Tommy Loughran
6. Bob Foster

Middleweight

1. Tom Sayers
2. Jack Dempsey (the Non-pareil
3. Stanley Ketchel
4. Harry Greb
5. Mickey Walker
6. Ray Robinson
7. Carlos Monzon

Welterweight

1. Joe Walcott
2. Dixie Kid
3. Ted Lewis
4. Jack Britton
5. Jimmy McLarnin
6. Emile Griffith

Lightweight

1. Dutch Sam Elias
2. Napoleon Jack McAuliffe
3. Joe Gans
4. Benny Leonard
5. Ike Williams
6. Joe Brown

Featherweight

1. Young Griffo
2. Johnny Kilbane
3. Jem Driscoll
4. Abe Attell
5. Henry Armstrong
6. Johnny Dundee
7. Willie Pep
8. Vincente Saldivar

Bantamweight

1. George Dixon
2. Jimmy Barry
3. Terry McGovern
4. Joe Lynch
5. Manuel Ortiz
6. Arnold Taylor

Flyweight

1. Jimmy Wilde
2. Pancho Villa
3. Midget Wolgast
4. Frank Genaro
5. Fidel LaBarba
6. Pascual Perez

227

2.

MOST FAMOUS POEM IN BOXING

The Nonpareil's Grave

I

Far out in the wilds of Oregon,
   On a lonely mountain side,
Where Columbia's mighty waters,
   Roll down to the ocean tide;
Where the giant fir and cedar
   Are imaged in the wave,
O'ergrown with firs and lichens,
   I found Jack Dempsey's grave.

II

I found no marble monolith
   No broken shaft, or stone,
Recording sixty victories,
   This vanquished victor won;
No rose, no shamrock could I find
   No mortal here to tell
Where sleeps in this forsaken spot
   Immortal Nonpareil.

III

A winding wooded canyon road
   That mortals seldom tread,
Leads up this lonely mountain,
   To the desert of the dead.
And the Western sun was sinking
   In Pacific's golden wave,
And those solemn pines kept watching,
   Over poor Jack Dempsey's grave.

IV

Forgotten by ten thousand throats,
   That thundered his acclaim,
Forgotten by his friends and foes,
   Who cheered his very name.
Oblivion wraps his faded form,
   But ages hence shall save
The memory of that Irish lad
   That fills poor Dempsey's grave.

V

Oh, Fame, why sleeps thy favored son
   In wilds, in woods, in weeds,
And shall he ever thus sleep on,
   Interred his valiant deeds?
'Tis strange New York should thus forget
   Its "bravest of the brave"
And in the fields of Oregon,
   Unmarked, leave Dempsey's grave.

—M. J. McMahon

3.

BARE-KNUCKLE HEAVYWEIGHT CHAMPIONS OF ENGLAND

1719	James Figg	1804	Henry Pierce
1730	No Champion	1806	John Gully
1734	Jack Broughton	1809	Tom Cribb*

1750	Jack Slack	1822	No Champion
1760	Billy Stevens	1823	Tom Spring
1761	Tom Faulkner	1825	Jem Ward
1762	George Millsom	1831	No Champion
1763	Tom Juchau	1833	James Burke
1766	Bill Darts	1839	Bendigo
1769	Tom Lyons	1850	No Champion
1771	Peter Corcoran	1856	Tom Sayers*
1776	Harry Sellers	1861	Jem Mace
1780	Duggan Fearns	1862	Tom King
1783	Tom Johnson	1864	No Champion
1791	Ben Brain	1865	Jem Mace
1795	Bill Hooper	1873	No Champion
1795	Jack Jackson		(Jem Smith, Claimant)
1800	Jem Belcher	1873	Jem Mace
		1890	Charlie Mitchell*

* World's title claim by British based on win or draw with Molyneux, Heenan and Sullivan, respectively.

4.

BARE-KNUCKLE HEAVYWEIGHT CHAMPIONS OF THE UNITED STATES

1810	Tom Molyneux	1852	John C. Morrissey
1812	No Champion	1859	John C. Heenan*
1816	Jacob Hyer	1863	Joe Coburn
1817	No Champion	1865	No Champion
1841	Yankee Sullivan	1869	Tom Allen
1847	Tom Hyer	1876	Joe Goss
1849	No Champion	1880	Paddy Ryan
		1882	John L. Sullivan*

* Fought draw with English Champions Sayers and Mitchell respectively.

5.

WORLD'S HEAVYWEIGHT CHAMPIONS

During transition period between Bare-Knuckles and Glove Competition and English and United States Control.

(English Control of World's Championship)
   1864   Tom King retires
   1865   Jem Mace
   1873   Jem Mace retires

(Recognized by U.S.)		(Recognized by British)	
1873	Tom Allen (claims title on basis of loss to Mace in 1870)	1873	Jem Smith claimant after Mace retires
1876	Joe Goss	1873	Jem Mace (retired but returns and loses to)
1880	Paddy Ryan		
1882	John L. Sullivan	1890	Charlie Mitchell
1892	Corbett K.O.'s Sullivan	1894	Corbett K.O.'s Charlie Mitchell

(American Control of World's Championship)
   1894   James J. Corbett*

6.

WORLD'S HEAVYWEIGHT CHAMPIONS

London Prize Ring Rules

1880	Paddy Ryan	1882	John L. Sullivan

Marquis of Queensberry Rules

1888	John L. Sullivan		
1892	James J. Corbett*	1926	Gene Tunney
1897	Robert L. Fitzsimmons	1930	Max Schmeling
		1932	Jack Sharkey
1899	James J. Jeffries	1933	Primo Carnera
1906	Tommy Burns	1934	Max Baer
1908	Jack Johnson	1935	James J. Braddock
1915	Jess Willard	1937	Joe Louis
1919	Jack Dempsey	1949	Vacant
1950	Ezzard Charles		
1951	Jersey Joe Walcott		
1952	Rocky Marciano		
1956	(vacant) Rocky Marciano, retired		
1956	Floyd Patterson		
1959	Ingemar Johansson		
1960	Floyd Patterson (first man to ever regain title)		
1962	Sonny Liston		
1964	Cassius Clay		
1967	(Grand Jury indictment for Clay's refusal to accept service with Armed Forces—Result—Both New York and world boxing organizations banned Clay from title)		
1970	(Various tournaments and claimed title holders by various organizations and states with Jimmy Ellis and Joe Frazier recognized as champions in 1968)		
1970	Joe Frazier		
1973	George Foreman		
1974	Cassius Clay (Ring Name: Muhammed Ali) (U.S.)		

* First clear title to World's Championship by defeating Charlie Mitchell accepted then as World's Champion in England and Europe. Sullivan and Mitchell fought a draw in France in 1888.

7.

WORLD'S LIGHT HEAVYWEIGHT CHAMPIONS

(175 pounds) Division established in 1903

1903	George Gardner	1927	Tommy Loughran
1903	Bob Fitzsimmons	1930	Jimmy Slattery
1905	Philadelphia Jack O'Brien	1930	Maxie Rosenbloom
1907	Tommy Burns	1934	Bob Olin
1912	Jack Dillon	1935	John Henry Lewis
1916	Battling Levinsky	1939	Melio Bettina
1920	Georges Carpentier	1939	Billy Conn
1922	Gene Tunney	1941	Gus Lesnevich
1922	Battling Siki	1948	Freddie Mills
1923	Mike McTigue	1950	Joey Maxim
1925	Paul Berlenbach	1952	Archie Moore
1926	Jack Delaney	1962	Harold Johnson
1927	Mike McTigue	1963	Willie Pastrano
		1965	Jose Torres

1966	Dick Tiger		W.B.C.
1968	Bob Foster (U.S.)		Victor Galindez (Argentina) W.B.A.
1975	Bob Foster Retires		
1975	John Conteh (England)		

8.

WORLD'S MIDDLEWEIGHT CHAMPIONS

(158—now 160 pounds) Division established in 1867

1874	Mike Donovan	1949	Jake La Motta
1884	Jack Dempsey, the Nonpareil	1951	Ray Robinson
		1951	Randy Turpin
1891	Bob Fitzsimmons	1951	Ray Robinson
1897	Tommy Ryan	1952	Ray Robinson retires
1907	Stanley Ketchel		Tournaments and various claimants
1907	Billy Papke		
1908	Stanley Ketchel	1953	Carl Olson
1911	Billy Papke	1955	Ray Robinson
1913	Frank Klaus	1957	Gene Fullmer
1913	George Chip	1957	Ray Robinson
1914	Al McCoy	1957	Carmen Basilio
1917	Mike O'Dowd	1958	Ray Robinson
1920	Johnny Wilson	1959	Gene Fullmer
1923	Harry Greb	1960	Paul Pender and Gene Fullmer
1926	Tiger Flowers		
1926	Edward "Mickey" Walker	1961	Terry Downes
		1962	Paul Pender, Dick Tiger
1932	Marcel Thil		
1937	Fred Apostoli, Fred Steele	1963	Pender Retires
		1963	Dick Tiger
1938	Fred Steele, Al Hostak, S. Krieger	1963	Joe Giardello
		1965	Dick Tiger
1939	Al Hostak	1966	Emile Griffith
1940	Tony Zale	1967	Nino Benvenuti
1947	Rocky Graziano	1967	Emile Griffith
1948	Tony Zale	1968	Nino Benvenuti
1948	Marcel Cerdan	1970	Carlos Monzon (Argentina)

9.

WORLD'S WELTERWEIGHT CHAMPIONS

(145—now 147 pounds). Division established in 1792, lapsed in 1795, revised in 1815

1892	"Mysterious Billy" Smith	1919	Jack Britton
		1922	Mickey Walker
1894	Tommy Ryan	1926	Pete Latzo
1897	Billy Smith	1927	Joe Dundee
1900	"Rube" Ferns	1929	Jackie Fields
1900	Matty Matthews	1930	Young Jack Thompson, Jackie Thompson, Jackie Fields
1901	Rube Ferns		
1901	Joe Walcott		
1904	"Dixie Kid"	1931	Tommy Freeman, Young Jack Thompson, Lou Brouillard
1906	Honey Melody		
1907	Mike (Twin) Sullivan		
1910	Jimmy Clabby	1932	Jackie Fields
1911	Ted Lewis	1933	Young Corbett III,

	Jimmy McLarnin	1956	Johnny Saxton
1934	Barney Ross, Jimmy McLarnin	1956	Carmen Basilio
1935	Jimmy McLarnin, Barney Ross		Basilio vacates title after winning middleweight title
1936	Barney Ross	1958	Virgil Atkins
1938	Henry Armstrong	1958	Don Jordan
1940	Fritz Zivic	1960	Benny Paret
1941	Fred Cochrane	1961	Emile Griffith
1946	Marty Servo	1961	Benny Paret
1946	Ray Robinson	1962	Emile Griffith
1951	Robinson vacates title after winning middleweight title	1963	Louis Rodriguez
		1963	Emile Griffith
		1966	Emile Griffith (gives up title for middleweight title)
1951	Johnny Bratton		
1951	Kid Gavilan	1966	Curtis Cokes
1954	Johnny Saxton	1969	Jose Napoles
1955	Tony DeMarco	1970	Billy Backus
1955	Carmen Basilio		
	1971 Jose Napoles (Mexico)		

1923	Eugene Criqui	1949	Willie Pep
1924	Johnny Dundee	1950	Sandy Saddler
1925	Louis "Kid" Kaplan	1957	Saddler relinquishes title due to anto accident
1927	Red Chapman		
1928	Tony Canzoneri, Andre Routis	1957	Kid Bassey
		1959	Davey Moore
1929	Christopher "Battling" Battalino	1963	Sugar Ramos
		1964	Vincente Saldivar
1932	Kid Chocolate	1968	Saldivar retires
1933	Freddie Miller	1969	Johnny Famechon
1934	Baby Arizmendi	1970	Vincente Saldivar
1936	Pete Sarron	1970	Kuniaki Shibata
1937	Henry Armstrong	1970	Clemente Sanchez
1938	Joey Archibald	1972	Sanchez retires
1940	Harry Jeffra	1973	Ernesto Marcel and Jose Legra
1941	Joey Archibald		
1941	Chalky Wright	1974	Ruben Olivares
1946	Willie Pep	1975	Alexis Arguella (Nicaragua)
1948	Sandy Saddler		
	David Katey (Ghana)		

10.

WORLD'S LIGHTWEIGHT CHAMPIONS

(133—now 135 pounds) Division established in 1868

1872	Arthur Chambers	1941	Sammy Angott
1882	Jack Dempsey	1944	Sammy Angott, Juan Zurita
1884	Jack McAuliffe		
1893	Kid Lavigne	1945	Ike Williams (N.B.A.) Bob Montgomery (N.Y.)
1899	Frank Erne		
1902	Joe Gans		
1908	Battling Nelson	1947	Ike Williams
1910	Ad Wolgast	1951	James Carter
1912	Willie Ritchie	1952	Lauro Salas
1914	Freddie Welsh	1952	James Carter
1917	Benny Leonard	1954	Paddy DeMarco
1925	Jimmy Goodrich	1954	James Carter
1925	Rocky Kansas	1955	Bud Smith
1926	Sammy Mandell	1956	Joe Brown
1930	Al (Abraham) Singer	1962	Carlos Ortiz
1930	Tony Canzoneri	1965	Ismael Laguna
1933	Barney Ross	1965	Carlos Ortiz
1935	Tony Canzoneri	1968	Carlos Cruz
1936	Lou Ambers	1969	Mando Ramos
1938	Henry Armstrong	1970	Ismael Laguna
1939	Lou Ambers	1970	Ken Buchanan
1940	Lew Jenkins	1972	Roberto Duran (Panama)

11.

WORLD'S FEATHERWEIGHT CHAMPIONS

(118, then 122—now 126 pounds) Division established in 1885

1890	Billy Murphy	1904	"Brooklyn" Tommy Sullivan
1892	George Dixon		
1899	Terry McGovern	1908	Abe Attell
1901	Young Corbett	1911	Johnny Kilbane

12.

WORLD'S BANTAMWEIGHT CHAMPIONS

(105, then 112, then 116—now 118 pounds) Division established in 1885

1887	Tom Kelly	1937	Harry Jeffra
1890	George Dixon	1938	Sixto Escobar
1894	Jimmy Barry	1940	Lou Salica
1899	Terry McGovern	1942	Manuel Ortiz
1900	Harry Forbes	1947	Harold Dade
1903	Frankie Neil	1948	Manuel Ortiz
1904	Joe Bowker	1950	Vic Toweel
1904	Digger Stanley and Jimmy Walsh	1952	Jimmy Carruthers
		1954	Jimmy Carruthers retires
1907	Johnny Coulon	1954	Robert Cohen
1914	Kid Williams	1956	Mario D'Agata
1915	Johnny Ertle	1957	Alphonse Halimi
1917	Pete Herman	1959	Joe Becerra
1920	Joe Lynch	1960	Joe Becerra retires
1921	Pete Herman	1960	Alphonse Halimi and Elder Joffre
1921	Johnny Buff		
1922	Joe Lynch	1962	Elder Joffre
1924	Abe Goldstein	1965	Fighting Harada
1924	Eddie Martin	1968	Lionel Rose
1925	Charles "Phil" Rosenberg	1969	Ruben Olivares
		1970	Chucho Castillo
1927	Bud Taylor, Kid Francis, Al Brown	1971	Ruben Olivares
		1972	Rafael Herrera
		1972	Enrique Pinder
1931	Eugene Huat	1973	Romeo Anaya
1932	Al Brown	1973	Arnold Taylor
1936	Sixto Escobar	1974	Soo Hwan Hong
	1975 Alfonso Zamora (Mexico)		

13.

WORLD'S FLYWEIGHT CHAMPIONS

1916	Jimmy Wilde	1954	Pascual Perez
1921	Johnny Buff	1960	Pone Kingpetch
1922	Pancho Villa	1962	Fighting Harada
1923	Frankie Genaro	1963	Pone Kingpetch
1923	Pancho Villa		(first to regain
1925	Fidel La Barba		this title)
1927	Corporal Izzy	1963	Hiroyuki Ebihara
	Schwartz	1964	Pone Kingpetch
1930	Midget Wolgast	1965	Salvatore Burruni
1930	Frankie Genaro	1966	Walter McGowan
1931	Young Perez	1966	Chartchai Chionoi
1932	Jackie Brown	1969	Efren Torres
1935	Benny Lynch	1970	Chartchai Chionoi
1938	Peter Kane	1970	Erbito Salvarria
1941	Vacant	1973	Venice Burkorsor
1943	Jackie Patterson	1973	Borkorsor (resigned
1948	Rinty Monaghan		title to fight as ban-
1950	Monaghan retires		tamweight)
1950	Terry Allen	1974	Susumo Hanagata
1950	Dado Marino		Shoji Oguma
1952	Yoshio Shirai	1975	Miguel Canto (Mexico)

14.

MODERN OLYMPIC BOXING CHAMPIONS

Light Flyweight

1968	Fran Rodriguez, Venezuela	1972	G. Gedo, Hungary
		1976	Jorge Hernandez, Cuba

Flyweight

1904	George V. Finnegan, U.S.	1948	Pascual Perez, Argentina
1920	Frank Genaro, U.S.	1952	Nate Brooks, U.S.
1924	Fidel La Barba, U.S.	1956	Terence Spinks, Great Britain
1928	Anton Kocsis, Hungary	1960	G. Torck, Hungary
1932	Stephen Enekes, Hungary	1964	Fernando Atzori, Italy
		1968	Ricardo Delgado, Mexico
1936	Will Kaiser, Germany	1972	G. Kostadinov, Bulgaria
	1976 Leo Randolph, U.S.A.		

Bantamweight

1904	O. L. Kirk, U.S.	1936	Ulderico Sergo, Italy
1908	H. Thomas, Gr. Britain	1948	T. Csik, Hungary
1920	C. Walker, So. Africa	1952	Pentti Hamalainen, Finland
1924	W. H. Smith, So. Africa	1956	Wolfgang Behrendt, Germany
1928	Vittorio Tamagnini, Italy	1960	O. Grigoryev, Russia
		1964	Takao Sakurai, Japan
1932	Horace Gwynne, Canada	1968	Valery Sokolov, Russia
		1972	Orlando Martinez, Cuba
	1976 Yong Jo Gu, North Korea		

Featherweight

1904	O. L. Kirk, U.S.	1948	Ernesto Formenti, Italy
1908	R. K. Gunn, Gr. Britain	1952	Jan Zachara, Czechoslovakia
1920	R. Fritsch, France		
1924	Jack Fields, U.S.	1956	Vladimir Sefronov, Russia
1928	L. Van Klaveren, Holland	1960	F. Musso, Italy
1932	Carmelo Robledo, Argentina	1964	Stanislav Stepashkin, Russia
1936	Oscar Casanovas, Argentina	1968	Antonio Roldan, Mexico
		1972	Boris Kousnetsov, Russia
	1976 Angel Harrera, Cuba		

Lightweight

1904	H. J. Spangler, U.S.	1948	Jerry Dreyer, So. Africa
1908	F. Grace, Gr. Britain	1952	Aureliano Bolognesi, Italy
1920	Samuel Mosberg, U.S.		
1924	Harold Nielsen, Denmark	1956	Richard McTaggart, Gr. Britain
1928	Carlo Orlandi, Italy	1960	K. Pazdzier, Poland
1932	Lawrence Stevens, So. Africa	1964	Jozef Grudzein, Poland
		1968	Ronnie Harris, U.S.
1936	Imre Harangi, Hungary	1972	Jan Szczepanski, Poland
		1976	Howard Davis, U.S.A.

Light Welterweight

1952	Charles Adkins, U.S.	1964	Jerzy Kulei, Poland
1956	Vladimir Engoibarian, Russia	1968	Jerzy Kulei, Poland
		1972	Ray Seales, U.S.
1960	B. Nemecek, Czechoslovakia	1976	Ray Leonard, U.S.A.

Welterweight

1904	Al Young, U.S.	1952	Zygmunt Chychia, Poland
1920	Tom Schneider, Canada	1956	Necolae Linca, Rumania
1924	J. S. DeLarge, Belgium	1960	Giovanni Benvenuti, Italy
1928	Edward Morgan, New Zealand	1964	Giovanni Benvenuti, Italy
1932	Edward Flynn, U.S.		
1936	Sten Suvio, Finland	1968	Manfred Wolke, E. Germany
1948	Julius Torma, Czechoslovakia	1972	Emilio Correa, Cuba
	1976 Jochen Bachfield, East Germany		

Light Middleweight

1952	Laszlo Papp, Hungary	1964	Marian Kasprzyk, Poland
1956	Laszlo Papp, Hungary	1968	Boris Lagutin, Russia
1960	W. McClure, U.S.	1972	Dieter Kettysch, W. Germany
	1976 Jerzy Rybicki, Poland		

Middleweight

1904	Charles Mayer, U.S.	1920	H. W. Malin, Gr. Britain
1908	J.W.N.T. Douglas, Gr. Britain		
		1924	H. W. Malin,

	Gr. Britain		Russia
1928	Piero Toscani, Italy	1960	E. Crook, U.S.
1932	Carmen Barth, U.S.	1964	Valery Popenchenko,
1936	Jean Despeaux,		Russia
	France	1968	Chris Finnegan,
1948	Laszlo Papp, Hungary		Gr. Britain
1952	Floyd Patterson, U.S.	1972	V. Lemechev, Russia
1956	Guennaddi Chatkov,	1976	Mike Spinks, U.S.A.

Light Heavyweight

1920	Edward Eagan, U.S.	1948	George Hunter,
1924	H. J. Mitchell,		So. Africa
	Gr. Britain	1952	Norvel Lee, U.S.
1928	Victor Avendano,	1956	James Boyd, U.S
	Argentina	1960	C. Clay, U.S.
1932	David E. Carstens,	1964	Cosimo Pinto, Italy
	So. Africa	1968	Dan Rozniak, Russia
1936	Roger Michelot,	1972	Mate Parlov, Yugoslavia
	France	1976	Leon Spinks, U.S.A.

Heavyweight

1904	Sam Berger, U.S.	1936	Herbert Runge,
1908	A. L. Oldham,		Germany
	Gr. Britain	1948	Rafael Iglesias,
1920	R. R. Rawson,		Argentina
	Gr. Britain	1952	Edward Sanders, U.S.
1924	Otto Von Porat,	1956	Pete Rademacher, U.S.
	Norway	1960	F. DePiccoli, Italy
1928	J. Rodriguez Jurado,	1964	Joseph Frazier, U.S.
	Argentina	1968	George Foreman, U.S.
1932	Santiago A. Lovell,	1972	T. Stevenson, Cuba
	Argentina	1976	Teofilo Stevenson, Cuba

(Unofficial) Team Champions

1904	United States	1952	United States
1908	Great Britain	1956	Russia
1920	Great Britain	1960	Italy
1924	United States	1964	Russia
1928	Italy	1968	Russia
1932	United States	1972	Cuba
1936	Germany	1976	U.S.A.
1948	Italy		
	South Africa		

15.

RECORD GATES OF BOXING BOUTS

Pre-Worldwide and Television Era

Date	Bout	Site of Contest	Receipts	Attend.
27 Sept. 1927	Tunney-Dempsey	Soldiers' Field	$2,658,660	104,943
19 June 1946	Louis-Conn	Yankee Stadium	1,925,564	45,266
23 Sept. 1926	Tunney-Dempsey	Sesquicentennial		
		Std.	1,925,733	120,757
2 July 1921	Dempsey-Carpentier	Boyle's 30 Acres	1,789,238	80,000
14 Sept. 1923	Dempsey-Firpo	Polo Grounds	1,188,603	82,000
21 July 1927	Dempsey-Sharkey	Yankee Stadium	1,083,530	75,000
22 June 1938	Louis-Schmeling	Yankee Stadium	1,015,012	70,000
	(2nd)			
25 Sept. 1935	Louis-Max Baer	Yankee Stadium	1,000,832	88,150
25 June 1948	Louis-Joe Walcott	Yankee Stadium	841,739	
12 June 1930	Schmeling-Sharkey	Yankee Stadium	749,935	79,222
	(1st)			
22 June 1937	Louis-Braddock	Comiskey Park	715,470	45,500
26 July 1928	Tunney-Heeney	Yankee Stadium	691,014	45,890
29 Sept. 1941	Louis-Nova	Polo Grounds	583,711	56,549
19 June 1936	Schmeling-Louis	Yankee Stadium	547,541	42,088
11 Sept. 1924	Firpo-Wills	Jersey City	509,135	70,000
16 July 1926	Berlenbach-Delaney	Ebbets Field	461,789	49,186
23 July 1923	Leonard-Tendler	Polo Grounds	452,648	58.250
4 July 1919	Dempsey-Willard	Toledo, Ohio	452,224	19,650
18 June 1941	Louis-Conn	Yankee Stadium	451,743	60,071
12 June 1923	Firpo-Willard	Jersey City, N. J.	434,269	62,500
21 June 1932	Sharkey-Schmeling	L. I. Bowl	432,365	61,863
14 June 1934	Baer-Carnera	L. I. Bowl	428,000	56,000
16 July 1947	Graziano-Zale	Chicago Stadium	422,918	
27 Feb. 1929	Sharkey-Stribling	Flamingo Park,		
		Fla.	405,000	40,000

16.

RECORD GATES OF YESTERDAY

1892	Sullivan-Corbett	$ 60,318
1896	Fitzsimmons-Sharkey	21,000
1897	Corbett-Fitzsimmons	22,000
1899	Jeffries-Sharkey	60,300
1901	Jeffries-Rublin	30,800
1902	Jeffries-Fitzsimmons	31,800
1903	Jeffries-Corbett	63,340
1904	Nelson-Brett	48,311
1904	Brett-Corbett	32,345
1906	Gans-Nelson	**69,715**
1908	Nelson-Gans	32,000
1908	Johnson-Burns	131,000
1909	Johnson-Ketchel	**28,000**
1910	Wolgast-Nelson	37,000
1910	Corbett-McCoy	**56,350**

17.

WORLD WIDE AND TELEVISION ERA STATISTICS
RECORD RECEIPTS INCLUDING TV, CLOSED CIRCUIT THEATRE COVERAGE

				Receipts	Gate
21	Sept.	1955	Marciano-Moore	$ 2,248,177	61,574
20	June	1960	Johansson-Patterson	2,468,278	31,890
25	Sept.	1962	Patterson-Liston	4,655,420	18,890
22	July	1963	Liston-Patterson	4,747,690	7,816
25	May	1965	Clay-Liston	1,602,190	2,424
22	Nov.	1965	Clay-Patterson	3,570,000	7,402
2	May	1966	Clay-Cooper	1,200,000	42,000
8	Mar.	1971	Frazier-Clay (Ali) 1	20,000,000*	20,455
23	Jan.	1974	Frazier-Ali 2	18,000,000*	20,750
30	Oct.	1974	Foreman-Ali	19,000,000*	48,000*
30	Sept.	1975	Ali-Frazier 3	18,000,000*	24,000*

* Estimated and unconfirmed.

18.

VITAL STATISTICS OF MODERN HEAVYWEIGHT CHAMPIONS

Champion	Height	Weight (Pounds)	Reach (Inches)	Chest, Normal (Inches)	Chest, Expanded (Inches)	Waist (Inches)	Biceps (Inches)	Neck (Inches)	Wrist (Inches)	Calf (Inches)	Ankle (Inches)	Thigh (Inches)	Fist (Inches)	Forearm (Inches)
James J. Corbett	6'1"	184	73	38	42	33	14½	17	6½	14½	8¼	21	12¾	11½
Bob Fitzsimmons	5'10½"	172	71¾	41	44	32	12	15	7½	13½	8¼	20	12½	11½
James J. Jeffries	6'1½"	225	76½	43	48½	35	16	18¼	7¾	17	10	25	13½	13½
Tommy Burns	5'7"	179	74¼	40	43¾	33	14½	16	7¼	16½	8¼	22	12	13
Jack Johnson	6'1¼"	222	74	37½	42¾	36	16	17½	10½	15	9½	22½	14	14½
Jess Willard	6'6¼"	252	83	46	49½	35½	17½	17½	10	17½	10½	26	14	14
Jack Dempsey	6'1½"	191	77	42	46	33	16¼	16½	9	15	9	23	11¼	14½
Gene Tunney	6'1"	192	77	42	45	34½	14½	17	9	15½	9	22	11¼	13½
Max Schmeling	6'1"	188	76	43	47	33¾	16	17½	8	16	10	23½	12	12¾
Jack Sharkey	6'1"	205	74½	40½	45½	34½	14½	17	7¾	16	10¼	24¾	12¾	15¾
Primo Carnera	6'5¾"	267	85½	48	54	38	18½	20	9½	20	11½	30	14¾	16
Max Baer	6'2½"	214	81	44	47½	32½	14½	17½	8	15	9½	21	12	14
Jimmy Braddock	6'3"	197	75	41	44	34½	13	17	8	16	10	22¾	11½	12½
Joe Louis	6'1½"	211¼	77	42	45	35	15	18	9	16½	11	23½	13	13¾
Ezzard Charles	6'	184½	74	39	42	33	15½	16½	7	13	8½	20	12	12
Joe Walcott	6'	194	74	40	43	35	16	17	7¾	14	9¾	21	12	13
Rocky Marciano	5'10½"	184	68	39	42	32	14	16¾	7½	14¾	10	22	11½	12
Ingemar Johansson	6'½"	197	72½	43	45	34	16½	17	7	16	10	24	13½	15
Floyd Patterson	6'	190	71	40	42	32½	14¼	17	6	15½	9½	21½	12¾	12
Sonny Liston	6'1"	212	84	44	46½	33	16½	17½	8½	16	12	25½	15	14½
Cassius Clay	6'3"	215	82	42	44½	34	15	17	7½	17	9½	25	12	13½
Joe Frazier	5'11½"	202	73½	42	44	34	15	17½	7	13	11	26	13	13
George Foreman	6'3"	220	78½	43	45½	34	15½	17½	8	17	10	25	12½	15

233

19

MAJOR INDOOR AND OUTDOOR ARENAS WORLDWIDE

Astrodome	Houston, Tex., U.S.	62,000
Araneta Coliseum	Quezon City, Philippines	36,000
Aztec Stadium	Mexico City, Mexico	60,000
Briggs Stadium	Detroit, Mich., U.S.	60,000
Buffalo Stadium	Buffalo, N.Y., U.S.	70,000
Busch Memorial Stadium	St. Louis, Mo., U.S.	55,000
Comisky Park	Chicago, Ill., U.S.	50,000
Dodger Stadium	Los Angeles, Cal., U.S.	60,000
Ebbets Field	Brooklyn, N.Y., U.S.	45,000
Fenway Park	Boston, Mass., U.S.	40,000
Forbes Field	Pittsburgh, Pa., U.S.	60,000
Gabriel Stadium	Port-au-Prince, Haiti	30,000
Gran Stadium	Havana, Cuba	35,000
Griffith Stadium	Washington, D.C., U.S.	50,000
Kampfbahn Rote Erde	Dortmund, Germany	40,000
Kezar Stadium	San Francisco, Cal., U.S.	85,000
Korakuen Stadium	Tokyo, Japan	50,000
Kosnien Stadium	Osaka, Japan	60,000
Lumpinee Boxing Stadium	Bangkok, Thailand	60,000
Luna Park	Buenos Aires, Argentina	29,000
Madison Square Garden	New York, N.Y., U.S.	19,500
Mario Filho (Maracama)	Rio de Janeiro, Brazil	220,000
Memorial Stadium	Baltimore, Md., U.S.	100,000
Memorial Park	Los Angeles, Cal., U.S.	120,000
Merdeka Stadium	Singapore	30,000
Miami Stadium	Miami, Fla., U.S.	16,000
Municipal Stadium	Cleveland, Ohio, U.S.	77,700
Namba Stadium	Osaka, Japan	30,000
National Stadium	Bangkok, Thailand	70,000
New Domed Stadium	Seattle, Wash., U.S.	80,000
Olympia Stadion	Berlin, Germany	55,000
Olympic Domed Stadium	Montreal, Canada	75,000
Olympic Stadium	Boston, Mass., U.S.	60,000
Pacaembu Stadium	Sao Paulo, Brazil	60,000
Philadelphia Stadium	Philadelphia, Pa., U.S.	120,000
Pontiac Domed Stadium	Pontiac, Mich., U.S.	65,000
Radreenbahn	Cologne, Germany	25,000
Rajadamern Stadium	Bangkok, Thailand	72,000
Rand Stadium	Johannesburg, S. Africa	30,000
River Front Stadium	Cincinnati, Ohio, U.S.	56,000
River Plate Stadium	Buenos Aires, Argentina	110,000
Roosevelt Stadium	Jersey City, N.J., U.S.	40,000
Rugby Stadium	Tokyo, Japan	40,000
Shea Stadium	Flushing, N.Y., U.S.	55,600
Sicks' Stadium	Seattle, Wash., U.S.	25,000
Soldiers Field	Chicago, Ill., U.S.	120,000
Sportsmen Park	St. Louis, Mo., U.S.	50,000
Stadio Olympic	Caracas, Venezuela	40,000
Stadion Mungersdorf	Cologne, Germany	50,000
Superdome	New Orleans, La., U.S.	100,000
Tiger Stadium	Detroit, Mich., U.S.	60,000
Triboro Stadium	New York, N.Y., U.S.	45,000
Ullevi Stadium	Gothenburg, Sweden	55,000
VFR Platz	Mannheim, Germany	30,000
Wembley Stadium	London, England	100,000
White City Stadium	London, England	46,000
Wrigley Field	Chicago, Ill., U.S.	38,690
Yankee Stadium	New York, N.Y., U.S.	72,000

20

ODD STATISTICS

LONGEST FIGHT, BARE KNUCKLES: James Kelly—Jonathan Smith, 6 hours, 15 minutes, Melbourne, Australia, 1 November, 1855.

LONGEST FIGHT WITH GLOVES: A. Bowen—J. Burke, draw, 6 April 1893, 110 rounds (7 hours, 19 minutes), New Orleans, Louisiana.

SHORTEST FIGHT WITH GLOVES: 1928, Al Foreman of England knocked out Ruby Levine in 11½ seconds, including count, landing three punches.

KNOCKOUT RECORDS: (Most) W. L. Stribling fighting from bantam to heavyweight knocked out 137 men 1920–1933. Rocky Marciano has highest "batting" average; knocked out 43 men in 49 fights without a single loss or draw.

SHORTEST BOXING SHOW: Dreamland Arena, San Francisco, 19 July 1929, 7 bouts completed in 22 minutes, 7 KO's, 4 in 1st round, 2 in 2nd round, 1 in 3rd round.

21.

BOXING ATTENDANCE IN UNITED STATES 1946

Newspaper Estimate
(All Boxing)

Approximate Paid Attendance	$26,500,000
Total Expenses	15,500,000

N. Y. State Athletic Commission Estimate
(Professional Fights Only)

Paid Attendance

United States at Large—Total	$14,000,000
New York State	7,000,000

22.

1974 NO OFFICIAL NEWSPAPER ESTIMATE AVAILABLE

Author's Estimate

U.S. Approx. Paid Attendance	$14,500,000
U.S. Total Expenses	9,250,000
N.Y. State Paid Attendance	4,000,000

These figures are not guaranteed but at least show the tremendous drop in boxing interest, promotions and receipts in the U.S. alone and even more so in New York state.

Official gross receipts including Television and closed circuit in State of New York..........$3,097,893.46
(N.Y. State Athletic Commission)

23.

PRE WORLDWIDE AND TELEVISION ERA

Top Approximate Earnings* World Boxing Champions

1. Jack Dempsey† $5,000,000
2. Joe Louis 4,715,000
3. Gene Tunney 3,015,000
4. John L. Sullivan‡........................1,500,000

* Includes movies, radio, theatre, vaudeville, referee tours, etc. Does not include monies made after retirement.

† Since 1934 conservative estimates of Dempsey's earnings to 1974—as most popular former boxing champion—average another $5,000,000.

‡ There are probably a number of heavyweights whose earnings top Sullivan in more recent years, but because boxing finances and value of money in late nineteenth century were so different, it is believed Sullivan is entitled to fourth place. Many people believe that the purchasing power of John L. Sullivan's million and a half at the end of the nineteenth century was far greater than Dempsey's five million.

24.

WORLDWIDE AND TELEVISION ERA

Estimated Gross Earnings World Boxing Champions

1. Rocky Marciano..........................$ 4,060,000
2. Floyd Patterson...........................7,738,010
3. Joe Frazier................................10,100,000
4. George Foreman..........................6,270,000
5. Cassius Clay (Muhammed Ali)....21,250,000

NOTE: Because of the tremendous taxes for major annual incomes and the devaluation of money throughout the world there cannot be any real comparison between pre World War II five million dollars gross with even twenty million dollars today.

25.

LEADING BOXER-ACTOR STATISTICS

Boxer-Actor	Major Plays, Pictures, or Radio Serials	Managers-Producers
John L. Sullivan	"Honest Hearts and Willing Hands" (Boxed with villain at Irish Fair) "East and West"	Billy Madden (Theatre and fight bookings) Duncan B. Harrison (Producer)
Peter Jackson	"Uncle Tom's Cabin"	Parson Davis (Fights)
Terrible Terry McGovern	"The Road to Ruin"	Sam Harris (Theatre and fights, manager and producer)
James J. Corbett	"After Dark" "Gentleman Jim" "A Naval Cadet"	William A. Brady (Theatre and fights, manager and producer)
Bob Fitzsimmons	"The Honest Blacksmith" (Would forge horseshoes on stage, imprint his name and hand out to the audience) "Ruby Robert"	Martin Julian (Fights)
James J. Jeffries	"The Man from the West"	William A. Brady (Theatre and fights, manager and producer)
Joe Walcott	Canterbury Music Hall, London	Chas. B. Cochran (Theatre and fights, manager and producer)
Jack Dempsey	"The Idol of Millions" (Picture) "The Idol of Millions" (Coast-to-coast radio serial)	Jack Kearns ⎫ Fights and Max Waxman ⎭ business John V. Grombach (Radio manager and producer)
Georges Carpentier	"French Revues"	Descamps (Fights and theatre)
Gene Tunney	"The Fighting Marine" (Picture)	Billy Gibson (Fights)
Max Baer	"The Prizefighter and the Lady" (Picture) "Lucky Smith (Coast-to-coast radio serial tied up with Braddock fight) "Taxi" Coast-to-coast radio serial tied up with Carnera fight)	Ancil Hoffman (Fights) John V. Grombach (Radio and theatrical manager and producer)
Billy Conn	"The Pittsburgh Kid" (Picture)	
Joe Louis	"The Spirit of Youth" (Picture)	M. Jacobs
Muhammad Ali	"The Greatest" (Picture)	Columbia Pictures

26.

NEW YORK STATE ATHLETIC COMMISSION CHAIRMEN

Aug.	1920 to April	1921	Joseph Johnson
June	1921 to April	1923	William Muldoon
April	1923 to Feb.	1924	George L. Brower
Feb.	1924 to Feb.	1933	Joseph A. Farley
Feb.	1933 to June	1945	John J. Phalen
June	1945 to Sept.	1951	Edward Eagan
Sept.	1951 to Dec.	1954	Robert K. Christenberry
Jan.	1955 to Dec.	1958	Julius Helfand
Jan.	1959 to June	1966	Melvin L. Krulewitch
June	1966 to April	1975*	Edwin Dooley
Aug.	1975 to		James A. Farley, Jr.

* N. Y. Athletic Commission scheduled for possible termination then continued.

27.

REVISED LONDON PRIZE RING RULES

RULE 1. The ring shall be made on turf, and shall be four-and-twenty feet square, formed of eight stakes and ropes, the latter extending in double lines, the uppermost line being four feet from the ground, and the lower two feet from the ground. That in the centre of the ring a mark be formed, to be termed a "Scratch."

RULE 2. Each man shall be attended to the ring by two seconds and a bottle-holder. The combatants, on shaking hands, shall retire until the seconds of each have tossed for choice of position, which adjusted, the winner shall choose his corner according to the state of the wind or sun, and conduct his man thereto; the loser taking the opposite diagonal corner.

RULE 3. Each man shall be provided with a handkerchief of a color suitable to his own fancy, and that the seconds shall entwine these handkerchiefs at the upper end of one of the centre stakes. That these handkerchiefs shall be called "colors," and that the winner of the battle at its conclusion shall be entitled to their possession as the trophy of victory.

RULE 4. Two umpires shall be chosen by the seconds or backers to watch the progress of the battle, and take exception to any breach of the rules hereafter stated. A referee shall be chosen by the umpires, unless otherwise agreed on, to whom all disputes shall be referred, and that the decision of this referee, whatever it may be, shall be final and strictly binding on all parties, whether as to the matter in dispute or the issue of the battle. This official shall receive out of the stakes a sum of 5 per cent, for officiating, such sum to be deducted by the stakeholder either from the amount of the winnings in the case of a win, or in equitable proportions from each stake in the event of a draw. No payment to be made in the event of a forfeit or if the referee not being called upon to act. The umpires shall be provided with a watch for the purpose of calling time; and that they mutually agree upon which this duty shall devolve, the call of that umpire only to be attended to, and no other person whatever, except the referee when appealed to, shall interfere in calling time. The referee shall withhold all opinion till appealed to by the umpires, and the umpires strictly abide by his decision without dispute.

RULE 5. The men, being stripped, it shall be the duty of the seconds to examine their drawers, and if any objection arises as to insertion of improper substances therein, they shall appeal to their umpires, who, with the concurrence of the referee, shall direct what alterations shall be made.

RULE 6. The spikes in the fighting boots shall be confined to three in number, which shall not exceed three-eighths of an inch from the sole of the boot, and shall not be less than one-eighth of an inch broad at the point; two to be placed in the broadest part of the sole and one in the heel; and that in the event of a man wearing any other spikes either in the toes or elsewhere, he shall be compelled either to remove them or provide other boots properly spiked, the penalty for refusal to be a loss of the stakes.

RULE 7. Both men being ready, each shall be conducted to that side of the scratch next his corner previously chosen; and the seconds on the one side, and the men on the other, having shaken hands, the former shall immediately leave the ring, and there remain till the round be finished, on no pretense whatever approaching their principals during the round, without permission from the referee. The penalty to be the loss of the battle to the offending parties.

RULE 8. At the conclusion of the round, when one or both of the men shall be down, the seconds shall step into the ring and carry or conduct their principal to his corner, there affording him the necessary assistance, and that no person whatever be permitted to interfere in this duty.

RULE 9. On the expiration of thirty seconds the umpire appointed shall cry "Time," upon which each man shall rise from the knee of his second and walk to his own side of the scratch unaided; the seconds immediately leaving the ring. The penalty for either of them remaining eight seconds after the call of time to be the loss of the battle to his principal; and that either man failing to be at the scratch within eight seconds shall be deemed to have lost the battle.

RULE 10. On no consideration whatever shall any person, except the seconds or the referee, be permitted to enter the ring during the battle, nor till it shall have been concluded; and that in the event of such unfair practice, or the ropes or stakes being disturbed or removed, it shall be in the power of the referee to award the victory to that man who, in his honest opinion, shall have the best of the contest.

RULE 11. The seconds shall not interefre, advise, or direct the adversary of their principal, and shall refrain from all offensive and irritating expressions, in all respects conducting themselves with order and decorum, and continue themselves to the diligent and careful discharge of their duties to their principals.

RULE 12. In picking up their man, should the seconds willfully injure the antagonist of their principal, the latter shall be deemed to have forfeited the battle on the decision of the referee.

RULE 13. It shall be a fair "stand up" fight, and if either man shall willfully throw himself down without receiving a blow, whether blows shall have previously been exchanged or not, he shall be deemed to have lost the battle; but that this rule shall not apply to a man who in a close slips down from the grasp of his opponent to avoid punishment, or from obvious accident or weakness.

RULE 14. Butting with the head shall be deemed foul, and the party resorting to this practice shall be deemed to have lost the battle .

RULE 15. A blow struck when a man is thrown, or down, shall be deemed foul. A man with one knee and one hand on the ground, or with both knees on the ground, shall be deemed down and a blow given in either of those positions shall be considered foul, providing always that when in such position, the man so down shall not himself strike, or attempt to strike.

RULE 16. A blow struck from below the waistband shall be deemed foul, and while in a close, the seizing of an antagonist below the waist, by the thigh, or otherwise, shall be deemed foul.

RULE 17. All attempts to inflict injury by gouging, or tearing the flesh with the fingers or nails, and biting, shall be deemed foul.

RULE 18. Kicking, or deliberately falling on an antagonist with the knees or otherwise when down, shall be deemed foul.

RULE 19. All bets shall be paid as the battle money, after a fight, is awarded.

RULE 20. The referee and umpires shall take their positions in front of the center stake, outside the ropes.

RULE 21. Due notice shall be given by the stakeholder of the day and place where the battle money is to be given up, and that he be exonerated from all responsibility upon obeying the direction of the referee; that all parties be strictly bound by these rules, and that in future all articles of agreement for a contest be entered into with a strict and willing adherence to the letter and spirit of these rules.

RULE 22. In the event of magisterial or other interference, or in case of darkness coming on, the referee (or stakeholder, in case no referee has been chosen) shall have the power to name the time and place for the next meeting, if possible on the same day, or as soon after as may be. In naming the second or third place, the nearest spot shall be selected to the original place of fighting where there is a chance of its being fought out.

RULE 23. Should the fight not be decided on the day all bets shall be drawn, unless the fight shall be resumed the same week, between Sunday and Sunday, in which case the referee's duties shall continue, and the bets shall stand and be decided by the event. The battle money shall remain in the hands of the stakeholder until fairly won or lost by a fight, unless a draw be mutually agreed upon, or, in case of a postponement, one of the principals shall be absent, when the man in the ring shall be awarded the stakes.

RULE 24. Any pugilist voluntarily quitting the ring, previous to the deliberate judgment of the referee being obtained, shall be deemed to have lost the fight.

RULE 25. On any objection being made by the seconds or umpire the men shall retire to their corners, and there remain until the decision of the appointed authorities shall be obtained; that if pronounced "foul," the battle shall be at an end; but if "fair," "time" shall be called by the party appointed, and the man absent from the scratch in eight seconds after shall be deemed to have lost the fight. The decision in all cases to be given promptly and irrevocably, for which purpose the umpires and the referee should be invariably close together.

RULE 26. If a man leaves the ring, either to escape punishment or for any other purpose, without the permission of the referee, unless he is involuntarily forced out, he shall forfeit the battle.

RULE 27. The use of hard substances, such as stones, or sticks, or of resin in the hand during the battle, shall be deemed foul, and that on the requisition of the seconds of either man the accused shall open his hands for the examination of the referee.

RULE 28. Hugging on the ropes shall be deemed a foul. A man held by the neck against the stakes, or upon or against the ropes, shall be considered down, and all interference with him in that position shall be foul. If a man in any way makes use of the ropes, or stakes, to aid him in squeezing his adversary, he shall be deemed the loser of the battle; and if a man in a close reaches the ground with his knees, his adversary shall immediately loose him or lose the battle.

RULE 29. All glove, or room fights, to be as nearly as possible in conformity with the foregoing rules.

28.

MARQUIS OF QUEENSBERRY RULES DRAFTED IN 1865— OFFICIALLY ADOPTED 1892

RULE 1. To be fair stand-up boxing match in a twenty-four foot ring, or as near that size as practicable.

RULE 2. No wrestling or hugging allowed.

RULE 3. The rounds to be of three minutes' duration, and one minute's time between rounds.

RULE 4. If either man fall through weakness or otherwise, he must get up unassisted, ten seconds to be allowed him to do so, the other man meanwhile to return to his corner, and when the fallen man is on his legs the round is to be resumed, and continued till the three minutes have expired. If one man fails to come to the scratch in the ten seconds allowed, it shall be in the power of the referee to give his award in favor of the other man.

RULE 5. A man hanging on the ropes in a helpless state, with his toes off the ground shall be considered down.

RULE 6. No seconds or any other person to be allowed in the ring during the rounds.

RULE 7. Should the contest be stopped by any unavoidable interference, the referee to name the time and place as soon as possible for finishing the contest; so that the match must be won and lost, unless the backers of both men agree to draw the stakes.

RULE 8. The gloves to be fair-sized boxing gloves of the best quality and new.

RULE 9. Should a glove burst, or come off, it must be replaced to the referee's satisfaction.

RULE 10. A man on one knee is considered down, and if struck is entitled to the stakes.

RULE 11. No shoes or boots with springs allowed.

RULE 12. The contest in all other respects to be governed by revised rules of the London Prize Ring.

29.

NEW YORK STATE ATHLETIC COMMISSION BOXING RULES 1975

The Ring Officials

SECTION 210.1 THE REFEREE. (a) The referee shall inspect each boxer's gloves and make sure that no foreign detrimental substances have been applied to either the gloves or the bodies of the boxers.

(b) The boxing referee shall have the following exclusive powers:

(1) To stop a bout or contest at any stage on the grounds that it is too one-sided. In such event, he may award the bout

to the superior contestant as a technical knockout.

(2) To stop a bout or contest at any stage if he considers one or both of the boxers are not competing in earnest. In such event he may disqualify one or both of the contestants, and if only one contestant is disqualified, he may award the bout as a technical knockout to the other.

(3) To stop a bout or contest at any stage on account of a major foul being committed by either contestant and to award the decision, under such circumstances, to the fouled boxer.

(c) Referees are required to stop any bout in which a boxer has been knocked down three times in one round from the result of a blow as distinguished from a slip or a fall from being off balance.

210.2 THE RING ANNOUNCER. (a) No individual will be permitted to act as a ring announcer at any boxing bouts held under the supervision and authority of the commission without having first obtained a license to so act from the commission, and no licensed promoting corporation may employ any unlicensed person to act as such announcer.

(b) The announcer of the bout shall be the master of ceremonies and at the conclusion of each bout must collect the score cards from the judges and referees and submit them to the commission representative in attendance for inspection before making any announcement of the decision.

(c) Introductions from the ring of persons not connected with the sport of boxing is forbidden and the announcer must receive the advance approval from the commission representative in attendance as to each of the persons introduced from the ring. After such introductions are completed, the announcer shall announce the name of the contestants and their correct weights, and any other matters he is directed to announce by the commission.

210.3 THE TIMEKEEPER. (a) The timekeeper must sit outside the ring platform and close to the gong.

(b) Each timekeeper must have either a whistle or a buzzer and a stopwatch, which shall be submitted for approval to the commission representative in attendance at the boxing program.

(c) In the event that a bout terminates by a knockout during any round, the timekeeper shall inform the announcer of the exact duration of such round.

(d) The timekeeper must not signal during the progress of a round except to indicate that only 10 seconds remain in the round. He shall also signal 10 seconds prior to the beginning of any round and at such signal all seconds must leave the interior of the ring and all stools and equipment must be removed from the ring platform. The timekeeper must strike the gong with a metal hammer to indicate the beginning and ending of each round.

210.4 REFEREES, JUDGES AND TIMEKEEPERS. (a) At all boxing and wrestling programs each ring official on duty directed by the commission to be in attendance thereat, shall be paid by the licensed promoting corporation in such sum and amounts as the commission shall order the licensed promoting corporation to pay, in accordance with the schedule furnished to the said promoting corporation and on file with the commission.

(b) Without the special permission of the commission, no licensed referee, judge or timekeeper may officiate in any way at any boxing or wrestling program which is not conducted under the authority or supervision of the commission.

(c) All judges and referees for bouts or exhibitions conducted by promoting corporations must be assigned by the commission, and the number of officials required to be in attendance or the substitution of officials for any reason at any time during the bout or exhibition is solely within the power and discretion of the commission.

(d) Semi-annual and annual medical examinations must be given to all licensed judges and referees by the commission physician and such examination must be of the same type and thoroughness as is outlined in section 209.1 above.

The Premises, Its Facilities and Equipment

SECTION 215.1 [APPROVAL OF PREMISES FOR BOXING REQUIRED.] Licensed promoting corporations may only arrange for and hold boxing bouts in premises approved by the commission.

215.2 [NOTICE CONCERNING GAMBLING.] In all such premises there shall be prominently displayed in at least four places and during the entire course of the bouts, as well as the period of one hour preceding the commencement of the bouts, the following notice:

NO GAMBLING ALLOWED

215.3 [POSTING OF LICENSE IN BOX OFFICE.] The license issued to the promoting corporation shall be posted in the box office of the premises where the boxing bouts are taking place and shall at all times be enclosed in a suitable frame so as to be completely visible for inspection.

215.4 [PROVIDING SEATS FOR RING OFFICIALS AND COMMISSION REPRESENTATIVES.] The premises must provide suitable raised and separate ringside seats for the judges and timekeeper, which must be approved by the commission representative in attendance before the commencement of any boxing program. The licensing promoting corporation must also provide two seats in each boxer's corner for the occupancy of the commission representatives on duty at the program.

215.5 [ADVERTISING ON ROUND CARDS.] Round cards exhibited in the ring between rounds must not bear advertising matter of any kind whatsoever.

215.6]PROVISION FOR CLEAN BUCKET AND BOTTLE IN BOXER'S CORNER.] For each bout there must be a clean bucket and a clean bottle in each boxer's corner.

215.7 [EMERGENCY MEDICAL FACILITIES AND EQUIPMENT.] All licensed corporations promoting boxing must provide medical facilities and equipment adequate for emergency occasions and all such medical facilities and equipment must be approved in advance by the commission. Specifications of the commission for the platform, the padding and the covering shall be prescribed by the commission from time to time by bulletin and forwarded by the commission to each licensed promoting corporation.

215.8 [INSPECTION OF RING BY COMMISSION.] The ring and platform must conform to the specified requirements submitted to the licensed corporation by the commission and no boxing contest shall be permitted in any ring unless such ring has been inspected and approved by the commission.

215.9 [SPECIFICATIONS FOR RING POSTS AND ROPES.] Ring posts shall be made of metal not more than three inches in diameter, extending from floor of building to a height of 58 inches above the ring floor. There shall be three ring ropes and each not less than one inch thick in diameter; the lower rope shall be 18 inches above the ring floor, the second rope 35 inches above the floor and the third rope 52 inches above the floor. Such ropes shall be wrapped in soft material.

215.10 [THE GONG.] The gong must not be less than 10 inches in diameter, adjusted securely on a level with the ring platform.

215.11 [CONDITION AND SIZE OF GLOVES.] The gloves shall be new for all main and semi-final events and also for all bouts scheduled for 10 or more rounds and are to be furnished by the licensed promoting corporation. In all bouts not less than eight-ounce gloves shall be used.

215.12 [TYPES OF SHOES BARRED FROM RING.] No shoes with spikes, cleats, hard soles or hard heels are permitted in the ring.

215.13 [MISCELLANEOUS EQUIPMENT.] Licensed promoting corporations must provide water buckets, powdered resin for the canvas, second's stools for each corner and such other articles as are required by the commission for the proper conduct of any boxing program.

215.14 [SCALES.] All scales used for any weigh-in must be approved in advance by the commission.

215.15 [PERSONS AUTHORIZED TO ENTER BOXER'S DRESSING ROOM.] No one shall be allowed in a boxer's dressing room except his manager, his seconds, the commission representatives, members of the press and such members of the promoting corporation as are permitted by the commission. This section must be posted by such corporation at the entrance of all dressing rooms.

Conduct of Boxing Bouts

SECTION 216.1 [NUMBER OF OFFICIALS REQUIRED.] At each boxing bout the officials shall consist of one referee, two judges, one timekeeper, one knockdown counter and one announcer. In addition, for all bouts there shall be two physicians in attendance.

216.2 [POSITION OF JUDGES AND PHYSICIANS.] The judges shall be stationed at opposite sides of the ring and the physicians shall be stationed at places designated by the commission representative in charge.

216.3 [NUMBER OF SECONDS.] Each contestant may have no more than three seconds and each such second while assisting in the boxer's corner may wear only such costume as may be prescribed by the commission from time to time. Only one of such seconds may be inside the ring ropes between rounds.

216.4 [CONDUCT OF SECONDS.] No second may coach any of the boxers during the progress of any round and must remain seated and silent during each round.

216.5 [EXCESSIVE SPRAYING OF WATER ON BOXER.] Any excessive or undue spraying or throwing of water on any boxer between rounds is forbidden.

216.6 [THROWING TOWEL INTO RING.] All seconds are pro-

hibited from throwing any towel into the ring as a token of defeat.

216.7 [APPLICATION OF MONSEL'S SOLUTION.] The application of Monsel's solution or any of its derivatives on the body of a boxer between rounds is prohibited.

216.8 [APPROVAL OF SECONDS BY COMMISSION.] Each boxer must submit to the commission for approval the name of his chief second and his assistant seconds and no other persons other than his approved seconds shall be permitted in the corner of the boxer.

216.9 [REFEREE'S INSTRUCTIONS TO CONTESTANTS.] Before the start of each bout the referee must call the contestants together for final instructions at which time each contestant shall be accompanied by his chief second only, except in the case of a boxer who also requires the services of an interpreter. After receiving the referee's instructions, the boxers shall shake hands and retire to their corners to await the gong for the first round.

216.10 [TIME FOR STARTING MAIN BOUTS.] All main bouts shall start no later than 10 p.m. unless otherwise ordered or approved by the commission.

216.11 [NUMBER OF BOXING ROUNDS ALLOWED IN ONE PROGRAM.] There shall be no less than 30 and no more than 40 rounds of boxing on any one program unless otherwise approved by the commission. Emergency bouts must be provided by the licensed promoting corporation in case the arranged program cannot be fulfilled. Boxers in the emergency bout if not used must be paid a minimum stand by fee of $25, and each such boxer must be engaged for a preliminary bout within a reasonable time thereafter by such licensed corporation.

216.12 [TIME WHEN BOXERS MUST REPORT TO DRESSING ROOMS.] All boxers participating in a boxing program must report to the dressing room of the premises no later than 7:30 p.m. except the contestants in the main bout, who may report at or before 8 p.m. All boxers will remain in their dressing rooms until ordered to the ring by the commission representative in charge. Before entering the ring, boxers must have a clean appearance, must be cleanly shaven and their hair must be trimmed.

216.13 [CHANGES IN ANNOUNCED OR ADVERTISED PROGRAMS.] A notice of any change in the announced or advertised programs for any main-bout contest must be filed with and approved by the commission at least 48 hours before the weighing-in time of the contest. Notices of such change or substitution must also be conspicuously posted at all box offices on the premises and announced from the ring before the opening bout, and if any of the patrons apply for refunds on tickets already purchased, the promoting corporation shall make such refunds upon demand, provided such tickets are presented at the box office on the day or night of the contest.

216.14 [PERSONS DISQUALIFIED FROM OFFICIATING.] No official, director, matchmaker or stockholder of any promoting corporation or licensed club shall officiate in any capacity at any boxing bout conducted by such corporation, or interfere in any way with the contestants participating in such boxing program.

216.15 [REFEREE'S WEARING APPAREL.] The type, style and color of apparel of all referees shall be as the commission may from time to time prescribe and all such referees must conform their apparel accordingly while on duty at the boxing bout.

216.16 [WEIGHING-IN CEREMONIES.] The times and places of all weigh-in ceremonies for indoor and outdoor shows shall be as determined by the commission and all contestants shall be weighed in on scales approved by the commission and in the presence of their opponents, the matchmaker and representatives of the commission. In the event of a postponement of the bout in excess of 24 hours for any reason whatsoever a second weigh-in and additional physical examinations may be required on the day to which the bout has been adjourned.

216.17 [BOXER'S RING COSTUME.] Each boxer on a program must provide himself with the ring costume selected and approved by the commission and such costume must include a foulproof guard of the boxer's own selection, type to be approved by the commission which will obviate the necessity of any claims being made for a low blow during the contest.

216.18 [ADJUSTMENT OF BOXER'S GLOVES.] In all nonchampionship bouts, the gloves of each boxer will be adjusted in the dressing room under the supervision of the commission representative in charge, and the laces of each glove shall be knotted on the back of the wrists and there shall be placed on the wrists of the glove, over the laces, a strip of one-inch adhesive tape. In championship bouts, the gloves shall be adjusted in this manner in the ring before the commencement of the bout. Except in championship bouts, the gloves must be removed in the dressing room after the bout.

216.19 [ANNOUNCEMEUT OF DECISION.] After the decision of any bout has been announced, both contestants and their seconds must leave the ring at once and retire to their dressing rooms, and a contestant is prohibited from indicating in any way to the officials or to the spectators his opinion as to whether he won or lost the bout.

216.20 [PERSONS FORBIDDEN TO COACH CONTESTANT.] The employees of any licensed promoting corporation and the matchmaker are forbidden from coaching any contestant at any time during the progress of any bout.

216.21 [DURATION OF MATCHES.] In nonchampionship matches, boxers can only be matched for four, six, eight, 10 or 12 rounds, unless otherwise approved by the commission. All world championship matches must be of 15 rounds duration. State championships may be conducted at either 12 or 15 rounds, at the discretion of the commission.

216.22 [INTERMISSION BETWEEN ROUNDS.] There shall be a one-minute intermission between rounds.

216.23 [AGE OF BOXERS AS AFFECTING DURATION OF MATCHES.] Unless special permission otherwise is granted by the commission, boxers 18 years of age are permitted to box six rounds; boxers 19 years of age, eight rounds; boxers 20 years of age, 10 rounds and for all bouts over 10 rounds each boxer in such bout must be at least 21 years of age.

216.24 [OUTDOOR BOXING SHOWS.] The following special rules and regulations (sections 216.25 through 216.28) pertain to outdoor boxing shows only, and all other rules and regulations of the commission not affected or modified below remain in force and effect for all such shows.

216.25 [POSTPONEMENT OF BOXING EVENT.] In the event of rain immediately before or during the course of any outdoor show, except during the course of the main bout, the promoting corporation may postpone the show to such time and at such place as is approved by the commission. An announcement giving the full details of the postponement shall forthwith be made by the promoting corporation and any patron desiring a refund of the purchase price of his ticket may apply for the same at the box office of the promoting corporation on the premises, except when the main bout is held on the scheduled or one of the successive rainout dates indicated on the ticket. However, all contestants who have fulfilled their boxing contracts before the event of the rain shall be paid in full, and on the postponed date, substitute bouts in such number and of such duration as is approved by the commission must be provided by the promoting corporation.

216.26 [REARRANGEMENT OR SHORTENING OF PROGRAM.] In the event of threatening weather and rain, the program of bouts may be rearranged or shortened by the promoting corporation with the consent of the commission representative in charge.

216.27 [REIMBURSEMENTS OF EXPENSES TO CONTESTANTS.] All contestants in bouts other than the main bout who were unable to compete because of weather conditions or a rearrangement or shortening of the boxing program, shall have such of their expenses and other fees paid by the promoting corporation as the commission may direct.

216.28 [STOPPING OF MAIN BOUT BECAUSE OF RAIN.] In the event that rain occurs after the main bout is completed, the boxing program shall be considered as having been completed. In the event of rain during the progress of the main bout, such bout shall be continued or stopped at the discretion of the commission representative in charge. If the main bout is stopped, the provisions of section 216.25 above as to postponement and refunds shall apply.

Scoring System

SECTION 217.1 [POINTS.] The following scoring system shall be used by the referee and judges in each boxing bout to determine which, if any, contestant has won a round. In each round, such officials must observe (a) clean hitting, (b) effective aggressiveness, (c) defense, and (d) ring generalship. At the conclusion of each round, each official must score each contestant's performance on these four items, and if the boxer is just slightly superior to his opponent in such round, one point must be scored for such boxer and the score of zero posted for his opponent. If a boxer is clearly superior to his opponent in any one round, two points should be scored for such boxer and the score of zero posted for his opponent. If a boxer is overwhelmingly the winner of a round and the round is therefore one-sided, three points should be scored for such boxer and the score of zero posted for his opponent. If in a one-sided round, a boxer also scores one or more knockdowns, four points should be posted for the boxer and the score of zero posted for his opponent.

217.2 [KNOCKDOWNS.] The officials may score a knockdown in any one round as either one or two points in favor of a boxer who scored such knockdown, and each official must determine for himself which value shall be placed on the knockdown.

217.3 [THE TALLY AND DECISION.] At the conclusion of the bout, each official must tally up the rounds and points he has awarded each contestant and submit his score card to the announcer. After such score cards have all been checked by the commission representative, they must be returned to the announcer, who shall announce the decision of the officials from the ring, and in main events the announcer shall call out the rounds and points awarded by each official. The boxer who has won the most number of rounds on the score cards of two of the officials is the winner of the bout. If the score cards when tallied do not establish a winner by rounds, the decision must be awarded to the boxer with the greatest number of points on two of the score cards, or if the rounds and points are both inconclusive, the winning boxer is the one who has been awarded the decision on two of the officials' score cards.

217.4 [Award of decision.] In the event that any official has scored the rounds and points of each boxer as even, such official may award his decision to the boxer who, in his opinion, is in the better physical condition at the end of the bout. In addition, even when a boxer has not been credited with the greatest number of rounds, he may be declared the winner of the bout on an official's score card if, in the judgment of the official, such boxer has definitely proven his superiority over his opponent, has finished in better physical condition than his opponent, and has been awarded by such official a greater number of points than those awarded by such official to the opponent.

217.5 [Score cards.] Judges and referees must mark their cards in ink or in indelible pencil, at the end of each round, with the symbols of W or L or E; a capital W in a boxer's column indicates the win of that round, a capital L, the loss of that round, and a capital E that the round was even.

217.6 [Major fouls.] The following are major fouls and upon the occurrence of any major foul in any round, the referee may disqualify the offending boxer and award the bout or any round thereof to the fouled boxer:
(a) hitting an opponent who is down or who is rising from down;
(b) using the knee against the opponent;
(c) purposely going down without being hit;
(d) failure to heed the referee's warnings concerning low blows or other minor fouls;
(e) any dangerous and unsportsmanlike conduct in the ring.

217.7 [Minor fouls.] The following are minor fouls and it is within the discretion of the referee as to whether the offending boxer should merely be warned or should lose the round because of the commission of a minor foul:
(a) holding an opponent;
(b) deliberately maintaining a clinch;
(c) hitting with the inside or butt of the hand, the wrist or the elbow;
(d) backhand blows;
(e) low blows;
(f) hitting or "flicking" with the open gloves;
(g) wrestling or roughing at the ropes;
(h) deliberately striking at that part of the body over the kidneys;
(i) use of a pivot blow or rabbit punch;
(j) hitting on the break.

217.8 [Referee's notice to judges concerning foul.] In the event that the referee has awarded the round to the fouled boxer, he must so notify the judges at the end of that round and in addition to the loss of the round because of such foul, the boxer who was fouled shall also be awarded one point in such round.

217.9 [When referee must count boxer out.] A referee must count a boxer out who falls to the floor claiming foul because of a low blow.

217.10 [Report to commission because of fouls.] If in any bout a boxer is penalized with the loss of three or more rounds because of fouls, the referee and each judge must report the matter in writing to the commission within 24 hours.

217.11 [Technical knockout.] A technical knockout is the ending of a bout by a referee for any reason other than a count-out or a disqualification. When a referee stops a contest to save any boxer from further punishment, he must award the other boxer the decision by technical knockout and must inform the announcer of the name of the boxer who was unable to continue, and direct the announcer to declare the other boxer the winner by technical knockout.

217.12 [When boxer is down.] A boxer is down if (a) any part of his body other than his feet is on the ring floor, or (b) he is hanging helplessly on the ring ropes, or (c) he is rising from a down position.

217.13 [Counting.] (a) When a contestant is "down" the timekeeper shall at once commence calling off the seconds, indicating the count with a motion of his arm. The referee must immediately order the other boxer to a neutral corner and shall thereafter pick up the count from the timekeeper and indicate it with a motion of his arm. If a contestant is unable to continue at the count of 10, the referee shall declare the other boxer the winner by a knockout. If a contestant who has been knocked or has fallen out of the ring during a contest fails to be on his feet in the ring before the expiration of 10 seconds, the referee shall count him out as if he were down. A contestant who has fallen or has been knocked out of the ring must return to the ring unassisted.
(b) When a round in any boxing contest, except the last round, shall terminate before a contestant who has been knocked down shall have risen from the floor of the ring, the timekeeper's count shall be continued and, if the fallen contestant shall fail to rise before the count of 10, he shall be considered to have lost the bout by a knockout in the round lately concluded.

217.14 [When contest terminates.] If the contest is terminated between rounds, the knockout must be recorded as having taken place in the round just terminated. However, if the bell for the subsequent round has already sounded, the contest ends in the subsequent round.

Boxing Classes and Championships

Section 218.1 [When boxer must defend title.] With the exception of champions in the armed forces, a boxer holding a championship title must defend his title against a suitable contender within a period of six months after winning or after last defending it, or his title may be vacated by the commission. In the event that a champion fails to so defend his title, any boxer in the same class who is considered by the commission to be a suitable contender, may, at the lapse of the said six months, forward to the commission a challenge. Such challenge must be accompanied by deposits of the following amounts for the following classes:
$1,000—flyweight, bantamweight and featherweight;
$1,500—lightweight;
$2,000—welterweight and middleweight;

$2,500—light heavyweight;
$5,000—heavyweight;
and each such deposit must be by certified check or by a bank cashier's check drawn to the order of the commission.

218.2 [Procedure when commission receives challenge.] Upon receipt of such challenge, the commission shall forward it to the champion and announce the challenge at the office of the commission. Thereafter such champion must, within 20 days after such announcement, enter into articles of agreement to defend his championship title against the contender. In the event the champion does not enter into such articles of agreement as specified above or capriciously refuses promptly to defend his title against such contender, his license shall be suspended by the commission until he either defends his title against the challenger or against some other contender considered suitable by the commission, or until his title is otherwise vacated, unless he is prevented by circumstances beyond his control, in which case the time may be extended.

218.3 [Champion's selection between challengers.] In the event that more than one suitable contender's challenge is received by the commission and forwarded to the champion, the champion may select to defend his title against any one of such challengers.

218.4 [When championship is forfeited.] In the event that the champion is permanently unable to physically qualify for the defense of his title, the commission shall forfeit his championship and declare the title vacant. In each defense of his title, the champion must be at the weight required by the class for which he holds the title.

218.5 [Contracts for championship bouts.] All contracts for chamionship bouts must be signed at a commission meeting. On the date of the signing of the contracts, the two contestants and the licensed corporation promoting the bout will each post forfeits with the commission in the following amounts per class:
$1,000—flyweight, bantamweight and featherweight;
$1,500—lightweight;
$2,000—welterweight and middleweight;
$2,500—light heavyweight;
$5,000—heavyweight.
Such forfeits are to insure that each of the contestants will appear at the championship contest and to make the proper weight, and that the promoting corporation will fulfill its obligations. In the event that a forfeit is declared, the deposit or deposits so forfeited will be distributed equally between the nondefaulting depositors.

218.6 [Individual may hold only one championship title at a time.] No individual may hold a world's championship title in two or more classes at the same time, but the holder of one such championship title may enter a contest for the world's championship title of another class. In the event that such individual wins such world's championship title in such other class, his original world championship is automatically vacated.

218.7 [Weight limits for contestants in championship bouts.] The weight limit for each contestant in a championship bout must be as listed below, and championships are recognized in the following classes only:

112	fyweight
118	bantamweight
126	featherweight
135	lightweight
147	welterweight
160	middleweight
175	light heavyweight
over 175	heavyweight

In the heavyweight class there is no maximum weight limit for any contestant.

218.8 [Weight limits in nonchampionship bouts other than four-round contests.] In nonchampionship bouts, other than four-round contests, the following limitations of weights between contestants may be permitted:

flyweights (112 lbs.)	5 lbs.
bantamweights (118 lbs.)	7 lbs.
featherweights (126 lbs.)	8 lbs.
lightweights (135 lbs.)	10 lbs.
welterweights (147 lbs.)	12 lbs.
middleweights (160 lbs.)	13 lbs.
light heavyweights (175 lbs.)	14 lbs.
heavyweights, all over 175 lbs.	no limitation

218.9 [Weight limits in four-round bouts.] In all four-round bouts, except in the light-heavyweight and heavyweight classes, the difference between the weights of the contestants shall not exceed five pounds.

218.10 [Weights at which matchmakers are permitted to make matches.] Matchmakers are permitted to make matches at the following weights only:

109	126	150
112	130	155
115	135	160
118	140	165
122	147	175

218.11 [Boxers overweight in non-title bout.] In non-title bouts, boxers overweight under the terms of the contract may be suspended after the match for such period as the commission may from time to time decide.

218.12 [Weight of holder of championship in contest of title.] Whenever a recognized holder of a championship engages in a championship contest in this State he must be at the weight required by the class for which he holds the championship except where a champion of one class competes as a contender for the championship in another class.

218.13 [How championship can be lost.] A championship can be lost by default, forfeit or inability to pass the scale, but a championship can only be won by a contender in a contest.

218.14 [When contestants in championship bout must "pass the scale".] All contestants in a championship bout must pass the scale at noon of the contest or at an additional weigh-in two hours thereafter.

Index